EBI Studies in Banking and Capital Markets Law

The European Banking Institute
The European Banking Institute based in Frankfurt is an international centre for banking studies resulting from the joint venture of Europe's preeminent academic institutions which have decided to share and coordinate their commitments and structure their research activities in order to provide the highest quality legal, economic and accounting studies in the field of banking regulation, banking supervision and banking resolution in Europe. The European Banking Institute is structured to promote the dialogue between scholars, regulators, supervisors, industry representatives and advisors in relation to issues concerning the regulation and supervision of financial institutions and financial markets from a legal, economic and any other related viewpoint.

As of May 2021, the Academic Members of the European Banking Institute are the following: Universiteit van Amsterdam, University of Antwerp, University of Piraeus, Alma Mater Studiorum–Università di Bologna, Universität Bonn, Academia de Studii Economice din București (ASE), Trinity College Dublin, University of Edinburgh, Goethe-Universität, Universiteit Gent, University of Helsinki, Universiteit Leiden, KU Leuven University, Universidade Católica Portuguesa, Universidade de Lisboa, University of Ljubljana, Queen Mary University of London, Université du Luxembourg, Universidad Autónoma Madrid, Universidad Carlos III de Madrid, Universidad Complutense, Madrid, Johannes Gutenberg University Mainz, University of Malta, Università Cattolica del Sacro Cuore, University of Cyprus, Radboud Universiteit, BI Norwegian Business School, Université Panthéon - Sorbonne (Paris 1), Université Panthéon-Assas (Paris 2), University of Stockholm, University of Tartu, University of Vienna, University of Wrocław, Universität Zürich.

Jan A. Jans

Electronic Payments in the European Market

Creating a Level Playing Field between Banks and Non-Banks

palgrave
macmillan

Jan A. Jans
Amsterdam, The Netherlands

ISSN 2730-9088 ISSN 2730-9096 (electronic)
EBI Studies in Banking and Capital Markets Law
ISBN 978-3-031-64337-8 ISBN 978-3-031-64338-5 (eBook)
https://doi.org/10.1007/978-3-031-64338-5

Cover credit: Teekid/gettyimages

This Palgrave Macmillan imprint is published by the registered company Springer Nature Switzerland AG
The registered company address is: Gewerbestrasse 11, 6330 Cham, Switzerland

Contents

About the Author

Jan A. Jans is a specialist in financial regulatory law with a focus on the regulatory framework covering banks, insurance companies, payment service providers, investment firms and investment funds. Prior to joining Regulatory Counsel I Financial Services as partner in 2022, Dr. Jans has been working as a financial regulatory lawyer at Linklaters LLP. He graduated from Nijmegen University in 2008. In addition to law, he studied financial economics and business administration. He obtained his PhD in payments at the Vrije Universiteit Amsterdam in 2023. Dr. Jans publishes regularly in national law journals.

Abbreviations

AISP	Account Information Service Provider
AML	Anti-Money Laundering
AML/CTF	Anti-Money Laundering and Counter Terrorist Financing
API	Application Programming Interface
AS-PSP	Account Servicing Payment Service Provider
ATM	Automated Teller Machine
B2B	Businesses to Business
Bank	Credit institution within the meaning of Article 4 of Regulation (EU) No 575/2013 on prudential requirements for Banks and investment firms
BIC	Bank Identifier Code
CDD	Customer Due Diligence
CJEU	The Court of Justice of the European Union
CNP	Card-Not-Present
Commission	The European Commission
CP	Card-Present
CPSS	Committee on Payment and Settlement Systems
DDoS	Distributed Denial of Service
DMA	Digital Markets Act
DORA	Digital Operational Resilience Act
DoS	Denial of Service
EBA	European Banking Authority
ECB	European Central Bank

EEA	European Economic Area, which consists of the 27 EU Member States plus Iceland, Lichtenstein and Norway
EMI	Electronic Money Institution
E-money	Electronic Money
EPC CT Rulebook	Rulebook developed by the European Payments Council for the SEPA Credit Transfer Scheme
EPC CT Scheme	Credit Transfer Scheme developed by the European Payments Council
EPC DD B2B Rulebook	Rulebook developed by the European Payments Council for the SEPA Direct Debit Business to Business Scheme
EPC DD B2B Scheme	SEPA Direct Debit Business to Business Scheme developed by the European Payments Council
EPC DD Core Rulebook	Rulebook developed by the European Payments Council for the SEPA Direct Debit Core Scheme
EPC DD Core Scheme	SEPA Core Direct Debit Scheme developed by the European Payments Council
EPC ICT Rulebook	Rulebook developed by the European Payments Council for the SEPA Instant Payments Scheme
EPC ICT Scheme	Instant Payments Scheme developed by the European Payments Council
EPC	European Payments Council
ESA	European Supervisory Authority
EU	European Union, which consists of the following 27 Member States: (i) Austria; (ii) Belgium; (iii) Bulgaria; (iv) Croatia; (v) Cyprus; (vi) Czech Republic; (vii) Denmark; (viii) Estonia; (ix) Finland; (x) France; (xi) Germany; (xii) Greece; (xiii) Hungary; (xiv) Ireland; (xv) Italy; (xvi) Latvia; (xvii) Lithuania; (xviii) Luxembourg; (xix) Malta; (xx) Netherlands; (xxi) Poland; (xxii) Portugal; (xxiii) Romania; (xxiv) Slovakia; (xxv) Slovenia; (xxvi) Spain; and (xxvii) Sweden
Euro area Member States	The Member States of the European Union that have adopted the euro as their currency. These Member States are: (i) Belgium; (ii) Croatia; (iii) Cyprus; (iv) Germany; (v)

	Estonia; (vi) Finland; (vii) France; (viii) Greece; (ix) Ireland; (x) Italy; (xi) Latvia; (xii) Lithuania: (xiii) Luxembourg; (xiv) Malta; (xv) the Netherlands; (xvi) Austria; (xvii) Portugal; (xviii) Slovenia; (xix) Slovakia; and (xx) Spain
E-wallet	Electronic Wallet
FATF	Financial Action Task Force
FIU	Financial Intelligence Unit
FSB	The Financial Stability Board
Home CA	Competent Authority of the Home Member State
Host CA	Competent Authority of the Host Member State
IBAN	International Bank Account Number
ICT	Information and Communications Technology
IFR	Interchange Fee Regulation
IOSCO	International Organization of Securities Commission
ISO	International Organization for Standardization
LVPS	Large-value Payment System
MIF	Multilateral Interchange Fee
ML/TF	Money laundering and Terrorist Financing
NCA	National Competent Authority
NFC	Near Field Communication
Non-euro area Member States	The Member States of the European Union that have not adopted the euro as their currency. These Member States are: (i) Bulgaria; (ii) Czech Republic; (iii) Denmark; (iv) Hungary; (v) Poland; (vi) Romania; and (vii) Sweden
Non-SIPS	Non-Systemically Important Payment System
P2P	Person-to-Person
Payment	Electronic Payment
PI	Payment Institution
PIN	Personal Identification Number
PISP	Payment Initiation Service Provider
POS	Point-of-Sale
PSP	Payment Service Provider
PSU	Payment Service User
RTGS	Real-Time Gross Settlement
SCA	Strong Customer Authentication
SecuRe Pay	The European Forum on the Security of Retail Payments

SEPA	Single Euro Payments Area
SIPS	Systemically Important Payment System
SIRA	Systematic Integrity Risk Analysis
TIPS	Target Instant Payments Settlement System
TPP	Third Party Payment Service Provider

List of Figures

List of Tables

CHAPTER 1

Introduction: Banks and Non-Banks in the European Market for Payments

1.1 General Introduction

Credit institutions ('**Banks**') have traditionally played a role in the circulation of money (bank notes and coins). In the fourteenth century, Italian merchant bankers first started offering services whereby money was received in a particular currency in a particular place and paid out in another place in another currency.[1] These merchant bankers settled their payment obligations in a manner very similar to the interbank clearing and settlement systems that we use today.[2] Making a payment did not immediately result in the transfer of money between merchant bankers. Instead, net positions between merchant bankers were calculated after a certain period and were subsequently settled by means of cash payment. These merchant bankers are generally regarded as the predecessors of Banks as we know them today.

In times when cash served as the most important means of payment in society, this was a role assigned to the private sector, under the preconditions and requirements defined by the public authorities.[3] In fact, this

[1] See Geva (2011, p. 356).

[2] Ibid.

[3] Including the requirement of close supervision of institutions involved in the circulation of money.

J. A. Jans, *Electronic Payments in the European Market*, EBI Studies in Banking and Capital Markets Law,
https://doi.org/10.1007/978-3-031-64338-5_1

classic role of Banks also gave rise to a new role for Banks, in which means of payment in the form of somewhat more abstract concepts, such as checks, exchange letters, letters of credit and other alternatives to cash, played a more important role in society, especially when large payments were involved. Banks played an important intermediary role as a provider of assurance that such means of payment represented value, for example by guaranteeing the cover of the alternative means of payment as used by their customers.

Since the nineties of the last century, Banks have developed a large variety of different electronic payment (**'Payment'**) solutions, which involve payment products that enable payment service users (**'PSUs'**) to transfer funds electronically, i.e., by means of book-entries in non-physical accounts.[4] For Payment products, Banks used to be responsible for the execution of all relevant steps in the transaction process, such as the authorisation, clearing and settlement of payment transactions.[5]

The more or less logical consequence of the rise of Payment solutions has been that in recent decades Banks have played a prominent role in this area and have therefore also been able to build up an almost monopolistic position in the development and establishment of systems, infrastructure, payment methods and means that were highly interoperable within the banking community, but whose functions were of very limited use outside the banking environment. The role of Banks in this field, which has grown almost organically based on the foundations of the organisation of the (traditional) payment systems over the last centuries, has started to become subject to challenge in recent decades. Amongst others because Non-Banks that intended to compete with Banks in the market for Payments were forced to adhere to the rules and regulations that were developed by Banks and to apply the Banks' technical communication standards.

The question is increasingly being asked whether the position of the Banks does not stand in the way of fair market forces for products and services in the field of Payments, both in terms of the functionality of those products and services and the price setting thereof. The fundamental question is, amongst other things, to what extent this monopolistic role of Banks has resulted in innovation in the field of

4 See Euro Banking Association (2017, p. 7).

5 As was the case with cash payments.

Payments being held back, whether the interests of customers of the financial industry have not been unnecessarily neglected as a result, and whether the opening of the market could not lead to a better balance between the interests of PSUs. In addition, the interests of fair pricing, optimal service to PSU needs and the application of innovation could be better served by a more open market than by retaining the monopolistic role of the Banks in the field of Payments, traditionally accepted by society and the authorities.

During the nineties of the last century, anti-competitive behaviour by Banks was only scrutinised under the European and national competition law frameworks. Until the adoption of Directive 2000/46/EC on the taking up, pursuit of and prudential supervision of the business of electronic money institutions (‘**EMD**’)[6] in 2000 and Directive 2007/64/EC on payment services in the internal market (‘**PSD**’)[7] in 2007, there was no European legislative framework focussing on Non-Bank competition from a financial services regulatory perspective. Absent a European legislative framework on market access by Non-Banks, Non-Banks that intended to enter the market for Payments were often compelled to apply for a banking licence. Since the licence requirements for Banks are disproportionately cumbersome for payment service providers (‘**PSPs**’) that do not obtain repayable funds from the public nor offer other regulated services than payment services, Non-Banks were facing substantial barriers to enter the market for Payments.

To stimulate sound competition between Banks and Non-Banks, it is of paramount importance to have a profound European legal framework supportive of Non-Bank participation. The European legislature considers in particular the reduction of market entry barriers for Non-Banks to be a *condicio sine qua non* for increasing Non-Bank participation and enhancing competition between Banks and Non-Banks in the field of Payments. The line of thinking is that with lower barriers to market entry, Non-Banks are better positioned to enter the market and start offering Payment solutions that PSUs consider to be a substitute of the Payment solutions offered by Banks.

[6] Directive 2000/46/EC of 18 September 2000 “on the taking up, pursuit of and prudential supervision of the business of electronic money institutions”, OJ L 275, 27.10.2000, pp. 39–43.

[7] Directive 2007/64/EC of 13 November 2007 “on payment services in the internal market amending (...)”, OJ L 319, 5.12.2007, pp. 1–36.

1.2 The Rise of FinTechs and BigTechs

Since the 2010s, the pace of technological innovation has accelerated considerably, creating new business opportunities for PSPs. Amongst others, the introduction of mobile technologies, such as near field communication (‘**NFC**’)[8] and quick response (QR) codes[9] have had a significant impact on the direction in which the Payment market has developed.[10] With technological innovation, customer behaviour and customer expectations *vis-à-vis* PSPs have also changed. Nowadays, PSUs demand 24/7 availability, fast, cheap and secure Payment products.[11] Further to the offering of low-cost Payment products, maximising customer convenience has become a requisite for PSPs that wish to strengthen their competitive position.[12] To stay ahead of the competition, the overall focus of PSPs has generally shifted from a product-centred approach towards a customer-centred approach, whereby the term ‘frictionless payment experience’ has become the new buzzword.

Nowadays, technology focussed service providers such as FinTechs and BigTechs are taking the Payments market by storm. The Financial Stability Board (‘**FSB**’) defines ‘FinTech’ as ‘*technology enabled financial innovation that could result in new business models, applications, processes or products with an associated material effect on financial markets and institutions and the provision of financial services*’.[13] Notable FinTechs that offer payment services in the European market include Adyen, Nexi, Klarna and Monzo. BigTechs are ‘*large technology companies with extensive established customer networks*’.[14] Well-known BigTechs that are

[8] NFC technology is used by *inter alia* Apple Pay, Google Pay and Payconiq.

[9] QR code technology is used by *inter alia* Google Pay, Apple Pay, Samsung Pay and Payconiq.

[10] See OXERA (2020, p. 23).

[11] See EBA (2019, p. 11).

[12] See ACM (2020, p. 43).

[13] See FSB (2019a, p. 1).

[14] See FSB (2019b, p. 3).

active in the Payments market are Facebook[15], Google[16], Alipay[17] and Amazon.[18] Certain BigTechs, such as Apple, operate in the Payments market as a technical service provider and are therefore not licensed as a PSP.[19]

Market entrance by FinTechs and BigTechs increases competition and can therefore offer social welfare benefits such as: (i) a reduction in the costs of payment services for PSUs; and (ii) a positive stimulus for innovation in the Payments market.[20] However, one must not neglect the fact that FinTechs and BigTechs can also stifle innovation and competition if they are too big. An example of a BigTech that appears to have such effect because of its dominant market position is Apple. Banks cannot offer electronic wallet (**'E-wallet'**) solutions other than Apple Pay to PSUs that use an iOS device instead of an android smartphone. Incumbent Banks and Non-Banks face competitive challenges as a result of FinTech and BigTechs entering the market. Especially BigTechs seem to be an immediate competitive threat for incumbent PSPs since BigTechs can provide (payment) services at a large scale during the start-up phase using their high investment capacity, extensive technological knowledge and well-developed client network.[21] The business operations of Non-Banks are generally smaller and less complex than the business operations of Banks and Banks are often hindered by the legacy of their automated platforms and technical infrastructures developed in decades. As a result, incumbent Non-Banks are more flexible and can therefore more easily adapt to the changing competitive environment, which gives them a competitive edge over Banks.[22] Indeed, Banks have developed different strategies to cope with the changing environment than Non-Banks. Whereas Non-Banks

[15] In 2018, Facebook Payments International Limited obtained a licence to operate as an EMI from the Central Bank of Ireland (Ireland).

[16] In 2018, Google Payment Lithuania UAB obtained a licence to operate as an EMI from the Lietu-vos Bankas (Lithuania).

[17] In 2018, Alipay (Europe) Limited S.A. obtained a licence to operate as an EMI from the Commission de Surveillance du Secteur Financier (Luxembourg).

[18] In 2010, Amazon Payments Europe S.C.A. obtained a licence to operate as an EMI from the Commission de Surveillance du Secteur Financier (Luxembourg).

[19] See ACM (2020, p. 5).

[20] See FSB (2019b, p. 22).

[21] See FSB (2019a, p. 1).

[22] See EBA (2019, p. 3).

seem to focus primarily on innovating their own product offering, Banks more often choose to partner with FinTechs and BigTechs to develop new technologies or jointly offer payment solutions.[23] Such arrangements, which are called horizontal cooperation agreements under the European competition law framework, are according to **Article 101 of the Treaty on the Functioning of the European Union** ('TFEU')[24] allowed from a competition law perspective provided that they do not restrict competition.[25] An alternative strategy often applied by Banks is to invest in FinTechs via venture capital funds or direct acquisitions.[26]

With these market dynamics, it is as important as ever to have a better understanding of the elements of the European financial services regulatory framework for the Payments market that contribute to the level playing field between Banks and Non-Banks in the field of Payments.

1.3 The Importance of Having a Level Playing Field Between Banks and Non-Banks

1.3.1 The Main Policy Objectives of the European Legislature

Since the early 2000s, the European legislature has adopted numerous directives and regulations to establish an internal market for Payments. Most of these directives and regulations contain both activity- and entity-based rules. Activity based rules involve legal requirements that apply to all types of PSPs conducting a certain activity whereas entity-based rules provide for different legal requirements for different types of PSPs (i.e., regardless of the type of activity conducted by these PSPs).

[23] An example of a Payment solution that is offered by a BigTech in collaboration with Banks is Apple Pay. Apple pay is a bank-led solution, which means that the bank is responsible for: (i) the authentication of the payment transaction; and (ii) the transfer of funds.

[24] Treaty on the Functioning of the European Union (OJ C 326, 26.10.2012).

[25] According to **Paragraph 42 of the Guidelines on Horizontal Agreements**, the degree of market power required for an infringement under **Article 101 TFEU** is less than the degree of market power required for having a dominant position within the meaning of **Article 102 TFEU**.

[26] Direct acquisitions are generally not the preferred option because it requires the Bank to keep the FinTech on its balance sheet. This brings the FinTech within the scope of inter alia the Bank's consolidated supervision requirement.

One of the main objectives of public policy is to enhance social welfare.[27] In the market for Payments, public policy contributes to this objective, amongst others, by promoting a competitive market. In general, having a competitive Payments market enhances social welfare by increasing the variety of available Payment solutions and decreasing the average costs charged for these solutions.

In order to establish a European Payments market that enhances social welfare, the European legislature developed a financial services regulatory framework containing legal requirements that can be divided into six different categories, each of them pursuing their own intermediate objectives. The first intermediate objective is the facilitation of market access by Non-Banks that intend to provide payment services. With the adoption of PSD in 2007, a separate licensing regime has been introduced for payment institutions (**'PIs'**) to boost market entrance by Non-Banks. The second intermediate objective involves the safeguarding of the security of the Payments market. To ensure the security of the Payments market, each participant in the payment chain must take responsibility for guaranteeing the safety of their involvement in the execution process. For this purpose, Directive (EU) 2015/2366 on payment services in the internal market ('PSD2')[28] PSD2 contains rules on security related requirements and the allocation of these requirements between the participants in the payment chain. The third intermediate objective is the safeguarding of the integrity of the Payments market. When providing payment services, PSPs are exposed to different (integrity) risks, such as the risk of being used for money laundering and terrorist financing (**'ML/TF'**) purposes. A legislative framework on the prevention of ML/TF has been adopted by the European legislature to minimise the ML/TF risk exposures of PSPs. The fourth intermediate objective involves the enhancement of PSU protection in case of an unauthorised or erroneous Payment. In the financial services regulatory framework, PSU protection is, amongst others, ensured by providing clear rules on the allocation of rights and obligations between PSPs and PSUs in case of unauthorised or erroneous Payments. The fifth intermediate objective involves allowing Non-Banks access to payment systems. The European legislature considers payment system access to be essential for Non-Banks in order to compete with Banks on an equal footing. However, the European legislature should

[27] See BIS (2021, p. 5).

not strive to establish Non-Bank payment system access at all costs. If in a particular situation the objective of achieving Non-Bank payment system access is at odds with the objective of ensuring financial stability of the Payments market, imposing restrictions on payment system access by Non-Banks for the benefit of enhancing financial market stability would be beneficial to social welfare. The sixth intermediate objective covers collaboration between competing PSPs to develop standards for the Payments market that reflect the interests of both Banks and Non-Banks. In order to stimulate efficient processing of Payments, it is essential that PSPs develop standards that are used by all PSPs for communicating with each other and exchanging information. The development of such standards requires collaboration between competing PSPs.

The above-mentioned intermediate objectives are addressed in different directives and/or regulations. For example, PSD2 on payment services in the internal market (‘**PSD2**’)[28] covers legal requirements on enhancing competition by Non-Banks and consumer protection but does not so much focus on addressing intermediate objectives such as safeguarding market integrity (e.g., addressing ML/TF risk exposures). In general, there does not appear to be a hierarchy between these intermediate objectives from the perspective of the European legislature.

Regulations are directly applicable in every Member State and come into effect after they are adopted by the European parliament and Council, or if it concerns delegated regulations by the Commission. Directives must be implemented into the local laws of each of the Member States in order to take effect. Based on the duty of consistent interpretation, Member States are obliged to interpret national law consistently with European law. However, it is in principle for each Member State to determine how it ensures compliance with the legal requirements imposed by directives. Ultimately, the Court of Justice of the European Union (‘**CJEU**’) is responsible for determining how a particular legal provision of EU law must be interpreted.[29]

At the European level, an important role has been assigned to the European Banking Authority (‘**EBA**’) in relation to Payments. One of the

[28] Directive (EU) 2015/2366 of 25 November 2015 “on payment services in the internal market, amending (...)”, OJ L 337, 23.12.2015, pp. 35–127.

[29] This means that national deviations may be set aside in case of an incorrect interpretation.

main objectives of the EBA is to contribute to the consistent interpretation of the European Payments framework. Although it is ultimately the CJEU that determines how European law provisions must be interpreted, **Article 8(1)(b) EBA Regulation**[30] enables the EBA to contribute to the consistent application of the European Payments framework by developing and issuing amongst others: (i) regulatory technical standards within the meaning of **Article 10(1) EBA Regulation**; (ii) implementing technical standards within the meaning of **Article 15 EBA Regulation**; (iii) guidelines and recommendations within the meaning of **Article 16 EBA Regulation**; and (iv) opinions within the meaning of **Article 16a EBA Regulation**. Regulatory technical standards and implementing technical standards must be endorsed by the Commission in order to be legally binding and directly applicable. Guidelines, recommendations and opinions are not legally binding. However, **Article 16(3) EBA Regulation** requires that National Competent Authorities ('**NCAs**') and PSPs make every effort to comply with EBA guidelines and recommendations. The content of standards, guidelines, recommendations and opinions must always be within the boundaries of the legislative framework for Payments as referred to in **Article 1(2) EBA Regulation**[31], being: (i) PSD2; (ii) Directive 2009/110/EC on the taking up, pursuit and prudential supervision of the business of electronic money institutions ('**EMD2**')[32]; and (iii) Directive 2014/92/EU on the comparability of fees related to payment accounts, payment account switching and access to payment accounts with basic features ('**PAD**').[33] These directives contain several provisions providing the EBA with a legal basis to develop such standards, guidelines, recommendations and opinions on specific topics covered by these directives. However, this legal framework appears to be at odds

[30] Regulation (EU) 1093/2010 of 24 November 2010 "establishing a European Supervisory Authority (European Banking Authority), amending (...)", OJ L 331, 15.12.2010, pp. 12-47.

[31] Regulation (EU) 2019/2175 of 18 December 2019 "amending Regulation (EU) No 1093/2010 establishing a European Supervisory Authority (European Banking Authority), (...)", OJ L 334, 27.12.2019, pp. 1-145, Recital 5.

[32] Directive 2009/110/EC of 16 September 2009 "on the taking up, pursuit and prudential supervision of the business of electronic money institutions (...)", OJ L 267, 10.10.2009, pp. 7-17.

[33] Directive 2014/92/EU of 23 July 2014 "on the comparability of fees related to payment accounts, payment account switching and access to payment accounts with basic features", OJ L 257, 28.8.2014, pp. 214-246.

with the catch all provision of **Article 1(3) EBA Regulation**, which states that the EBA shall also act in the field of activities of PSPs in relation to issues not directly covered in the directives mentioned in **Article 1(3) EBA Regulation** provided that such involvement is considered necessary to ensure the effective and consistent application of these directives (e.g., matters of corporate governance). Given that there is no hierarchy between directives and regulations from a European law perspective, this contradiction creates uncertainty as to the mandate of the EBA with regard to the issuing of standards, guidelines, recommendations and opinions on Payments related topics.

Further to the issuing of standards, guidelines, recommendations and opinions, the EBA also contributes to the consistent interpretation of the European Payments framework by investigating differences in supervision by NCAs.[34] In case an NCA has not applied, or incorrectly applied the provisions of PSD2, EMD2 or the PAD,[35] **Article 17(2) EBA Regulation** allows that the EBA can at its own volition[36] or upon request of an NCA, the European Parliament, the Council, the Commission or the Banking Stakeholder Group investigate an alleged breach or non-application by an NCA of EU law.[37] For this purpose, the EBA has established rules of procedure containing criteria that are taken into account when the EBA receives a request to initiate an investigation.[38] Since **Article 17(2) EBA Regulation** allows the EBA discretion as to whether or not it will pursue investigations based on information received from a natural or legal person regarding an alleged breach or non-application of EU law by an NCA, these rules of procedure also clarify under what conditions the EBA may decide to close a particular case without opening an investigation.[39] In the recently published

[34] See Gortsos and Lagaria (2020, p. 6).

[35] Or any of the directives or regulations based on these acts.

[36] Where relevant, based on information provided by legal- or natural persons.

[37] The EBA may, not later than 2 months from initiating its investigation address a recommendation to the NCA on the action required for the NCA to comply with EU law. If these recommendations are not followed, this can lead to infringement procedure by the Commission.

[38] See EBA (2020).

[39] European Court of Justice. (2016). Case C-577/15 P, *SV Capital OU v EBA* (EU:C:2016:947), paragraph 46.

proposal for a regulation on payment services (**'PSR Proposal'**),[40] the Commission suggests to amend the EBA Regulation to allow the EBA the authority to temporarily prohibit or restrict the offering of certain payment services, payment instruments or electronic money (**'E-money'**) products if these potentially harm consumers or threaten the functioning and integrity of financial markets.[41] According to **Article 104(2) PSR Proposal** such decision can only be taken provided that all of the following conditions are fulfilled: (i) it involves a significant number of PSUs or E-money holders or a threat to the functioning, integrity or stability of the Payments or E-money market; (ii) these threats are not addressed by the applicable legislative framework; and (iii) no (adequate) action has been taken by the NCA(s) to address the threat.

1.3.2 A Level Playing Field Between Banks and Non-Banks

To create a Payments market in which a variety of different Payment solutions are offered at a price that is not too distant from the price that would be charged in a perfectly competitive market (where price equals marginal costs), there needs to be sound competition between Banks and Non-Banks. Having a so-called 'level playing field' between Banks and Non-Banks in the market for Payments is a requisite for achieving such sound competition.

There is no consensus as to the definition of a level playing field at present. The Cambridge dictionary defines a level playing field as '*a situation in which everyone has the same chance of succeeding*'.[42] This definition seems to suggest that a level playing field is a market situation whereby PSPs sharing similar characteristics are subject to the same rules and requirements and, as a result thereof, have the same starting position for competing with each other.

In legal literature, the concept of a 'level playing field' is mostly described as a measure for having relatively low barriers to market entry for Non-Banks. In general, a level playing field is believed to exist if different types of PSPs are subject to market entry requirements that

[40] See Commission (2023).

[41] PSR Proposal, Recital 140.

[42] See Cambridge Dictionary (n.d.).

are proportionate to the size and complexity of their business model. Legal requirements are considered proportionate if they: (i) are suitable to protect the interest that requires protection[43], which means that the requirement must be appropriate to protect said interest[44]; (ii) are necessary, which means there are no legal alternatives with which the same objective can be achieved that are less stringent[45]; and (iii) are in proportion to the intended objective.[46] Whether or not a particular legal requirement can be considered in proportion to the intended objective very much depends on different factors such as the type of PSP to which the requirement in question applies. Because the business of a Non-Bank is typically smaller and less complex than the business of a Bank, the principle of proportionality implies that Non-Banks should not face the exact same market access requirements as Banks and that the requirements applicable to Non-Banks must be aligned with *inter alia* the services they provide and the security and integrity risks to which their businesses are exposed. As a result of having proportionate entity-based market entrance requirements, different types of PSPs are assumed to be able to compete with each other on a more equal footing.

The premise of this book is that having proportionate market entry barriers for Non-Banks is only one of the elements that constitute the level playing field between Banks and Non-Banks. When assessing the level playing field between Banks and Non-Banks, the rules and regulations covering all of the intermediate objectives described in **Paragraph 1.3.1** are of relevance since they all entail regulations that may enhance or hamper Non-Bank market participation. Therefore, all these regulations are covered by this book from the proportionality perspective for Non-Banks.

This book applies a holistic interpretation of the concept 'level playing field' that takes into account the six intermediate objectives described in **Paragraph 1.3.1**. A level playing field is defined as the extent to which the rules and regulations covering the intermediate objectives are proportionate in the context of competition between Banks and Non-Banks.

[43] See Jans (2000, p. 240).

[44] Ibid., p. 243.

[45] Ibid., p. 240.

[46] Ibid., p. 241.

This means that if the restrictions imposed on Non-Banks by regulations covering these intermediate objectives are in proportion to these objectives, such regulations are considered proportionate and therefore contribute to the level playing field between Banks and Non-Banks. In other words, the level playing field between Banks and Non-Banks is therefore determined by the extent to which the financial services regulatory framework covering the market for Payments is in proportion to the objective of: (i) facilitating Payment market access by Non-Banks; (ii) safeguarding the security of the Payments market; (iii) safeguarding the integrity of the Payments market; (iv) enhancing PSU protection in case of an unauthorised or erroneous Payment; (v) allowing Non-Banks access to payment systems; and (vi) providing for collaboration between competing PSPs to develop standards for the Payments market that reflect the interests of both Banks and Non-Banks. It is relevant to note that a level playing field does not always mean less regulation. A level playing field can also mean more legislation provided that it is proportionate for all market participants.

With technological innovation and the fast changing competitive environment for PSPs, it is important to have a better understanding of the extent to which these legislative initiatives have contributed to the envisaged level playing field between Banks and Non-Banks. With continuously changing market conditions, it is challenging for the European legislature to develop legislation that contributes to the establishment of a level playing field between Banks and Non-Banks. When observing how the Payments market has developed over the last decades, the European legislature had made certain choices that appears to have had an impeding effect on the level playing field between Banks and Non-Banks.

This book provides an overview of the legislative framework regulating the European Payments market. The Payments market covers all non-cash payment solutions offered by PSPs in the European Economic Area (**'EEA'**), with the exception of the digital euro, which involves a central bank digital currency project the European Central Bank (**'ECB'**) is currently working on together with the national central banks that aims to offer PSUs another electronic equivalent to cash.[47] For the sake of clarity, Payments covered by this book do also not include E-money transactions nor crypto assets, which are unregulated digital currencies that are

[47] See Commission (n.d.).

not issued by a central bank.[48] Like Payments, crypto assets do not constitute legal tender within the meaning of **Article 128 TFEU**.[49] However, unlike Payments, crypto assets are not (yet) broadly accepted as a means for making payments.[50]

Secondary Sources

ACM. (2020). *Rapportage BigTechs in het betalingsverkeer*, pp. 5, 43.

BIS. (2021). *Fintech Regulation: How to Achieve a Level Playing Field*. Occasional Paper No. 17, p. 5.

Cambridge Dictionary. (n.d.). *A Level Playing Field. Cambridge Dictionary*. https://dictionary.cambridge.org/dictionary/english/a-level-playing-field. Accessed: April 13, 2024.

Commission. (2023). *Proposal for a Regulation of the European Parliament and of the Council on Payment Services in the Internal Market and Amending Regulation (EU) No 1093/2010*, COM(2023) 367 final.

Commission. (n.d.). *Digital Euro. European Commission*. https://finance.ec.europa.eu/digital-finance/digital-euro_en. Accessed April 13, 2024.

EBA. (2019). *EBA Report on the Impact of Fintech on Payment Institutions' and E-Money Institutions' Business Models*, pp. 3, 11.

EBA. (2020). *Decision of the European Banking Authority Concerning Rules of Procedure for Investigation of Breach of Union Law*. EBA/DC/2020/312 (consolidated version).

Euro Banking Association. (2017). *Open Banking: Advancing Customer-Centricity—Analysis and Overview*. Open Banking Working Group, p. 7.

European Court of Justice. (2016). Case C-577/15 P, *SV Capital OU v EBA* (EU:C:2016:947), paragraph 46.

FSB. (2019a). *FinTech and Market Structure in Financial Services: Market Developments and Potential Financial Stability Implications*, p. 1.

FSB. (2019b). *BigTech in Finance: Market Developments and Potential Financial Stability Implications*, pp. 3, 22.

Geva, B. (2011). *The Payment Order of Antiquity and the Middle Ages: A Legal History*. Hart Monographs in Transnational & International Law, Bloomsbury Publishing Plc, p. 356.

[48] Examples of crypto assets include Bitcoin, Bitcoin Cash and Litecoin.

[49] Only Euro banknotes and coins have the status of legal tender in Europe.

[50] Crypto assets are however being accepted as means for making payments at an increasing rate. For example, in 2021 Tesla announced that it accepts bitcoin as a means for payment. Moreover, in 2021 PayPal launched a crypto checkout service.

Gortsos, C. V., & Lagaria, K. (2020). *The European Supervisory Authorities (ESAs) as "Direct" Supervisors in the EU Financial System*. EBI Working Paper Series 2020—No. 57, p. 6.

Jans, J. H. (2000). Proportionality Revisited. *Legal Issues of Economic Integration, 27*(3), 239–265, pp. 240, 241, 243.

OXERA. (2020). *The Competitive Landscape for Payments: A European Perspective*, p. 23.

CHAPTER 2

Payments

2.1 Background

Prior to the introduction of Payment solutions as a means for making payments, cash used to be the primary means of payment for EU consumers at the point-of-sale ('**POS**'). Cash offers real-time settlement and is particularly convenient for making low value payments. As a result, cash continues to be a relatively popular means for making payments in the EU at present, albeit that large differences in the use of cash are observed between Member States. Whereas, for example, in Germany cash payments accounted for 63% of the total number of POS transactions in 2022, cash payments accounted for only 21% of the POS transactions during that year in the Netherlands.[1]

Despite the wide acceptance of cash payments, there are several disadvantages to the use of cash as a means for making payments. An important disadvantage is that cash is not suitable for making payments in a digital context. Another key disadvantage is that cash is less suitable for making businesses to business ('**B2B**') payments. Since B2B transactions generally involve high value payments, using cash leaves both the payer and

[1] See ECB (2022b, p. 19).

J. A. Jans, *Electronic Payments in the European Market*, EBI Studies in Banking and Capital Markets Law,
https://doi.org/10.1007/978-3-031-64338-5_2

beneficiary exposed to significant security risks.[2] Moreover, the handling of cash payments comes with substantial storage and transportation costs. In addition, it is difficult for companies to maintain adequate administration records for large value cash payments. For these reasons, companies commonly used paper cheques for B2B payments. Cheques are payment instruments in written form which instruct the issuing PSP to pay the amount specified on the cheque when it is presented to the issuing PSP.[3] Cheque payments are less susceptible to fraud, cheaper to process and provide for a paper trail which is helpful for administration purposes. A key risk with cheques however is that there are no guarantees for the beneficiary regarding the creditworthiness of the payer.[4]

During the early nineties of the last century, new electronic communication techniques were developed, such as the internet and NFC technology, which paved the way for the introduction of Payment products. Examples of Payment products that were introduced during that period include debit cards and credit cards. These Payment products provide for an efficient and cheap alternative for cash and paper cheques. As a result, the use of cash and paper cheques decreased considerably over the last decades and continues to decrease at present. This trend has been further accelerated as a result of the measures taken by Member States during the COVID-19 pandemic. As a result of the COVID-19 restrictions imposed by EU governments, there has been an increasing demand for contactless Payment solutions which further stimulated the migration from cash payments towards the use of Payment solutions.[5] In 2022, contactless payments represented 62% of the card payments at the POS.[6]

In general, Payment products consist of four different layers, called the product layer, the payment scheme layer, the clearing layer and the settlement layer.

[2] Companies that receive low value cash payments from consumers face similar risks, albeit that these risks are lower due to the limited transaction amount. Regardless of the risks involved, it is not allowed for companies to receive high value payments in cash due to AML/CTF requirements.

[3] See Bank of England (1996, p. 15).

[4] Ibid.

[5] See Commission (2020, p. 13).

[6] See ECB (2022b, p. 23).

2.1.1 The Product Layer

The product layer covers the Payment solution that the PSP offers to its PSUs. During the last decades, a variety of different Payment products have been developed which can in general be classified in one of the following categories: (i) credit transfers (**Paragraph 2.2**); (ii) direct debit collections (**Paragraph 2.3**); (iii) card payments (**Paragraph 2.4**); and (iv) E-money payments (**Paragraph 2.5**). As part of the Payment solution offered to a PSU, the PSP provides the payer (in case of a credit transfer, card payment or E-money payment) or the beneficiary (in case of a direct debit collection) with a payment instrument that enables the payer respectively the beneficiary to submit payment orders[7] to its PSP for processing.

2.1.2 The Payment Scheme Layer

The Payment scheme consists of the rules and procedures that apply to a particular Payment product.[8] These rules are generally developed and enforced by the service provider that owns the Payment product in question. The scheme rules determine *inter alia* the manner in which participants in the ecosystem of the Payment product exchange data (e.g., the technical standards that PSPs must apply when sending Payment messages to other PSPs and payment systems) and the conditions under which funds are transferred between PSPs. Well-known examples of Payment schemes include: (i) credit transfer schemes such as the EPC CT Scheme (**Paragraph 2.2**)and the EPC ICT Scheme (**Paragraph 2.2.1**); (ii) direct debit schemes such as the EPC DD Core Scheme and the EPC DD B2B Scheme (**Paragraph 2.3**); and (iii) card schemes such as the Visa card scheme and the American Express card scheme (**Paragraph 2.4**).

[7] **Article 4(13) PSD2** defines a 'payment order' as an instruction by a payer or beneficiary to its PSP requesting the execution of a Payment.

[8] **Article 2(7) SEPA Regulation** defines a 'payment scheme' as a single set of rules, practices, standards and/or implementation guidelines agreed between PSPs for the execution of Payments.

2.1.3 *The Clearing Layer*

When a payer or beneficiary initiates a Payment with its PSP, the payer's PSP owes the beneficiary's PSP the corresponding transaction amount. The clearing process involves the calculation of the net positions between PSPs on the basis of which settlement takes place (**Paragraph 8.2.2**). If both the payer and beneficiary of a particular transaction have their payment account with the same account servicing PSP (**'AS-PSP'**)[9], the Payment is cleared by said AS-PSP. In situations where the payer and beneficiary have their payment account with different AS-PSPs, the clearing responsibility is commonly assigned to a payment system (**Paragraph 8.2**).[10]

2.1.4 *The Settlement Layer*

Settlement is the process whereby the net positions calculated by the payment system or AS-PSP are transferred to the relevant PSPs respectively beneficiaries. It involves an act of discharging financial obligations between two or more PSPs.[11] As with the clearing process, Payments between payers and beneficiaries holding their payment account with the same AS-PSP are settled by this AS-PSP. Such transactions are merely book-entry transactions, whereby the AS-PSP debits and credits the balance on the payment accounts of the payer respectively the beneficiary.

The settlement of fund transfers between payment accounts held with different AS-PSPs requires the involvement of a payment system or correspondent banking arrangement (**Paragraph 8.2**).[12] The services of a payment system or correspondent Bank are also needed if the payer and beneficiary of a Payment have a payment account with different branches of the same PSP.

[9] Such transaction is commonly referred to as an in-house payment.

[10] Examples of payment systems that provide clearing services to AS-PSPs in Europe include equensWorldline (the Netherlands and Germany), NETS (Denmark) and STET (France).

[11] See ECB (2010, p. 43).

[12] A combination of correspondent banking arrangements and payment systems is also possible.

2.2 Credit Transfers

A credit transfer involves the service of making funds available in a designated payment account.[13] In 2021, over 22% of the non-cash payment transactions were executed by means of a credit transfer.[14] The most frequently used credit transfer product is the SEPA credit transfer, which was developed by the European Payments Council (**'EPC'**) in 2008 (**Paragraph 3.5**). Figure 2.1 illustrates the processing of a credit transfer.

If a payer wants to transfer funds electronically to a beneficiary (**1**), the payer can make such transfer by means of a credit transfer. A credit transfer is executed by the payer's PSP on the basis of a payment order that the payer submits to its PSP (**2**). Upon receipt of such order, the payer's PSP transfers the transaction amount electronically from the payer's payment account via its own payment account to the payment account of the beneficiary's PSP (**3**).[15] **Article 83(1) PSD2** requires that the transaction

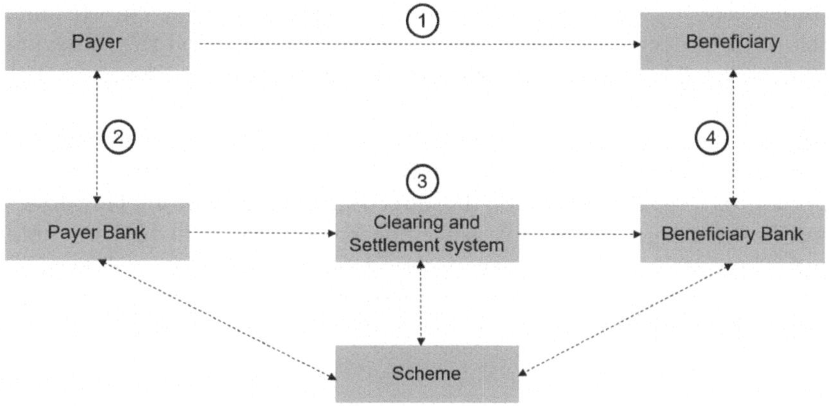

Fig. 2.1 Flowchart credit transfer

[13] **Article 4(24) PSD2** defines a 'credit transfer' as a payment service for crediting a beneficiary's payment account with a payment transaction or a series of payment transactions from a payer's payment account by the PSP which holds the payer's payment account, based on an instruction given by the payer.

[14] See ECB (2022a).

[15] The beneficiary can maintain its payment account with the same PSP (an in-house payment) or with a different PSP.

amount is credited to the payment account of the beneficiary's PSP by the end of the following business day[16] (D + 1) after the moment the payer's PSP received the instruction from the payer.[17] After the funds have been credited to the payment account of the beneficiary's PSP, the beneficiary's PSP is obliged to credit the beneficiary's payment account with the transaction amount on the same business day (**4**).

Given that **Article 78(1) PSD2** provides that the time limit for a credit transfer commences the moment the payer's PSP receives the payment order from the payer, it is of paramount importance to have clear rules as to when such order is deemed to be received by the payer's PSP.[18] Since certain payment orders, such as paper initiated orders, cannot be processed automatically nor 24/7/365, PSPs often impose restrictions on the moment until which PSUs can submit payment orders that are to be processed the same day. This moment is called the cut-off time and represents according to **Article 78(1) PSD2** the latest point in time on which an instruction is deemed to be received by the PSP on a particular business day.[19] In case a payment order is received after the cut-off time, such order is deemed to be received by the payer's PSP on the following business day. There is also the option for payers to submit payment orders to their PSP which must be executed at a future date. If a PSU submits an order for the execution of a fund transfer at a specific date, the payment order is warehoused by the payer's PSP and the time of receipt of the payment order is deemed to be the agreed date for execution. This makes sense from a legal perspective since the payer's PSP will have to hold on to the instruction for a certain period of time before it is allowed to execute the transaction. A different interpretation of the concept 'time of receipt of the payment order' would result in the payer's PSP breaching

[16] **Article 4(37) PSD2** defines a 'business day' as a day on which the relevant PSP of the payer or the PSP of the beneficiary involved in the execution of a Payment is open for business as required for the execution of a Payment. The definition of business day can therefore differ depending on the Payment product and system required for processing.

[17] This time limit may be extended by one business day for paper initiated payment transactions. For national Payments, Member States are allowed to impose a shorter maximum execution time limit.

[18] If the payment order is received on a non-business day, the payment order is deemed to be received on the following business day.

[19] If the Bank applies such cut-off time, it must inform the PSU thereof.

the mandatory time limit when acting in accordance with the payment instruction.

Further to the legal requirements imposed by PSD2 and Regulation (EU) No 260/2012 establishing technical and business requirements for credit transfers and direct debits in euro ('**SEPA Regulation**')[20], a credit transfer is also subject to the scheme rules of the Payment product used by the PSU for executing the transfer. Nowadays, the vast majority of credit transfers are processed on the basis of the EPC CT Scheme developed by the EPC. Credit transfers that are executed under this scheme have to comply with the requirements laid down in the EPC CT Rulebook.[21]

2.2.1 Fast Payments

Although PSD2 requires credit transfers to be processed within a relatively short time limit (i.e., within one business day), Payment products have been developed that cater for the 'perceived' need of consumers and companies to receive incoming payments in near real time. These Payment products, which are known as fast payments, are in essence credit transfers that provide for close to immediate clearing and settlement 24/7/365.

Payment products that offer near real-time processing have certain advantages over conventional credit transfers. For example, fast payments guarantee instant processing of time-sensitive payments.[22] Moreover, fast payments improve cash flow management of companies because it provides them with near immediate access to incoming payments.

Interoperability between PSPs is an absolute necessity when processing payments in near real time. It is therefore of paramount importance to have an EU-wide payment scheme that provides for reachability of PSPs in all Member States. The first EU-wide solution facilitating fast payments was developed by the EPC in 2017. The EPC ICT Rulebook, which refers to fast payments as 'instant payments', was developed on the basis of the EPC CT Scheme and enables near real-time processing of credit transfers

[20] Regulation (EU) No 260/2012 of 14 March 2012 "establishing technical and business requirements for credit transfers and direct debits in euro and amending Regulation (EC) No 924/2009", OJ L 94, 30.3.2012, pp. 22–37.

[21] The EPC CT Rulebook provides harmonised standards that enable PSPs to offer standardised SEPA credit transfer services (single and bulk payments) to their PSUs.

[22] See BIS (2016, p. 1).

denominated in euros.[23] In case a payer submits a payment order to its PSP for the processing of an instant payment, the EPC ICT Rulebook requires that the relevant funds be credited to the beneficiary's payment account within ten seconds after the transaction was initiated.[24] Payments exceeding a value of €100,000[25] cannot be processed on the basis of the EPC Instant CT Scheme.[26] Contrary to the market's expectations, the number of PSPs that adhered to the EPC Instant CT Scheme remains relatively limited. In August 2020, only 62.4% of the PSPs offering SEPA credit transfers adhered to the EPC Instant CT Scheme.[27] As a consequence, Payments that are initiated with the intention to be executed as a fast payment are often executed as a standard credit transfer because the Bank of the beneficiary is not a member of the EPC Instant CT Scheme.[28] One of the objectives of the Commission is however to have fast payments as the 'new standard' in the EU.[29] On 26 October 2022, the Commission therefore published a proposal for an Instant Payments Regulation, which amends the SEPA Regulation, to further enhance the adoption of fast payments by PSPs established in the EU.[30] The Instant Payments Regulation was published in the Official Journal of the European Union on 19 March 2024 and will enter into force in 2025 (**Paragraph 3.6**).

2.3 Direct Debit Collections

Like credit transfers, direct debit collections are a commonly used method for transferring funds electronically between a payer's payment account and the payment account of a beneficiary. In 2021, direct debit collections

[23] Non-euro Payments are not (yet) eligible under the EPC ICT Scheme.

[24] This is the processing time limit. PSPs are however allowed to agree with their clients that even shorter processing time limits are applied.

[25] The maximum amount was €15,000 until 1 July 2020.

[26] The EPC ICT Scheme does allow Banks to agree with their PSUs to apply a higher maximum transaction amount. Agreeing a higher amount would however only work in case both the payer's PSP and beneficiary's PSP agree to process instant payments representing such higher amount.

[27] See Commission (2020, p. 5).

[28] See ECB (2022c).

[29] See Commission (2020, p. 5).

[30] See Commission (2022).

accounted for 20% of the executed non-cash payments.[31] Unlike credit transfers, direct debit collections are initiated by the beneficiary via the beneficiary's PSP.[32] Figure 2.2 illustrates the processing of a direct debit collection.

A direct debit collection is initiated on the basis of an authorisation provided by the payer to the beneficiary called the mandate (**1**). The mandate sets out the characteristics of the collections that the beneficiary is allowed to initiate on behalf of the payer. For example, the mandate sets out the amount of each collection and whether the beneficiary is allowed to initiate a one-off (a single) collection or recurring (multiple) collections. The direct debit mandate is signed by the payer and stored by the beneficiary as evidence in case the payer questions the authorisation of a particular direct debit collection.[33] To process direct debit collections in an efficient manner, it is essential that the PSPs involved in the execution of these collections apply the same standards. To this end, the EPC

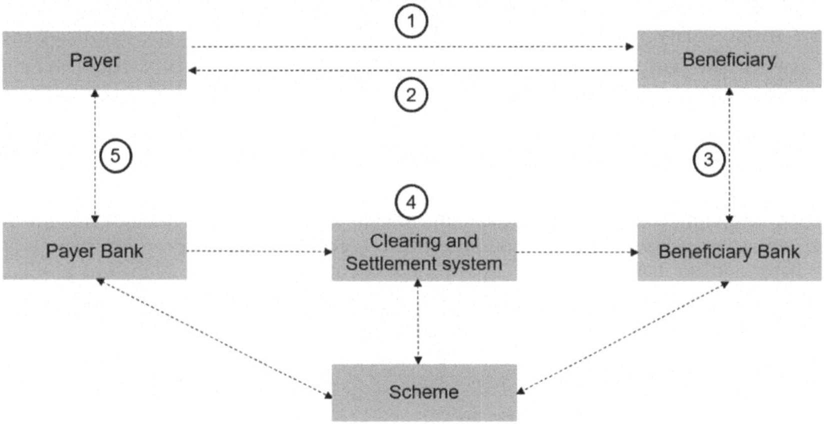

Fig. 2.2 Flowchart direct debit collection

[31] See ECB (2022a).

[32] A transaction is considered to be initiated by the beneficiary if the beneficiary initiates the transaction without any interaction of the payer.

[33] If the mandate does not meet the standards agreed between the payer and the payer's PSP, the beneficiary runs the risk that the payer's PSP considers the direct debit collection to be unauthorised.

developed direct debit schemes for direct debit collections processed by PSPs established in the SEPA area.[34] The EPC developed two schemes, namely the EPC DD Core Scheme and the EPC DD B2B Scheme. The EPC DD Core Scheme is available for processing direct debit collections whereby the payer is a company or consumer.[35] If a direct debit collection is processed under the EPC DD Core Scheme, the payer's PSP is not obliged to verify the direct debit collection against the mandate.[36] The reason for this is that the EPC DD Core Scheme allows the payer eight weeks to claim a refund in case it questions the authorisation of a particular collection. If the payer's PSP receives such request, it must refund the payer on a no-questions-asked basis.[37] To ensure support for the SEPA project, it was considered essential to establish a high level of protection for payers by providing for a legal refund right on a no-questions-asked basis for consumers (with this refund right potentially being withheld in the event of a corporate opt-out).[38] For this reason, **Article 5(6) SEPA Regulation** provides that if the framework contract between the payer and the payer's PSP does not include the right to a refund, the payer's PSP must verify for each direct debit collection whether the transaction is authorised on the basis of the mandate before it debits the payer's payment account. This provision does not work well with the refund provisions of PSD2 and the EPC DD Core Rulebook. On the basis of

[34] A SEPA direct debit is a payment instrument that enables beneficiaries to initiate national or cross-border euro denominated direct debit collections provided that both the payer and the beneficiary hold a payment account with a PSP established in a SEPA country.

[35] The EPC DD Core Scheme is mandatory for all PSPs that offer SEPA direct debit products.

[36] It is optional for the payer's PSP to verify the mandate prior to execution of the transaction under the EPC DD Core Scheme.

[37] Legacy non-euro direct debit schemes used to exist in the Non-euro area Member States since these countries were out of scope of the EPC DD Core Scheme. According to Recital 76 PSD2 these legacy direct debit schemes did not always provide for an unconditional refund right since this was not required under PSD. **Article 76(1) PSD2** addresses this issue by introducing the unconditional right to a refund as a general requirement for direct debit collections in all Member States. However, since the PSD2 unconditional refund right only covers euro-denominated direct debit collections and it were primarily the non-euro legacy direct debit schemes that did not provide for such refund right, PSD2 has not brought the envisaged harmonisation of the refund right for direct debit collections in the Non-euro area Member States.

[38] SEPA Regulation, Recital 32.

PSD2 and the EPC DD Core Rulebook, there is no requirement for the payer's PSP to verify each direct debit collection in case a refund right has not been explicitly provided for in the framework contract. Therefore, a direct debit collection whereby the framework contract does not provide for a refund right is nevertheless covered by the refund rights under PSD2 and the EPC DD Core Rulebook in case the collection is not verified by the payer's PSP.

The EPC DD B2B Scheme is only available for the processing of direct debit collections whereby the payer is a company.[39] Unlike the EPC DD Core Scheme, there is no obligation for PSPs to offer their clients direct debit collections on the basis of the EPC DD B2B Scheme. For direct debit collections governed by the EPC DD B2B Scheme, it is mandatory for the payer's PSP to verify the collection against the mandate prior to transferring the corresponding funds to the beneficiary's PSP since this scheme does not provide for a right of refund for the payer. Not having a right of refund for payers reduces the credit risk exposures of beneficiaries vis-à-vis payers, which gives companies an incentive to use direct debit collections under the EPC DD B2B Scheme.

Two weeks before the execution of a direct debit collection, the beneficiary notifies the payer of the forthcoming collection. This is a requirement often carried out by the beneficiary's PSP (**2**).[40] The beneficiary initiates the collection by sending a payment order to its PSP (**3**). When the beneficiary's PSP receives the payment order, it verifies whether the order contains all relevant information regarding the identity of the payer and the characteristics of the collection as set out in the mandate.[41]

[39] PSPs are not allowed to offer SEPA direct debit products to consumers under the EPC DD B2B Scheme.

[40] The beneficiary's PSP informs the payer's PSP of the forthcoming collection. The payer's PSP subsequently informs the payer.

[41] According to **Article 5(3) SEPA Regulation**, such data includes: (i) the type of direct debit collection (recurrent, one-off, first, last or reversal); (ii) the beneficiary's name; (iii) the IBAN of the beneficiary's payment account to be credited for the collection; (iv) where available, the payer's name; (v) the IBAN of the payer's payment account to be debited for the collection; (vi) the unique mandate reference; (vii) the date on which it was signed; (viii) the amount of the collection; (ix) where the mandate has been taken over by a beneficiary other than the beneficiary who issued the mandate, the unique mandate reference as given by the original beneficiary who issued the mandate; (x) the beneficiary's identifier; (xi) where the mandate has been taken over by a beneficiary other than the beneficiary who issued the mandate, the identifier of the original beneficiary who issued the mandate; (xii) any remittance information from the beneficiary to the

Subsequently, the beneficiary's PSP transmits the order to the payer's PSP within the time limits agreed between the beneficiary and its PSP (**4**) in accordance with **Article 83(3) PSD2**. Upon receipt of the payment order by the payer's PSP, the corresponding funds are transferred to the beneficiary's PSP within the time limits applicable to credit transfers (**Paragraph 2.2**). Regardless of whether the collection is governed by the EPC DD B2B Scheme or the EPC DD Core Scheme, the execution time for the collection is D−1/D + 1.[42] This means that when the beneficiary instructs its PSP (D-1), the payer's payment account is debited the following business day (D). The beneficiary's payment account is credited the business day following the debit value date of the payer's payment account (D + 1). In other words, SEPA direct debit collections are executed within two business days after the moment on which the beneficiary's PSP receives the beneficiary's order to initiate a collection, or the scheduled date for the beneficiary's PSP pull transaction in the event of recurring direct debit collections (**5**).

2.4 Card Payments

2.4.1 Background

When a PSU opens a payment account with an AS-PSP, the PSU often receives a debit card and/or credit card, which enables the PSU to *inter alia*: (i) access the funds standing to the credit of its payment account; (ii) initiate fund transfers from its payment account to the payment account of a beneficiary; and (iii) withdraw cash from an automated teller machine ('**ATM**'). A card provides the cardholder with a safe and efficient means for transferring funds electronically. Moreover, it offers merchants the

payer; (xiii) any purpose of the collection; and (xiv) any category of the purpose of the collection.

[42] Prior to 20 November 2016, the execution time limits used to be considerably shorter for direct debit collections executed under the EPC DD B2B Scheme, (D-1 time cycle for requesting collections and D + 1 time cycle for crediting the beneficiary's payment account) compared to direct debit collections executed under the EPC DD Core Scheme (D-5/D-2) time cycle for requesting collections and D + 3 time cycle for crediting the beneficiary's payment account).

advantage of receiving incoming payments quickly, safely and at a relatively low cost.[43] Debit cards and credit cards are therefore the most used non-cash payment instruments in the EU at present.[44] In 2021, over 49% of the non-cash payments were executed using a debit or credit card.[45]

According to **Article 2(4) IFR** a debit card transaction is a card-based Payment whereby the transaction amount is immediately charged to the cardholder. This means that the corresponding funds are debited from the payer's payment account instantly the moment after the transaction is initiated. According to **Article 2(5) IFR** credit card transactions are card-based Payments whereby the transaction amount is debited in full or in part at a pre-agreed specific calendar month date in accordance with a prearranged credit facility. Credit cards can be categorised as a deferred debit card or other credit card. With deferred debit cards, the total amount of the transactions initiated by the cardholder during a period of time is debited from the cardholder's payment account without interest on a pre-agreed date (e.g., once a month).[46] With other credit cards, the cardholder can use a credit facility to reimburse part of the amounts with interest due at a later date than specified and typically beyond a one-month horizon.[47]

In Europe, national card payments are processed primarily on the basis of national card schemes. At the moment, there is no European-wide card scheme that facilitates the processing of cross-border card payments in Europe. Cross-border acceptance of cards issued under national card schemes currently relies on co-badging agreements with international card schemes such as Visa and Mastercard.[48] As a result, the market for cross-border card payments in Europe is dominated by non-European card schemes.[49]

In order to reduce the dependence on non-European card schemes for the processing of cross-border card payments, European Banks launched

[43] The merchant is not required to keep large amounts of cash nor does it have to incur any expenses for secure cash transportation.

[44] See Ernst & Young and Copenhagen Economics (2020, p. 41).

[45] See ECB (2022a).

[46] IFR, Recital 17.

[47] Ibid.

[48] See ECB (2020b).

[49] See ECB (2019a, p. 9).

the European Payments Initiative (EPI) to enhance the reachability of cards in Europe.[50] In July 2020, the EPI Interim Company was established, which aims to create a pan-European card payment solution for consumers and merchants, a digital wallet and person-to-person (**'P2P'**) payments.[51]

In general, card payments are processed on the basis of a three-party card scheme or a four-party payment card scheme.[52]

2.4.2 Three-Party Card Scheme

A three-party card scheme, such as American Express, is a card scheme that involves the following three participants: the cardholder, the merchant and the issuer/acquirer. The card scheme is the manager of the payment network of the relevant card and determines *inter alia* the technical standards applicable to card payments, POS terminals and ATMs. Furthermore, the card scheme provides the rules on the allocation of liability between the participants in the scheme.[53] In a three-party card scheme, the card scheme also assumes the roles of issuer and acquirer. This means that the card scheme issues cards to PSUs and is responsible for authorising transactions on behalf of merchants. Three-party card schemes have contractual arrangements with both cardholders and merchants but do not hold payment accounts for these PSUs. Figure 2.3 illustrates the processing of a card payment under a three-party card scheme.

[50] See ECB (2020c).

[51] See Credit Agricole (n.d.). The EPI initiative is built on the EPC ICT Scheme.

[52] **Article 2(18) IFR** defines a 'three-party payment card scheme' as a payment card scheme in which the scheme itself provides acquiring and issuing services and card-based Payments are made from the payment account of a payer to the payment account of a beneficiary within the scheme. When a three-party payment card scheme licenses other PSPs for the issuance of card-based payment instruments or the acquiring of card-based Payments, or both, or issues card-based payment instruments with a co-branding partner or through an agent, it is considered to be a four-party payment card scheme. **Article 2(17) IFR** defines a 'four-party payment card scheme' as a payment card scheme in which card-based Payments are made from the payment account of a payer to the payment account of a beneficiary through the intermediation of the scheme, an issuer (on the payer's side) and an acquirer (on the beneficiary's side).

[53] See ECB (2010, p. 55).

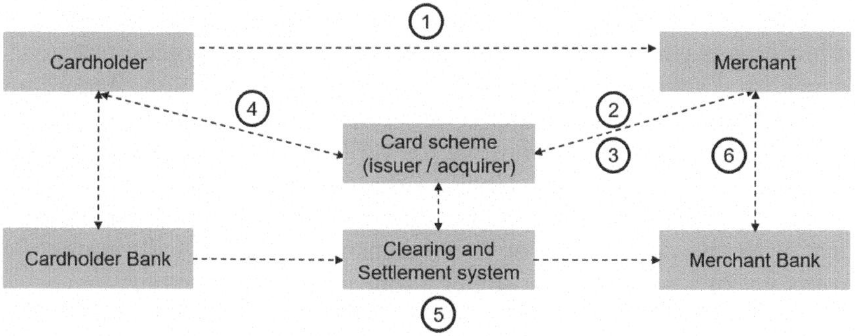

Fig. 2.3 Flowchart three-party card scheme

To initiate a Payment using a card governed by a three-party scheme, the cardholder first offers his card to a merchant's payment terminal in the merchant's physical store (Card-Present (**'CP'**) transaction) or web shop (Card-Not-Present (**'CNP'**) transaction[54]) (**1**). Subsequently, the merchant sends an authorisation request for the transaction to the card scheme (**2**). The card scheme informs the merchant of the outcome of the authorisation process (**3**). The card scheme informs the cardholder if the transaction is authorised, the transaction amount involved and the name of beneficiary (**4**). The transaction amount is transferred electronically from the cardholder's payment account to the payment account of the merchant Bank (**5**). After the funds have been credited to the payment account of the merchant Bank, the merchant Bank credits the merchant's payment account with the transaction amount on the same business day (**6**).

2.4.3 Four-Party Card Scheme

In a four-party card scheme, such as Mastercard and Visa, the issuing and acquiring roles are assumed by separate issuers and acquirers. According to **Article 2(2) IFR** the issuer is the PSP that: (i) provides the cardholder with a card to initiate payment transactions; and (ii) processes transactions

[54] CNP transactions are Payments whereby the PSU is not physically presenting the payment card to the merchant when initiating the Payment. In other words, CNP transactions are card-based transactions that are not initiated at POS.

that have been initiated with such card. The issuer provides services like authorising payment transactions initiated by the cardholder and guaranteeing the acquirer payment of the card-based transaction. According to **Article 2(1) IFR** the acquirer processes card transactions on behalf of the merchant and is responsible for verifying the cardholder's creditworthiness and authenticity. Unlike a three-party card scheme, the card scheme of a four-party card scheme does not have a contractual arrangement with the cardholders or the merchants. Figure 2.4 illustrates the processing of a card payment under a four-party card scheme.

To initiate a Payment using a card governed by a four-party card scheme, the cardholder first offers his card to a merchant's payment terminal in the merchant's physical store (CP transaction) or web shop (CNP transaction) (**1**). Subsequently, the merchant sends an authorisation request for the transaction to the acquirer (**2**). The acquirer forwards the relevant payment information, which it received from the merchant's (digital) terminal, via the card scheme to the issuer for authorisation (**3**).[55] If the transaction is authorised by the issuer, the transaction amount will be reserved, which means that the cardholder

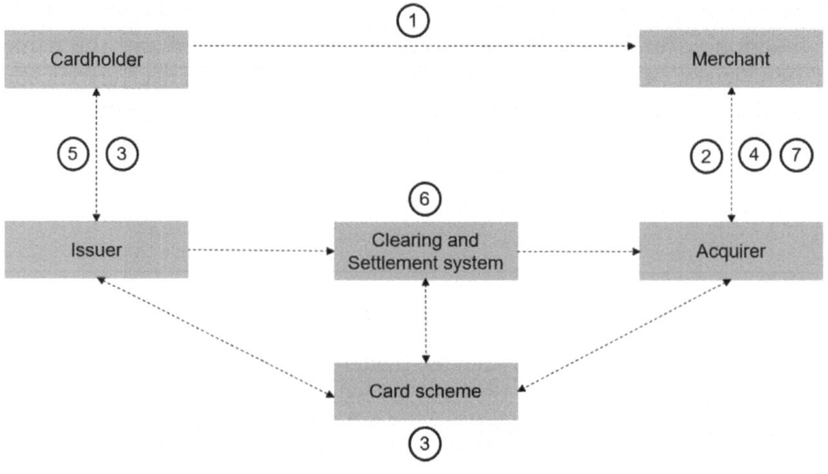

Fig. 2.4 Flowchart four-party card scheme

[55] The acquirer can also forward said information to the issuer via a switching center.

can no longer dispose of that amount for making other payments, and the issuer informs the acquirer that the transaction has been authorised (**3**). The acquirer informs the merchant on the outcome of the authorisation process (**4**). The issuer informs the cardholder regarding the outcome of the authorisation process, the transaction amount involved and the name of beneficiary (**5**). The transaction amount is transferred electronically from the issuer's payment account to the payment account of the acquirer (**6**). When the funds are credited to the payment account of the acquirer, the acquirer credits the merchant's payment account with the transaction amount on the same business day (**7**).

2.5 Payments Connected to E-money Transactions

An E-money instrument is an electronic device on which a monetary value can be stored and which can be used to make payments with merchants that have accepted the E-money instrument as a payment method. E-money instruments can be hardware-based or software (server)-based, depending on the technology used to store the monetary value. With hardware-based E-money instruments, the monetary value is loaded on a physical device before it can be used to make payments. Examples of hardware-based E-money instruments include prepaid cards[56] such as gift cards and loyalty cards, which can be used for making low value payments. These cards are also known as 'pay early' cards.[57] With software-based E-money instruments, the monetary value is stored on a remote server. The most commonly known provider of software-based E-money instruments is PayPal.

A further distinction can be made with regard to the functionality of E-money instruments. Depending on the scope of use, E-money instruments are categorised as closed-loop or open-loop instruments. Closed-loop E-money instruments can only be used by the E-money holder to purchase: (i) a single category of products or services within an unrestricted geographical area; or (ii) various products or services within a restricted geographical area. With an open-loop E-money instrument,

[56] Prepaid cards were initially used as a single-purpose payment instrument whereby the card issuer and the merchant accepting these cards were the same entity (e.g., telephone cards).

[57] See Sienkiewicz, S. (2007, p. 10).

the E-money holder has more flexibility for making payments. Open-loop E-money instruments can be used for a wide range of products and services and are often designed to be used on an international scale.[58] Furthermore, open-loop E-money cards often allow the E-money holder to withdraw cash from an ATM.[59]

E-money instruments have numerous advantages over other payment methods. Compared to cash, E-money instruments provide a safer means to make payments. For merchants, the costs of accepting E-money payments are considerably lower than the costs of accepting cash payments. An important advantage of E-money instruments over other cashless instruments, such as credit cards and cheques is that the credibility of the payer is guaranteed with an E-money instrument. Since the transaction value must be loaded to the E-money instrument before it can be used to initiate payments, the beneficiary has certainty that payment will not be refused due to a lack of funds. Despite these advantages, E-money instruments are not very popular in Europe. In 2018, E-money transactions accounted for only 3% of the executed non-cash payments.[60] Moreover, fast payments are expected to replace E-money products for P2P, POS and e-commerce payments since fast payments also provide for near real-time fund transfers in a closed-loop system.[61]

Figure 2.5 illustrates the processing of an E-money payment.

The E-money issuer[62] is responsible for loading the monetary value on an E-money instrument in exchange for money.[63] When loading monetary value on an E-money instrument, the holder of such instrument

[58] See FATF (2010, p. 29).

[59] Open-loop cards are often branded with Visa or Mastercard, as a result of which prepaid cards can be used for making payments anywhere where Visa or Mastercard is accepted.

[60] See Ernst & Young and Copenhagen Economics (2020, p. 42).

[61] See ECB (2019b, p. 23).

[62] According to **Article 1(1) EMD2**, an E-money issuer can be: (i) a Bank; (ii) an EMI; (iii) a post office giro institution (iv) the ECB or a national central bank not acting in their capacity as monetary authority or other public authority; or (v) a Member State or its national authority when acting in its capacity as public authority.

[63] The E-money issuer is generally also the E-money system operator. In its capacity as system operator, the E-money issuer is responsible for providing the technical platform for the execution of Payments using E-money products and managing the E-money scheme program. To this end, the E-money issuer often enters into contractual arrangements with the distributors, acquirers, PSUs and merchants.

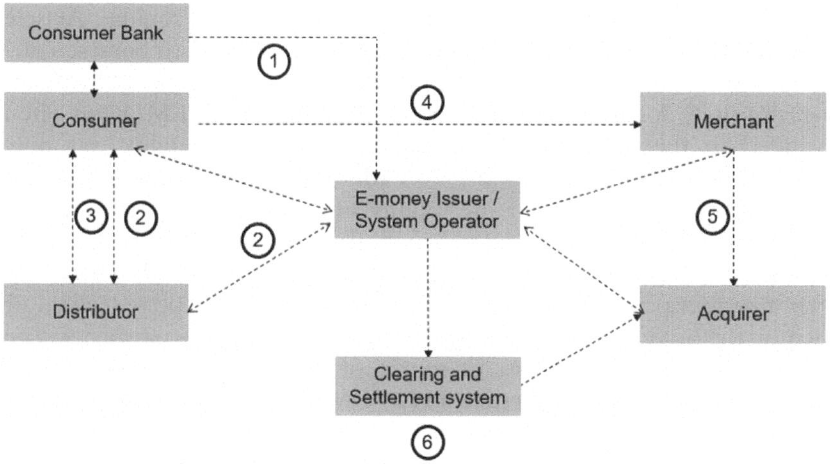

Fig. 2.5 Flowchart E-money scheme

obtains a claim on the E-money issuer. There are several ways in which money can be uploaded in an E-money system. This can, for example, be done by transferring funds from a payment account held with a Bank (**1**) or by purchasing a pre-paid card on which a certain amount of E-money is loaded (**2**). For Non-Bank E-money issuers, it is essential that the funds received from the E-money holder are instantly converted into E-money. If the funds are not immediately converted, such funds constitute repayable funds, which Non-Bank E-money issuers are not allowed to attract or hold from the public (**Paragraph 4.1**). The monetary value stored on the E-money instrument must be equal to the value of the funds transferred to the E-money issuer in exchange for the E-money instrument.

It is common practice for E-money issuers to use distributors, such as merchants, for the distribution of E-money instruments. **Article 3(4) EMD2** provides that distributors are responsible for selling E-money instruments to E-money holders (**2**) and/or redeeming E-money on behalf of E-money issuers (**3**). As such, distributors are not required to obtain a licence as an electronic money institution (**'EMI'**) or PI.[64] Redeeming E-money is a process whereby E-money is converted back to

[64] See Voerman, J. A., and Baukema, J. (2017, p. 196).

money and paid out to the consumer. Under the EMD regime, **Article 3(2) EMD** provided that E-money issuers were allowed to contractually agree with E-money holders under which conditions they could redeem their funds.[65] A condition required under **Article 3(3) EMD** and often included in the terms & conditions was that redeemability was only allowed for a minimum amount.[66] In addition, it was common practice for E-money issuers to limit the validity of their E-money instruments, which enabled E-money issuers to benefit from the so-called 'freefall'. The freefall represents the value of outstanding E-money that loses validity after a certain period (e.g., one year) and can no longer be redeemed or used by the holder of the E-money instrument for making payments. The freefall used to be an important source of income for E-money issuers under the EMD regime. **Article 11(2) EMD2** stipulates that E-money holders can request their E-money issuer to redeem their funds at any time at par value.[67] E-money issuers are no longer allowed to impose a minimum threshold on the redeemability of the E-money instruments issued. Furthermore, E-money issuers are no longer allowed to limit the validity of the E-money instrument as a result of which EMD2 does not allow E-money issuers to benefit from a freefall of their issued E-money instruments.

When an E-money holder uses an E-money instrument for initiating a payment to a merchant (**4**), the E-money holder's claim on the E-money issuer is transferred to the merchant.[68] The acquirer provides the IT-infrastructure needed for the merchant's acceptance of E-money payments (**5**) and obtains a credit risk exposure vis-à-vis the E-money

[65] EMD was in effect from October 27, 2000 until October 30, 2009.

[66] E-money issuers were not allowed to impose a minimum threshold for redeemability exceeding €10.

[67] However, **Article 11(4) EMD2** allows EMIs to make redeemability subject to a fee provided that this is included in the contract with the E-money holder and: (i) redemption is requested before the termination of the contract; (ii) the contract provides for a termination date and the E-money holder terminates the contract before that date; or (iii) redemption is requested more than one year after the date of termination of the contract (in that case, the total monetary value of the E-money held must be redeemed when redemption is requested within one year after the date of the termination of the contract). In case an E-money issuer imposes such fee, it must be proportionate with the actual costs incurred by the EMI for redemption.

[68] See Voerman, J. A., and Baukema, J. (2017, p. 194).

issuer equal to the transaction amount.[69] The corresponding funds are transferred electronically from the E-money issuer's payment account to the payment account of the acquirer (**6**) and subsequently to the payment account of the merchant.

Secondary Sources

Bank of England. (1996). *Payment Systems*. Handbooks in Central Banking No. 8, p. 15.

BIS. (2016). *Fast Payments—Enhancing the Speed and Availability of Retail Payments*, p. 1.

Commission. (2020). *Communication from the Commission to the European Parliament, the Council, the European Economic and Social Committee and the Committee of the Regions on a Retail Payments Strategy for the EU*, COM(2020) 592 final, pp. 5, 13.

Commission. (2022). *Proposal for a Regulation of the European Parliament and of the Council amending Regulations (EU) No 260/2012 and (EU) 2021/1230 as regards instant credit transfers in euro*, COM(2022) 546 final.

Credit Agricole. (n.d.). *EPI: The European Payments Initiative*. Credit Agricole Press Room. https://pressroom.credit-agricole.com/news/epi-the-european-payments-initiative-1d9b-94727.html Accessed April 13, 2024.

ECB. (2010). *The Payment System*, pp. 43, 55.

ECB. (2019a). *Card Payments in Europe—Current Landscape and Future Prospects: A Eurosystem Perspective*, p. 9.

ECB. (2019b). *Implications of Digitilisation in Retail Payments for the Eurosystem's Catalyst Role*, p. 23.

ECB. (2020a). *ECB Announces Changes to Collateral Framework for Eurosystem Credit Operations*. https://www.ecb.europa.eu/press/pr/date/2020/html/ecb.pr200702~214c52c76b.en.html. Accessed 14 April 2024.

ECB. (2020b). *From the Payments Revolution to the Reinvention of Money*, Speech by F. Panetta at the Deutsche Bundesbank conference on the "Future of Payments in Europe.

ECB. (2020c). *ECB Announces Changes to Its Supervisory and Supervisory Board*. https://www.ecb.europa.eu/press/pr/date/2020/html/ecb.pr200702~214c52c76b.en.html. Accessed April 13, 2024.

ECB. (2022a). *Payments Atatistics: 2021*, Press release.

ECB. (2022b). *Study on the Payment Attitudes of Consumers in the Euro Area (SPACE)—2022*, pp. 19, 23.

[69] The acquirer has a contractual arrangement with the merchants that accept the relevant E-money product.

ECB. (2022c). *Speech by Fabio Panetta, Member of the Executive Board of the ECB, at the Eurofi Financial Forum 2022.* European Central Bank. https://www.ecb.europa.eu/press/key/date/2022/html/ecb.sp220616~9f8d1e277b.en.html#footnote.24. Accessed April 13, 2024.

Ernst & Young and Copenhagen Economics. (2020). *Study on the Application of the Interchange Fee Regulation*, Commission Final Report, pp. 41, 42.

FATF. (2010). *Money Laundering Using New Payment Methods*, FATF Report, p. 29.

Sienkiewicz, S. (2007). *Prepaid Cards: Vulnerable to Money Laundering* (Discussion Paper Payment Cards Center, p. 10).

Voerman, J. A., & Baukema, J. (2017). *Het toenemend belang van electronisch geld voor FinTech ondernemingen*, Tijdschrift voor Financieel Recht No. 5, pp. 194, 196.

CHAPTER 3

Key Legislative Initiatives on the Establishment of an Internal Market for Payments

3.1 Background

It was the banking sector that first developed self-regulations on the execution of Payments as well as the conditions under which Non-Bank service providers were allowed to participate in the Payments ecosystem. Since these regulations were developed by Banks instead of the national or European legislature, they were not so much in favour of enhancing the competitive position of Non-Banks *vis-à-vis* Banks. As a consequence, Non-Banks often encountered disproportionate barriers when trying to enter the European market for Payments as a banking competitor. One could therefore not speak of a level playing field between Banks and Non-Banks.

The lack of a level playing field between Banks and Non-Banks did not remain unnoticed by the European legislature. However, it was the large growth of cross-border credit transfers that occurred during the nineties of the last century which turned out to be the trigger for the European legislature to become more active in regulating the European market for Payments.[1] The ambitious target set by the European legislature was to

[1] Moreover, an integrated European market for Payments also contributes to the objective of establishing an internal market as set out in **Article 3(3) Treaty on European Union** (OJ C 202, 7.6.2016).

J. A. Jans, *Electronic Payments in the European Market*, EBI Studies in Banking and Capital Markets Law,
https://doi.org/10.1007/978-3-031-64338-5_3

establish an internal market for Payments, which matched perfectly with the objectives of the Financial Services Action Plan that the EU heads of government signed up to at the Lisbon summit in March 2000.[2]

Before the adoption of the Financial Services Action Plan in 2000, the first modest steps were taken by the Commission. In 1997, the Commission called for legislative action at a European level in order to boost the market for Payments.[3] Four key areas were identified by the Commission that required attention from the European legislature. First, the Commission considered it essential to develop a profound legal framework for the issuance of E-money instruments. Second, clear rules were needed on transparency, liability and redress procedures for payment instruments. Third, clarification regarding the applicability of EU competition law in the Payments market was required in order to strike an adequate balance between PSP interoperability and sound competition. Fourth, the security of the processing of Payments had to be improved to reduce the market's exposure to security risks such as payment fraud. The European legislature picked up the gauntlet, which resulted in a transition from the self-regulation framework developed by the banking sector towards a European-wide legislative framework aimed at creating equivalent standards for PSPs that process Payments in the EU.

The European legislature has a range of different legal instruments at its disposal of which the most important ones are regulations and directives.[4] According to **Article 288, TFEU** Regulations are legal acts that are binding in their entirety[5] and directly applicable in all Member States. This means that a regulation applies *vis-à-vis* PSPs and PSUs in the EU/EEA without the necessity of being transposed into national laws. A regulation is therefore the better legal instrument if the goal is to ensure a uniform application of legal requirements in all Member States. Unlike a regulation, **Article 288 TFEU** requires a directive to be transposed into national law before it applies in the Member States. As a result, there is a significant risk that the requirements set out in a directive do not apply homogenously in all Member States nor at the same time, which

[2] See European Parliament. (n.d.).

[3] See Commission (1997, p. 3).

[4] An example of an alternative instrument available to the European legislature that is not covered in this study is a 'decision'. A decision is a binding act which can have a specific addressee or be of general application.

[5] This element distinguishes a regulation from a decision.

in itself may impose a barrier for PSPs to enter a certain geographical market.[6] A directive can be a minimum harmonisation directive or a maximum harmonisation directive. A minimum harmonisation directive only provides for minimum requirements that national legislatures must adopt into their national legislation.[7] Minimum harmonisation directives allow Member states to impose more stringent requirements when deemed necessary. With a maximum harmonisation directive, Member States are not allowed to impose requirements that are more stringent than those set out in the directive.[8] Consequently, a maximum harmonisation directive is an obvious choice in case the main objective is to create a uniform legal framework in all Member States.

The first legislative initiatives developed by the European legislature covered the processing of cross-border Payments and the issuance of E-money products. Although these initiatives contributed to a more efficient processing of cross-border Payments and an increasing use of E-money products as an alternative to cash transactions, these initiatives did not so much focus on enhancing competition between Banks and Non-Banks. Sound competition between PSPs is however of paramount importance since it incentivises PSPs to innovate.[9] In addition, higher levels of competition between PSPs tend to increase the variety of Payment products available in the market and reduces the prices charged for these products.

With the adoption of EMD in 2000 and PSD in 2007, sound competition between Banks and Non-Banks first became a main priority for the European legislature from a financial services regulatory perspective. EMD and PSD were the first financial services regulatory directives incorporating competition law requirements for PSPs. As such, these directives marked the beginning of the transition towards a level playing field between Banks and Non-Banks.

[6] See Rosa (2018, p. 422).

[7] See EUR-Lex (n.d.).

[8] Ibid.

[9] A potential disadvantage of increased competition is that it can exert pressure on the profitability of PSPs and as a result incentivise risk-taking behavior.

3.2 EU Rules on Cross-Border Payments

The processing of cross-border Payments, which are Payments whereby the payer's PSP and the beneficiary's PSP are established in different Member States, used to be relatively complex and expensive compared to national Payments, which are Payments whereby both the payer's PSP and the beneficiary's PSP are established in the same Member State. PSPs used to apply different communication standards for Payment messaging as well as different arrangements for the clearing of Payments. Moreover, before the introduction of the euro in 2002[10], the execution of cross-border Payments between Member States required a currency conversion, which further complicated the processing of these transactions. As a result, the execution time for cross-border Payments used to be substantially longer compared to national Payments and the fees for processing cross-border Payments were considerably higher. In other words, large differences were observed regarding processing efficiency between national Payments and cross-border Payments.[11]

In 1990, the Commission published a discussion paper on Payments in the EU in which it concluded that the internal market's true potential for Payments could only be realised if the systems for processing cross-border Payments operate as efficient as the systems used for national Payments.[12] Efficient processing of cross-border Payments requires *inter alia* that PSPs in different Member States apply the same standards. To this end, the Commission adopted in 1990 Recommendation 90/109/EEC on the transparency of banking conditions relating to cross-border financial transactions[13], which introduced several transparency principles that Member States were recommended to impose on the service providers that processed retail cross-border Payments in their jurisdiction.[14] These principles did not only apply to PSPs, but were also relevant to other

[10] Council Regulation (EC) No 974/98 of 3 May 1998 "on the introduction of the euro", OJ L 139, 11.5.1998, pp. 1–5.

[11] See Commission (2003, p. 5).

[12] See Commission (1990, p. 1).

[13] Commission Recommendation 90/109/EEC of 14 February 1990 "on the transparency of banking conditions relating to cross-border financial transactions", OJ L 67, 15.3.1990, pp. 39–43.

[14] Recommendation 90/109/EEC focussed on retail cross-border Payments and did not cover wholesale cross-border Payments.

service providers involved in the ecosystem of cross-border Payments. Commission Recommendation 90/109/EEC covered different types of cross-border Payments, including credit transfers and direct debit collections.[15] The Commission recommended Member States to adopt the following six principles:

Principle 1:	Service providers should provide their clients with understandable information on cross-border Payments prior to executing such transactions
Principle 2:	After the execution of a cross-border Payment, service providers should inform their clients of the fees charged[16]
Principle 3:	The payer's service provider should inform the payer if the payer, the beneficiary or both of them incur charges for the execution of the cross-border Payment
Principle 4:	Intermediary service providers, that do not have a direct client relationship with the payer or the beneficiary, should process payment orders within two business days after receipt of the funds[17]
Principle 5:	The payer's service provider should fulfil its obligations arising from a transfer instruction no later than the business day following receipt of the funds[18]
Principle 6:	All service providers should swiftly deal with complaints

These principles merely provided the market with insight into what the Commission considered to be desired behaviour since recommendations issued by the Commission do not create enforceable legal obligations. Especially with regard to cross-border Payments, it would have resorted more effect if these principles had been adopted in a regulation or directive. However, these legislative instruments were not available at the time the Commission issued Recommendation 90/109/EEC.

In 1992, the Commission published a working document in which it concluded that substantial improvements were needed in relation to

[15] Recommendation 90/109/EEC covered Payments denominated in ecus or in an EU currency.

[16] Where relevant, clients should also be informed about the exchange rate for the execution of a cross-border Payment.

[17] In case this is not possible, the intermediary service provider should give prior notification to the service provider that issued the payment order of the expected delay. In case of a delay in the processing of the transaction, the payer should obtain a refund for part of the costs of the Payment.

[18] This is only different in case the order provides for a later date of execution.

the transparency, speed, reliability and costs of cross-border Payments.[19] Since the fees charged for cross-border Payments were approximately ten to 20 times higher than the fees charged for corresponding national Payments, the European Parliament adopted Resolution A3/0029/93 concerning the systems of payments in the context of the Economic and Monetary Union in 1993. According to Resolution A3/0029/93, the following requirements had to be covered in a directive: (i) an obligation for PSPs to inform prospective PSUs of the means available for initiating Payments and the costs associated therewith; (ii) a right for the PSU to incur all charges associated with a cross-border Payment[20]; (iii) cross-border Payments should be settled within four business days; and (iv) PSUs should have access to a redress procedure.

3.2.1 Directive 97/5/EC on Cross-Border Credit Transfers

The establishment of a European legal framework for the execution of cross-border Payments was one of the first initiatives taken by the European legislature to regulate the market for Payments. To reduce the execution time and costs for cross-border Payments, the European legislature adopted Directive 97/5/EC on cross-border credit transfers ('**Directive 97/5/EC**')[21], which had to be transposed into national law by 14 August 1999 according to **Article 11 Directive 97/5/EC**.[22] Directive 97/5/EC introduced, amongst others, transparency requirements and standards for execution times and charges that PSPs had to apply when processing cross-border credit transfers. Directive 97/5/EC only covered: (i) cross-border credit transfers executed in euro, or the currency of a Non-euro area Member State; (ii) that represented a

[19] See Commission (1992, p. 2).

[20] Thereby eliminating the market practice of 'double charging'.

[21] Directive 97/5/EC of 27 January 1997 "on cross-border credit transfers", OJ L 43, 14.2.1997, pp. 25–30.

[22] Directive 97/5/EC was in effect from February 14, 1997 until October 31, 2008.

maximum value of €50,000; and (iii) which were executed by institutions[23] established in the EEA.[24] Like Commission Recommendation 90/109/EEC, Directive 97/5/EC referred to institutions instead of credit institutions to cover all service providers involved in the execution of cross-border credit transfers. Not bringing other service providers than Banks within the scope of Directive 97/5/EC was considered inadequate since this would be detrimental to the efficient processing of cross-border credit transfers. Although the Commission also recognised the importance of having efficient processing of cross-border direct debit collections[25], the Commission did not consider it necessary to bring these collections within the scope of Directive 97/5/EC since cross-border direct debit collections accounted for only a small part of all cross-border Payments executed at that time.[26] Moreover, cross-border direct debit collections were excluded from the scope of Directive 97/5/EC because of the different responsibilities that the service providers involved in the processing of these collections fulfilled compared to their responsibilities regarding cross-border credit transfers.[27]

3.2.1.1 Execution Time Limit for Cross-Border Credit Transfers

Article 6(1) Directive 97/5/EC required institutions to execute cross-border credit transfers within the time limits agreed between the payer's institution and the payer. If the payer's institution and the payer did not agree on a specific time limit, the payer's institution was obliged to execute cross-border transfers within five business days after acceptance of the payment order.[28] When the funds were received by the beneficiary's institution, **Article 6(2) Directive 97/5/EC** required said

[23] Institutions within the meaning of Directive 97/5/EC are natural or legal persons involved in the execution of cross-border credit transfers.

[24] Decision by the EEA Joint Committee No 1/98 of 30 January 1998 "amending Annex IX (Financial Services) and Annex XIX (Consumer Protection) to the EEA Agreement", OJ L 272, 8.10.1998, pp. 1–2.

[25] See Commission (1992, p. 3).

[26] Directive 97/5/EC, Recital 1.

[27] See Commission (1994, p. 21).

[28] Prior to the processing of a cross-border credit transfer, the payer's institution had to provide the payer with an indication of the time required for the funds to be credited to the payment account of the beneficiary's institution as well as the time needed for the funds to be credited to the account of the beneficiary.

institution to credit the beneficiary's payment account within the time limit agreed with the beneficiary or, in the absence of such agreement, at the end of the business day following the day on which the funds were credited to the institution's payment account. If the payer's institution or the beneficiary's institution did not meet the applicable time limit, the relevant institution had to compensate its own PSU for the damages caused thereby.[29] In case a cross-border credit transfer was not successfully executed, **Article 8(1) Directive 97/5/EC** required the payer's institution to refund the payer: (i) the transaction amount of the cross-border credit transfer; and (ii) interest and charges paid by the payer regarding the cross-border credit transfer. The refund liability was capped at €12,500 to ensure that such liability would not have an undesirable impact on the solvency position of the payer's institution.

3.2.1.2 Charging Fees for Cross-Border Credit Transfers

In general, institutions can apply three different methods for charging fees for the execution of cross-border credit transfers.[30] First, institutions can apply BEN charging, which means that all transaction fees are charged to the beneficiary. If BEN charging is applied, the beneficiary's institution deducts the fees from the incoming transaction amount before crediting the beneficiary's payment account. Second, institutions can apply OUR charging, which means that all transaction fees are charged to the payer. Third, institutions have the option to apply SHA charging, which is a charging method whereby the payer and beneficiary share the costs for the execution of the transaction. In the case of SHA charging, the payer and the beneficiary each pay the fees of their own institution. As a default setting, **Article 7(1) Directive 97/5/EC** applied OUR charging for cross-border credit transfers. However, PSUs acting as payer were allowed to request their institution to apply BEN or SHA charging for a particular payment.

It was not uncommon for institutions to double charge fees for the execution of cross-border credit transfers. In such cases, the payer paid all fees to ensure that the beneficiary received the full transaction amount and the beneficiary was additionally charged by its own institution for the crediting of its payment account. To eliminate the practice of double

[29] Such compensation covered only payment of interest.

[30] These charging options are also used for other types of Payments.

charging for cross-border credit transfers, **Articles 7(2) and 7(3) Directive 97/5/EC** imposed an obligation on institutions to refund any fees it charged in breach of the charging instructions given by the payer.

3.2.2 Regulation 2560/2001 on Cross-Border Payments in Euro

In 2001, Retail Banking Research Ltd published a research report on the application of Directive 97/5/EC in the Member States (Retail Banking Research 2001).[31] This report revealed that the implementation of Directive 97/5/EC has had a positive effect on the average costs for cross-border credit transfers, which decreased from €25.41 to €24.09.[32] Moreover, the implementation of Directive 97/5/EC resulted in a reduction of the average execution time of cross-border credit transfers from 4.79 business days to 2.97 business days.[33] Despite these improvements, there were still large differences with regard to costs and execution times between national and cross-border credit transfers.[34] Cross-border transfers remained expensive compared to national credit transfers and the processing times of such transactions were relatively long. These high costs and long execution times withheld the Payments market from achieving its full potential.

Alignment of the fees charged for cross-border Payments and corresponding national Payments is a prerequisite for the realisation of an efficient European market for Payments. To bridge the gap between the fees charged for national and cross-border Payments, the European legislature adopted Regulation (EC) No 2560/2001 on cross-border payments in euro (**'Regulation 2560/2001'**)[35], which covered according to **Article 2(a) Regulation 2560/2001** cross-border credit transfers, cross-border card payments, cross-border cash withdrawals with a payment instrument, the (un)loading of E-money instruments at ATMs

[31] See Retail Banking Research (2001).

[32] Ibid., p. 1.

[33] Ibid.

[34] See Simona (2011, p. 69).

[35] Regulation (EC) No 2560/2001 of 19 December 2001 on cross-border payments in euro", OJ L 344, 28.12.2001, pp. 13–16. Regulation 2560/2001 was in effect from December 31, 2001 until October 31, 2009.

and cross-border cheques.[36] **Article 1 Regulation 2560/2001** excluded cross-border Payments between institutions made for their own account excluded from the scope of application. **Article 3 Regulation 2560/2001** required charges levied in respect of euro-denominated Payments executed in the EEA[37] for a maximum amount of €12,500 to be the same as the charges levied by the same PSP for corresponding national transactions.[38] To ensure homogenous application of the equal charging principle throughout the EU, the European legislature resorted to the use of a regulation instead of a directive.

A reason why the processing of cross-border Payments used to be relatively expensive compared to national Payments was because it often required manual intervention. PSPs applied different communication standards, which made it impossible for them to use automated processing. To promote standardisation in the market for Payments, **Article 5(1) Regulation 2560/2001** required institutions to provide customers upon request with the International Bank Account Number ('**IBAN**') and Bank Identifier Code ('**BIC**'). Moreover, **Article 5(2) Regulation 2560/2001** obliged customers to provide their institution upon request with the IBAN of the beneficiary and the BIC of the beneficiary's institution. Regulation 2560/2001 did however not oblige institutions to use the IBAN and BIC standards *vis-à-vis* each other.

[36] Pursuant to **Article 2(a)(iii) Regulation 2560/2001** cross-border cheques are cheques as defined in the Geneva Convention providing uniform laws for cheques of 19 March 1931. According to Recital 8 Regulation 2560/2001, the principle of uniform charges did not apply to paper cheques since these payments could not be processed efficiently. However, the principle of transparent charges did apply to paper cheques.

[37] Non-euro area Member States were however also allowed to apply Regulation 2560/2001 if it notified the Commission thereof. This option was applied by the Swedish authorities, who notified the Commission that it also applied Regulation 2560/2001 to the Swedish Kronor as of 25 July 2002 (Communication from the Commission pursuant to **Article 9 Regulation 2560**, OJ C 165, 11.7.2002). As of 2003, the application of Regulation 2560/2001 was expanded to cover all EEA Member States as a result of Decision by the EEA Joint Committee No 154/2003 of 7 November 2003 " amending Annex XII (Free movement of capital) to the EEA Agreement", OJ L 41, 12.2.2004, pp. 51–52.

[38] Cross-border transfers to euro-denominated payment accounts held in a Non-euro area Member State were also covered by Regulation 2560/2001. Currency conversion fees imposed by an institution where a cross-border transaction involved a non-euro payment account were not subject to Regulation 2560/2001. In these situations, institutions were free to determine the fees it charged for conversion services.

3.2.3 Regulation 924/2009/EC on Cross-Border Payments

In 2008, the Commission published an evaluation report on the impact of Regulation 2560/2001 on costs and execution times of cross-border Payments in the EEA.[39] One of the Commission's main conclusions was that the costs of processing cross-border euro-denominated Payments decreased significantly as a result of Regulation 2560/2001.[40] The average cost of a €100 cross-border Payments went down from €24 to €2.50.[41] The evaluation report also revealed that Regulation 2560/2001 incentivised the European Payments sector to invest in a pan-European IT-infrastructure for the execution of cross-border Payments, thereby increasing the processing efficiency of these payments.[42]

However, the evaluation report also identified several shortcomings that required further attention from the European legislature. First, it appeared that a number of Banks in Non-euro area Member States applied the provisions on equality of charges for cross-border credit transfers and national transfers to increase the charges for national Payments instead of to decrease the charges for cross-border Payments.[43] Second, the introduction of new cross-border Payment products that were not covered by Regulation 2560/2001, such as cross-border direct debit collections,[44] resulted in the applicability of different standards and requirements for different types of cross-border transactions.[45] Third, the definitions applied in Regulation 2560/2001 were not aligned with the definitions used in PSD.[46]

To ensure alignment with PSD and to boost the rollout of new cross-border Payment products, such as the SEPA direct debit collections, the

[39] See Commission (2008).

[40] Ibid., p. 13.

[41] See Commission (2006b, p. 3).

[42] See Commission (2008, p. 13).

[43] Ibid., p. 6.

[44] Prior to the adoption of Regulation 924/2009, direct debit products were only available on a national level.

[45] See Commission (2008, pp. 9–10).

[46] Ibid., p. 13.

European legislature adopted Regulation (EC) No 924/2009 on cross-border payments (**'Regulation 924/2009'**).[47] Regulation 924/2009 entered into force in 2009 and introduced a number of amendments to the equal charging principle of Regulation 2560/2001 to further align charges for national and cross-border Payments.[48] First, Regulation 924/2009 applied the principle of equal charging to cross-border Payments that was initiated by the beneficiary's PSP, such as direct debit collections.[49] Second, **Article 3(1) Regulation 924/2009** increased the maximum value of cross-border Payments covered by the equal charging principle from €12,500 to €50,000. Third, the equal charging principle covered fees that were linked to cross-border Payments.[50] Fourth, **Article 6 Regulation 924/2009** imposed a cap on the fees that the payer's PSP could charge to the beneficiary's PSP for the execution of a cross-border direct debit collection.[51]

As with Regulation 2560/2001, the provisions of Regulation 924/2009 were only binding for PSPs established in Euro area Member States. Regulation 924/2009 did however allow Non-euro area Member States to extend the scope of applicability of the regulation to their national currency if it notified the Commission thereof.[52]

[47] Regulation (EC) No 924/2009 of 16 September 2009 "on cross-border payments in the Community and repealing Regulation (EC) No 2560/2001", OJ L 266, 9.10.2009, pp. 11–18.

[48] According to Recital 7 Regulation 924/2009 one should take, amongst others, the following criteria into consideration when comparing cross-border Payments with 'corresponding' national Payments: (i) the payment channel (e.g., internet banking) used for initiating the Payment; (ii) rules and regulations for executing and terminating the Payment; and (iii) the degree of automation of the relevant Payment.

[49] Payment products covered by Regulation 924/2009 included: (i) credit transfers; (ii) direct debit collections; (iii) cash withdrawals at ATM's; (iv) payments by means of debit cards and credit cards; and (v) money remittance. As with Regulation 2560/2001, Articles 1(3) and 3(4) Regulation 924/2009 stipulates that the provisions of Regulation 924/2009 did not apply to payments made by PSPs for their own account or on behalf of other PSPs nor did it apply to currency conversion charges.

[50] As with Regulation 2560/2001, currency conversion charges were not in scope of Regulation 924/2009.

[51] A fee of €0.088 had to be applied for each cross-border direct debit collection executed before 1 November 2012, unless a lower fee was agreed between the PSPs of the payer and beneficiary.

[52] Among others Romania opted for the option to extend the application of Regulation 924/2009 to the Romanian Lei on 29 July 2011. **Article 14(3) Regulation 924/2009**

3.2.3.1 Regulation 2019/518 Amending Regulation 924/2009

Since approximately 80% of the cross-border euro-denominated Payments appeared to involve a PSP established in a Non-euro area Member State, the equal charging requirement of Regulation 924/2009 only covered around 20% of the cross-border euro-denominated transactions executed in the EU.[53] For these transactions, charges have decreased considerably as a result of the adoption of Regulation 924/2009. However, the charges for cross-border euro Payments to or from Non-euro area Member States remained relatively high. This imbalance was addressed with the adoption of Regulation (EU) 2019/518 as regards certain charges on cross-border payments in the Union and currency conversion charges ('**Regulation 2019/518**')[54], which amended Regulation 924/2009. Regulation 2019/518 expands the scope of the equal charging requirement of Regulation 924/2009 by also covering cross-border euro Payments from or to PSPs established in a Non-euro area Member State. To be subject to the equal charging requirement, a particular cross-border Payment must be 'equivalent' to a corresponding national Payment. Regulation 2019/518 does however not provide any guidance as to what 'equivalent' means in practice. The European Banking Federation (EBF) suggested that PSPs must assess whether transactions correspond in their nature based on transaction characteristics such as processing time, transaction value, degree of automation, customer status, urgency of the payment and system used for clearing and settlement.[55]

Another shortcoming of Regulation 2019/518 is that it appears to be based on the assumption that fees charged for cross-border Payments are always higher than the fees charged for corresponding national Payments.

states that Non-euro area Member States that already notified the Commission of the extension of the scope of application in accordance with **Article 9 Regulation 2560/2001** (such as Sweden), were not required to submit a new notification within the meaning of Regulation 924/2009. Following the decision of the EEA Joint Committee Decision (No. 86/2013 of 3 May 2013 amending Annex XII (Free movement of capital) to the EEA Agreement (OJ L 291, 31.10.2013)), Regulation 924/2009 has been inserted into Annex XII of the EEA Agreement. The effect of this decision is that as of 4 May 2013, Regulation 924/2009 applies to all EEA Member States.

[53] Regulation 2019/518, Recital 2.

[54] Regulation (EU) 2019/518 of 19 March 2019 "amending Regulation (EU) 924/2009 as regards certain charges on cross-border payments in the Union and currency conversion charges", OJ L 91, 29.3.2019, pp. 36–41.

[55] See EBF (2020), pp. 1–2.

In the wholesale payments market, this is however not always the case. In practice, PSPs often enter into bespoke contracts with larger corporate clients and negotiate prices that are lower than the prices it charges consumers and companies for national Payments. Since Regulation 2019/518 demands equal pricing and applying different fees for national Payments harms a PSP's competitive position in the national market, such PSP is bound to increase its fees for cross-border Payments to comply with Regulation 2019/518. This is contrary to Regulation 2019/518's objective of reducing fees for cross-border Payments.

3.2.3.2 Regulation 2021/1230 on Cross-Border Payments in the Union

As Regulation 924/2009 has been amended several times, the European legislature decided that Regulation 924/2009 and its amendments should be codified.[56] For this purpose, Regulation 924/2009 has been repealed by Regulation (EU) 2021/1230 on cross-border payments in the Union (**'Regulation 2021/1230'**)[57] on 18 August 2021. The objective of Regulation 2021/1230 is to clarify the European law provisions applicable to cross-border Payments without introducing substantive amendments to Regulation 924/2009.

3.3 EU Rules on E-money

3.3.1 Commission Recommendation on E-money Instruments

In the early nineties of the last century, Banks and Non-Banks started offering E-money products in the form of loyalty programmes and prepaid cards. Initially, these E-money products did not have a wide range of usability since they were only accepted as a means of payment within restricted merchant networks. Given the limited usability of E-money products at that time, Non-Bank issuers of E-money were not considered to be serious competition by the banking sector. This sentiment changed however when PSUs also started to use E-money products as an alternative for debit cards and credit cards.

In February 1993, the Committee of Governors of the Central Banks requested the Working Group on EU Payment Systems to investigate how

[56] Regulation 2021/1230, Recital 1.

[57] Regulation (EU) 2021/1230 of 14 July 2021 "on cross-border payments in the Union", OJ L 274, 30.7.2021, pp. 20–31.

the risks associated with E-money products issued by Non-Bank E-money issuers should be addressed.[58] In its report on prepaid cards published in May 1994, the Working Group on EU Payment Systems recommended that only Banks should be allowed to issue E-money products.[59] The main reason for this is that E-money products issued by Non-Banks were not subject to banking regulations.[60] Legal safeguards that the clients of a Bank have as a result of these regulations, such as the deposit guarantee scheme, were therefore not available to clients of Non-Bank E-money issuers.

The first rules on E-money products were introduced in July 1997 by means of a recommendation issued by the Commission on transactions initiated with E-money instruments.[61] The Commission defined an E-money instrument in **Article 2(c) Commission Recommendation 97/489/EC** as '*a reloadable payment instrument other than a remote access payment instrument, whether a stored-value card or a computer memory, on which value units are stored electronically, enabling its holder to effect transactions*'. The objective of this recommendation was to improve consumer protection by imposing *inter alia*: (i) standards for the obligations and liabilities applicable to the service providers involved in the processing of E-money payments; and (ii) minimum information requirements for E-money issuers. Since a Commission recommendation does not have legal binding status, the service providers that applied the recommendation did so on a voluntary basis.

The absence of a European legal framework for E-money instruments raised concerns with the ECB, such as its potential impact on the efficient functioning of payment systems, the lack of confidence in the market for E-money instruments and the protection of consumers and merchants. In 1998, the ECB published a report on E-money which addressed these concerns by identifying several key requisites for the development of a European E-money market.[62] First, the ECB considered it elementary

[58] See Working Group on EU Payment Systems (1994, p. 1).

[59] Ibid., p. 3.

[60] Ibid., p. 8.

[61] Commission recommendation 97/489/EC of 30 July 1997 "concerning transactions by electronic payment instruments and in particular the relationship between issuer and holder", OJ L 208, 2.8.1997, pp. 52–58.

[62] See ECB (1998, pp. 1–2).

that issuers of E-money are subject to prudential supervision. For this purpose, the definition of 'credit institution' in Directive 77/780/EEC (First Banking Directive) was to be amended to ensure that this directive would also cover Non-Bank issuers of E-money.[63] With this amendment, Non-Bank issuers were subject to the same level of prudential supervision as Banks, even though their business models and risk profiles were very different. Second, the rights and obligations of all service providers involved in an E-money payment transaction had to be clearly defined and enforceable in all Member States. Third, E-money schemes should maintain adequate technical safeguards to prevent and detect threats to the security of the scheme. Fourth, E-money issuers should provide the central bank with relevant information that may be required for the purpose of monetary policy. Fifth, E-money issuers must be obliged to redeem E-money upon request. Sixth, central banks must have the possibility to impose reserve requirements on E-money issuers.

The first European legal framework for E-money issuers was introduced with the adoption of Directive 89/646/EEC on the coordination of laws, regulations and administrative provisions relating to the taking up and pursuit of the business of Banks ('**Second Banking Directive**').[64,65] Since the issuance of E-money was considered to be an activity similar to deposit taking, both Banks and Non-Bank issuers of E-money were subject to the Second Banking Directive. The applicability of these banking regulations on Non-Bank issuers increased the legal burden for these issuers in a disproportionate manner. As a result, the market for E-money instruments did not live up to its full potential under the Second Banking Directive.

[63] The First Banking Directive was in effect from December 15, 1977 until June 14, 2000.

[64] Directive 89/646/EEC of 15 December 1989 "on the coordination of laws, regulations and administrative provisions relating to the taking up and pursuit of the business of credit institutions and amending Directive 77/780/EEC", OJ L 386, 30.12.1989, pp. 1–13.

[65] The Second Banking Directive was in effect from December 22, 1989 until June 14, 2000.

3.3.2 The E-Money Directive (EMD)

Non-Bank E-money issuers were amongst the first Non-Banks to compete with the banking sector in the market for Payments. Under the Second Banking Directive, Non-Bank E-money issuers encountered prudential requirements that were disproportionately high given the size and complexity of their businesses. Non-Bank E-money issuers were obliged to meet the same prudential requirements as Banks, even though their less complex business models and limited risk exposures justified a less stringent prudential regime.

Taking into account the risks associated with the issuance of E-money, the European legislature recognised that the prudential requirements for Non-Bank E-money issuers should be less cumbersome than the prudential requirements applicable to Banks.[66] To this end, the European legislature adopted a separate directive for Non-Bank E-money issuers called EMD.[67] **Article 1(3)(a) EMD** defined an EMI as any undertaking or legal person, other than a credit institution within the meaning of Directive 2000/12/EC relating to the taking up and pursuit of the business of Banks (**'Banking Consolidation Directive'**),[68] that issues E-money instruments. **Article 4 EMD** required EMIs in the EEA[69] to have an initial capital of EUR1 mln. and minimum own funds equal to at least 2% of the outstanding E-money supply. E-money within the meaning of **Article 1(3)(b) EMD** is a monetary value represented by a claim on the EMI that: (i) is stored on an electronic device; (ii) representing the same value as the funds received in exchange for the E-money issued; and (iii) is accepted as a means for making payment with legal entities other than the issuer of the E-money instrument.

To safeguard the financial soundness of EMIs, EMD also provided for a restriction on the business activities that EMIs were allowed to conduct. Further to the issuance of E-money, **Article 1(5) EMD** allowed EMIs

[66] EMD, Recital 11.

[67] The EU Member States were obliged to transpose EMD into national legislation by April 2002 the latest.

[68] Directive 2000/12/EC of 20 March 2000 "relating to the taking up and pursuit of the business of credit institutions", OJ L 126, 26.5.2000, pp. 1–59. The Banking Consolidation Directive was in effect from June 15, 2000 until July 19, 2006.

[69] Decision by the EEA Joint Committee No 45/2001 of 30 March 2001 "amending Annex IX (Financial Services) to the EEA Agreement", OJ L 158, 14.6.2001, p. 59.

only to provide financial and non-financial services closely related to the issuing of E-money, such as the administering of E-money and the issuing and administering of other means of payment or services relating to the storing of (financial) data. In addition, excessive risk taking by EMIs was restricted as EMD limited the investment possibilities and hedging activities of EMIs. **Article 5(1) EMD** required EMIs to maintain at all times investments of at least the value of outstanding E-money in highly liquid asset items.

3.3.3 The Revised E-money Directive (EMD2)

Notwithstanding the introduction of a new prudential framework for Non-Bank E-money issuers under the EMD regime, the E-money market did not develop as expected.[70] In its report on the application of the EMD requirements in the Member States, the Commission concluded that the prudential requirements for EMIs continued to be too stringent given the risks inherent to the issuance of E-money.[71] The prudential requirements imposed by EMD on EMIs were disproportionately cumbersome compared to the prudential requirements applicable to the banking sector. Moreover, the EMD prudential requirements were implemented very differently in the Member States. This imbalance opposed the development of an internal market for E-money products as new market entrants continued to struggle to meet the prudential requirements. In addition, it was often unclear whether a particular product qualified as E-money and, as a result thereof, was subject to the EMD provisions. Applying different interpretations of the concept of E-money did not contribute to the rollout of a harmonised legal framework for EMIs in the Member States.

The European legislature therefore considered it essential to establish a level playing field between EMIs and Banks. EMD2, which repealed EMD with effect from 30 April 2011, aims to create this level playing field by *inter alia* reducing the prudential burden for EMIs (**Paragraph 4.2.3**). Moreover, EMD2 provides further clarification on the concept of E-money and imposes unified legal requirements for EMIs established

[70] See Commission (2006a, p. 3).

[71] Ibid., p. 5.

in the EEA.[72] To foster a harmonised interpretation of the definition of E-money and to ensure legal certainty regarding the products that are covered by this definition, EMD2 introduced a technologically neutral definition. **Article 2(2) EMD2** defines 'E-money' as '*electronically, including magnetically, stored monetary value as represented by a claim on the issuer which is issued on receipt of funds for the purpose of making payment transactions as defined in point 5 of Article 4 PSD, and which is accepted by a natural or legal person other than the e-money issuer*.'

In order for an activity to qualify as the issuance of E-money, there must be a contractual agreement between the E-money issuer and the holder of the E-money which states that the E-money issuer will issue a separate monetary asset up to the monetary value of the funds paid by the E-money holder.[73] This means that when a Non-Bank merely receives funds from a PSU without a concrete payment order, such activity does not constitute the issuance of E-money.[74]

In addition, EMD2 expanded the scope of ancillary business activities that EMIs are allowed to conduct. A key ancillary service that EMIs can provide according to **Article 6(1) EMD2** includes the offering of payment services within the meaning of PSD2. When providing payment services, EMIs are also allowed to grant credit in relation to these services.[75] Furthermore, EMIs are allowed to offer operational services and closely related ancillary services in respect of the issuance of E-money or the provision of payment services.

3.4 EU Rules on Payment Services

3.4.1 The Payment Services Directive (PSD)

Notwithstanding the efforts taken by the European legislature to create a profound legal framework for cross-border credit transfers, regulations covering other types of Payments remained fragmented in the EU until

[72] Decision by the EEA Joint Committee No 120/2010 of 10 November 2010 "amending Annex IX (Financial Services) to the EEA Agreement", OJ L 58, 3.3.2011, pp. 77–78.

[73] See European Court of Justice (2024, paragraph 48).

[74] Ibid., paragraph 52.

[75] Granting credit is only allowed in connection with the payment services referred to in points 4, 5 or 7 of the Annex to PSD2.

the adoption of PSD.[76] National Payment products were subject to very different legal requirements depending on the Member State in which the PSP was established. As a result, large differences were observed between Member States in terms of the efficiency and costs with which Payments were being processed. The costs of a basic payment service were up to eight times higher than the costs charged for the same service in the most cost-efficient Member State.[77] Furthermore, large differences existed in terms of the execution time limits that PSPs applied for processing Payments.

In 2007, PSD entered into force, which changed the European Payments landscape fundamentally.[78] PSD aimed to harmonise the European legislative framework for Payments and to enhance competition between Banks and Non-Banks. To this end, PSD introduced a harmonised set of rules covering payment services (national and cross-border) offered in the EEA (**Paragraph 3.4.1.2**). PSD provided new standards on the information that PSPs had to provide to PSUs with regard to the offering of payment services as well as standards on the rights and obligations applicable between PSPs and PSUs. More importantly, PSD intended to remove legal obstacles preventing Non-Banks from entering the European market for Payments. To this end, a new licensing regime was introduced for Non-Banks named PIs (**Paragraph 4.1**).

When developing the PSD framework, the European legislature recognised the value of having self-regulation initiatives in the Payments market. The European legislature aimed to allow maximum flexibility for self-regulation by the payments industry and to only regulate what was considered necessary to overcome the legal barriers for the establishment of an internal market.[79]

[76] PSD, Recital 2.

[77] See Commission (2005b, p. 2).

[78] PSD was in effect from December 25, 2007 until January 12, 2018.

[79] See Commission (2005c, p. 8).

3.4.1.1 Introduction of Payment Services

PSD was the first directive to introduce the concept 'payment services', which are services provided by PSPs to PSUs for the purpose of effectuating Payments. The following categories of payment services were introduced by PSD:

1. Services that enable cash to be credited to a payment account, including all services required for operating a payment account

   This payment service is typically provided by PSPs that offer payment accounts. A payment account is an account held with a PSP in the name of one or more PSUs, which is used for the execution of Payments. It is important to emphasise that only accounts whose main objective is the execution of Payments fall within the scope of the PSD definition of a payment account.[80] When determining if an account qualifies as a payment account within the meaning of PSD, one must take a principle-based approach that focusses on the underlying objective and functionality of the relevant account.[81] Examples of accounts that qualify as payment accounts are current accounts, credit card accounts and e-money accounts. A savings account qualifies as a payment account unless payment and withdrawal transactions can only be made via a linked current account.[82]

   The cash that is credited to the payment account can be received by the PSP electronically, over-the-counter or via an ATM. The crediting of interest to the payment account of a PSU does not constitute this payment service.

   Services that enable cash to be credited to a payment account, including all services required for operating a payment account, also constitute a payment service under PSD2.

[80] In the PSD Q&A published by the Commission it is for example clarified that a mortgage account should not be considered a payment account within the meaning of PSD. This could be different when such account combines mortgage and saving or payment facilities.

[81] See PSD Expert Group (2009, p. 11).

[82] See European Court of Justice (2018a). To clarify the definition of 'payment account', **Articles 3(15) PSR Proposal and 2(13) PSD3 Proposal** require an account to allow for the sending and receiving of funds to and from third parties in order to qualify as a 'payment account'.

2. Services enabling cash withdrawals from a payment account as well as all the operations required for operating a payment account

   This service is provided if, for example, a PSP offers a payment instrument in addition to a payment account, which enables the holder of the payment instrument to withdraw cash from an ATM. **Article 4(23) PSD** defined a payment instrument as a personalised device and/or set of procedures agreed upon between a PSU and PSP and used by the PSU to initiate a payment order.[83] A payment instrument can be tangible (e.g., a card or smartphone) or intangible (e.g., a Personal Identification Number ('**PIN**') or login/ password/authorisation code). For example, arrangements whereby a telephone call in combination with a password is used for initiating payment orders may qualify as a payment instrument.[84]

   In the EU, ATM withdrawals are the primary means for consumers to withdraw cash from their payment accounts.[85] Companies that offer cash withdrawal services via a terminal in a physical store and which do not carry out any operation on the PSU's payment account do not provide this payment service.[86] The activities of such a company must be limited to making these terminals available and loading them with cash.

   Services enabling cash withdrawals from a payment account as well as all the operations required for operating a payment account also constitute a payment service under PSD2.

3. Execution of fund transfers

   This payment service is provided when PSPs transfer funds electronically on behalf of a payer or beneficiary. This service covers credit transfers, direct debit collections, debit card payments and the execution of an instruction to deposit funds to a payment account or withdraw funds from a payment account. The PSP executing

[83] Since anonymous pre-paid cards do not contain the name of the cardholder, the Commission considered that the current definition of 'payment instrument' could lead to anonymous cards remaining outside the scope of the definition of payment instrument. **Article 2(15) of the PSD3 Proposal** therefore suggests to amend the definition of payment instrument by referring to 'individualised' devices instead of 'personalised' devices.

[84] See European Court of Justice (2014).

[85] See Ernst & Young and Copenhagen Economics (2020, p. 50).

[86] See European Court of Justice (2018b).

the transaction does not have to be the PSP providing the payer's payment account as such order can be initiated by the payer, the beneficiary or a third party. Examples of PSPs offering this payment service include companies offering escrow services, issuers of debit cards and acquirers. Moreover, providers of electronic communication networks, such as a mobile operator offering the option to purchase digital content via SMS services, can provide this payment service in case such a provider is ineligible for the digital services exemption described below.

The execution of fund transfers also constitutes a payment service under PSD2.

4. Execution of fund transfers where the funds are covered by a credit line

   This payment service is very similar to the payment services described under 3 above albeit that this payment service involves the transfer of funds that are covered by a credit line. This service is typically provided by credit card issuers and often triggers other licensing requirements, such as a licence for the offering of consumer credit.[87] It should be noted that PSD allowed the granting of credit lines that are closely linked to this payment service without the need for the PI to apply for an additional licence.[88]

   The execution of fund transfers where the funds are covered by a credit line also constitutes a payment service under PSD2.

5. Issuing and acquiring payment instruments

   Providing a payer with a payment instrument for initiating payment orders and processing payment transactions constitutes the payment service 'issuing of payment instruments'. This payment service is mostly provided in combination with other payment services, such as the execution of funds transfers as described under 3 above.

[87] In certain Member States (e.g., the Netherlands) only the offering of credit to consumers (natural persons not acting in their professional capacity) triggers a licence requirement. In other Member States (e.g., Germany) the offering of credit triggers a licence requirement regardless of whether such credit is offered to consumers or non-consumers.

[88] For a more detailed overview of the requirements for this exemption see **Paragraph 3.4.1.3**.

Examples of PSPs that offer this payment service include debit card and credit card issuers. Issuing direct debit mandates does not qualify as issuing a payment instrument. Moreover, the mere distribution of cards or provision of technical services (e.g., processing of data) with regard to cards does also not constitute issuing.[89]

Further to the issuing of payment instruments, the offering of acquiring services to merchants is also covered by this payment service. Acquiring is a service provided by a PSP contracting with a merchant to accept and process payment transactions, which results in the crediting of the merchant's payment account. Intermediaries that do not have a contractual relationship with the merchant but offer services that are part of the acquiring services also qualify as acquirer. Technical services provided to PSPs, such as the processing of data or the operation of POS terminals do not constitute acquiring.[90]

PSD allowed the granting of credit lines that are closely linked to this payment service without the need for the PI to apply for an additional licence.[91]

The issuing and acquiring of payment instruments also constitute a payment services under PSD2.

6. Money remittance

Money remittance is a service whereby the payer transfers funds electronically to a beneficiary without any payment account being created in the name of the payer or the beneficiary. The payer's PSP typically receives the funds from the payer in cash and remits the corresponding amount, for example via a telecommunication network, to a beneficiary or a PSP acting on behalf of a beneficiary.[92] The definition of this payment service in **Article 4(13) PSD** is technology neutral, which means that the payer's PSP does not have to receive the funds in cash in order to provide this service.

Money remittance also constitutes a payment service under PSD2.

[89] IFR, Recital 29.

[90] IFR, Recital 30.

[91] For more detail on the requirements for this exemption see **Paragraph 3.4.1.3**.

[92] PSD, Recital 7.

7. Execution of Payments where the consent of the payer to execute a Payment is given by means of any telecommunication, digital or IT device and the payment is made to the telecommunication, IT system or network operator, acting only as an intermediary between the payment service user and the supplier of the goods and services.

   This payment service was typically offered by network operators[93] acting as an intermediary between the payer and a merchant. The payer's consent was given via a telecommunication device[94] and the Payment was made to the telecommunication operator. It was essential that the network operator acted solely as an intermediary with regard to the Payment between the payer and the merchant and did not add any value to the goods or services for which the Payments were executed. This service was not provided if a payer used his smartphone for authenticating a Payment and the Payment was not routed via the telecom provider. PSD allowed the granting of credit lines that were closely linked to this payment service without the need for the PI to apply for an additional licence.[95]

   This service no longer constitutes a payment service under PSD2 and has therefore been removed from the PSD2 list of regulated payment services.

Certain payment-related services did not qualify as a payment service within the meaning of PSD and were explicitly excluded from the scope of applicability. These services included amongst others:

1. Cash-based payments

   Payments made exclusively in cash directly from the payer to the beneficiary without any intermediary intervention did not constitute a payment service under PSD according to **Article 3(a) PSD**. Cash-based payments are transactions that have a cash component and do not involve the use of a payment account. These transactions only involve coins, banknotes, paper cheques, bills of exchange, paper-based vouchers, paper-based traveller's

[93] E.g., telecommunications operators and internet providers.

[94] E.g., a telephone or computer.

[95] For more detail on the requirements for this exemption see **Paragraph 3.4.1.3**.

cheques, paper-based postal money orders or comparable instruments. Examples of cash-based payments are: (i) cash processing; (ii) non-professional cash collection and delivery within the framework of a non-profit or charitable activity; and (iii) cashback transactions.[96]

In case one of the above-mentioned transactions involved a non-cash component, e.g., because cash was temporarily held on a payment account, such transaction was no longer exempted from the PSD requirements.

Cash-based payments are also excluded from the scope of applicability under PSD2.

2. Payment services provided to others than end users

   Payment services that did not involve any direct end users were exempted from the PSD requirements according to **Article 3(h) PSD**. This exemption applied to payment transactions executed: (i) within a payment or securities settlement system or between settlement agents; (ii) between central counterparties, clearing houses and/or central banks; or (iii) between PSPs.

   Payment services provided to others than end users are also excluded from the scope of applicability under PSD2.

3. Payment services provided by intragroup

   According to **Article 3(n) PSD**, payment services between a parent undertaking and its subsidiary or between subsidiaries of the same parent undertaking, without any intermediary intervention by a PSP other than an undertaking belonging to the same group, were exempted from PSD.

   Payment services provided intragroup are also excluded from the scope of applicability under PSD2. Under **Article 2(2)(m) PSR Proposal**, it is clarified that the collection of Payment orders on behalf of a group by a parent or subsidiary for onward transmission to another PSP does not constitute a payment service.

4. Commercial agent exemption

   Article 3(b) PSD stipulated that PSD did not apply to Payments that were facilitated by a commercial agent involved in negotiating the exchange of goods or services on behalf of the

[96] Cashback transactions are services offered to customers whereby a customer can request a merchant to add an amount to the purchase price, which is paid using a debit card, and pay out the additional amount to the customer in cash.

seller (beneficiary) or the buyer (payer). To qualify as a 'commercial agent', there had to be a business relationship between the agent and the payer/beneficiary covering more than one payment transaction. If the business relationship covered only one transaction, the intermediary qualified as a 'broker' to which the exemption did not apply.

The commercial agent exemption has been amended under PSD2 to clarify that a commercial agent can only act on behalf of the payer or only on behalf of the beneficiary (**Paragraph 3.4.3.3**).

5. Provision of services in connection with securities

   Payments relating to securities asset servicing, such as dividend distributions, were out of the scope of the PSD requirements according to **Article 3(i) PSD**. The payment transactions could only be executed in connection with the main activity of providing investment services in order to be eligible for this exemption. Cash deposits and fund transfers to a securities account fall within the scope of this exemption.

   Services in connection with securities are also excluded from the scope of applicability under PSD2.

6. Technical service providers

   Service providers offering technical services, which support the provision of payment services and never enter into a business relationship with PSUs, did not qualify as a PSP according to **Article 3(j) PSD**, provided that such service providers would never be in the possession of any funds. Such supporting services include *inter alia*: (i) data processing and storage; (ii) data and entity authentication; and (iii) IT maintenance services.

   Technical service providers are also excluded from the scope of applicability under PSD2.

7. Money exchange services

   Money exchange services are cash-to-cash exchange services where funds are not held in a payment account. These services were not covered by PSD according to **Article 3(f) PSD**.

   Money exchange services are also excluded from the scope of applicability under PSD2.

8. Digital services exemption

   Article 3(l) PSD exempted certain Payments that were executed using a telecom or IT device where the network operator acted as an intermediary for the delivery of digital goods and services through the device and added value to these goods or services. This exemption focussed on micro-payments for digital content and allowed for example offerors of ring tones to operate outside the PSD framework. This exemption only applied when the service provider added value to the relevant service or product and did not only act as an intermediary. Examples of services that were considered to add value to the payment service included the provision of information regarding the products or services provided or the provision of a search tool for clients to facilitate their decision making.

The scope of the digital services exemption has been substantially narrowed under PSD2 (**Paragraph 3.4.3.3**).

9. Limited network exemption

Payment services using a payment instrument that could only be used to pay within a restricted network or for a limited range of goods or services were exempted from the PSD requirements according to **Article 3(k) PSD**.

The scope of the limited network exemption has been further clarified under PSD2 (**Paragraph 3.4.3.3**).

10. Operation of an ATM

Independent service providers operating an ATM, which enable cardholders to withdraw cash from an ATM, were exempted from PSD according to **Article 3(o) PSD** provided that they were not a party to a framework contract[97] with the cardholder withdrawing cash from his payment account.

The operation of an ATM exemption has been amended under PSD2 (**Paragraph 3.4.3.3**). In the proposal for a new Payment Services and Electronic Money Services Directive (**'PSD3 Proposal'**),[98] independent ATM deployers will be subject to a registration requirement. In **Article 37 PSD3 Proposal** it is suggested that operators of retail stores are exempted from a PI licence requirement when offering cash withdrawal services without purchase if the amount of cash distributed does not exceed EUR 50.

[97] **Article 4(12) PSD** defined a 'framework contract' as a payment service contract which governs the future execution of individual and successive Payments and which may contain the obligation and conditions for setting up a payment account.

[98] See Commission (2023).

Table 3.1 Scope of application PSD

	Two-leg Payments	*One-leg Payments*
Payment in Euro	PSD applied fully	Only PSD provision on value dating applied
Payment service in non-euro EEA currency	PSD applied fully	Only PSD provision on value dating applied
Other currency	PSD did not apply	PSD did not apply

3.4.1.2 Scope of Applicability

The PSD provisions applied to Payments denominated in an EEA Member State currency[99] that were executed in the EEA.[100] The scope of the PSD provisions that applied to a particular Payment was determined on the basis of where the payer's PSP and the beneficiary's PSP were established. Pursuant to **Article 2(1) PSD** so-called two-leg Payments, which are Payments whereby both the payer's PSP and the beneficiary's PSP are established in the EEA, were subject to all PSD requirements. One-leg Payments, which are Payments whereby one of the PSPs involved is established outside the EEA, were only subject to the PSD requirements regarding value dating.

Table 3.1 provides a summary of the applicability of the PSD provisions with respect to one-leg and two-leg Payments.

3.4.1.3 Introduction of a Licensing Regime for Non-Banks

Prior to the adoption of PSD, there was no European legislative framework on market access by Non-Banks other than EMIs (**Paragraph 3.3.2**). Adopting legal requirements for market access by Non-Banks other than EMIs was a matter reserved for the national legislatures. As a result, there was a considerable degree of fragmentation between the national legal frameworks regulating market access by Non-Banks involved in the offering of payment services. Non-Banks were facing different authorisation requirements in different Member States when

[99] Non-euro area Member State currencies include: (i) Czech koruna; (ii) Norwegian krone; (iii) Danish krone; (iv) Icelandic króna; (v) Swedish krona; and (vi) Swiss Francs (because Liechtenstein is part of the EEA and uses Swiss Francs as currency).

[100] Decision by the EEA Joint Committee No 114/2008 of 7 November 2008 "amending Annex IX (Financial Services) and Annex XIX (Consumer Protection) to the EEA Agreement", OJ L 339, 18.12.2008, pp. 103–104.

providing similar payment services.[101] Depending on the characteristics of the services provided, such Non-Banks often provided payment services on the basis of a national exemption or were required to apply for a banking licence. An exemption was often available since Non-Banks did not attract repayable funds from the public and were therefore ineligible for a banking licence. For example, service providers in the Netherlands were allowed to offer payment services on the basis of an exemption prior to the implementation of PSD provided that they processed payment transactions within five business days. These service providers were not considered to attract repayable funds from the public and did therefore not require a banking licence.[102]

Given the limited size and complexity of the business of a Non-Bank, requiring a banking licence imposes disproportionate barriers for these PSPs to enter the market. In particular, the capital requirements that apply to Banks were considered too onerous for PSPs that were not involved in granting loans and attracting repayable funds from the public. The Commission, therefore, received numerous complaints from Non-Banks about substantial entry barriers and an unlevel playing field.[103]

To level the playing field between Banks and Non-Banks, the European legislature considered it essential to have a separate licensing regime for PSPs that did not attract repayable funds from the public or issued E-money.[104] To this end, PSD introduced a licencing regime for PIs, which involves according to **Article 4(4) PSD** legal persons that have been granted authorisation to provide and execute payment services throughout the EEA.[105] According to **Article 16(1) PSD**, PIs are, further to the provision of payment services, also allowed to carry out certain operational and ancillary services that are closely related to the provision of payment services.[106] Moreover, **Article 16(3) PSD** allowed PIs to grant short-term credit to their clients in relation to certain

[101] See Commission (2003, p. 23).

[102] See Jans (2010, p. 154).

[103] See Commission (2005a, p. 6).

[104] Bringing these service providers within the scope of a banking licence would be disproportionally burdensome and impose barriers to market entry.

[105] PSD, Recital 10.

[106] Such services include foreign exchange services, safekeeping activities, and the storage and processing of data.

payment services provided that the following requirements were met: (i) the credit was ancillary and granted exclusively in connection with the execution of a Payment; (ii) the PSU needed to repay the full amount of the debt by the end of the twelve-month period at the latest; (iii) the PSP could not use any funds received or held for the purpose of executing a Payment for granting credit and (iv) the PI's own funds had to be sufficient at all times in view of the overall amount of credit granted.[107]

3.4.1.4 Transparency and Information Requirements

The majority of the payment services provided by PSPs are governed by a framework contract entered into between the PSP and a PSU. A framework contract is required if a client opens a payment account or requests a specific payment instrument.[108] Certain payment services, such as money remittances, are typically executed on a stand-alone basis and are therefore not always covered by such framework contract. To enhance the transparency *vis-à-vis* PSUs of the payment services provided under both types of contractual arrangements, PSD introduced transparency and information requirements for PSPs regarding one-off Payments and Payments covered by a framework contract. To a large extent, these requirements continue to apply under the PSD2 regime. The transparency and information requirements that are currently in force are set out in **Annex I**.

3.4.1.5 Rights and Obligations

Further to the introduction of a licensing regime for PIs and transparency requirements for PSPs, PSD was also the first directive to set out the rights and obligations applicable to PSPs and PSUs. The main requirements introduced by PSD revolved around the: (i) prohibition on value dating; (ii) obligation of timely execution of Payments; (iii) use of payment instruments by PSUs; and (iv) fees charged by the PSP for the execution of Payments.

[107] As far as the granting of such loans, the national laws on conduct requirements for the offering of credit also applied.

[108] PSD, Recital 24.

Prohibition on Value Dating

When funds are transferred electronically between payment accounts, Banks apply a 'value date' to determine: (i) the moment until which interest accrued on the amount debited from the payer's payment account (the debit value date); and (ii) the moment from which interest starts to accrue for the funds credited to the beneficiary's payment account (the credit value date).

Prior to PSD, the value date used to be a different date than the date on which funds were debited from the payer's payment account (in case of the debit value date) or credited to the beneficiary's payment account (in case of the credit value date). This was caused by a practice known as value dating, which Banks commonly applied for the purpose of generating additional profit. The principle of value dating works as follows. When a €100 credit transfer was initiated on day D, the payer's Bank used to set a debit value date several days prior to day D, for example, D-3. As a result, the payer's Bank instead of the payer collected the interest accrued on the €100 for the intermediate period of three days (i.e., the period between D-3 and D). The same technique was applied by the Bank acting for the beneficiary, which used to hold on to the incoming funds for a couple of days before crediting the beneficiary's payment account. The beneficiary would have the funds at his disposal and start earning interest on the amount transferred several days after the date on which the amount was received by the beneficiary's Bank (e.g., D + 3). The interest accrued on the €100 between the moment the beneficiary's Bank received the funds (e.g., D + 1) and the moment the beneficiary's payment account was credited (D + 3) provided for an additional source of income for the beneficiary's Bank.

With PSD, a prohibition on value dating was introduced, which continues to apply under the PSD2 regime. This means that the payer's Bank must apply a debit value date that is no earlier than the date on which the transaction amount is debited from the payer's payment account. Furthermore, **Article 87 PSD2** stipulates that the beneficiary's Bank must apply a credit value date that is no later than the business day on which the transaction amount is credited to the payment account of the beneficiary's Bank. The transaction amount must be at the beneficiary's disposal immediately after the funds have been received by the beneficiary's Bank.[109]

Timely Execution of Payments

A PSU initiates a Payment by submitting a payment order to its PSP. The payment order sets out the characteristics of the proposed transaction. Provided that the payment order meets all the requirements that have been agreed between the PSP and the PSU in the framework contract, the PSP has a legal obligation to execute the transaction within a certain time limit after the moment it received the payment order.[110] This is only different in case the payment order is revoked in accordance with the applicable requirements.[111]

With Directive 97/5/EC, a first step was taken to harmonise the execution times for cross-border Payments at a European level (**Paragraph 3.2**). However, since PSPs were allowed to contractually agree on a particular maximum execution time, the implementation of Directive 97/5/EC did not bring the desired level of harmonisation. With PSD, a more comprehensive solution was presented to harmonise execution time limits for (national and cross-border) credit transfers and direct debit collections, which took into account: (i) who initiates the Payment (the payer or the beneficiary); (ii) the means by which the payment order is submitted by the PSU to its PSP (e.g., electronically or

[109] This is only different in case the transaction involves a currency conversion between: (i) the euro and a non-Member state currency; or (ii) two non-Member State currencies.

[110] The PSP is allowed to refuse the execution of a payment order in case not all conditions of the framework contract are met. In case the PSP refuses to execute the transaction, that particular payment order is deemed not to be received. Therefore, the refusal to execute the transaction does not constitute a breach by the PSP of the obligation to execute the Payment within the required timeline. In case of a refusal, the payer's PSP must notify the payer regarding the refusal, the reasons for the refusal and the procedure for correcting any factual mistakes that caused the refusal. The PSP may charge the payer for such a notification in case: (i) this is provided for in the framework contract; and (ii) the refusal is justified.

[111] In principle, the PSU is allowed to revoke a payment order until the moment the order has been received by its PSP. In case of a warehoused payment order, which is a payment whereby the execution of the transaction starts on a specified day, the PSU can revoke the order until the end of the business day preceding the day on which the order is planned to be executed.

paper-based) and (iii) whether the transaction involves a currency conversion. These time limits for (national and cross-border) credit transfers and direct debit collections continue to apply under the PSD2 regime.

The Use of Payment Instruments

To safeguard the use of payment instruments, PSD introduced new security measures that continue to apply under the PSD2 regime (**Paragraph 5.5.3**). A PSU is obliged to use its payment instrument in accordance with the terms and conditions of the framework contract and to take all reasonable measures to keep the security features of its payment instrument safe. Furthermore, **Article 56(1) PSD** requires a PSU to notify its PSP without undue delay if it notices that its payment instrument is lost or stolen. Further to the requirements that were introduced for PSUs, **Article 57 PSD** also provided for safety requirements for PSPs, such as: (i) the PSP has to ensure that the personalised security features, which are according to **Article 4(31) PSD2** personalised features provided by the PSP to a PSU for the purposes of authentication, of the instruments issued cannot be accessed by others than the PSU; (ii) the PSP must refrain from providing a PSU with an unsolicited payment instrument[112]; (iii) the PSP must make means available for PSUs to notify the PSP when becoming aware of loss, theft, misappropriation or unauthorised use of a payment instrument; (iv) the PSP must ensure that a payment instrument cannot be used after receiving such notification; and (v) the PSP is to be held liable in case something goes wrong when sending a payment instrument or its personalised security features to a PSU.

Charges

SHA charging for the execution of a Payment

Article 52(2) PSD no longer allowed PSPs to deduct charges for the execution of Payments, which did not involve a currency conversion, from the amount transferred to the beneficiary's PSP.[113] This prohibition is

[112] Except where a payment instrument of a PSU is to be replaced.

[113] The payer's PSP was however allowed to deduct its charges from the amount transferred in case the transaction involved a currency conversion on the payer's side.

known as the full amount principle or SHA principle and continues to apply under the PSD2 regime.

Although the default setting for charging is SHA, **Article 67(2) PSD** allows the beneficiary to agree with its PSP that the PSP deducts its charges from the amount that will be credited to the beneficiary's payment account. In any other situation where charges are deducted from the transaction amount, the payer's PSP is responsible for ensuring that the beneficiary receives the full amount of the Payment.

In case a PSP or third party requests a charge for the use of a specific payment instrument to initiate a Payment, **Article 50(2) PSD** requires said PSP or third party to inform the PSU thereof before it initiates the Payment.

Charges for non- or incorrectly executed Payments

In situations where a credit transfer could not be executed correctly and straight-through processing (STP) was not possible, it was common practice for Banks to charge reject, return or repair fees.[114] These charges are also known as 'R-charges'. Since R-charges were not covered by Regulation 2560/2001, most PSUs were not aware of these costs being charged by the Banks. **Article 52(1) PSD** stipulated that Banks were only allowed to impose R-charges if the PSU agreed in the framework contract to pay for such charges. Furthermore, these charges were only allowed when imposed for objectively justified reasons and if these were in line with the Bank's costs.[115]

Charges for information obligations

To enable PSUs to compare the product conditions of the payment services provided by different PSPs, PSUs must receive relevant product information from their PSPs without being charged for such information. **Article 32(1) PSD** therefore stipulated that PSPs were not allowed to charge PSUs for providing the information set out in **Annex I**. **Article 32(2) PSD** allowed PSPs to agree with their PSUs to charge a fee for

[114] See Commission (2008, p. 5).

[115] **Article 51(1) PSD** allowed PSPs to agree with non-consumer PSUs that this provision shall not apply in whole or in part (corporate opt-out).

providing additional or more frequent information provided that these charges were in line with the additional costs incurred by the PSP for providing such information.[116]

Charges for termination of framework contract

To facilitate customer mobility, **Article 45(2) PSD** allowed PSUs to terminate their framework contract without incurring any costs after the expiry of a year provided that the contract was concluded for: (i) a fixed period exceeding one year; or (ii) an indefinite period. For other framework contracts, PSPs were allowed to charge the PSU for the termination of the contract provided that these charges were in line with the actual costs incurred by the PSP for terminating the contract.

3.4.1.6 The Corporate Opt-Out and Its Impact on Competition

The transparency requirements and rules on rights and obligations were introduced primarily to improve consumer protection. Companies that enter into a contractual arrangement with a PSP generally have extensive knowledge and experience regarding the processing of Payments and the rights and obligations in relation thereto. Moreover, large companies often have a strong bargaining position when contracting with a PSP, which enables them to negotiate the terms of the framework contract.

As a result, corporate PSUs generally do not require a similar level of protection as consumer PSUs. Applying the PSD requirements in full regarding payment services provided to corporate PSUs would therefore have been disproportionate given the more balanced nature of the business relationship between PSPs and corporate PSUs. For this reason, **Articles 30 and 51 PSD** allowed PSPs to agree with their corporate clients (i.e., non-consumers) that certain PSD requirements on transparency and/or rights and obligations did not apply in whole or in part. This option is known as the corporate opt-out and continues to apply under the PSD2 regime.

PSD contained a Member State option that allowed Member States to disapply the corporate opt-out option regarding framework contracts that PSPs enter into with so-called 'micro enterprises'. Micro enterprises are enterprises that employ fewer than ten persons and whose annual turnover

[116] **Article 30(1) PSD** allowed PSPs to agree with non-consumer PSUs that this provision shall not apply in whole or in part (corporate opt-out).

and/or annual balance sheet total does not exceed €2 mln.[117] Several Member States adopted this Member State option into their national legislation, which required PSPs established in their jurisdiction to treat micro enterprises in the same manner as consumers.[118] Member States that transposed this option into national legislation increased the administrative burden of the PSPs in that Member State. Since most PSPs tend to apply the corporate opt-out for all corporate clients, these PSPs were obliged to have ongoing monitoring measures in place to identify corporate clients that needed to be reclassified as a micro enterprise. PSPs established in a Member State that did not apply this Member State option did not face this practical inconvenience.

3.4.2 The Payment Accounts Directive (PAD)

The majority of the Payment solutions offered in Europe require the involvement of a payment account. Not having payment account access would therefore deprive consumers of the possibility to use these Payment solutions. In 2010, Professor M. Monti published a report in which he suggested that the Commission should propose a regulation stipulating that all consumers in the EU have the right to obtain access to basic banking services.[119] This suggestion was not well received by the banking sector. The banking sector took the view that such regulation would not add substantial value to the initiatives already undertaken by Banks themselves to provide large groups of consumers access to basic banking services.[120] Notwithstanding the arguments provided by the banking sector against the introduction of a legal right for all consumers to obtain

[117] Commission Recommendation 2003/361/EC of 6 May 2003 "concerning the definition of micro, small and medium-sized enterprises", OJ L 124, 20.5.2003, pp. 36–41.

[118] Member States that treat micro enterprises in the same way as consumers in relation to the provisions on rights and obligations are: (i) the Czech Republic; (ii) Italy; (iii) Cyprus; (iv) Hungary (if decided by the PSP); (v) Malta; (vi) Portugal; (vii) Slovakia; and (viii) Sweden. Member States that treat micro enterprises in the same way as consumers in relation to the provisions on transparency are: (i) the Czech Republic; (ii) Ireland; (iii) Italy; (iv) Cyprus; (v) Hungary; (vi) Malta; (vii) Portugal; and (viii) Slovakia (if decided by the PSP).

[119] See Monti (2010, p. 74).

[120] See Commission (2011, p. 6).

access to basic banking services, the Commission adopted a recommendation in 2011 on basic payment accounts which set out that each consumer should be able to open and use a basic payment account at a reasonable cost.[121] Only a few Member States adopted legal requirements regarding basic payment account access on the basis of this recommendation. Since the majority of the Member States did not take any legislative action to guarantee that each consumer in their jurisdiction could have access to a basic payment account, the Commission introduced new requirements on the accessibility of a basic payment account by means of a directive called the PAD. The legal requirements introduced by the PAD apply to so-called 'basic payment accounts' that are provided by Banks established in the EU.[122] **Article 17(1) PAD** defines basic payment accounts as payment accounts that provide consumers access to the following services: (i) placing funds on the payment account; (ii) withdrawing cash from the payment account at the POS or ATM; and (iii) executing direct debit collections, credit transfers and card initiated Payments.[123] The PAD allows Member States to extend the scope of applicability of the PAD requirements to other payment accounts than basic payment accounts.

According to **Article 1(1) PAD**, the key provisions of the PAD are: (i) the right for consumers to access a basic payment account; (ii) the option of payment account switching within Member States; and (iii) increased transparency and comparability of fees charged to consumers in relation to such basic payment account.

3.4.2.1 Right of Access to a Basic Payment Account

Prior to the PAD, each Member State applied its own legal requirements for consumers who wanted to obtain access to a payment account. Moreover, Banks tended to only provide consumers with a payment account if certain eligibility criteria were met, such as the requirement for the applicant to have a certain financial position, nationality or place of residence. To ensure that Banks cannot deny consumers access to a basic

[121] Commission Recommendation 2011/442/EU of 18 July 2011 "on access to a basic payment account", OJ L 190, 21 July 2011, pp. 87–91, p. 87.

[122] Publication of Joint Committee Decision incorporating the act into the EEA Agreement pending.

[123] According to **Article 17(2) PAD**, Member States are allowed to add additional services to a basic payment account. Such additional service could for example include an overdraft facility or a credit card.

payment account on the basis of inappropriate eligibility criteria, the PAD provides an exhaustive list of criteria on the basis of which Banks can refuse a consumer access to a basic payment account. **Article 16(4) and (5) PAD** only allows Banks to refuse a particular consumer access to a basic payment account if: (i) the opening of such account would result in a violation of an AML/CTF requirement; or (ii) the consumer requesting the basic payment account already has a basic payment account with another Bank in the same Member State. **Article 16(6) PAD** allows Member States to allow Banks to refuse consumers access to a basic payment account in other situations on the basis of national law requirements regarding abuse by a PSU.

Further to a list of limitative grounds for refusal, the PAD provides for other safeguards to ensure that consumers have access to a basic payment account. First, **Article 16(9) PAD** prohibits Banks from requiring that consumers can only have a basic payment account if they also purchase additional services or products from that Bank. Second, **Article 18(1) PAD** requires that Banks offer basic payment account services free of charge or at a reasonable cost. What reasonable costs are must according to **Article 18(3) PAD** be determined on the basis of national income levels and average fees charged by Banks in that Member State. Third, **Article 17(4) PAD** prohibits Banks from imposing a limit on the maximum number of Payments that PSUs are allowed to execute using a basic payment account. Fourth, Banks can only terminate a framework contract for a basic payment account in limitative circumstances.[124] According to **Article 19(3) PAD** Member States can allow Banks to terminate a basic payment account on other grounds than those set out in the PAD provided that such situations are aimed at preventing consumers from abusing their right to a basic payment account.

Prior to the adoption of the PAD, it was difficult for consumers to open a payment account in another Member State since Banks were often

[124] According to **Article 19(2) PAD**, Banks are allowed to terminate a framework contract for a basic payment account if at least one of the following conditions is met: (i) the PSU has deliberately used its payment account for illegal purposes; (ii) the PSU has not executed a Payment using the payment account for more than 24 consecutive months; (iii) the PSU has misinformed the Bank to obtain the basic payment account where such account would not have been provided in case correct information would have been provided; (iv) the PSU is no longer legally resident in the EEA; and (v) the PSU has opened a second payment account which allows him to make use of the same services in the same Member State where he already holds a basic payment account.

reluctant to offer payment accounts to residents of other Member States. With the development of the internal market, we observe an increasing number of EU citizens working in other Member States. The possibility of opening a payment account in another Member States has therefore become even more relevant for EU citizens. The PAD addresses this issue by introducing an obligation for Banks to assist their consumer clients with the opening of a payment account with a Bank established in another Member State.[125]

3.4.2.2 Switching of Payment Accounts Within a Member State

Consumers should be able to select the Payment products and services from the Bank that best meet their needs. It is therefore essential that consumers can switch easily between Banks if they are no longer satisfied with their current Bank. Prior to the PAD, Banks used to apply different requirements for payment account switching, which made it difficult for consumers to switch between Banks.[126] The difficulties of payment account switching were also noticed by the European Banking Industry Committee, which published a set of principles in 2008 that the banking sector had to apply to facilitate the process of payment account switching.[127] Notwithstanding the best intentions of this self-regulation initiative, payment account switching continued to be an onerous process for consumers.

Articles 9 and 10 PAD oblige Banks to offer payment account switching services to any consumer who opens or holds a payment account with a Bank provided that the payment accounts are held in the same currency. The Bank that offers the new payment account, which is called the receiving Bank, is responsible for initiating the switching process.[128] **Article 10(5) PAD** requires the receiving Bank to have the

[125] This means according to **Article 11(1) PAD** that upon the PSU's request the Bank: (i) informs the PSU free of charge about all active standing orders for credit transfers/direct debit mandates and recurring incoming credit transfers/direct debit collections executed on the PSU's payment account in the previous 13 months; (ii) transfers any positive balance on the payment account to the payment account held by the PSU with the new Bank; and (iii) close the original payment account.

[126] PAD, Recital 25.

[127] See EBIC (2008).

[128] Within two business days after receipt of the authorisation, the receiving Bank requests the transferring Bank to: (i) provide a list of the existing standing orders for credit transfers and available information on direct debit mandates that are switched. This

new payment account operational within five business days after it receives all relevant information from the transferring Bank. For this purpose, the receiving Bank sets up the standing orders for credit transfers requested by the consumer and makes the required preparations to ensure that it can accept direct debit collections.

3.4.2.3 Transparency and Comparability of Fees Charged to Consumers

The level of detail of the information provided by Banks regarding fees for the execution of Payments must be sufficient to enable PSUs to compare the costs of corresponding payment services provided by different Banks. Although PSD provided fee transparency requirements for Banks, it was difficult for PSUs to compare fees charged by different Banks for similar Payment products. The information provided by Banks was often complex, presented in different formats and contained different terminology, which made it difficult for consumers to compare the characteristics of Payment Products.

Because PSD did not prescribe how relevant information should be presented, Banks did not breach any fee transparency requirements under PSD when it provided information in a different manner. However, the lack of a uniform presentation of fees charged by Banks hindered competition in the European retail banking sector.[129] For this reason, **Article 7(1) PAD** stipulates that consumers have to have access to websites that provide a clear overview of the fees charged by Banks for the most commonly used payment services. Furthermore, **Article 4(1) PAD** requires Banks to provide their clients with a fee information document before they enter into a framework contract for a payment account.

information will have to be provided within five business days; (ii) provide the available information about recurring incoming credit transfers and creditor-driven direct debit collections executed on the consumer's payment account in the previous 13 months. This information will have to be provided within five business days; (iii) stop accepting direct debit collections and incoming credit transfers with effect from the date specified in the authorisation in case the transferring Bank does not automatically redirect incoming credit transfers and direct debit collections to the new payment account; (iv) cancel standing orders with effect from the date specified in the authorisation; (v) transfer any remaining positive balance to the payment account opened or held with the receiving Bank on the date specified by the consumer; and (vi) close the payment account held with the transferring Bank on the date specified by the consumer if the consumer has no outstanding obligations on that payment account and the actions set out above have been completed.

[129] PAD, Recital 4.

Unfortunately, the PAD allows Member States to decide on the fee terminology to be used in the fee information document. Allowing for different fee terminology makes it difficult for consumers to compare fees charged by different Banks on a cross-border basis.

3.4.3 The Revised Payment Services Directive (PSD2)

In 2012, London Economics published an evaluation report on the impact of PSD on the development of the internal market for Payments.[130] This report shows that the introduction of a new licencing regime for PIs appeared to have lowered barriers to market entry.[131] In addition, the costs and execution time limits for Payments have been reduced considerably as a result of PSD. Moreover, substantial improvements were realised in relation to the information provided by PSPs to their PSUs.

Further to these positive developments, the PSD evaluation report also revealed numerous shortcomings that required further attention from the European legislature. PSD did for example not take account of the development of new technologies such as Application Programming Interfaces ('**APIs**') and the Payment products that was introduced on the basis of these technologies (**Paragraph 3.4.3.2**). These developments were not foreseen at the time PSD was adopted and, as a result thereof, numerous Payment solutions were developed after the adoption of PSD which was not covered by PSD. Other main concerns include the large number of member states options and the fact that many PSD requirements and exemptions were interpreted differently in Member States. Because of these shortcomings, the internal market for Payments was not able to reach its full potential.

On 20 November 2012, the European Parliament adopted a resolution to further align the national legislative frameworks for Payments.[132] The European Parliament concluded that legislative action was required at a European level to address the shortcomings of PSD. On 8 October

[130] See London Economics and iff in association with PaySys (2013).

[131] Ibid., p. 196.

[132] European Parliament resolution of 20 November 2012 on 'Towards an integrated European market for card, internet and mobile payments, OJ C 419, 16.12.2015, pp. 19–28.

2015, the European Parliament adopted PSD2, which had to be implemented by the Member States into their national legislation by 13 January 2018 the latest. As with PSD, the European legislature decided to use the instrument of a directive rather than a regulation. By adopting a directive instead of a regulation, the European legislature missed the opportunity to fully harmonise the PSD2 requirements for PSPs and PSUs in the EEA.[133]

3.4.3.1 Increased Scope of Applicability

The PSD requirements did not apply to so-called one-leg Payments, except for the provisions on value dating and the availability of funds (**Paragraph 3.4.1.2**). Although PSD allowed Member States to apply the PSD requirements to one-leg Payments, only a few Member States have used this option. Consequently, the legal safeguards for PSUs were adversely affected in Member States where the majority of the PSD's conduct of business requirements, such as transparency and conduct of business requirements, did not apply to one-leg transactions. PSD2 addressed this issue by applying a broader scope of applicability. According to **Article 2(1) PSD2**, PSD2 requirements also cover one-leg Payments in relation to the part of the transaction that is being carried out in the EEA.[134] Unfortunately, PSD2 does not provide any guidance on how to determine which part of a transaction is being carried out in the EEA. In my opinion, further guidance from the European legislature would be helpful to ensure a harmonised interpretation as to where parts of a cross-border transaction are being carried out.

Moreover, the PSD transparency and information requirements only applied to Payments denominated in an EEA currency. With PSD2, the scope of the transparency and information requirements for PSPs has been broadened and also covers Payments denominated in non-EEA currencies. Table 3.2 provides a summary of the scope of application of the PSD2 provisions regarding one-leg and two-leg transactions.

[133] Even though PSD2 is primarily a maximum harmonisation directive.

[134] Decision by the EEA Joint Committee No 165/2019 of 14 June 2019 "amending Annex IX (Financial Services) to the EEA Agreement", OJ L 291, 10.11.2022, pp. 50–52.

Table 3.2 Scope of application PSD2

	Two-leg Payments	*One-leg Payments*
Payment in Euro	PSD2 applies fully	PSD2 requirements apply with the exceptions listed in Article 2(4) PSD2[135]
Payment service in non-euro EEA currency	PSD2 applies fully	PSD2 requirements apply with the exceptions listed in Article 2(4) PSD2[136]
Other currency	PSD2 requirements apply with the exceptions listed in Article 2(3) PSD2[137]	PSD2 requirements apply with the exceptions listed in Article 2(4) PSD2[138]

3.4.3.2 Extension of the Definition of Payment Services

The PSD definitions of the different payment services were not technologically neutral. As a result, new services have been developed after the adoption of PSD that contained characteristics of a payment service but nevertheless fell outside the scope of PSD. PSD did for example not account for the development of open banking solutions, which are Payment products that can be used to, amongst others, initiate Payments on behalf of a payer whereby the service provider will never be in the possession of the funds that are transferred as a result of the execution of that transaction.[139] With these products, funds are transferred directly from the payer's payment account held with his AS-PSP[140] to the payment account of the beneficiary.

Since open banking services were not regulated by PSD, service providers offering these services were neither obliged to hold a PI licence

[135] Title III PSD2 applies except for point (b) of Article 45(1), point (2)(e) of Article 52, point (5)(g) of Article 52 and point (a) of Article 56. Title IV PSD2 applies except for Article 62(2) and (4), Articles 76, 77, 81, 83(1), 89 and 92.

[136] *See* Footnote 158.

[137] Title III PSD2 applies except for point (b) of Article 45(1), point (2)(e) of Article 52 and point (a) of Article 56. Title IV PSD2 applies except for Articles 81 to 86.

[138] *See* Footnote 158.

[139] Open banking services are also referred to as access to the account (XS2A) services.

[140] **Article 4(17) PSD2** defines an 'AS-PSP' as a PSP providing and maintaining payment accounts for a payer. These are mostly Banks but can also be PIs offering current accounts.

nor to comply with the legal requirements imposed by PSD on PSPs for safeguarding consumer protection and ensuring sound competition between PSPs. The fact that these service providers were not obliged to be licensed as a PI resulted in unsound competition between PSPs. It may appear that open banking service providers used to have a competitive advantage over Non-Banks that were required to hold a licence. However, the opposite turned out to be the case since Banks were (rightfully) preventing open banking service providers from accessing the payments accounts of their PSUs. Since there was no legal basis for open banking service providers to demand payment account access from Banks, it was difficult for service providers to successfully rollout open banking services in the market at a large scale.[141] Service providers that did manage to offer open banking services did so by obtaining payment account access using the PSU's authentication procedures (**Paragraph 5.5.2**).

The licensing regime for PIs needed to have a broader scope of applicability to bridge this legal gap. One of the main objectives of PSD2 is to address this issue without imposing restrictions that are too onerous for the development of new innovative Payment products. To this end, PSD2 expanded the list of regulated payment services set out in Annex I PSD by adding two payment services based on open banking. These payment services are 'payment initiation services' and 'account information services'.

Payment Initiation Service

Article 4(15) PSD2 defines a payment initiation service as a payment service whereby the PSP obtains access to a PSU's payment account held with an AS-PSP for the purpose of initiating credit transfers on behalf of the PSU. Payment initiation services are only available in relation to credit transfers and cannot cover other types of Payments such as credit card transactions or direct debit collections. Payment initiation services are also known as overlay services and can be offered by Banks, EMIs and PIs. A payment initiation service provider (**'PISP'**), which is a PSP that solely provides payment initiation services, does not provide the PSU with a payment account. Instead, the PISP assists the PSU with the initiation of a credit transfer from a payment account that the PSU holds with its AS-PSP. In essence, the AS-PSP receives the payment order from the PISP on

[141] Furthermore, it often created confusion in the market since these service providers were sometimes perceived by consumers to be regulated PSPs.

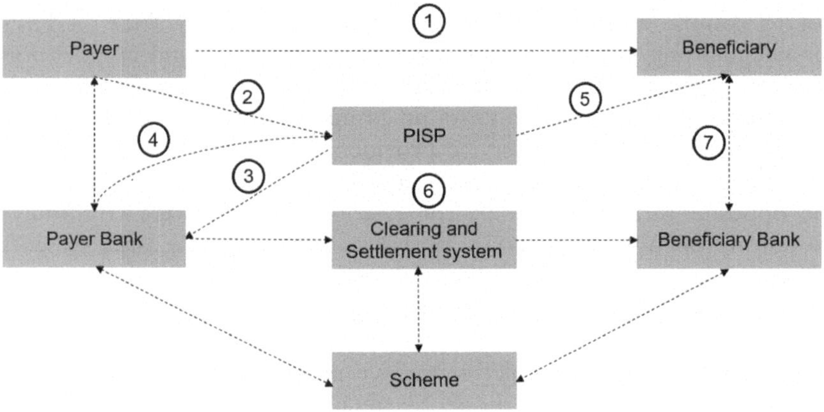

Fig. 3.1 Flowchart payment initiation service

behalf of a PSU instead of from the PSU directly. The PSU gives explicit consent to a PISP allowing the PISP to access its payment account and to initiate credit transfers on its behalf.[142] Figure 3.1 illustrates the processing of a payment initiation service.

The payer holds a payment account with his Bank (AS-PSP) and uses a payment initiation product to initiate credit transfers. When the payer wants to make a Payment (e.g., when purchasing a good or service from a merchant) (**1**), the payer can use the payment initiation product offered by the PISP to initiate the transaction (**2**). The payer provides his consent to the PISP for the execution of the credit transfer and the PISP accesses the payer's payment account held with his Bank to initiate the credit transfer to the beneficiary's payment account (**3**).[143] The PISP is not allowed to change any of the transaction characteristics, such as the amount to be transferred or the beneficiary of the transaction. The role

[142] In order for the PSU to monitor and manage the permissions it has given to PISPs for the purpose of payment initiation services, **Article 43(1) PSR Proposal** requires AS-PSPs to provide the PSU with a permissions dashboard that is integrated into its user interface.

[143] **Article 45(2) PSD2** stipulates that before a PISP initiates a Payment, it informs the payer about: (i) the name of the PISP; (ii) the address of the PISP's office; (iii) the address of the PISP's agent or branch established in the Member State where the payment service is provided (if applicable); (iv) contact details that are relevant for the payer to be able to communicate with the PISP; and (v) the NCA under PSD2.

of the PISP is strictly limited to the forwarding of the payment order to the payer's Bank. Each time the PISP initiates a credit transfer on behalf of the payer, the PISP must identify itself *vis-à-vis* the payer's Bank. **Article 66(4)(c) PSD2** obliges the Bank to treat payment orders received from a PISP in the same manner as payment orders that it receives from payers directly. When the payer's Bank receives a payment order from a PISP, the Bank notifies the PISP that it received the order and confirms whether the payer has sufficient funds on his payment account for the execution of the transaction (**4**).[144] After receipt of this confirmation, the PISP informs the beneficiary that the payment has been successfully initiated (**5**). Subsequently, the payer's Bank transfers the corresponding funds directly from the payer's payment account to the beneficiary's Bank (**6**). After the funds have been credited to the payment account of the beneficiary's Bank, the beneficiary's Bank must credit the beneficiary's payment account with the transaction amount on the same business day (**7**). It is important to emphasise that the PISP is only involved in the communication between the payer and his Bank and that the PISP is not allowed to be in possession of the funds that are transferred to the beneficiary's Bank at any moment according to **Article 66(3)(a) PSD2**.

PISPs are only capable of offering competitive payment initiation products if they have instant and reliable access to payment accounts.[145] Prior to the implementation of PSD2, Banks were not obliged to provide third parties access to the payment accounts of their PSUs. To be able to offer payment initiation services, such service providers commonly applied a technique called screen scraping to obtain access to the payment account of a Bank's PSU (**Paragraph 5.5.2**).[146] Given the security risks involved

[144] Such notification must be made without delay.

[145] **Article 66(3) PSD2** stipulates that a PISP is not allowed to request other data from the PSU than it strictly requires for providing payment initiation services and it must ensure that any information it obtains regarding a particular PSU is only provided to the beneficiary with the PSU's explicit consent. Furthermore, data obtained from the PSU cannot be stored for other purposes than the provision of the payment initiation service.

[146] An example of a service provider that used a different method for obtaining payment account access prior to PSD2 was Payconiq. Payconiq structured its payment initiation product as a combination of a SEPA credit transfer and a SEPA direct debit collection. The payer would sign a direct debit mandate on the basis of which Payconiq could initiate direct debit collections from the payer's payment account. When the payer provided Payconiq with an instruction to process a fund transfer from its payment account held with

in screen scraping, PSD2 provides PISPs with a legal basis to demand access to a PSU's payment account, which makes screen scraping no longer necessary. **Article 66(1) PSD2** stipulates that PSUs have a right to use the services of a PISP if such PSU holds a payment account with an AS-PSP.[147] Since Banks themselves can also offer payment initiation services, there is a risk that Banks foreclose PISPs by imposing barriers to payment account access.[148] To ensure that Banks do not impose barriers for PISPs to access their IT-infrastructure, **Article 66(5) PSD2** states that Banks are not allowed to make the provision of payment initiation services by a PISP dependent on the existence of a contractual arrangement between the PISP and the Bank. PSUs should be free to use payment initiation services provided by a PISP and requiring approval from the Bank to use the services of a PISP would contradict that principle. It is however not desirable to allow PISPs payment account access under all circumstances. Banks are allowed to deny a PISP payment account access under strict conditions. **Article 68(5) PSD2** stipulates that Banks can only refuse payment account access for objective reasons related to unauthorised or fraudulent access to the payment account by the PISP.[149]

Account Information Service

Further to the payment initiation service, PSD2 introduced a new payment service called the account information service. According to **Article 4(16) PSD2**, account information services enable PSUs to obtain (consolidated) information on their payment account(s), such as bank accounts, credit card accounts and investment accounts, from a PSP other than their AS-PSP. These services are also known as account aggregation services since they typically compile payment information from more than one payment account. Account information services were not regulated

an AS-PSP to, for example, a merchant, Payconiq would obtain the relevant funds from the payer's payment account by initiating a direct debit collection. Subsequently, Payconiq transferred the transaction amount from its own payment account to the merchant's payment account.

[147] A PSU only has such right if it holds a payment account with an AS-PSP that is accessible online.

[148] See ACM (2017, p. 4).

[149] If the AS-PSP denies a PISP access to a payment account, the AS-PSP informs the PSU thereof (unless this would compromise objectively justified security reasons or if this is prohibited under national law).

under PSD and service providers offering these services were not subject to the licensing regime for PIs at that time. This made it difficult for account information service providers (**'AISPs'**) to provide these services since Banks were not obliged to accede to an AISP's request to provide access to payment account information. To enable AISPs to offer account information services, **Article 67(1) PSD2** provides PSUs with a right to make use of account information services if the PSU holds a payment account with an AS-PSP that is accessible online. Figure 3.2 illustrates the processing of an account information service.

The PSU gives its consent to an AISP allowing the AISP to access its payment account(s) held with one or more Banks (**1**).[150] The AISP is only allowed to obtain access to information from payment accounts designated by the PSU.[151] There are limitations on the information that an AISP is legally entitled to receive. An AISP cannot request information regarding a PSU that is not relevant to the provision of the account information service. Furthermore, AISPs are not allowed to request 'sensitive payment data'[152] relating to payment accounts. After the PSU has given its consent to the AISP, the AISP requests payment account access from the PSU's Bank(s) (**2**). As with PISPs, it is essential that Banks do not impose barriers for AISPs to access their IT-infrastructure for the provision of account information services. To this end, **Article 67(4) PSD2** prohibits Banks from making the provision of account information services by an AISP dependent on the existence of a contractual arrangement between the AISP and the Bank. Moreover, **Article 67(3)(b) PSD2** stipulates that Banks have to treat data requests from an AISP without any discrimination for other than objective reasons. According to **Article 68(5) PSD2**, a Bank is only allowed to deny an AISP access to its

[150] In order for the PSU to monitor and manage the permissions it has given to AISPs for the purpose of account information services, **Article 43(1) PSR Proposal** requires AS-PSPs to provide the PSU with a permissions dashboard that is integrated into its user interface.

[151] Furthermore, **article 94(1) PSD2** requires that any processing of personal data shall be carried out in accordance with the requirements set out in Regulation (EU) 2016/679 (GDPR).

[152] **Article 4(32) PSD2** defines 'sensitive payment data' as data, including personalised security credentials which can be used to carry out fraud. For the activities of AISPs and PISPs, the name of the account owner and the account number do not constitute sensitive payment data.

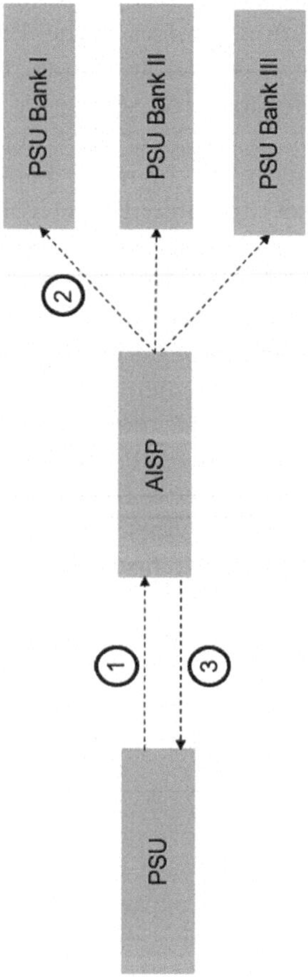

Fig. 3.2 Flowchart account information service

payment accounts for objective reasons related to unauthorised or fraudulent access to the payment account by the AISP.[153] After the AISP obtains access to the PSU's payment account, the AISP provides the PSU with financial information regarding its payment accounts, such as information regarding its spending behaviour (**3**). The AISP can provide the payment account information in the original form or in a processed form. An AISP can also provide payment account information to a third party with the PSU's explicit agreement.[154]

3.4.3.3 Clarification of Related Services that Are Out of Scope of PSD2

Under the PSD regime, certain services were explicitly excluded from the PSD requirements (**Paragraph 3.4.1.1**). For some of these exempted services, there was a lot of ambiguity on what the relevant characteristics were to remain outside the scope of PSD. The characteristics that these services were allowed to have to be exempted from PSD were interpreted differently by NCAs. As a result, service providers offering similar services could require a licence in certain Member States and be exempted from such requirements in other Member States.[155] PSD2 addressed this issue by further clarifying which Payment related services do not constitute payment services within the meaning of PSD2. The most relevant PSD exemptions that have been amended under PSD2 are (i) the limited network exemption; (ii) the commercial agent exemption; (iii) the digital services exemption; and (iv) the ATM exemption.

1. Limited Network Exemption

Under the PSD regime, the limited network exemption was often applied by large networks processing relatively high payment volumes.[156] Since it was not the intention of the European legislature to allow large payment volumes to be processed outside of the financial services regulatory framework, PSD2 tried to clarify which payment instruments can be used under

[153] In case an AS-PSP denies an AISP payment account access, the AS-PSP informs the relevant PSU thereof, unless this would compromise objectively justified security reasons or if it is not allowed under national law.

[154] See EBA (n.d.).

[155] This was particularly relevant with regard to the commercial agent exemption.

[156] PSD2, Recital 13.

this exemption. According to **Article 3(k) PSD2**, payment instruments are only eligible for the limited network exemption if their usability is restricted to a 'very' limited range of goods or services. Since PSD2 does not provide any further guidance as to how the concept of a 'very' limited range of goods or services should be interpreted, the eligibility requirements for this exemption were interpreted very differently by NCAs. To ensure a harmonised interpretation of the limited network exemption, the EBA published its final guidelines on the limited network exemption under PSD2 on 24 February 2022. These guidelines apply as of June 2022 and contain certain indicators that NCAs must take into account when reviewing an application for the limited network exemption.[157] Moreover, according to these guidelines, there must be a functional connection between the goods and/or services that can be acquired with the payment instrument in order for the payment instrument to qualify as limited for acquiring a very limited range of goods or services under PSD2.[158]

To prevent the limited network exemption from being used by networks processing high payment volumes, **Article 37(2) PSD2** stipulates that service providers operating under this exemption have to notify their NCA of the total value of the Payments executed during the preceding 12 months if the total value exceeds €1 mln. On the basis of such notification, the NCA determines whether the service provider remains eligible to rely on the exemption based on the indicators set out in the EBA guidelines on the limited network exclusion under PSD2. In my opinion, this discretionary power contradicts the European legislature's objective of harmonising the use of the limited network exemption throughout the EEA.

Given that services provided under this exemption often involve substantial Payment volumes, the PSR Proposal clarifies that it is not possible to use a particular instrument under the exemption to acquire goods/services within more than one limited network or for acquiring an unlimited range of goods/services.[159]

[157] See EBA (2022).

[158] Ibid., p. 21.

[159] PSR Proposal, Recital 12.

2. Commercial Agent Exemption

Under the PSD regime, it was not entirely clear whether an exempted commercial agent was allowed to act on behalf of both the seller and the buyer of a particular good or service. It was therefore not uncommon for agents, such as e-commerce platforms, to act on behalf of both parties without being licensed as a PI.[160] **Article 3(b) PSD2** clarified that this exemption is only available to agents acting solely for the payer or the beneficiary and not for agents acting on behalf of both parties. Given that the concept of a commercial agent is typically defined in national civil law, it is proposed in the PSR Proposal to harmonise the use of the concept commercial agent by referring to Directive 86/653/EEC on self-employed commercial agents.[161] Moreover, in order to be eligible for the exemption, **Article 2(2)(b) PSR Proposal** requires the agent to be authorised via an agreement with either the payer of the beneficiary to negotiate or conclude the sale or purchase of goods/services on behalf of only the payer or only the beneficiary.

3. Digital Services Exemption

The digital services exemption was often used more broadly than envisaged by the European legislature and covered relatively high transaction volumes.[162] As with the limited network exemption, the use of the digital services exemption for high transaction volumes triggered undesirable consumer protection risks. Furthermore, this exemption was implemented differently by Member States due to the ambiguous wording of PSD. To address these concerns, PSD2 substantially narrowed the scope of the digital services exemption by stipulating that it only applies to 'ancillary payment services' carried out by providers of electronic communications

[160] See London Economics and iff in association with PaySys (2013, p. 125).

[161] PSR Proposal, Recital 11.

[162] See London Economics and iff in association with PaySys (2013, p. 123).

networks[163] or services.[164] According to **Article 3(l) PSD2**, payment services provided by a provider of electronic communication networks or services in addition to electronic communication services are only exempted in case these transactions are: (i) made for purchasing digital content[165] and voice-based services, regardless of the device used for the purchase or consumption of the digital content and charged to the related bill; or (ii) performed using an electronic device and charged to the related bill within the framework of a charitable activity or for the purchase of tickets.[166] **Article 3(l)(ii) PSD2** stipulates that the value of any single Payment may not exceed €50 and the total value of Payments for one single user is not allowed to exceed €300 on a monthly basis.

[163] **Article 4(41) PSD2** defines an 'electronic communications network' as a network within the meaning of **Article 2(1) of Directive (EU) 2018/1972** (OJ L 321, 17.12.2018). Electronic communications networks are transmission systems, whether or not based on a permanent infrastructure or centralised administration capacity, and, where applicable, switching or routing equipment and other resources, including network elements which are not active, which permit the conveyance of signals by wire, radio, optical or other electromagnetic means, including satellite networks, fixed (circuit- and packet-switched, including internet) and mobile networks, electricity cable systems, to the extent that they are used for the purpose of transmitting signals, networks used for radio and television broadcasting, and cable television networks, irrespective of the type of information conveyed.

[164] **Article 4(42) PSD2** defines an 'electronic communication service' as a service as defined in **Article 2(4) of Directive (EU) 2018/1972** (OJ L 321, 17.12.2018). An electronic communication service is a service normally provided for remuneration via electronic communications networks, which encompasses, with the exception of services providing, or exercising editorial control over, content transmitted using electronic communications networks and services, the following types of services: (a) 'internet access service' as defined in point (2) of the second paragraph of **Article 2 of Regulation (EU) 2015/2120**; (b) interpersonal communications service; and (c) services consisting wholly or mainly in the conveyance of signals such as transmission services used for the provision of machine-to-machine services and for broadcasting.

[165] **Article 4(43) PSD2** defines 'digital content' as goods or service which are produced and supplied in digital form whose use or consumption is restricted to a technical device and which do not include in any way the use or consumption of physical goods or services.

[166] According to Recital 16 PSD2, a clear reference to the purchase of electronic tickets has been introduced to cover the development in payments where, in particular, customers can order, pay for, obtain and validate electronic tickets from any location and at any time using smartphones or other devices.

4. ATM Exemption

Under **Article 3(o) PSD**, payment services provided by ATM deployers that operated independently from Banks or other PSPs (e.g., ATMs in supermarkets and stores) were exempted from the PSD requirements. The rationale behind this exemption was to stimulate the availability of ATM's in remote and less populated areas. By allowing ATM deployers to charge higher fees, ATM deployers were provided with an incentive to also operate ATMs in remote areas. In practice, this exemption appeared to incentivise ATM deployers to terminate their contractual arrangements with PSPs as this enabled them to charge higher fees for ATM cash withdrawals in general. This was never intended when the exemption was introduced. It was believed that this practice of charging higher fees could be restricted by requiring ATM deployers to comply with specific transparency provisions in relation to the charges it applies.[167] For that purpose, **Article 3(o) PSD2** requires ATM deployers to inform persons making a cash withdrawal of the fees charged for such withdrawal before it carries out the withdrawal and upon receipt of the cash from the ATM.

3.4.3.4 Refined Transparency and Information Requirements

To enhance the transparency of both single payment transactions and payment transactions covered by a framework contract, PSD introduced transparency and information requirements for PSPs (**Paragraph 3.4.1.4**. To a large extent, these requirements continue to apply under the PSD2 regime. The transparency and information requirements that are currently in force are set out in **Annex I**.

3.4.3.5 Refined Rights and Obligations of PSPs and PSUs

PSD introduced rights and obligations for both PSPs and PSUs which continue to apply under the PSD2 regime (**Paragraph 3.4.1.5**). However, with PSD2 certain rights and obligations have been refined to better safeguard the interests of consumers. The most relevant consumer protection measures that have been refined under PSD2 relate to (i) surcharging; (ii) strong customer authentication; and (iii) value date and availability of funds.

[167] PSD2, Recital 18.

Surcharging

Article 52(3) PSD allowed merchants to charge customers a fee for using a particular payment instrument to initiate Payments.[168] These charges, which are called 'surcharges', together with rebates, which involve a price reduction for using a particular payment instrument, provide merchants with a tool to incentivise customers to use a payment instrument that is cheaper to accept for the merchant. Card schemes used to counterbalance the effects of surcharging and rebate practices by imposing contractual obligations on merchants such as the 'no discrimination rule' and the 'honour all cards rule'.[169] The no discrimination rule prohibits merchants from steering customers to use the Payment instrument of their preference. The honour all cards rule obliges merchants to accept all cards of the same brand, regardless of the fees charged for using these cards (**Paragraph 3.7.3.2**).[170]

PSD allowed Member States to implement different rules on surcharging, thereby creating heterogeneity in the European market for card payments. For example, the Member State option to implement a prohibition on the use of surcharges was applied by no more than 14 Member States.[171] With **Article 62 PSD2**, the option for merchants to apply surcharging has been limited. **Article 62(3) PSD2** allows surcharging only if the fees of a particular payment instrument do not exceed the costs borne by the beneficiary for the use of that instrument.[172] According to **Article 60(3) PSD2**, the payer is only bound to pay such surcharge provided that he has been informed of the costs before initiating the Payment. Furthermore, **Article 62(4) PSD2** introduced a prohibition to apply surcharging regarding credit cards or other instruments for which interchange fees are regulated by Regulation (EU)

[168] PSD allowed Member States to forbid surcharging, taking into account its objective to encourage competition and promote the use of efficient payment instruments.

[169] See Commission (2012, p. 14).

[170] IFR, Recital 37.

[171] These Member States were Austria, Bulgaria, Cyprus, Czech Republic, France, Greece, Hungary, Italy, Latvia, Lithuania, Luxembourg, Portugal, Romania and Sweden.

[172] The amount of a surcharge must be limited to the costs incurred by the merchant when the customer chooses a particular Payment product. **Article 19 of Directive 2011/83/EU** on consumer rights stipulates that surcharging should not be used by merchants as an additional source of income.

2015/751 on interchange fees for card-based payments ('**IFR**')[173] or the SEPA Regulation. Given the considerable reduction in the fees that merchants have to pay to their Bank due to the IFR, surcharging was no longer considered to be justified for cards that are covered by this Regulation.[174] Surcharging is only prohibited for payment instruments that are issued under a four-party card scheme. Cards that operate on the basis of a three-party card scheme are generally more expensive, which justifies that merchants should be able to charge a customer for the additional costs incurred when using such an instrument.

Strong Customer Authentication (SCA)

PSD2 introduced an advanced method of authentication called strong customer authentication ('**SCA**') (**Paragraph** 5.4.2). The PSD2 SCA requirement reflects to a large extent the SCA requirement set out in the SecuRe Pay[175] Recommendations, which PSPs were obliged to implement by February 2015. However, with **Article 97(4) PSD2**, the requirement to apply SCA also covers payment initiation services and account information services.

Value Date and Availability of Funds

Article 73(2) PSD obliged the beneficiary's PSP to ensure that the amount of an incoming Payment was at the beneficiary's disposal immediately after the amount was credited to the beneficiary's PSP's payment account. Under **Article 87(2) PSD2**, this obligation only applies where on the part of the beneficiary's PSP there is: (i) no currency conversion; or (ii) there is a currency conversion between the euro and a Non-euro area Member State currency or between two Non-euro area Member State currencies. This obligation also applies to payments where the payer's payment account and the beneficiary's payment account are held with the same PSP.

[173] Regulation (EU) 2015/751 of 29 April 2015 "on interchange fees for card-based payment transactions", OJ L 123, 19.5.2015, pp. 1–15.

[174] PSD2, Recital 66.

[175] The European Forum on the Security of Retail Payments (SecuRe Pay) is a voluntary initiative established in 2011 between relevant EEA authorities, the EBA and its members and the European System of Central Banks. SecuRe Pay was established in 2011 to facilitate common knowledge and understanding of issues related to the security of electronic retail payment services and instruments and to issue recommendations.

3.5 The Single Euro Payments Area (SEPA) Regulation

Before the European legislature introduced mandatory standards for the processing of cross-border credit transfers and direct debit collections, the European banking sector developed its own standards for the processing of national and cross-border Payments on a voluntary basis. This self-regulation initiative, known as SEPA[176], aims to create an integrated market for euro-denominated Payments by replacing national standards for Payments with SEPA standards. The intention to develop the SEPA project was first announced by the European banking sector in May 2002. In an EPC white paper, the banking sector expressed its ambition to migrate all national standards used for Payments in the EU to SEPA standards by 2010.[177] The SEPA standards that participating PSPs have to apply when processing SEPA transactions are issued by the EPC. These standards are based on standards developed by international standardisation bodies such as the International Organization for Standardization ('**ISO**') and apply only with regard to euro-denominated credit transfers (EPC CT Rulebook), direct debit collections (EPC DD Core Rulebook and the EPC DD B2B Rulebook) and instant payments.[178] These rulebooks are binding for PSPs established in a SEPA country[179] that have adhered to these rulebooks.

A point of criticism is that the SEPA project is mainly a banking project and there are only limited possibilities for Non-Bank involvement. For example, Non-Banks do not have a say in the development of the EPC rulebooks and are confronted with the EPC requirements as a matter of fact. In the first instance, Non-Bank were only allowed to participate in the EPC's Stakeholder Forums, which were in essence information

[176] The EPC applies the following definition of SEPA: "*SEPA will be the area where citizens, companies and other economic actors will be able to make and receive payments in euro, within Europe, whether between or within national boundaries under the same basic conditions, rights and obligations, regardless of their location*".

[177] See EPC (2002, p. 6).

[178] EPC ICT Rulebook. Although the EPC also provides for standards and recommendations regarding mobile payments, cash handling and card payments, the EPC has not (yet) established rulebooks for these types of Payments.

[179] The SEPA countries include: (i) EEA Member States; (ii) Switzerland; (iii) Monaco; (iv) Mayotte; (v) St Pierre-et-Miquelon; (vi) San Marino; (vii) the Principality of Andorra; (viii) Vatican City; and (ix) Saint Pierre and Miquelon.

sessions and did not offer a platform to provide input or propose changes to the rulebooks.[180] Nowadays, Non-Banks are becoming more involved since several PIs, such as Conotoxia and eQuire, have become an EPC member within the meaning of the EPC By-laws.[181] Furthermore, PIs are represented in the EPC via the interest groups the European Payment Institutions Federation (EPIF) and the Electronic Money Association (EMA). According to **Article 5.4.2 of the EPC By-laws** this allows PIs to attend the EPC's general assembly and cast votes.[182] Since each member has one vote in the general assembly, and Banks are represented by over 64 members, there continues to be an imbalance with regard to the representation of the different stakeholders.

Moreover, it is essential for Non-Banks to have direct access to the EPC schemes in order to compete with Banks on an equal footing. For Banks it is relatively easy to become a direct participant in the EPC schemes since Banks are deemed to automatically satisfy all eligibility criteria.[183] This is however not the case for PIs. The most difficult adherence criterion for PIs to comply with is the requirement to provide payment accounts to PSUs.[184] Since payment accounts are typically not offered by PIs, the practical outcome of the EPC's adherence policy is that PIs cannot join the EPC schemes as a direct participant. This means that PIs can only obtain indirect access via a Bank.

The self-regulation SEPA initiative proved to be insufficiently successful in ensuring that all EU based PSPs apply the same standards.[185] To stimulate a uniform rollout of the SEPA standards throughout the EU, the European Parliament and the Council of the EU adopted the SEPA Regulation in 2012, which introduced end-dates for the migration to the SEPA standards.[186] According to **Article 1(1) SEPA Regulation**, the

[180] See Payment System End-Users Committee (EUC) (2009, p. 14).

[181] See EPC (2020a).

[182] Ibid., Article 5.4.2.

[183] See EPC (2020b, pp. 8–10).

[184] Ibid., p. 10.

[185] SEPA Regulation, Recital 5.

[186] Further to the SEPA Regulation, Regulation 924/2009 facilitated the rollout of the SEPA by introducing the reachability requirement for direct debit collections and the principle of equal charges for cross-border direct debit collections. In addition, PSD introduced international standards regarding the processing of credit transfers and direct debit collections.

SEPA Regulation covers credit transfers and direct debit collections[187] denominated in euro[188] whereby both the payer's PSP and the beneficiary's PSP are established in the EEA.[189] The SEPA Regulation does not cover all jurisdictions that are subject to the EPC rulebooks.[190] Consequently, PSPs established in a jurisdiction that is not covered by the SEPA Regulation do not have to meet the legal requirements of the SEPA Regulation other than those to which they have committed themselves under the EPC rulebooks.

The key provisions of the SEPA Regulation include: (i) the introduction of an obligation for PSPs to replace the conventional payment account numbers with the IBAN and BIC standards; (ii) the technical interoperability and reachability requirement; (iii) an amendment of Regulation 924/2009 to remove the limitation that only Payments up to €50,000 are subject to the same charging requirement for national and cross-border corresponding Payments; and (iv) a prohibition on (multilateral) interchange fees for cross-border direct debit collections.[191]

[187] **Article 1(2) SEPA Regulation** excludes the following Payments from its scope of application: (i) payments carried out between and within PSPs for their own account, including their agents or branches; (ii) payments that are processed and settled through LVPSs, excluding direct debit collections which the payer has not explicitly requested be routed via an LVPS; (iii) payments initiated through a card or similar device, including cash withdrawals, unless the card or similar device is only used to generate the information required to directly make a credit transfer or direct debit; (iv) payments initiated via any telecommunication, digital or IT device, if such Payments do not result in a credit transfer or direct debit to and from a payment account; (v) money remittance; and (vi) transferring of E-money, unless such transactions result in a credit transfer or direct debit to and from a payment account.

[188] Unlike PSD2, the SEPA Regulation does not apply to Payments executed in a non-euro EEA currency.

[189] Decision by the EEA Joint Committee No 86/2013 of 3 May 2013 "amending Annex XII (Free movement of capital) to the EEA Agreement", OJ L 291, 31.10.2013, pp. 51–52. Decision by the EEA Joint Committee No 283/2014 of 12 December 2014 "amending Annex XII (Free movement of capital) to the EEA Agreement", OJ L 311, 26.11.2015, p. 36.

[190] Although Monaco, Switzerland, Mayotte, St Pierre and Miquelon are also part of the SEPA area according to the EPC, the SEPA Regulation does not apply in these countries.

[191] Regulation 924/2009/EC has been substantially amended multiple times. In the interest of clarity, this regulation has been codified in Regulation 2021/1230 on cross-border payments in the Union.

3.5.1 *Introduction of the IBAN and BIC Standards*

As part of the migration to the SEPA standards, **Article 5(1) SEPA Regulation** required the SEPA countries had to replace the conventional 9-digit Basic Bank Account Number (BBAN) by the 18-digit IBAN standard and BIC by 1 February 2014.[192] **Article 2(16) SEPA Regulation** defines 'BIC' as a business identifier code that unambiguously identifies a PSP, the elements of which are specified by ISO standard 9362. IBAN together with the BIC allow for the identification of payment accounts held with PSPs in the SEPA countries. Since one can identify a payment account using only IBAN, it was considered too burdensome to require payers and beneficiaries to always provide both IBAN and BIC.[193] The obligation to also provide BIC was therefore abandoned under **Article 5(7) SEPA Regulation** for national Payments on 1 February 2014 and for cross-border Payments on 1 February 2016.

3.5.2 *Interoperability and Reachability*

To establish an internal market for Payments, it is essential that PSPs do not have to process Payments on the basis of different IT standards or are in other ways hindered by incompatible IT payment infrastructures. It is therefore essential to have interoperability between payment systems. The Committee on Payments and Market Infrastructures (CPMI) defines interoperability as the '*technical, semantic or business compatibility that enables a system or mechanism to be used in conjunction with other systems or mechanisms*'.[194] According to the CPMI, interoperability consists of three elements. The first element covers the technical infrastructure. The 'technical' element requires the adoption of a common IT-infrastructure and the use of common standards, such as the standard for exchanging Payment messages. An example of a standard introduced by the SEPA Regulation is the ISO 20022 XML standard[195], which is used by PSPs for

[192] For Non-euro area Member States, the migration deadline was set for 31 October 2016.

[193] SEPA Regulation, Recital 8.

[194] See BIS (n.d.).

[195] **Article 2(17) SEPA Regulation** defines the 'ISO 20022 XML standard' as a standard for the development of electronic financial messages as defined by the ISO, encompassing the physical representation of the Payments in XML syntax, in accordance

sending Payment messages to other PSPs or payment systems (**Paragraph 8.2.3**). According to **Article 5(1)(b) SEPA Regulation** the obligation to use the ISO 20022 XML standard only applies with regard to credit transfers and direct debit collections.[196] On 19 November 2023, all ISO 20022 based messages used under the SEPA payment scheme rulebooks will migrate to the 2019 standard.[197] The second element of interoperability involves the interpretative ability of payment systems and PSPs.[198] In order to have interoperability, the 'semantic' element ensures that all participants exchange similar data in a similar manner and interpret these data in a similar way. The third element involves the business rules of the payment system. The 'business' element covers *inter alia* the requirements for payment system access and the rights and obligations of its participants. **Article 4(1)(a) SEPA Regulation** requires that the rules of the payment scheme[199] used by PSPs for processing credit transfers and direct debit collections have to be the same for national and cross-border transactions carried out within the EEA. Furthermore, **Article 4(1)(b) SEPA Regulation** requires that payment schemes are only used in case the participants in that particular scheme represent a majority of PSPs[200] within a majority of the Member States and constitute a majority of PSPs within the EEA. Only PSPs that provide credit transfers or direct debit collections are taken into consideration in this regard.

Further to interoperability, the execution of Payments requires that payment accounts are reachable. **Article 8 Regulation 924/2009** first introduced a 'reachability' obligation for the payer's payment account

with business rules and implementation guidelines of EU-wide schemes for Payments falling within the scope of the SEPA Regulation.

[196] The ISO 20022 XML standard is also required in case the PSU, which is not a consumer or a micro-enterprise, initiates or receives an individual credit transfers or direct debit collections which are bundled in a batch file.

[197] See EPC (2023, p. 4).

[198] Jans (2023, p. 17).

[199] **Article 2(7) SEPA Regulation** defines a 'payment scheme' as a single set of rules, practices, standards and/or implementation guidelines agreed between PSPs for the execution of Payments and which is separated from any infrastructure or payment system that supports its operation.

[200] In case neither the payer nor the beneficiary is a consumer, only the Member States where such services are made available by PSPs and only PSPs providing such services are to be taken into account for this requirement.

under the EPC DD Core Scheme.[201] Regulation 924/2009 required the payer's PSP to be reachable for euro-denominated direct debit collections initiated by a beneficiary via a PSP established in a Member State.[202] **Article 3 SEPA Regulation** provides for a reachability obligation for PSPs with regard to both credit transfers and direct debit collections, provided that these Payments are initiated via a PSP established in a Member State.[203] On the basis of this reachability obligation, PSPs are not allowed to reject a SEPA credit transfer or SEPA direct debit collection if they accept equivalent national Payments. **Article 3(3) SEPA Regulation** provides that the reachability requirement for direct debit collections only applies if the payer is a consumer.

3.5.3 Charges Levied by a PSP

Regulation 924/2009 stipulated that charges levied by a PSP for a cross-border Payment up to €50,000 had to be the same as the charges levied by that PSP for a corresponding national Payments of the same value and in the same currency (**Paragraph 3.2.3**). **Article 17 SEPA Regulation** amended Regulation 924/2009 by removing the threshold for payments that are subject to the principle of 'same charges'. Consequently, cross-border Payments exceeding €50,000 are also covered by the principle of same charges.

3.5.4 Prohibition on Multilateral Interchange Fees (MIFs) for Direct Debit Collections

Article 2(13) and 2(12) SEPA Regulation introduced a definition of multilateral interchange fees ('**MIFs**') for direct debit collections, which are fees paid between the payer's PSP and the beneficiary's PSP for a direct debit collection that is subject to an arrangement between more than two PSPs. The SEPA Regulation stipulates that MIFs are no longer

[201] To harmonise the definitions applied in payment services regulations throughout the EU, Regulation 924/2009 refers to PSPs instead of institutions.

[202] Since the reachability requirement was also covered by the SEPA Regulation, this provision was removed from Regulation 924/2009 in 2012.

[203] To improve the transparency regarding the reachability requirement, the SEPA Regulation set aside the Regulation 924/2009 reachability requirements for direct debit collections per 2012.

allowed for cross-border direct debit collections after 1 November 2012 and for national direct debit collections after 1 February 2017. An exception is made for MIFs charged in relation to R-transactions for direct debit collections. **Article 2(25) SEPA Regulation** defines R-transactions as transactions that cannot be properly executed by a PSP.[204] The European legislature considered that MIFs can help allocate the costs of executing R-transactions in relation to a direct debit collection to the party responsible for the R-transaction.[205] According to **Article 8(2) SEPA Regulation** MIFs for R-transactions are allowed provided that the following four conditions are met. First, the MIFs do not exceed the actual costs incurred by the PSP for handling the R-transaction. Second, the costs of the R-transaction are allocated to the PSP or PSU responsible for the R-transaction. Third, PSPs do not charge PSUs additional fees to cover costs for which it has already been compensated by the MIF. Fourth, MIFs are only allowed if there is no viable alternative at an equal or lower cost for the PSU.

3.6 The Instant Payments Regulation

Given that fast payments must be executed within a time limit of 10 seconds, it is essential that these Payments are processed in accordance with a common set of rules.[206] Although fast payments were already covered by the SEPA Regulation and PSD2, said the legislative framework was not developed with a view to the specific characteristics of these Payments as they were developed after the adoption of PSD2 and the SEPA Regulation.[207]

In order to better align the legislative framework with the requirements for the execution of fast payments, the Commission published a proposal for an Instant Payments Regulation on 26 October 2022 as part of the

[204] Examples of R-transactions include payments: (i) where the payer does not have sufficient funds on its payment account; (ii) that have been revoked; (iii) for which a wrong amount or date has been used; (iv) executed without a valid mandate (direct debit collection); and (v) executed using the wrong or a closed payment account.

[205] SEPA Regulation, Recital 20.

[206] See Commission (2022, p. 13).

[207] Instant Payments Regulation, Recital 3.

2020 Retail Payments Strategy.[208] The Instant Payments Regulation[209] was published in the Official Journal of the European Union on 19 March 2024 and introduces *inter alia* four amendments to the requirements imposed by the SEPA Regulation on credit transfers in euro.

First, **Article 1(2) Instant Payment Regulation** requires that PSPs offering credit transfers in euro must also offer the service of sending and receiving instant payments in euro. PSPs (with the exception of EMIs and PIs) established in a euro Member State will be required to offer their PSU the possibility to receive instant payments in euro by 9 January 2025 and sending instant payments in euro by 9 October 2025.[210] This requirement will apply regarding all payment accounts, including basic payment accounts within the meaning of the PAD.[211] The European legislature considered that PIs and EMIs should also contribute to the adoption of instant payments.[212] Since PIs and EMIs are excluded from access to payment systems designated under Directive 98/26/EC on settlement finality in payment and securities settlement systems (**'SFD'**),[213] **Article 4 of the Instant Payments Regulation** amends the SFD to include PIs and EMIs in the term ínstitution′ for purposes of defining participants in a payment system. To ensure that PSUs have access to instant payments, all interfaces via which PSUs can initiate a payment order for credit transfers must also facilitate the initiation of instant payments.[214] In addition, **Article 1 of the Instant Payments Regulation** requires payment accounts to be reachable for

[208] See Commission (2022).

[209] Regulation (EU) 2024/886 of 13 March 2024 "amending Regulations (EU) No 260/2012 and (EU) 2021/1230 and Directives 98/26/EC and (EU) 2015/2366 as regards instant credit transfers in euro", OJ L, 2024/886, 19.3.2024.

[210] EMIs and PIs located in euro Member States will be obliged to offer their PSU the possibility to receive and sending instant payments in euro by 9 April 2027. PSPs (with the exception of EMIs and PIs) located in non-euro Member States will be obliged to offer their PSU the possibility to receive instant payments in euro by 9 January 2027 and sending instant payments in euro by 9 July 2027. EMIs and PIs located in non-euro Member States will be obliged to offer their PSU the possibility to receive instant payments in euro by 9 April 2027 and sending instant payments in euro by 9 July 2027.

[211] Instant Payment Regulation, Recital 7.

[212] Ibid., Recital 15.

[213] Directive 98/26/EC of 19 May 1998 "on settlement finality in payment and securities settlement systems", OJ L 166, 11.6.1998, pp. 45–50.

[214] Instant Payment Regulation, Recital 11.

instant payments 24/7/365. Second, **Article 1 of the Instant Payments Regulation** stipulates that charges applied by PSPs for sending and receiving instant payments in euro cannot be higher than the charges applied with regard to sending and receiving other credit transfers of the corresponding type, taking into account factors such as the payment initiation channel and customer status.[215]

Third, because instant payments do not allow the payer sufficient time to identify an error or fraud before the funds are credited to the payment account of the beneficiary, the payer's PSP is obliged to verify the name and the IBAN of the beneficiary. In case of a discrepancy, the payer's PSP notifies the payer before the payer authorises the transaction.[216] This requirement will apply to PSPs located in a euro Member State as of 9 October 2025 and to PSPs located in a non-euro Member State as of 9 July 2027. Fourth, the Instant Payment Regulation amends the sanctions screening procedure for instant payments. Since it is not possible for the payer's PSP to verify within 10 seconds whether the beneficiary of an instant payment is included on a sanctions list, **Article 1 Instant Payments Regulation** contains deviating measures regarding the moment at which sanctions screening must be conducted which will apply as of 9 January 2025. A practical solution is suggested which allows PSPs to screen their PSUs against the sanction lists on a daily basis and whenever the applicable lists are updated instead of applying transaction-based screening. This simplified sanction screening process for instant payments has also been supported by the ECB.[217]

3.7 EU Rules on Card Payments

3.7.1 The Cards Market: A Two-Sided Market

The market for card-based Payments is a so-called two-sided market. Two-sided markets are characterised by two different customer groups that need to participate in order for the market to work. For example, in the market for card Payments, card schemes act as an intermediary between cardholders and merchants.

[215] Ibid., Recital 17.

[216] If the transaction is authorised after the payer has been informed of the discrepancy, the PSP cannot be held liable under **Article 88 PSD2**.

[217] See ECB (2023, p. 2).

Two-sided markets are also characterised by indirect network effects[218], which means that the willingness of cardholders and merchants to participate in a card scheme is to a large extent determined by the participation rate of the other customer group. In other words, the value for merchants to accept a particular card increases when more consumers are using that card for receiving incoming Payments. Similarly, the value for consumers to use a card increases when more merchants accept that card for making payments. Industries with indirect network effects generally have higher levels of concentration[219] because they tend to increase the barriers for new market entrants by leveraging the advantage of their larger client base.[220] Incumbent card schemes have therefore been scrutinised by the Commission for compliance with European competition law requirements (**Paragraph 9.3.1**).

3.7.2 *Pricing in a Three-Party Card Scheme and Four-Party Card Scheme*

The indirect network effects in the cards market influence the price setting method applied by card schemes.[221] Compared to a one-sided market, pricing in a two-sided market is not based on a trade-off between marginal cost[222] and marginal revenue.[223] Instead, the fees charged to cardholders and merchants also depend on the strength of the network effects. Three-party card schemes and four-party card schemes apply different pricing mechanisms. In a three-party card scheme, the card scheme charges the cardholder a fee for the use of a particular card referred to as the 'cardholder fee'. For each Payment the cardholder initiates using that card, the scheme charges the merchant a fee for accepting the card payment, which is under **Article 2(12) IFR** called the 'merchant service charge'.

Figure 3.3 illustrates the fees charged in a three-party card scheme.

In a four-party card scheme, different PSPs assume responsibility for the issuing and acquiring of card transactions (**Paragraph 2.4.2**). As a

[218] See Economides (2008, p. 3).

[219] A high level of concentration means that the market is dominated by a small number of large PSPs.

[220] See OXERA (2020, p. 6).

[221] See Wismer et al. (2017, p. 258).

[222] Marginal cost represents the additional cost of producing one additional unit.

[223] Marginal revenue represents the additional revenue of selling one additional unit.

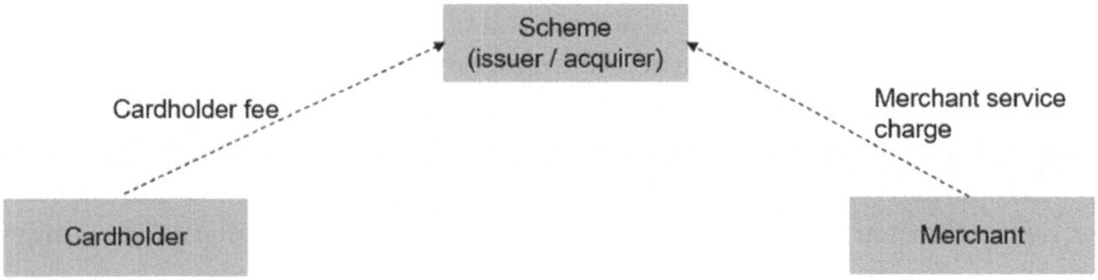

Fig. 3.3 Pricing in a three-party card scheme

result, four-party card schemes apply a pricing mechanism that works as follows. The cardholder pays the issuer a cardholder fee for the use of a particular card. For each Payment that the cardholder initiates using that card, the acquirer charges the merchant a merchant service charge. The merchant service charge in a four-party card scheme consists of: (i) a fee for the card scheme, also referred to as the scheme fee and (ii) a fee that the acquirer has to pay the issuer for the processing of a card transaction, which is according to **Article 2(10) IFR** called an interchange fee. If interchange fees are agreed between multiple issuers and acquirers, such a fee is called a MIF.

Interchange fees compensate the issuer for the costs it incurs when processing card payments, which include general service costs, payment guarantee costs and interest-free funding costs.[224,225] An interchange fee can be a flat fee, a percentage of the transaction amount or a combination of both.[226]

Figure 3.4 illustrates the fees charged in a four-party card scheme.

The existence of interchange fees is often claimed to be justified by the fact that a-symmetric pricing is essential to have an optimal pricing structure in a two-sided market.[227] With a-symmetric pricing, different fees are charged to merchants and cardholders for accepting and using a particular card. The fee for each customer group is based on the price elasticity of that customer group. Low price elasticity means that the demand

[224] Interest free funding costs are the costs that incur because the amount of the card transaction is not immediately debited from the payer's payment account. These costs are only relevant in case of a credit card payment.

[225] See Malaguti and Guerrieri (2014, p. 6).

[226] See Commission (2014, p. 1).

[227] See Malaguti and Guerrieri (2014, p. 6).

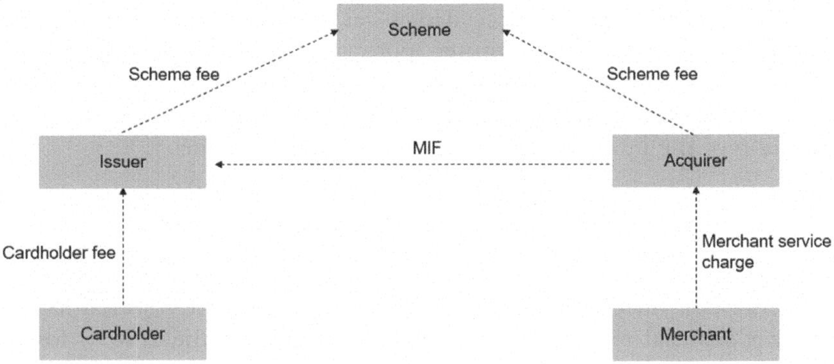

Fig. 3.4 Pricing in a four-party card scheme

of the customer group is less affected by a price increase. Cardholders appear to be more price sensitive than merchants, which means that the price elasticity of cardholders is relatively high compared to the price elasticity of merchants.[228] Merchants do not want to risk losing a sale due to the rejection of a certain card and may therefore feel obliged to accept a particular card regardless of the higher costs involved.[229] Since the price elasticity appears to be lower for merchants, optimum pricing means that the card scheme charges merchants relatively higher fees.[230] As a result, card schemes can, to a certain extent, increase the interchange fees without running the risk of losing substantial demand.[231]

The use of interchange fees in card schemes is subject to scrutiny by European and national competition authorities on the basis of competition law (**Paragraph 8**).[232] At a European level, the Commission has opened numerous investigations into card schemes regarding their pricing

[228] See Commission (2015, p. 18).

[229] Ibid., pp. 13–14.

[230] See ECB (2010, p. 58).

[231] See Commission (2015, p. 14).

[232] The Commission launched numerous antitrust investigations on the use of interchange fees in market for card payments. Although the use of these fees appears to restrict competition within the meaning of **Article 101(1) TFEU**, these fees can be eligible for an exemption under **Article 101(3) TFEU** provided that: (i) they have a positive effect on innovation and efficiency; and (ii) a part of these benefits are passed on to consumers.

structure but has not yet succeeded in taking a uniform approach and interpretation as to what constitutes appropriate pricing behaviour in card schemes.[233] The Commission's attempts to reduce interchange fees by means of antitrust enforcement have not (yet) resulted in a substantial reduction of the interchange fees charged by card schemes.[234]

3.7.3 *The Interchange Fee Regulation (IFR)*

Since competition law enforcement has not (yet) substantially enhanced competition in the cards market, the European legislature resorted to the use of a financial regulatory instrument and adopted the IFR to foster competition in the European market for card-based payments.[235] The IFR entered into force on 8 June 2015 and imposes requirements on PSPs that process card-based payment transactions whereby the payer's PSP and the beneficiary's PSP are located in the EEA.[236]

The key provisions of the IFR include (i) the introduction of a cap on interchange fees for debit card and credit card payments; (ii) rules on co-badging, the use of customer steering rules and a prohibition on the honour all cards rule; and (iii) the obligation for card schemes to separate the scheme from the card processor.

3.7.3.1 *Caps on Interchange Fees for Debit Card and Credit Card Payments*

The Commission took the position that interchange fees restrict competition and adversely affect retail prices.[237] The IFR addresses this concern by introducing a cap on the interchange fees that issuers can charge acquires for processing debit card transactions[238] and credit card transactions[239] under a four-party card scheme. To prevent circumvention of the

[233] See De Matteis and Giordano (2015, p. 86).

[234] Ibid., p. 91.

[235] IFR, Recital 8.

[236] Decision by the EEA Joint Committee No 21/2019 of 8 February 2019 "amending Annex IX (Financial Services) to the EEA Agreement", OJ L 60, 28.2.2019, p. 34.

[237] See Almunia (2013).

[238] **Article 2(4) IFR** defines a 'debit card transaction' as a card-based payment transaction, including those with prepaid cards that it not a credit card transaction. With a debit card transaction, the transaction amount will be immediately charged to the cardholder.

[239] **Article 2(5) IFR** defines a 'credit card transaction' as a card-based payment transaction where the transaction amount is debited in full or in part at a pre-agreed specific

IFR caps, **Article 5 IFR** stipulates that any remuneration with a similar objective as the interchange fee is considered to qualify as an interchange fee. This means that the total amount of payments or incentives received by an issuer from a card scheme with respect to the transactions less the fees paid by the issuer to the card scheme should be taken into account.[240] According to **Article 1(3) IFR**, the IFR caps do not apply to cards issued under a three-party payment card scheme unless such three-party scheme uses a separate PSPs as issuer and acquirer. It was argued that imposing these caps on three-party schemes would not be appropriate since competition rules do not apply to these schemes (the scheme operates both as issuer and acquirer).[241] Furthermore, **Article 1(3) IFR** provides that the caps imposed by the IFR do not apply to commercial cards[242]; and (ii) cash withdrawals at ATM's or at the counter of a PSP.

The caps in the IFR have been determined on the basis of the merchant indifference test. This test enables the legislature to estimate the maximum fee that a merchant is willing to pay if it would compare the cost of the PSU's use of a payment card (the merchant service charge and the interchange fee due to the acquirer) with the costs of accepting non-card payments.[243] In other words, the merchant indifference test provides an estimate of the maximum fee for a card payment at which the merchant

calendar month date to the payer, in line with a prearranged credit facility, with or without interest. With a credit card transaction, the cardholder can make a purchase up to a prearranged credit limit and will be charged afterwards. As set out in Recital 17 IFR, there are two main types of credit cards available in the market. With deferred debit cards, the total amount of transactions carried out in a specified period is debited from the payment account of the cardholder on a specific date (e.g., once per month) without the cardholder having to pay interest. With other credit cards, whereby the cardholder has a credit facility in order to reimburse part of the amounts due at a later date than specified, together with interest or other costs.

240 IFR, Recital 31.

241 See Juan et al. (2012, p. 5).

242 **Article 2(6) IFR** defines a 'commercial card' as any card-based payment instrument issued to undertakings or public sector entities or self-employed natural persons which is limited in use for business expenses where the payments made with such cards are charged directly to the account of the undertaking or public sector entity or self-employed natural person.

243 IFR, Recital 20.

would be indifferent between being paid by that particular card or by any other means (e.g., cash).[244]

Cap on Interchange Fees for Debit Card Transactions

The maximum per transaction interchange fee that PSPs are allowed to offer or request for debit card transactions has been set at 0.2% of the transaction amount pursuant to **Article 3 IFR**. For national debit card transactions, **Article 3(2)(a) IFR** allows Member States to impose stricter requirements on the use of interchange fees (e.g., by imposing a cap lower than 0.2%). This option was introduced because the interchange fees for debit card transactions were already below the 0.2% threshold in numerous Member States.[245] Setting a cap at 0.2%, could increase the interchange fees charged in these Member States instead of having a price reducing effect.

Cap on Interchange Fees for Credit Card Transactions

Article 4 IFR has set the maximum per transaction interchange fee that PSPs are allowed to offer or request for credit card transactions at 0.3% of the transaction amount. For national credit card transactions, **Article 4 IFR** allows Member States to apply a lower per transaction interchange fee cap.

In 2020, the Commission published an evaluation report on the effects of the IFR.[246] The caps on interchange fees turned out to be a considerable cost saving for acquirers. The total annual interchange fees paid by acquirers to issuers in the EU have declined by approximately €2,680 mln between 2015 and 2017.[247] The evaluation report also shows that acquirers have passed on these cost savings to merchants by imposing lower merchant service charges, which are subsequently passed on to

[244] See Commission (2015, p. 3).

[245] E.g., Denmark and the Netherlands.

[246] See Ernst & Young and Copenhagen Economics (2020). This study was conducted by Ernst & Young and Copenhagen Economics at the instruction of the Commission. According to **Article 17 IFR**, the Commission was obliged to submit a report to the European Parliament and to the Council on the application of the IFR.

[247] Ibid., p. 14.

consumers by means of lower retail prices.[248] Moreover, no evidence was found that issuers tried to compensate for the loss of income by increasing the charges for cardholders.[249]

3.7.3.2 Co-Badging, Steering Rules and the Honour All Cards Rule

Article 2(31) IFR defines co-badging as the inclusion of two or more payment brands or payment applications of the same brand on a single card. In Member States where mostly national card schemes are used, it is not uncommon that cards issued by such scheme carry a national card brand and an international card brand.[250] By combining these brands on a single card, the cardholder can also use his card for initiating Payments in other countries. Co-badging provides for cardholder convenience and increases competition between card schemes provided that cardholders can choose which card brand they want to use when initiating a particular transaction. Moreover, since there are significant price differences between card brands and payment applications, merchants may develop a strong preference for a particular brand or application. To protect their market share, card schemes therefore often included a prohibition on co-badging in their scheme rules. Under **Article 8(1) IFR**, card schemes are no longer allowed to prohibit an issuer to co-badge different payment brands or applications on a single card.

The IFR also provides for a prohibition on anti-steering rules. **Article 11(1) IFR** prohibits card schemes and acquirers from applying rules or entering into agreements that prevent merchants from steering cardholders to using a particular payment brand or application preferred by the merchant. The combination of the co-badging and steering rules allows cardholders and merchants to choose their preferred brands and applications for initiating Payments.

Further to the prohibition on co-badging and anti-steering rules, card scheme rules often included an honour all cards provision in their contracts, which obliged merchants accepting a particular card or brand to also accept the other cards and brands issued under the same card scheme. Such provision was non-negotiable and enforced by the scheme operators. The honour all cards rule forced merchants to also accept the

[248] Ibid., p. 16.

[249] Ibid., p. 130.

[250] Ibid., p. 190.

more expensive card applications issued by a particular scheme, which had a restrictive effect on price-based competition. Under **Article 10(1) and (2) IFR**, it is no longer allowed to oblige merchants accepting a card from a particular issuer to also accept other cards issued within the same card scheme unless these cards are of the same category and subject to the IFR caps on interchange fees. This means that merchants can decide to only accept the less expensive card applications issued by a particular card scheme in case the costs of such card are not restricted under the IFR.

3.7.3.3 Separation of Card Scheme and Card Processor

Card schemes used to have their own processing entities for handling payment instructions between acquirers and issuers. According to **Article 2(27) IFR**, such processing entities provided authorisation, clearing and settlement services.

To boost competition between independent processing entities and processing entities belonging to card schemes, the IFR requires independence between card schemes and processing entities.[251] The separation requirement of **Article 7(1)(a) IFR** means that card schemes and processing entities have to be independent in terms of accounting, organisation and decision making process. Moreover, **Article 7(1)(b) IFR** does not allow the card scheme and processing entity to present prices for the scheme and processing activities in a bundled manner or cross-subsidise such activities. In addition, separation is effected in **Article 7(1)(c) IFR** by not allowing the card scheme and processing entity to discriminate between subsidiaries or shareholders and users of card schemes. Ideally, card schemes and processing entities are two different legal entities. However, **Article 7 Commission Delegated Regulation (EU) 2018/72** allows for the card scheme and processing entity to be a single legal entity provided that these functions are organised in two separate internal business units.[252]

[251] IFR, Recital 32.

[252] Delegated Regulation (EU) 2018/72 of 4 October 2017 "supplementing Regulation (EU) 2015/751 of the European Parliament and of the Council on interchange fees for card-based payment transactions with regard to regulatory technical standards establishing the requirements to be complied with by payment card schemes and processing entities to ensure the application of independence requirements in terms of accounting, organisation and decision-making process", OJ L 13, 18.1.2018, pp. 1–7.

As a result of the separation requirement, card schemes have become solely responsible for setting rules and regulations and the processing entities are charged with the processing of card-based transactions. The European legislature envisaged that with the separation requirement, independent processing entities would be in a better position to compete for card scheme customers.[253] To date, the separation requirement has however not resulted in any observable improvements in the card processing market.[254]

Secondary Sources

ACM. (2017). *Report Fintechs in the Payment System: The Risk of Foreclosure* (p. 4). ACM.

Almunia, J. (2013). *Introductory Remarks on Proposal for Regulation on Interchange Fees for Cards, Internet and Mobile Payments*. SPEECH 13/660.

BIS. (n.d.). *Glossary*. https://www.bis.org/cpmi/publ/d00b.htm. Accessed April 13, 2024.

Commission. (1990). *Making Payments in the Internal Market*. Discussion Paper COM (90) 447 final, p. 1).

Commission. (1992). *Easier Cross-border Payments: Breaking Down the Barriers*. SEC (92) 621 final, pp. 2, 3.

Commission. (1994). *Proposal for a European Parliament and Council Directive on cross-border transfers*, COM (94) 436 final, p. 21.

Commission. (1997). *Communication from the Commission to the European Parliament, the Council, the European Monetary Institute and the Economic and Social Committee Boosting Customers' Confidence in Electronic Means of Payment in the Single Market*', COM (97) 353 final, p. 3.

Commission. (2003, December 2). *Communication from the Commission to the Council and the European Parliament Concerning a New Legal Framework for Payments in the Internal Market (Consultative Document)*. COM (2003) 718 final, pp. 5, 23.

Commission. (2005a, December 1). *Commission Staff Working Document: Annex to the Proposal for a Directive of the European Parliament and of the Council on Payment Services in the Internal Market—Impact Assessment*. SEC (2005) 1535, p. 6.

253 IFR, Recital 33.

254 See Ernst & Young and Copenhagen Economics (2020, p. 226).

Commission. (2005b, December 1). *Frequently Asked Questions (FAQs) on the Single Payments Area: Commission proposal for a 'New Legal Framework'*. MEMO/05/461, p. 2.

Commission. (2005c, December 1). *Implementing the Community Lisbon programme: Proposal for a Directive of the European Parliament and of the Council on Payment Services in the Internal Market and Amending Directives*. 97/7/EC, 2000/12/EC and 2002/65/EC, COM (2005) 603 final, p. 8.

Commission. (2006a, July 19). *On the Review of the E-Money Directive (2000/46/EC). Commission Staff Working Document*. SEC (2006) 1049, pp. 3, 5.

Commission. (2006b). *Addressed to the European Parliament and to the Council on the Impact of Regulation (EC) No 2560/2001 on Bank Charges for National Payments*, Commission Staff Working Document, SEC (2006) 1783, p. 3.

Commission. (2008). *Report from the Commission and the European Parliament and the Council on the Application of Regulation (EC) No 2560/2001 on Cross-border Payments in Euro*, COM (2008) 64 final, pp. 5, 6, 9, 10, 13.

Commission. (2011, July). *Impact Assessment Accompanying the Document Commission Recommendation on Access to a Basic Payment Account* (Working paper SEC [2011]) 906, 18, p. 6.

Commission. (2012). *Green Paper: Towards an integrated European market for card, internet and mobile payments*, COM (2011) 941 final, p. 14.

Commission. (2014, February 26). *Antitrust: Commission Makes Visa Europe's Commitments Binding—Frequently Asked Questions*. MEMO/14/138, p. 1.

Commission. (2015). *Survey on Merchants' Costs of Processing Cash and Card Payments*. Final results, pp. 3, 13, 14, 18.

Commission. (2022). *Proposal for a Regulation of the European Parliament and of the Council Amending Regulations (EU) No 260/2012 and (EU) 2021/1230 as Regards Instant Credit Transfers in Euro*. COM(2022) 546 final, p. 13.

Commission. (2023). *Proposal for a Directive of the European Parliament and of the Council on Payment Services and Electronic Money Services in the Internal Market Amending Directive 98/26/EC and Repealing Directives 2015/2366 and 2009/110/EC*. COM(2023) 366 final.

De Matteis, A., & Giordano, S. (2015). Payment Cards and Permitted Multilateral Interchange Fees (MIFs): Will the European Commission Harm Consumers and the European Payment Industry? *Journal of European Competition Law & Practice, 6*(2), pp. 85–95.

EBA. (2022). *Final Report on the EBA Guidelines on the Limited Network Exclusion Under PSD2', EBA/GL/2022/02*, p. 21.

EBA. (n.d.). *Single Rule Book Q&A*. https://eba.europa.eu/single-rule-book-qa/-/qna/view/publicId/2018_4098. Accessed April 13, 2024.

EBF. (2020). *Cross-Border Payments Regulation—Implementation Guidance* Version 1.0, pp. 1–2.

EBIC. (2008). *Common Principles for Bank Accounts Switching* (Position Paper).

ECB. (1998). *Report on Electronic Money*, pp. 1–2.

ECB. (2010). *The Payment System*, p. 58.

ECB. (2023). *Opinion of the European Central Bank of 1 February 2023 on a Proposal for a Regulation Amending Regulations (EU) No 260/2012 and (EU) 2021/1230 as Regards Instant Credit Transfers in Euro*. CON/2023/4, p. 2.

Economides, N. (2008). *Antitrust Issues in Network Industries*. The Reform of EC Competition Law, p. 3.

EPC. (2002). *Euroland: Our Single Payment Area!* White Paper summary, p. 6.

EPC. (2020a). *By-laws of the European Payments Council—Coordinated Version*, EPC148–19, Version 1.0, Article 5.4.2.

EPC. (2020b, October 28). *Guide for Adherence to the SEPA Credit Transfer Scheme, the SEPA Instant Credit Transfer Scheme and the SEPA Direct Debit Schemes (the 'Adherence Guide')*. EPC012–17, Version 5.0, pp. 8–10.

EPC. (2023). *Migration to the 2019 Version of the ISO 20022 Standard-based XML Messages*. EPC087–22, Version 3.1, p. 4.

Ernst & Young and Copenhagen Economics. (2020). *Study on the Application of the Interchange Fee Regulation*. Commission Final Report, pp. 14, 16, 50, 130, 190, 226.

EUR-Lex. (n.d.). *Legal Summary: Payment Services Directive 2 (PSD2)*. https://eur-lex.europa.eu/legal-content/EN/TXT/HTML/?uri=LEGISSUM:l14527&from=EN. Accessed April 13, 2024.

European Court of Justice. (2014). *T-Mobile Austria*. Judgment of 9 April 2014, Case C-616/11, EU:C:2014:242.

European Court of Justice. (2018a). *ING-DiBa Direktbank Austria*. Judgment of 4 October 2018, Case C-191/17, EU:C:2018:809.

European Court of Justice. (2018b). *Rasool*. Judgment of 22 March 2018, Case C-568/16, EU:C:2018:211.

European Court of Justice. (2024). Request for a Preliminary Ruling Under Article 267 TFEU of 22 February 2024. *ABC Projektai*, Case C-661/22, EU:C:2024:148, paragraphs 48, 52.

European Parliament. (n.d.). *Lisbon European Council*. https://www.europarl.europa.eu/summits/lis1_en.htm. Accessed April 13, 2024.

Jans, J. A. (2010). Harmonisering van regels voor markttoegang betaalinstellingen. *Tijdschrift Voor Financieel Recht, 6*, p. 154.

Jans, J. A. (2023). ISO 20022 als standaard voor interoperabiliteit tussen betalingssystemen. *Tijdschrift Voor Financieel Recht No., 1*(2), p. 17.

Juan, I., et al. (2012). *The Effects of the Mandatory Decrease of Interchange Fees in Spain* (MPRA Paper No. 43097), p. 5.

London Economics and Iff in Association with PaySys. (2013). *Study on the Impact of Directive 2007/64/EC on Payment Services in the Internal Market*

and on the Application of Regulation (EC) No 924/2009 on Cross-border Payments in the Community: Final Report, pp. 123, 125, 196.
Malaguti, M. C., & Guerrieri, A. (2014). *Multilateral Interchange Fees—Competition and Regulation in Light of Recent Legislative Developments* (European Credit Research Institute Research Report. *No., 14*, p. 6.
Monti, M. (2010). *A New Strategy for the Single Market—At the Service of Europe's Economy and Society* (Report to the President of the European Commission), p. 74.
OXERA. (2020). *The Competitive Landscape for Payments: A European Perspective*, p. 6.
Payment System End-Users Committee (EUC). (2009). *Position Paper on SEPA Direct Debit*, p. 14.
PSD Expert Group. (2009, August). *PSD Guidance for the Implementation of the Payment Services Directive, Versions, 1*, p. 11.
Retail Banking Research. (2001). *Study on the Verification of a Common and Coherent Application of Directive 97/5/EC on Cross-Border Credit Transfers in the 15 Member States* (Final Report), p. 1.
Rosa, M. M. (2018). Achieving Competition in the Financial Sector. *Journal of European Competition Law & Practice, 9*(7), p. 422.
Simona, G. (2011). Special Rules for the Cross-border Payment Services in Euro. *EuroEconomica, 3*(29), p. 69.
Wismer, S., et al. (2017). Multi-Sided Market Economics in Competition Law Enforcement. *Journal of European Competition Law & Practice, 8*(4), p. 258.
Working Group on EU Payment Systems. (1994). *Report to the Council of the European Monetary Institute on Prepaid Cards*, pp. 1, 3, 8.

CHAPTER 4

Non-Bank Market Access

4.1 Background

In order to create a level playing field between Banks and Non-Banks in the market for Payments, it is amongst others essential to have clear and consistent rules on market access by Non-Banks. The first European legislative initiatives on market access by PSPs were based on the assumption that one had to be a Bank in order to be involved in the offering and processing of Payments. As a result, PSPs that did not want to offer the full suite of banking services were nevertheless obliged to adhere to the market access requirements applicable to Banks. Non-Banks were therefore confronted with market access requirements that were disproportionate given the limited size and complexity of their business. An alternative to obtaining a banking licence was to structure the payments business in such a manner that the Non-Bank could rely on a national exemption (**Paragraph 3.4.1.3**). Although an exemption may have provided a viable solution for certain smaller Non-Banks, such an option was not available in all Member States. Moreover, the lack of a separate licensing regime for Non-Banks restricted the opportunities for these PSPs to expand their business on an international scale since a European passport for the cross-border provision of payment services was not available for Non-Banks operating without a licence.

J. A. Jans, *Electronic Payments in the European Market*, EBI Studies in Banking and Capital Markets Law,
https://doi.org/10.1007/978-3-031-64338-5_4

Besides the adverse effects that these market access barriers had on the business opportunities of Non-Banks, it also hampered the development of the European market for Payments in general. A market that lacks sufficient competition tends to reduce the incentive for market participants to innovate and operate on a cost-efficient basis. The limited competition between Banks and Non-Banks was therefore likely to have a restrictive effect on the variety of Payment products available in the market. Moreover, limited competition was likely to have an increasing effect on the costs that PSPs charged for these products.

To enhance market entrance by Non-Banks, the legal requirements for market entrance have to be proportionate to the size and complexity of the applicant's business and the scope of the services it intends to provide. With PSD and EMD, the European legislature aimed to introduce such proportionality for Non-Banks by introducing licensing regimes for PIs and EMIs, which have been refined under PSD2 and EMD2. Although it appears that these licensing regimes have enhanced market access by Non-Banks, the benefits of having these licensing regimes for the competitive position of Non-Banks *vis-à-vis* Banks must be put into perspective. Further to the obvious benefit of having to comply with less onerous market access requirements than Banks, being subject to a lighter licensing regime comes with restrictions regarding the business activities that Non-Banks are allowed to conduct. For example, PSPs holding a PI or EMI licence are according to **Article 16(4) PSD** and **Article 6(2) EMD2** respectively, not allowed to attract deposits or other repayable funds from the public. According to **Article 18(3) PSD2**, funds received from PSUs for the provision of payment services do not constitute deposits or other repayable funds within the meaning of Regulation (EU) No 575/2013 on prudential requirements for Banks and investment firms ('**CRR**').[1,2] This means in practice that Non-Banks can only offer payment accounts to PSUs if they receive funds with a view to the provision of payment services. Although PSD2 does not require such funds to be received by the Non-Bank together with a concrete order to be transferred at a particular date, there is an increasing risk of these funds qualifying as repayable funds the longer they are maintained on

[1] Regulation (EU) No 575/2013 of 26 June 2013 "on prudential requirements for credit institutions and investment firms and (...)". *OJ L* 176, 27 June 2013, pp. 1–337.

[2] **Article 18(3) PSD2** contains an omission since funds received from other PSPs for the provision of payment services do not seem to be covered.

the payment account as the duration could at a certain point in time be an indication that the funds have not been received with a view to the provision of payment services. To avoid a reclassification of such funds as repayable funds it is in any case recommended to credit these funds to accounts that can only be used for the execution of payment transactions.

Non-Banks tend to address this issue by using payment accounts provided by Banks. For EMIs, this restriction also implies according to **Article 6(3) EMD2** that they cannot delay the issuance of E-money instruments after they receive the corresponding funds from the client. As a result of the prohibition to attract deposits or other repayable funds from the public, most Non-Banks cannot provide payment services on a standalone basis without the involvement of a Bank.[3] Moreover, not being able to offer payment accounts disqualifies Non-Banks from becoming a direct participant in a payment system, such as an EPC SEPA scheme (**Paragraph 3.5**). Notwithstanding these limitations, the prohibition for Non-Banks to attract deposits or other repayable funds does in my opinion not weaken the level playing field between Banks and Non-Banks. Not being able to obtain repayable funds from the public justifies that Non-Banks are subject to less onerous prudential requirements (**Paragraph** 4.2.3). If Non-Banks were able to obtain repayable funds from the public without having to apply the appropriate prudential safeguards, this would in my opinion create unsound competition for Banks and unacceptable risks for PSUs that entrust Non-Banks with their money.

Further to the prohibition for Non-Banks to attract deposits or other repayable funds, the economic characteristics of the European Payments market also appear to have inhibitory effects on Non-Bank competition which have not been mitigated with the introduction of a licensing regime for Non-Banks. The market for Payments exhibits economies of scale, which means that the costs of an individual payment transaction decrease with an increased volume of executed transactions by that PSP.[4] Economies of scale exist because fixed costs do not vary with the number of Payments executed. Because of economies of scale, large PSPs have by default a competitive advantage over smaller PSPs since they can process

[3] Exceptions include end-to-end providers such as PayPal, which operate their own payment ecosystem.

[4] See Commission (2003, p. 12).

Payments at a lower cost per individual transaction. As a result, economies of scale can make it difficult for new market entrants to compete with incumbent PSPs. Non-Bank start-ups have to make substantial investments in order to obtain a minimum market share that allows them to offer competitive prices. To date, most FinTechs have not managed to obtain large market shares and therefore often seek partnerships with Banks.[5] BigTechs appear to be less affected by the economies of scale characteristic of the Payments market because they benefit from their large client networks when starting offering Payments.

4.2 Non-Bank Licences

4.2.1 Payment Institution (PI) and Electronic Money Institution (EMI) Licences for Providing Payment Services

Anyone providing payment services to PSUs in a Member State is in principle required to hold a licence as a PSP.[6] A service provider that does not intend to undertake other regulated activities than the provision of payment services can opt for a PI licence.[7] PSD only required service providers to hold a licence as a PI in case the payment services were: (i) offered as an independently identifiable activity, and (ii) not to support other core activities.[8] In other words, the PI licence requirement only applied to PSPs whose principal activity consisted of the offering of payment services. PSD did not take into account that providing payment services on a large scale as an ancillary service could trigger the same risk

[5] See Ernst and Young (2020, p. 81).

[6] **Article 33(1) PSD2** stipulates that service providers which only offer account information services are exempted from the PSD2 licensing requirement. AISPs do need to be registered with their NCA. The requirements for such registration are less cumbersome than the requirements for a licence. An AISP is, amongst others, not obliged to prepare a description of its internal control mechanisms setting out how it complies with AML regulations.

[7] In case a service provider intends to undertake other business activities, a licence as a Bank or EMI may be more suitable.

[8] PSD, Recital 6. Moreover, under PSD, service providers relied on their own assessment to determine whether or not their services constituted a payment service for which a PI licence was required. Although PSD2 also allows PSPs to make their own assessment, PSD2 requires that service providers which consider themselves exempted from the licence application notify their NCA so that the NCA can assess whether such service provider is indeed exempted from the licence requirement.

exposures. With PSD2, it is no longer required for payment services to be the main activity in order to be subject to the PI licensing requirement.

To avoid abuse of the right of establishment, **Article 11(3) PSD2** stipulates that a PI licence can only be obtained in a Member State if at least part of the activities will be conducted in that Member State. With this requirement, the European legislature aimed to minimise regulatory arbitrage by PIs. Regulatory arbitrage is a practice that involves Non-Banks obtaining their licence in a Member State that imposes less onerous market access requirements and subsequently offering payment services to PSUs in their own jurisdiction using a European passport.[9] It is unclear however how NCAs should determine if a particular PI meets the requirement of providing a part of its activities in the Member State where it holds its licence.[10] As a result, this requirement has been interpreted very differently by Member States, whereby some Member States require that most of the business must be conducted in their country.[11] According to **Article 13(3) PSD3 Proposal**, the Commission considers however that NCAs are not allowed to require PIs to carry out the majority of its business in the country were it holds its licence.

EMIs are permitted to provide payment services without holding a separate licence as a PI. EMIs can apply for a payment services top-up, which enables them to operate as a PSP on the basis of their EMI licence. Under EMD, the licensing regime for EMIs used to be much like a Bank 'light' licence since the vast majority of the CRD provisions also applied to EMIs.[12] However, the operational and financial risks to which EMIs are exposed are more akin to those of a PI.[13] With EMD2, the licensing regime for EMIs has therefore been aligned with the PI licensing regime of PSD2.[14] Contrary to PSD2, EMD2 does not require EMIs to conduct at least a part of their activities in the Member State where they obtain their licence. By not imposing such requirements on EMIs, service

[9] See Jans (2014, p. 409).

[10] See Van Duijvenbode and Salemans (2019, p. 527).

[11] PSD3 Proposal, Recital 38.

[12] A CRD provision that did not apply to EMIs was the own funds requirements (**Article 2(1) EMD**).

[13] See Van Esch (2012, p. 29).

[14] This means that EMD2 is no longer referring to banking legislation when it comes to market access requirements. Instead, reference is made to PSD2 whenever an EMI is involved in the provision of payment services.

providers that want to obtain a licence for providing payment services can apply regulatory arbitrage by resorting to an EMI licence instead of a PI licence. An interesting case involves the EMI licence that Google obtained in Lithuania. In 2019, Mr. Ferber (member of the European Parliament) shared his concerns with the EBA as to why Google decided to apply for an EMI licence in Lithuania given that Google has its headquarters in Dublin.[15] In other words, Mr. Ferber questioned whether Google applied for the EMI licence in Lithuania to benefit from what appears to be a lighter market access regime or whether Google had a genuine business reason for establishing its EMI in Lithuania. Although the EBA did not see any indication for regulatory arbitrage by Google,[16] Mr. Ferber did have a point in my opinion given that Google's primary target market does not seem to be Lithuania and the Lithuanian NCA promoted its licensing regime as being one of the least cumbersome. If this means that Google is subject to less stringent regulatory compliance requirements, such as AML/CTF obligations, unacceptable risk exposures may occur in other Member States where Google provides payment services based on its European passport.[17]

4.2.2 *The Licence Application Procedure*

The application for a PI or EMI licence must be submitted to the NCA of the Member State in which the applicant is established.[18] Among the main requirements for obtaining a PI or EMI licence are: (i) an obligation to maintain sufficient capital to cover for the short and medium term financial obligations; (ii) the requirement to safeguard funds received from PSUs or other PSPs when providing payment services; (iii) an integrity and/or suitability screening requirement for the (co) policy-makers of the applicant to ensure that these persons are fit and proper for their roles; and (iv) a screening requirement for shareholders holding

[15] See EBA (2019a).

[16] Ibid.

[17] See Joosen (2020, p. 112).

[18] According to the PSD3 Proposal, it is suggested that a PI licence will be required for both the offering of payment services and E-money services. Because of the proposed amendments to the licensing regimes for the provision of payment services and E-money services, the Commission suggests that existing licenses for PIs and EMIs will be grandfathered until 30 months after the moment PSD3 enters into force.

(in)directly a qualifying holding in the applicant to ensure that these shareholders are suitable for holding such interest. If an applicant submits an application for a PI licence to the NCA, such application must include at least the documentation and information set out in **Annex III**.[19] The documentation and information that needs to be submitted to the NCA for obtaining registration as an AISP are set out in **Annex IV**.[20] If an applicant submits an application for an EMI licence, the application must include the documentation and information set out in **Annex V**.[21]

The NCA has three months to complete its assessment after receipt of a licence application that is complete.[22] The NCA can extend the statutory consideration period in case it requires additional information or documentation to complete its assessment of the licence application. When assessing an application for a PI or EMI licence, NCAs take into account factors such as: (i) the type of Non-Bank (PI or EMI); (ii) the size of the envisaged business; (iii) the organisational set-up (national or cross-border); and (iv) the complexity of the services to be provided.[23] Because of the proportionality principle, certain applicants may be subject to less stringent requirements regarding *inter alia* their internal organisation, such as their compliance function or AML/CTF procedures. Neither PSD2 nor EMD2 provide for guidance as to whether NCAs are allowed to impose conditions or limitations on a PI or EMI licence.[24] Absent any guidance, NCAs tend to take the view that they are indeed allowed to impose conditions or limitations on such licences.[25] The fact that PSD2 leaves room for different interpretations has in my opinion adverse implications for the maximum harmonisation that is envisaged with PSD2 and EMD2.

[19] See EBA (2017, pp. 18–37). Under **Article 3 PSD3 Proposal** it is suggested to extent the list of documents that must be submitted with a description of the ICT arrangements, ICT business continuity plans and ICT response and recovery plans as required under DORA.

[20] Ibid., pp. 38–49.

[21] Ibid., pp. 50–70.

[22] To ensure a level playing field, the PSD3 Proposal suggests to allow NCAs a maximum period of three months to review a licence application (provided that all information has been provided).

[23] See EBA (2019b, p. 26).

[24] Ibid., p. 20.

[25] See European Court of Justice (2015).

4.2.3 Capital Requirements for Payment Institutions (PIs) and Electronic Money Institutions (EMIs)

As with Banks, safeguarding the sound and prudent business operations of Non-Banks is a key objective of the European legislature. To secure the stability of the financial system and to provide for adequate PSU protection, both PIs and EMIs are subject to capital requirements. Like Banks, PIs and EMIs are obliged to comply with an initial capital requirement and an own funds requirement.[26] Since AISPs and PISPs are never in the possession of any funds belonging to a PSU, there are different prudential requirements for third-party payment service providers (**'TPPs'**). The initial capital and own funds requirements do not apply to PIs that solely provide account information services (i.e., AISPs). Moreover, the own funds requirement does not apply to PIs that only offer payment initiation services (i.e., PISPs).

Prudential requirements ensure that PIs and EMIs maintain sufficient capital to meet their financial obligations in the short and medium term. There appears to be a trade-off when assessing the adequateness of the capital requirements for Non-Banks. On the one hand, imposing stringent capital requirements ensures that Non-Banks remain financially sound and capable of addressing risks to which their businesses are or may be exposed. On the other hand, imposing capital requirements that are too stringent hampers market access by Non-Banks and therefore harms competition in the market for Payments. It is therefore of paramount importance that the capital requirements for Non-Banks are proportionate to their business model and risk profile. A Non-Bank's business model and risk profile is generally less complex than the business model and risk profile of a Bank, which justifies having less stringent capital requirements for Non-Banks.[27] The prudential regimes of PSD2 and EMD2 have been designed to provide for proportionate capital requirements for PIs and EMIs, thereby stimulating market entrance by Non-Banks.

[26] The own funds requirement is also referred to as the solvency requirement. Unlike Banks, Non-Banks are not subject to liquidity requirements.

[27] In general, the payments business of most PIs is relatively small compared to the payment business of Banks. However, there are exceptions. An example of a Dutch Non-Bank whose payment business was comparable to that of the larger Banks was Adyen. Adyen was initially licensed as a PI but later obtained a banking licence in order to facilitate its growth.

Unlike Non-Banks, Banks are also subject to prudential supervision on a consolidated basis in accordance with **Article 18 CRR**. The rationale behind this requirement is to ensure that in case certain business activities of a Bank are conducted by different group entities, the core activities of the Bank remain sufficiently protected against the risks stemming from these ancillary activities.[28] An unintended side effect of consolidated supervision is however that it unlevels the playing field between Non-Banks that are part of a banking group and Non-Banks that are not part of such group.[29] Non-Banks that are an (indirect) subsidiary of a Bank are subject to the Bank's consolidated supervision, whereas the shareholder of a standalone Non-Bank with a similar business proposition does not have to meet such requirement. This can hamper Banks from acquiring a stake in a Non-Bank (e.g., a FinTech) to compete with other Non-Banks. Moreover, it hampers Non-Banks that do have a Bank as shareholder to compete with other Non-Banks on an equal footing. To level the playing field between Non-Banks that have a Bank as shareholder and Banks that do not have such shareholder, the Expert Group on Regulatory Obstacles to Financial Innovation (ROFIEG)[30] suggested that capital requirements for PSPs should be activity and risk based instead of institution based.[31] Having activity-based capital requirements would however not be the solution to this problem since the benefit of having consolidated supervision for the stability of Banks outweighs in my opinion the benefit of having all Non-Banks subjected to the exact same legal requirements.

4.2.3.1 Initial Capital Requirement

PSD2 and EMD2 require Non-Banks to maintain sufficient initial capital in the form of Common Equity Tier 1 (CET1) instruments within the meaning of **Article 26(1)(a)–(e) CRR**.[32] Non-Banks have to comply with the initial capital requirement on an ongoing basis, which means

[28] See BIS (2021, p. 8).

[29] See Expert Group on Regulatory Obstacles to Financial Innovation (2019, p. 68).

[30] The Expert Group on Regulatory Obstacles to Financial Innovation was founded by the Commission to review the suitability of the European legal framework to FinTech to identify issues that hamper the development of FinTech in the EU.

[31] See Expert Group on Regulatory Obstacles to Financial Innovation (2019, p. 67).

[32] Common Equity Tier 1 instruments include: (i) capital instruments meeting the requirements of **Article 28 CRR** (e.g. ordinary shares); (ii) share premium accounts; (iii) retained earnings; (iv) other comprehensive income; (v) other reserves.

that the capital of a Non-Bank should never fall below the initial capital threshold.[33]

Initial capital requirement for payment institutions (PIs)

The European legislature recognises the importance of having an initial capital requirement for PIs that is proportionate to the risks associated with the payment service(s) provided.[34] As a consequence, the initial capital requirement for PIs is considerably lower than the initial capital requirement for Banks. For PIs, the initial capital required varies with the type of payment services provided by the relevant PI as set out in **Article 7 PSD2**. Table 4.1 provides an overview of the initial capital requirements for PIs.

Initial capital requirement for electronic money institutions (EMIs)

Under **Article 4(1) EMD**, EMIs were required to have an initial capital of at least €1 mln.[35] EMD allowed Member States to impose an even higher initial capital requirement on EMIs established in their jurisdiction. As a result, large differences were observed regarding the initial capital requirements applicable to EMIs in different Member States. For example, EMIs established in Greece were even required to maintain an initial capital of at least €3 mln.[36] With EMD2, the European legislature lowered the barrier for market access for EMIs by reducing the initial capital requirement from €1 mln to €350,000.[37] According to **Article 4 EMD2**, the initial capital requirement of €350,000 applies regardless of the amount of outstanding E-money and the payment services provided. Despite the fact that the initial capital required under EMD2 has been reduced considerably, EMIs must comply with a substantially higher initial capital requirement than PIs. A justification for this difference is that the liabilities and risk exposures of EMIs are non-identical to the liabilities

[33] Non-Banks usually submit audited account statements to their NCA to evidence that the initial capital requirement is complied with.

[34] PSD2, Recital 34.

[35] The initial capital consisted of paid in capital and reserves.

[36] See The Evaluation Partnership (2006, p. 56).

[37] In **Article 5(d) PSD3 Proposal** it is suggested to increase the amount to €400,000.

Table 4.1 Initial capital requirement PIs

Payment service	*Initial capital requirement*
• Services enabling cash to be placed on a payment account; • Services enabling cash withdrawals from a payment account; • Execution of Payments; • Execution of Payments where the funds are covered by a credit line; and/or • Issuing of payment instruments and/or acquiring of Payments.	€125,000
Money remittance	€20,000[38]
• Money remittance; and • Services enabling cash to be placed on a payment account; and/or • Services enabling cash withdrawals from a payment account; and/or • Execution of Payments; and/or • Execution of Payments where the funds are covered by a credit line; and/or • Issuing of payment instruments and/or acquiring of Payments.	€125,000[39]
• Payment initiation services	€50,000
• Payment initiation services; and • Services enabling cash to be placed on a payment account; and/or • Services enabling cash withdrawals from a payment account; and/or • Execution of Payments; and/or • Execution of Payments where the funds are covered by a credit line; and/or • Issuing of payment instruments and/or acquiring of Payments.	€125,000[40]

and risks to which PIs are exposed. Another justification is that EMIs are, unlike PIs, obliged to redeem outstanding E-money at par at a certain point in time. In other words, the issuance of E-money creates a future

[38] In **Article 5(a) PSD3 Proposal** it is suggested to increase the amount to €25,000.

[39] In **Article 5(c) PSD3 Proposal** it is suggested to increase the amount to €150,000.

[40] In **Article 5(c) PSD3 Proposal** it is suggested to increase the amount to €150,000.

obligation for EMIs to redeem funds that it received in exchange for the E-money issued, which obligation does not exist for PIs.

4.2.3.2 Own Funds (Solvency) Requirement

Like Banks, Non-Banks have an obligation to ensure they remain solvent to cover their medium term financial obligations. Further to the initial capital requirement, Non-Banks are therefore required to maintain sufficient own funds.[41]

Own funds requirement for payment institutions (PIs)

Article 9 PSD2 distinguishes three methods for calculating a PI's own funds requirement, which are referred to as methods A, B and C. Method A is the least sophisticated method for calculating the own funds requirement and requires that the minimum level of own funds is 10% of a PI's fixed overhead costs over the preceding year.[42] This method is particularly unfavourable for PIs whose business model is not limited to the offering of payment services. The own funds that these PIs are required to have under method A are relatively high since the PI's non-payments business is also included in the calculation of the own funds requirement.[43] A more sophisticated method for calculating the own funds requirement is method B.[44] Method B calculates the minimum own funds requirement on the basis of a PI's payment volume, which is the total monetary value

[41] According to **Article 4(1)(118) CRR**, the own funds of a Non-Bank consist of Tier 1 capital and Tier 2 capital. Tier 1 capital consists of Common Equity Tier 1 items (capital instruments, share premium accounts, retained earnings, accumulated other comprehensive income, and other reserves) and Additional Tier 1 items (capital instruments that meet the conditions set out in **Article 52(1) CRR** and the share premium accounts related to these capital instruments). At least 75% of the Tier 1 capital must be held as Common Equity Tier 1 capital. Tier 2 capital consists of certain capital instruments, subordinated loans and share premium accounts. Tier 2 capital can be no more than 33.33% of the Tier 1 capital.

[42] Fixed overhead costs are expenses that do not vary as a result of sales.

[43] See Jans (2014, p. 409).

[44] In **Article 7(2) PSD3 Proposal** it is suggested that NCAs must apply method B by default and that method A or C can be applied if this would be more appropriate in the context of the PI's business model.

of the executed Payments.[45] Method C is the most sophisticated method and calculates the capital requirement on the basis of a PI's net operating income over the previous financial year using the following formula: (interest income + interest expenses + commissions and fees received + other operating income)[46] x multiplication factor[47] x scaling factor k.[48]

When an applicant submits a PI licence application to the NCA, the applicant indicates which method it intends to apply for calculating its own funds requirement. It is however for the NCA to decide which method provides for the most appropriate own funds calculation and should therefore be used. Since NCAs can take their own approach for selecting a calculation method for the own funds requirement, PIs with similar business models that apply for a licence with a different NCA can face different own funds requirements. Moreover, based on the evaluation of a PI's risk-management processes and internal control mechanisms, **Article 9(3) PSD2** provides that an NCA can require a PI to hold an amount of own funds which is up to 20% higher or lower than the amount calculated on the basis of the chosen method. If an NCA imposes more stringent requirements on a PI on the basis of such evaluation, the PI would have no legal basis for challenging the NCA's decision since this falls within the discretionary power of the NCA.

[45] Based on method B, own funds shall amount to at least the sum of the following elements multiplied by the scaling factor k, where payment volume (PV) represents one twelfth of the total amount of Payments executed by the PI in the preceding year: (i) 4% of the slice of PV up to €5 mln., plus (ii) 2.5% of the slice of PV above €5 mln. up to €10 mln., plus (iii) 1% of the slice of PV above €10 mln. up to €100 mln., plus (iv) 0.5% of the slice of PV above €100 mln. up to €250 mln., plus (v) 0.25% of the slice of PV above €250 mln. Scaling factor k is: (i) 0.5 where the PI provides only the payment service listed in point 6 of the Annex; (ii) 0.8 where the PI provides the payment service listed in point 7 of the Annex; and (iii) 1 where the PI provides any of the payment services listed in points 1–5 of the Annex.

[46] The sum of these indicators is calculated based on the previous financial year. When audited figures are not available, which is usually the case for new market entrants, it is allowed to use estimates.

[47] The multiplication factor is: (i) 10% of the slice of the relevant indicator up to €2,5 mln.; (ii) 8% of the slice of the relevant indicator from €2,5 mln. up to €5 mln.; (iii) 6% of the slice of the relevant indicator from €5 mln. up to €25 mln.; (iv) 3% of the slice of the relevant indicator from €25 mln. up to €50 mln.; and (v) 1.5% above €50 mln.

[48] Scaling factor k is: (i) 0.5 where the PI provides only the payment service listed in point 6 of the Annex; (ii) 0.8 where the PI provides the payment service listed in point 7 of the Annex; and (iii) 1 where the PI provides any of the payment services listed in points 1–5 of the Annex.

Own funds requirement for electronic money institutions (EMIs)

With regard to its E-money issuance business, **Article 5(3) EMD2** requires an EMI to hold an amount of capital representing 2% of its average E-money exposure.[49] **Article 5(4) EMD2** stipulates that where an EMI carries out other activities that are not linked to the issuance of E-money and the amount of outstanding E-money is unknown in advance, the EMI must calculate its own funds requirement on the basis of a representative portion assumed to be used for the issuance of E-money.[50] Based on the evaluation of the EMI's risk-management processes and internal control mechanisms, an NCA can require an EMI to hold a number of own funds which is up to 20% lower or higher than the amount representing 2% of its average E-money exposure pursuant to **Article 5(5) EMD2**.

If an EMI offers payment services that are not linked to the issuance of E-money, **Article 5(2) EMD2** stipulates that the EMI's own funds requirement is calculated as the sum of: (i) 2% of the average outstanding E-money; and (ii) the own funds calculated for the non-E-money linked payment services in accordance with PSD2. An example of a payment service that is linked to the issuance of E-money is a request from an E-money holder to carry out a single transaction which includes both the redemption or issuing of E-money and the transfer of funds to a third party's payment account.[51]

4.2.3.3 Professional Indemnity Insurance for AISPs and PISPs

TPPs that offer payment initiation services or account information services are never in the possession of funds belonging to a PSU. For this reason, the European legislature did not consider it proportionate to subject: (i) AISPs to the initial capital and own funds requirements; and (ii) PISPs to the own funds requirement. However, the business activities of a TPP can create liabilities *vis-à-vis* its PSUs, creditors or

[49] According to **Article 2(4) EMD2**, the average outstanding E-money exposure is the average total amount of financial liabilities related to E-money in issue at the end of each calendar day over the preceding six calendar months.

[50] Where an EMI has not completed a sufficient period of business, its own funds requirement is calculated based on projected outstanding E-money evidenced by its business plan.

[51] See European Court of Justice (2019).

other PSPs with which they have a business relationship. These stakeholders should not remain empty-handed in case a TPP does something wrong which gives rise to a claim against that TPP.[52] TPPs are therefore required to have safeguards in place should someone claim damages as a result of a liability on the side of the TPP. PSD2 requires TPPs to take out a professional indemnity insurance or similar guarantee.[53] With regard to payment initiation services, the insurance or guarantee must cover potential claims in relation to unauthorised Payments and non-execution or erroneous execution of Payments. For account information services, **Article 5(3) PSD2** requires the insurance or guarantee to cover potential claims from PSUs for unauthorised or fraudulent access to or use of payment account information. The minimum coverage required is calculated as the sum of: (i) the amount considered appropriate given the TPP's risk profile[54]; (ii) the amount considered appropriate to the type of activities carried out by the TPP[55]; and (iii) the amount appropriate to the size of activities of the TPP.[56]

[52] PSD2, Recital 35.

[53] In case a PI offers payment services in addition to account information services or payment initiation services, the insurance requirement applies in addition to the capital requirements. In **Article 36(5) PSD3 Proposal** it is suggested that the applicant of an AISP licence shall hold an initial capital of €50,000 which can be replaced by a professional indemnity insurance without undue delay after the moment the PI commences its activities.

[54] The amount considered appropriate represents the total value of reimbursement requests by PSUs and/or AS- PSPs over the past 12 months or an estimation thereof if the TPP is not yet active.

[55] In case business activities are conducted in addition to payment services, a value of €50,000 is added unless it can be demonstrated that the risks involvement in such business do not impact the payment services business because: (i) there is a guarantee in place; or (ii) the payment services business is incorporated in a separate entity.

[56] For PISPs, this amount is the sum of: (i) 40% of the share of the total value of aggregate transactions over the past 12 months (N) between €0 and €500,000; (ii) 25% of the share of N between €500,000 and €1 mln.; (iii) 10% of the share of N between €1 mln. and €5 mln.; (iv) 5% of the share of N between €5 mln. and €10 mln.; and (v) 0.025% of the share of N over €10 mln. Of AISPs, this amount is the sum of: (i) 40% of the share of the total number of users over the past 12 months (N) between 1 and 100; (ii) plus 25% of the share of N between 100 and 10,000 users; (iii) 10% of the share of N between 10,000 and 100,000 users; (iv) 5% of the share of N between 100,000 and 1 mln. users; and (v) 0.025% of the share of N over 1 mln. users. In case payment services were not yet provided in the past 12 months, estimated values and/or numbers must be provided.

4.2.4 *Safeguarding PSU Funds*

When providing payment services, Non-Banks often receive funds from PSUs which are to be transferred to a beneficiary. Moreover, EMIs receive funds from PSUs in exchange for the issuance of E-money. To safeguard these funds against the adverse effects of potential insolvency of the Non-Bank, it is important that the funds held by Non-Banks on behalf of PSUs are not commingled with the funds of any of the Non-Bank's other creditors. For PSUs serviced by Banks, the deposit guarantee scheme ensures that the funds entrusted to the Bank are secured against the insolvency of the Bank up to an amount of €100,000. Non-Banks are however not eligible to participate in the deposit guarantee scheme.[57] Moreover, the payment accounts that Non-Banks use to provide payment services are not covered by the deposit guarantee scheme since these accounts are held with a Bank in the name of the Non-Bank. Therefore, if no safeguards are put in place, the opening of an insolvency proceeding against a Non-Bank would result in the PSU funds being captured by the Non-Bank's insolvency estate.

To secure the PSU's funds after it has entrusted its funds to a Non-Bank, **Article 10 PSD2** obliges Non-Banks to safeguard the funds they receive from their PSUs. This requirement does not apply to TPPs since PIs that offer only payment initiation or account information services are never in the possession of PSU funds.

Article 10(1) PSD2 provides for two different methods by which Non-Banks can comply with the safeguarding requirement. Non-Banks can safeguard the relevant funds by ensuring that these are not commingled with the funds of other creditors or by entering into an insurance policy or comparable guarantee.

4.2.4.1 *Preventing PSU Funds from Being Commingled with the Funds of Other Creditors*

A common method for Non-Banks to secure the funds of their PSUs is to ensure that these are not commingled at any time with the funds of other (legal) person(s). This safeguarding method consists of two elements. First, the Non-Bank must keep the relevant funds segregated from any

[57] For this very reason, the Working Group on EU Payment Systems published a Report to the Council of the European Monetary Institute on prepaid cards in May 1994, in which it stated that only Banks should be allowed to issue electronic purses.

other funds it holds as soon as it receives the funds. Second, where these funds are held by the Non-Bank at the end of the following business day, the funds must be: (i) deposited in a separate account in a Bank; or (ii) invested in invested in secure, liquid low risk assets.

Segregating PSU Funds from Other Funds

PSD2 obliges Non-Banks to ensure that the funds it receives from PSUs or other PSPs remain segregated from the Non-Bank's own funds.[58] The funds that must be segregated include: (i) funds that PIs and EMIs[59] receive from PSUs for the execution of Payments as well as funds received from other PSPs for the execution of Payments on behalf of PSUs and (ii) the funds that EMIs receive in exchange for the issuance of E-money. Funds that are to be used for future Payments are according to **Article 10(2) PSD2** also subject to the segregation requirement. In case the amount of funds to be used for future Payments is variable or unknown in advance, Member States may allow Non-Banks to apply the segregation requirement on the basis of a representative portion.[60]

In Member States where national law does not provide that a Non-Bank's payment account held with a Bank is bankruptcy remote, the funds standing to the credit of such payment account are in fact not segregated from the Non-Bank's assets.[61] This incompatibility with the segregation obligation could be solved by obliging Non-Banks to receive all PSU funds directly in the depository's payment account.

Deposit Funds in Separate Account or Invest in Assets

Funds that are held by a Non-Bank on the following business day have to be deposited in a separate account in a Bank or invested in secure,

[58] These safeguards for third party monies held by PIs were first introduced by PSD. PSD allowed Member States to limit the safeguarding requirement to funds from PSUs whose funds individually exceeded a threshold of €600. With PSD2, this member state option has been abandoned.

[59] Under EMD, EMIs were subject to liquidity requirements since EMD brought EMIs within scope of the prudential requirements applicable to Banks. With EMD2, these liquidity requirements have been replaced by an obligation for EMIs to safeguard funds received from third parties in accordance with the safeguarding provisions set out in PSD2 (**Article 7(1) EMD2**).

[60] Such representative portion is an estimation based on historical data.

[61] This is for example the case in the Netherlands. See Van Zaal (2010, p. 234).

liquid low risk assets.[62] In some Member States, national law provides for a safeguarding account for Non-Banks.[63] In practice, Non-Banks often face difficulties applying this option for safeguarding funds given that Banks often refuse to open a payment account or close an existing payment account because of perceived high ML/TF risk exposures.[64] The Commission therefore considers it important to include in the legislative framework that Banks must provide PIs[65] and their agents and distributors with a payment account except in case there are serious grounds to refuse such account.[66] Situations where a payment account can be refused involve PIs conducting illegal activities or applying a risk profile that exposes the Bank to unacceptable risks or compliance costs.[67] As an alternative to the safeguarding account maintained with a Bank, **Article 9(1) PSD3 Proposal** suggests that PI's should also be able (at the discretion of the central bank) to deposit PSU funds in a separate account at a central bank. This alternative is suggested to extent the safeguarding options for Non-Banks and to limit concentration risk in safeguarding funds.[68]

In Member States that do not provide for a safeguarding account for Non-Banks, PSPs can safeguard funds via a depository established specifically for this purpose. When using a depository, the funds entrusted to the Non-Bank by PSUs are standing to the credit of a payment account held with a Bank in the name of the depository.[69]

[62] Such assets include: (i) cash; and (ii) government bonds with a long-term rating of no less than BBB which are traded on a stock exchange.

[63] E.g. the UK (until 31 December 2020).

[64] PSR Proposal, Recital 35.

[65] As well as applicants of a PI licence.

[66] PSR Proposal, Recital 36. In order to avoid concentration risk, it is suggested in **Article 9(2) PSD3 Proposal** that PIs must endeavor not to safeguard all funds with one Bank.

[67] Ibid.

[68] See Commission (2023, p. 8).

[69] See Rank and Tomé (2020, p. 621). In the Netherlands, such depository often has the form of a customer accounts foundation. On 7 July 2022, the concept of a 'statutory segregated client money account' was introduced into Dutch law, as a result of which the credit standing to the balance of a segregated client money account (which the PI/EMI holds with a bank in its own name for one or more customers) will serve by operation of law only to settle claims of: (i) the PSUs of the PI/EMI; and (ii) the bank in relation to the costs of the management of said account.

To ensure that other creditors of the Non-Bank cannot recover claims on funds held in safekeeping by a depository, such depository must meet certain requirements. For example, in the Netherlands, a key requirement for the depository is to include in its articles of association that its sole purpose is to receive, manage and distribute PSU funds for a particular Non-Bank. It is of paramount importance that the articles of association of the depository do not allow the depository to pursue commercial activities since such activities could give rise to claims by non-PSU creditors. Otherwise, PSUs may not have full recourse in case of an insolvency proceeding against the Non-Bank. Another requirement is that the Non-Bank must ensure that the liquid assets of the depository at all times equal the Non-Bank's financial liabilities *vis-à-vis* its PSUs.[70] Moreover, the depository is not allowed to pay out any funds to a PSU acting as beneficiary before it receives the corresponding funds from the payer. In other words, the depository is not allowed to issue any bridge financing to ensure that it can pay out all claims in case of the opening of an insolvency proceeding against the Non-Bank.

4.2.4.2 Insurance Policy or Comparable Guarantee

Alternatively, a Non-Bank can safeguard PSU funds by taking out an insurance policy or obtaining a comparable guarantee from an insurance company or a Bank. Such insurance policy or guarantee must cover the potential amount payable by the Non-Bank in the event that the Non-Bank would be unable to meet its financial obligations. According to **Article 10(1)(b) PSD2,** it is not allowed for a Non-Bank to take out an insurance policy or guarantee from an insurance company or Bank that belongs to the same group as the Non-Bank.

4.2.5 Fit and Proper Screening of Policymakers and Co-policymakers

The persons in charge of the management of a Non-Bank determine to a large extent the level of success of the Non-Bank's business. These persons are amongst others responsible for: (i) overseeing the day-to-day operations of the Non-Bank and (ii) developing the overall strategy of the organisation. Furthermore, these persons are to a large extent responsible for creating and managing the organisational culture. The persons

[70] This requirement is also known as reconciliation.

in charge of the management of the Non-Bank therefore have a great responsibility *vis-à-vis* the PSP, its employees and other stakeholders.

For this reason, the European legislature considered it to be of paramount importance that persons qualifying as day-to-day policymaker of a Non-Bank are fit and proper for their role. Day-to-day policymakers include *inter alia* the members of the management board in a two-tier board structure and the executive directors in a one-tier board structure.[71] A person does not necessarily need to hold the official title of a management board member or executive director to qualify as a day-to-day policymaker. Regardless of the formal position held by a particular person within a Non-Bank, such person can qualify as a day-to-day policymaker if he or she de facto acts as a day-to-day policymaker of the Non-Bank.[72]

When applying for a licence as a Non-Bank, the persons who will determine the day-to-day policy of the Non-Bank are subject to a fit and proper screening requirement as set out in **Article 5(1)(n) PSD2**.[73] Being fit and proper implies that day-to-day policymakers are suitable for their role and that their integrity is beyond any doubt. Whether a person is suitable to assume a particular role within the organisation of a Non-Bank is determined on the basis of his knowledge, experience and skills.[74] It is not required for each day-to-day policymaker to have substantial experience and knowledge regarding all focus areas of the Non-Bank's business. Responsibility for focus areas can be allocated between day-to-day policymakers as long as the collective satisfies all requirements. Further to

[71] Although EU legislation does not provide for a definition of day-to-day policymakers, day-to-day policymakers include in any case persons that are responsible for the (long term) strategy of the Non-Bank and its daily operations.

[72] Qualification as day-to-day policymaker requires a factual assessment of the case at hand. An example of a non- director that may qualify as a day-to-day policymaker is a person that is granted a power of attorney which does not contain any limitations. Such power of attorney allows the attorney to represent the Non-Bank as if he were a day-to-day policymaker.

[73] The fit and proper requirement is an ongoing requirement, which means that a re-screening of a person's suitability or integrity may be required under certain circumstances.

[74] When assessing the suitability of a candidate, the NCA takes into consideration his education, work experience and competences (e.g. general management skills). Furthermore, availability is an important element of the suitability requirement, which means that a person will not be suitable for a particular position in case he holds too many other positions.

the suitability screening, day-to-day policymakers are also screened for integrity by the NCA prior to their appointment to ensure that the trustworthiness of such policymakers is beyond any doubt.[75]

In addition, there may also be persons working for a Non-Bank who are not responsible for the day-to-day operations of the Non-Bank but can nevertheless exercise a certain level of influence over the management of such a Non-Bank. These persons are known as co-policymakers and include *inter alia* the members of the management board of the holder of a qualifying holding in the Non-Bank. Co-policymakers are not screened for suitability since they do not assume responsibility for the Non-Bank's day-to-day operations. However, as with day-to-day policymakers, it is essential that the integrity of these persons is beyond any doubt. Co-policymakers of Non-Banks are therefore screened for integrity by the NCA prior to their appointment.

4.2.5.1 Screening of Prospective Shareholders

Shareholders of a Non-Bank often find themselves in a position that enables them to exercise substantial influence over the strategy and day-to-day business operations of the Non-Bank. The influence exerted by shareholders can either have positive or adverse effects on the financial soundness of the Non-Bank. It is therefore of paramount importance to have legal safeguards in place to ensure that the influence exerted by shareholders will not endanger the stability and financial soundness of a Non-Bank. To this end, prospective shareholders holding a so-called 'qualifying holding' in a Non-Bank must be of good repute and financially sound in order to minimise the risk that a particular shareholder adversely impacts the financial soundness of the Non-Bank.

With regard to Non-Banks, **Article 3(3) EMD2** introduced the obligation for prospective shareholders to obtain prior approval for obtaining a qualifying holding in an EMI. It was not until PSD2 that a change in control approval requirement was imposed for prospective shareholders of PIs.[76] PSD2 and EMD2 stipulate that prospective acquirers of a 'qualifying holding' within the meaning of CRR in an EU based PI or EMI

[75] When assessing whether the integrity of a candidate is beyond any doubt, the NCA screens a person based on his criminal, financial, tax compliance, supervisory and administrative law antecedents.

[76] PSD did not contain an approval requirement for prospective shareholders of PIs.

require prior approval from the NCA.[77] A qualifying holding is defined in **Article 4(1)(36) CRR** as a direct or indirect holding in a Bank representing 10% or more of the Bank's capital or voting rights. Moreover, having the right to appoint the (majority of) the members of a Bank's management board or having other means of providing substantial influence over a Bank's management falls within the definition of a qualifying holding.[78] Although PSD2 and EMD2 refer to the CRR definition of qualifying holding, PSD2 and EMD2 apply a different threshold for the applicability of the change in control approval requirement. According to Articles 6(1) PSD2 and 3(3) EMD2, the relevant threshold for PIs and EMIs is 20% of the Non-Bank's issued share capital or voting rights whereas CRR applies a 10% threshold for Banks. Certain Member States also apply the 10% threshold for Non-Banks, even though PSD2 and EMD2 do not provide for a legal basis for Member States to impose a lower threshold.[79] As a result, group structures of Non-Banks can be subject to different changes in control approval requirements depending on the Member State of establishment.

4.2.5.2 *The Change in Control Approval Process*

Obtaining change in control approval for the shareholder of a Non-Bank is an important element of the licence application process of a Non-Bank.[80] Such approval requirement remains however relevant for Non-Banks since further changes to their shareholding structure may also need prior approval from the NCA. When reviewing a change in control application, the NCA assesses whether the envisaged holding imposes any risks on the prudent and sound management of the Non-Bank.[81] In this

[77] The same requirement applies to an entity or person that intends to (in)directly dispose of a qualifying holding, or to reduce its qualifying holding so that the proportion of the capital or of the voting rights held would fall below certain thresholds.

[78] See ECB. (n.d.).

[79] This is for example the case in the Netherlands.

[80] The implications of obtaining a qualifying holding without prior approval are severe. **Article 6(4) PSD2** stipulates that if a qualifying holding is obtained in a PI without prior approval from the NCA, the exercise of the corresponding voting rights is suspended and the votes cast by the holder of the qualifying holding are nullified or can be annulled.

[81] Upon receipt of a change in control application, the NCA confirms receipt thereof within two business days. The NCA has 60 business days to complete its assessment, which can be extended with a maximum of 30 business days in case the NCA requires additional information to complete its assessment.

regard, NCAs are particularly interested in understanding the shareholder's intentions with regard to its envisaged shareholding in the Non-Bank. Questions to which the NCA will seek answers relate amongst others to the willingness of the prospective shareholder to financially support the Non-Bank in the event of financial difficulties and the shareholder's long-term strategic objectives.

The criteria on the basis of which the suitability of a prospective shareholder is assessed have first been harmonised in the EU with the adoption of Directive 2007/44/EC as regards procedural rules and evaluation criteria for the prudential assessment of acquisitions and increase of holdings in the financial sector ('**Antonveneta Directive**').[82] The Antonveneta Directive provided for an exhaustive list of criteria on the basis of which NCAs had to assess the prospective acquisition of a qualifying holding in a Bank, which continues to be relevant to date.[83] First, the NCA verifies the reputation of the prospective acquirer. Is the proposed acquirer trustworthy, does he have criminal records or has he been involved in court proceedings? Another reputational aspect is the acquirer's professional competence, which can be evidenced by the acquirer's track record in financial sector investments. Second, the NCA verifies the suitability and integrity of the persons that will be appointed as members of the management board of the Non-Bank after the acquisition of the qualifying holding. Third, the NCA assesses the financial soundness of the prospective acquirer. Important elements of the financial soundness assessment are the capability of the prospective acquirer to finance the acquisition and the capability of the acquirer to financially support the Non-Bank should the need arise. Fourth, the NCA assesses what impact the acquisition will likely have on the continuity of the business operations of the Non-Bank. Will the Non-Bank still be able to comply with its prudential requirements after the acquisition has been completed? A

[82] Directive 2007/44/EC of 5 September 2007 "amending Council Directive 92/49/EEC and Directives 2002/83/EC, 2004/39/EC, 2005/68/EC and 2006/48/EC as regards procedural rules and evaluation criteria for the prudential assessment of acquisitions and increase of holdings in the financial sector", *OJ L* 247, 21 September 2007, pp. 1–16. The Antonveneta Directive was in force from September 21, 2007 until January 2, 2018.

[83] The Antonveneta Directive did not allow NCAs to refuse change in control approval based on arguments other than those set out in the directive.

Non-Bank should for example not be put under stress because the acquisition has been partly financed by debt.[84] Fifth, the NCA verifies whether the envisaged acquisition triggers unacceptable ML/TF risk exposures.

4.3 Waiver for Small Non-Banks

4.3.1 Payment Institutions (PIs)

Although the licensing requirements for PIs are less stringent than the licensing requirements for Banks, it can be too burdensome for certain smaller PIs to comply with the full-fledged PI licensing regime. For this reason, **Article 32(1) PSD2** provides Member States with the option to allow smaller PIs, which do not provide account information services or payment initiation services, to carry out their business under a lighter authorisation regime referred to as the waiver.[85]

PIs are eligible for the PSD2 waiver if: (i) the monthly average value of Payments executed in the preceding 12 months did not exceed €3 mln.; and (ii) none of the members of its management board has been convicted for ML/TF crimes or other financial crimes. Although the financial eligibility criterion is backward-looking, primarily new market entrants are keen to rely on this waiver. Since new market entrants have not yet commenced their business operations, registration under the waiver can also be obtained on the basis of a forecast of the monthly average value of Payments to be executed in the first year after commencement of the payments business.

Article 32(1)(a) PSD2 allows Member States to apply a threshold below €3 mln. for PIs in their jurisdiction to be eligible for the waiver. The European legislature considered that Member States should have flexibility, which allows them to strike an adequate balance between avoiding a regulatory burden that is too onerous for small PIs and ensuring an adequate level of protection for all stakeholders. Notwithstanding the legislature's good intentions, allowing Member States to apply a lower threshold harms the competitive position of PIs in at least

[84] Furthermore, the organisation structure of the acquirer should not be so complex that it hampers the NCA from carrying out effective supervision on the Non-Bank.

[85] When operating under the waiver, a PI is exempted from the application of all or part of the requirements set out in Sections 1, 2 and 3 PSD2, except for Articles 14, 15, 22, 24, 25 and 26 PSD2.

two ways. First, the introduction of this option was not without consequences for PIs that operated on the basis of the PSD waiver in Member States that decided to lower the threshold under PSD2. Such PIs were obliged to either reduce their turnover or apply for a PI licence. Second, a side effect of having this option is that PIs can operate without a licence in some Member States while requiring a licence for the same activities in other Member States.

Apart from the adverse effects of having different eligibility criteria for the waiver regime on market entrance by PIs, one can ask the more profound question of whether there is a benefit of having the option of the waiver. The PSD2 licensing regime for PIs allows NCAs to apply the principle of proportionality when imposing legal requirements on PIs. For example, the calculation methods B and C for the own funds requirement take into account the size of the PI's business operations and can be reduced by the NCA with a maximum of 20% based on the evaluation of a PI's risk-management processes and internal control mechanisms. In addition, PIs operating under the waiver cannot obtain a passport for carrying out payment services in other Member States and are therefore, by default, restricted in their options to expand their business.

4.3.2 E-Money Institutions (EMIs)

Like PSD2, **Article 9 EMD2** provides Member States with the option to allow smaller EMIs to carry out their business under a lighter authorisation regime referred to as the waiver.[86] **Article 9(1) EMD2** allows Member States to waive the application of the licence, prudential and/ or safeguarding requirements imposed under EMD2 provided that the

[86] Under the EMD regime, smaller EMIs were also allowed to rely on a waiver. **Article 8 EMD** allowed Member States to waive the application of some or all of the provisions of the EMD and the Banking Consolidation Directive for EMIs in cases where: (i) the total E-money business activities of the EMI generated a total amount of financial liabilities related to outstanding E-money that normally did not exceed €5 mln. and never exceeded €6 mln.; or (ii) the E-money issued was only accepted as a means of payment by: (a) subsidiaries of the EMI which performed operational or other ancillary functions related to E-money issued or distributed by the EMI; (b) any parent undertaking of the EMI; or (c) any other subsidiaries of that parent undertaking; or (iii) issued E-money was only accepted as payment by a limited number of undertakings (also known as the closed-loop principle), which could be clearly distinguished by: (a) their location in the same premises or other limited local area; or (b) their close financial or business relationship with the issuing EMI, such as a common marketing or distribution scheme.

following three requirements are met.[87] First, the business activities of the EMI generate an average outstanding amount of E-money, commonly referred to as the float, which does not exceed a limit set by the legislature in the Member State of the establishment. Such a limit can in any case not exceed €5 mln.[88] A consequence of this requirement is that EMIs operating on the basis of a waiver have to monitor on an ongoing basis whether they operate below the monetary threshold.[89] EMIs that rely on the waiver have to report periodically to their NCA on their E-money issuance activities and E-money-related financial liabilities.[90] Second, none of the persons responsible for the management of the EMI can have been convicted for offences relating to ML/TF or other financial crimes. Third, the underlying contractual arrangements provide that the maximum storage amount of E-money on the electronic storage device does not exceed €150.

EMIs that operate on the basis of a waiver are not exempted from the ongoing requirements, such as the obligation to safeguard funds that the EMI receives in exchange for the issuance of E-money and the AML/CTF requirements (**Paragraph 6.4.1**).[91] EMIs that operate under the waiver and want to provide payment services that are not connected to the issuance of E-money, are also eligible for the PI waiver under PSD2 provided that the EMI meets the requirements for PIs as set out in **Paragraph 4.2.1**.

[87] **Article 9(6) EMD2** stipulates that failing to comply with any of the waiver requirements results in an obligation for the EMI to submit a licence application within 30 calendar days.

[88] Where an EMI also carries out any activities that are not linked to the issuance of E-money and the amount of outstanding E-money is unknown in advance, NCAs allow EMIs to apply the limit on the average outstanding E-money on the basis of a representative portion assumed to be used for the issuance of e-money, provided that such a representative portion can reasonably be estimated on the basis of historical data and to the satisfaction of the NCAs. Where an EMI has not been in business for a sufficiently long period of time, this requirement shall be assessed based on projected outstanding E-money evidenced by its business plan (subject to any adjustment to that plan having been required by the NCAs).

[89] EMIs benefitting from the **Article 9 EMD2** waiver must however be registered with the NCA.

[90] **Article 9(5) EMD2** stipulates that the EMI notifies the NCA: (i) of any change in its situation which is relevant to the conditions regarding the waiver; and (ii) at least annually on the average outstanding E-money.

[91] See Joosen (2020, p. 109).

4.4 Cross-Border Services, Branches and Agents of Non-Banks

EEA-licensed PIs can request their NCA to grant a passport for the offering of payment services in any other Member State.[92] Although EMD2 does not provide for a European passport for EMIs, PSD2 allows licensed EMIs to apply the same passporting procedure available to PIs for the provision of payment services in other Member States.[93]

Providing payment services on the basis of a passport reduces market entry costs for Non-Banks and, as a result, increases competition between PSPs in the EEA. There is however no harmonised European approach for determining when you are providing payment services in a particular Member State. Different tests are applied by NCAs to assess whether someone is active in their jurisdiction. Some Member States apply the 'solicitation test', which looks at where the PSP's clients are located to determine in which Member State payment services are provided.[94] Other Member States apply the 'characteristic performance test', which looks at where the characteristic elements of the payment service take place instead of where the PSP's clients are located.[95] Because NCAs apply different standards to determine whether payment services are provided in their jurisdiction, it is often unclear to Non-Banks for which Member States it requires a passport.

Non-Banks have three different options for providing payment services in other Member States. First, the Non-Bank can request a passport for servicing PSUs in other Member States on a cross-border basis. Second, a Non-Bank can offer payment services in another Member State using a local physical presence called a branch. Third, a Non-Bank can engage an agent in a particular Member State who will act as a representative of the Non-Bank. In practice, it is not always clear whether payment

[92] Such passport is not available for Non-Banks having their head office outside the EEA.

[93] Recital 9 EMD2 states that for EMIs any reference in PSD (currently PSD2) to PIs must be interpreted as a reference to EMIs.

[94] The solicitation test is used in, amongst others, the Netherlands, Belgium and France.

[95] This test is applied in the United Kingdom, which is no longer a Member State. Germany applies a combination of the characteristic performance test and the solicitation test.

services are provided on a cross-border basis or under the right of establishment. To ensure a harmonised interpretation of these concepts, the EBA requested the Commission to issue guidance on the identification of cross-border digital services.[96] To date, no guidance has been published by the Commission however on when payment services are provided on a cross-border basis or via a branch.

It is elementary that the information requirements for passporting procedures for Non-Banks are the same in all Member States. To standardise the passporting procedure under PSD2, the Commission adopted a delegated regulation on passporting setting out which information must be submitted to the NCA in the event a Non-Bank intends to offer payment services in another Member State.[97]

4.4.1 Provision of Cross-Border Services

A Non-Bank that intends to provide payment services in another Member State on a cross-border basis sends a notification to the competent authority of the home Member State (‘**Home CA**’).[98] The Home CA forwards the notification to the competent authority of the host Member State (‘**Host CA**’) within one month after receipt and informs the Non-Bank that such communication has been made. The Non-Bank can commence providing payment services on a cross-border basis when it has been informed by the Home CA that the communication has been made. PSD2 is not entirely clear on whether the Host CA is authorised to assess the content of the application. In other words, PSD2 remains silent as to whether the Host CA can oppose the provision of cross-border payment

[96] See EBA (2019c, p. 12).

[97] Commission Delegated Regulation (EU) 2017/2055 of 23 June 2017 “supplementing Directive (EU) 2015/2366 of the European Parliament and of the Council with regard to regulatory technical standards for the cooperation and exchange of information between competent authorities relating to the exercise of the right of establishment and the freedom to provide services of payment institutions”, *OJ L* 294, 11 November 2017, pp. 1–25.

[98] When applying for a passport to provide payment services on a cross-border basis, **Article 28(1) PSD2** requires that the following information is submitted to the Home CA: (i) the name, address and authorisation number of the PI or EMI; (ii) the Member State in which the PI or EMI intends to operate; and (iii) the payment service(s) that the PI or EMI intends to provide in that Member State.

services in its jurisdiction by a particular Non-Bank. Based on the European concept of home and host Member State supervision, it would in my opinion not be appropriate to allow Host CAs to intervene in the application procedure for a cross-border services passport.

4.4.2 Establishment of a Branch

Alternatively, Non-Banks can offer payment services in other Member States via a local branch. **Article 4(39) PSD2** defines a branch is a place of business other than the head office, which is part of the Non-Bank and does not have a legal personality. A Non-Bank is considered to have a branch in a particular Member State if it has an infrastructure or physical presence, which allows it to participate in the economic life of that Member State on a 'stable and continuous basis' and to profit therefrom.[99] A branch must comply with the ongoing requirements applicable to the Non-Bank. This includes complying with the information and transparency requirements *vis-à-vis* PSUs and making sure that the same rights and obligations apply between the branch and its PSUs.[100] In addition, branches have to comply with the AML/CTF and consumer protection rules applicable in the host Member State.[101] According to **Article 20(2) PSD2** the Non-Bank remains fully liable in the event one of its branches does not comply with these legal requirements.

A Non-Bank that intends to establish a branch must notify the Home CA of its intention.[102] Within one month after receipt of the application, the Home CA forwards said application to the relevant Host CA(s).

[99] E.g. European Court of Justice (2003, 2010).

[100] **Article 30(1) PSD2** stipulates that in case the NCA of the Member State where the branch is established does not comply with these requirements, it immediately informs the Home CA thereof. The Home CA will take appropriate action to remedy the situation. In case of an emergency situation, the Host CA may already take precautionary measures if these are temporarily and proportionate.

[101] It is therefore key that EU legislation covering these subjects is implemented in a harmonised manner throughout the EEA.

[102] **Article 28(1) PSD2** requires Non-Banks that intend to provide payment services in another Member State via a branch to provide the Home CA with the following information: (i) the name, address and, where applicable, the authorisation number of the Non-Bank; (ii) the Member State(s) in which it intends to operate; (iii) the payment service(s) to be provided; (iv) a business plan (including a forecast budget calculation for the first three financial years); (v) a description of the governance arrangements and internal control mechanisms relating to the payment service business in the host Member

Article 28(2) PSD2 provides that the Host CA is entitled to carry out an assessment of the application to establish a branch in its jurisdiction. Within one month after receipt of the Home CA's notification, the Host CA will inform the Home CA if there are reasonable grounds for concern in connection with the establishment of the branch. Of particular interest is whether the Host CA anticipates that the branch will not meet the host Member State's AML/CTF requirements. In case of a disagreement between the Home CA and Host CA regarding the admissibility of establishing a branch in a particular Member State, PSD2 does not oblige the Home CA to follow the Host CA's advice. Ultimately, it is for the Home CA to decide whether the Non-Bank is allowed to establish the branch.[103]

4.4.3 Agents

Non-Banks can also provide payment services in other Member States via an agent. **Article 4(38) PSD2** defines an agent is a natural or legal person acting on behalf of a PI. Although EMD2 does not allow EMIs to use agents, EMIs can provide payment services via an agent under the PSD2 regime.[104] A main difference between an agent and a branch is that an agent is not part of the organisation of the Non-Bank. Moreover, Non-Banks can have agents in their home Member State, which is not possible with regard to branches.

A Non-Bank that intends to engage an agent for providing payment services will have to submit an application for registration to its Home CA.[105] As with the application for a branch, the Home CA forwards the

State; (vi) a description of the organisational structure of the branch; and (vii) the identity of those responsible for the management of the branch.

[103] In case the Home CA agrees with a negative advice received from the Host CA, the Home CA will refuse to register the branch.

[104] According to **Article 3(5) EMD2**, EMIs are not allowed to issue E-money via agents. **Article 3(4) EMD2** does allow EMIs to use agents for the distribution and redeeming of E-money.

[105] **Article 19(1) PSD2** requires Non-Banks that intend to provide payment services in another Member Sate via an agent to provide the Home CA with the following information: (i) the name and address of the agent; (ii) a description of the internal control mechanisms that are used by the agent to comply with the obligations in relation to ML/TF; (iii) the identity of the persons responsible for the management of the agent in relation to the provision of payment services and, for agents other than PSPs, evidence

application to the relevant Host CA(s) within one month of receipt.[106] The Host CA is entitled to carry out an assessment of the application to establish an agent in its jurisdiction.[107] In case the Host CA is not in favour of registering the agent, the Host CA informs the Home CA thereof and provides the reasons underlying its conclusion. Ultimately, it is for the Home CA to decide whether the Non-Bank will be allowed to register the agent.

The agent must comply with the ongoing requirements applicable to the Non-Bank on whose behalf the agent operates. This involves, complying with the information and transparency requirements *vis-à-vis* PSUs and making sure that the rights and obligations apply between the Non-Bank and its PSUs.[108] **Article 20(2) PSD2** stipulates that the Non-Bank remains fully liable in the event an agent does not comply with these legal requirements.

4.5 Technical Service Providers

4.5.1 What Is a Technical Service Provider?

Technological developments allowed for new technology-focussed firms, such as BigTechs, to become active in the market for Payments. In practice, BigTechs enter the market for Payments either as a licensed PSP or as a so-called 'technical service provider'. Technical service providers support PSPs with the provision of payment services by performing payment-related services, such as the offering of PSU interfaces for the initiation of Payments and the authorisation of Payments. Technical service providers often provide their services to PSUs free of charge because their objectives of being active in the Payments market revolve primarily around strengthening their ecosystem and the collection of data rather than making profits.

that they are fit and proper persons; (iv) the payment services for which the agent is mandated; and (v) the unique identification code or number of the agent (when available).

[106] This is only relevant in case the agent is established in a different Member State.

[107] The Host CA has one month to complete its assessment.

[108] **Article 30(1) PSD2** stipulates that in case the NCA of the Member State where the agent is located notices that the agent does not comply with these requirements, it immediately informs the Home CA thereof. The Home CA will take appropriate action to remedy the situation. In case of an emergency situation, the Host CA may already take precautionary measures if these are temporarily and proportionate.

Technical service providers are not subject to a PSD2 licence requirement according to **Article 3(j) PSD2** since their activities do not constitute payment services and these service providers are never in the possession of any PSU funds. An example of a BigTech that is active in the market for Payments as a technical service provider is Apple. With Apple Pay, Apple offers an E-wallet which allows Banks, which have a contractual arrangement with Apple, to offer their debit cards and credit cards in electronic form via an E-wallet to initiate contactless Payments at the POS.[109] Apple Pay is a bank-led solution, which means that the Bank conducts the verification of the Payment and the transfer of funds. Apple Pay provides a frictionless payment experience for PSUs, which makes it a popular solution amongst consumers. Since Banks are not (yet) able to offer the same customer experience as Apple Pay, Banks often feel compelled to partner with Apple and to offer their cards in the Apple E-wallet environment.

4.5.2 Technical Service Providers and the Level Playing Field for PSPs

BigTechs have contributed considerably to innovation in the market for Payments.[110] However, market entrance by BigTechs that operate as a technical service provider can have adverse effects on the level playing field for PSPs. Because of their network externalities, BigTechs are capable of obtaining a dominant position in the market for Payments. Consequently, significant risks for unsound competition are triggered if a BigTech with a dominant position abuses its position. For example, in case such BigTech dominates the customer interface of a particular Payment solution.[111] BigTechs such as Apple with Apple Pay dominate the customer interface for E-wallet solutions because Apple Pay is currently the only E-wallet solution that can use the NFC antenna installed on iOS devices (**Paragraph 9.4.1**).

[109] According to Recital 13 of the PSD3 Proposal, E-wallets, which are referred to in the PSD3 Proposal as 'pass- through wallets', are considered a technical service and therefore excluded from the definition of a 'payment instrument'. However, pre- paid E-Wallets are considered a 'payment instrument' and, as a result, the issuance thereof a 'payment service'.

[110] ACM (2017, p. 3).

[111] OECD (2020, p. 24).

Banks see both risks and opportunities with regard to BigTechs entering the market. An opportunity that is created as a result of BigTechs entering the market is the possibility for Banks to further improve the service offering to their PSUs and limit the costs of development of their own digital Payment solutions (e.g., E-wallets).[112] A main concern however is that BigTechs often take over the Banks' direct contact with the client.[113] In addition, Banks have become dependent on BigTechs as a result of BigTechs entering the market for Payments. Banks do not have access to the NFC antenna installed on iOS devices as a result they cannot develop their own E-wallet that can be installed on an iOS device and used for making contactless payments at the POS. Moreover, given their large customer base, BigTechs tend to have strong bargaining power, which may force Banks to accept terms with which they would normally not agree. Market entrance by BigTechs therefore gives rise to concerns regarding the level playing field.

4.6 Conclusion

A key requirement for a level playing field between Banks and Non-Banks is that Non-Banks are able to enter the market on the basis of objective and proportionate legal requirements. Prior to the adoption of PSD, service providers were often compelled to obtain a banking licence if they wanted to offer payment services in the European market. The European legislature considered that service providers, that do not obtain repayable funds from the public and are not engaged in other regulated services than payment services, should be able to enter the Payments market under a less stringent regulatory regime than Banks. With PSD, the European legislature aimed to lower the barriers to market entry for Non-Banks by providing such objective and proportionate market entry requirements. By introducing a licensing regime for Non-Banks that is tailored to the business model and risk exposures of service providers that only offer payment services, PSD marked a turning point in the competitive position of Non-Banks and significantly stimulated Non-Bank participation in the European market for Payments. With the PI licensing regime, the regulatory burden was reduced considerably for Non-Banks that were

[112] ACM (2020, p. 38).

[113] Ibid., p. 4.

otherwise required to obtain a banking licence. For example, the prudential requirements applicable to PIs are proportionate to the size and risk profile of their businesses and therefore less stringent than the prudential requirements that apply to Banks.

With PSD2, the scope of activities that qualify as a payment service has been extended, thereby also lowering the barriers of market entry for innovative service providers that require payment account access in order to provide their services. With PSD2, account information services and payment initiation services are also regulated as payment services. As a consequence, the scope of applicability of the PI licensing regime has been broadened and also covers service providers offering open banking solutions. In this regard, PSD2 has been a game changer for Non-Bank competition since it caters to new players, such as FinTechs, to enter the Payments market as a licensed PI.

The PSD2 licensing regime for PIs imposes limitations on PIs which appear to have an adverse effect on the competitive position of Non-Banks but which do not harm the level playing field between Banks and Non-Banks. For example, the fact that PIs are not allowed to obtain repayable funds from the public restricts PIs from offering payment accounts to their PSUs. This means that most PIs have to rely on Banks for the provision of payment accounts. Although this may appear to be a competitive disadvantage for PIs, allowing PIs to obtain repayable funds without participating in the deposit guarantee scheme or having to comply with the prudential requirements applicable to Banks would expose the market to unacceptable financial stability risks. Therefore, even though the limitation of not being able to obtain repayable funds limits the independence of Non-Banks *vis-à-vis* Banks, this restriction does not harm the level playing field between Banks and Non-Banks.

Nowadays, many BigTechs have become active in the market for Payments, some of them in the capacity of technical service provider. Technical service providers are not subject to the PI licence requirement since they are never in the possession of any PSU funds. As described in **Paragraph 3.4.1.1**, services that are typically offered by technical service providers include: (i) data processing and storage; (ii) data and entity authentication and (iii) IT maintenance services. Since these BigTechs do not operate on the basis of a PI or EMI licence, they are not subject to the financial services regulatory framework applicable to PSPs. Although these BigTechs are not receiving any PSU funds nor provide payment services, their business proposition often entails more than supporting PSPs in the back-end side of the Payments market with the provision of payment services. Some of these BigTechs operate at the front-end of the Payments market and offer PSU interfaces that have managed to acquire such large market shares that their services can no longer be considered to be supportive of the provision of payment services by PSPs. An example of a BigTech that offers such a widely used customer interface in the capacity of technical service provider is Apple with the E-wallet Apple Pay. Although the E-wallet Apple Pay in itself is not a payment service, the transactions that are initiated via the cards added to the Apple Pay E-wallet do qualify as payment services. Since Apple does not allow PSPs access to the NFC antenna installed on iOS devices, Banks nor Non-Banks can compete in this segment by developing their own E-wallet that provides the same frictionless Payment experience as Apple Pay. As a consequence, card-issuing PSPs are dependent on Apple for the use of their cards in an E-wallet environment. This means that if a company, such as BigTech, develops a PSU interface for which the market cannot provide alternatives, such a company can acquire a dominant position in a regulated market without being regulated themselves.

Secondary Sources

ACM. (2017). *Report Fintechs in the Payment System: The Risk of Foreclosure* (p. 3).

ACM. (2020). *Rapportage BigTechs in Het Betalingsverkeer* (pp. 4, 38).

BIS. (2021). *Fintech Regulation: How to Achieve a Level Playing Field* (Occasional Paper No 17), p. 8.

Commission. (2003). *Communication from the Commission to the Council and the European Parliament Concerning a New Legal Framework for Payments in the Internal Market (Consultative Document)*, COM (2003) 718 final, p. 12.

Commission. (2023). *Proposal for a Directive of the European Parliament and of the Council on Payment Services and Electronic Money Services in the Internal Market Amending Directive 98/26/EC and repealing Directives 2015/2366 and 2009/110/EC*, COM(2023) 366 final, p. 8.

EBA. (2017). *Final Report on the EBA Guidelines Under Directive (EU) 2015/2366 (PSD2) on the Information to Be Provided for the Authorisation of Payment Institutions and e-Money Institutions and for the Registration of Account Information Service Providers* (EBA/GL/2017/09), pp. 18–49.

EBA. (2019a). *Letter from Markus Ferber MEP Regarding E-money License for Google*. https://eba.europa.eu/sites/default/documents/files/documents/10180/2573549/4ce54ef2-8f27-49b6-8ac2-11891a8b12cf/2019%2001%2009%20Letter%20from%20Markus%20Ferber%20MEP%20re%20E-money%20License%20for%20Google.pdf. Accessed April 13, 2024.

EBA. (2019b). *EBA Report on Regulatory Perimeter, Regulatory Status and Authorisation Approaches in Relation to FinTech Activities* (pp. 20, 26).

EBA. (2019c). *EBA Report on Potential Impediments to the Cross-Border Provision of Banking and Payment Services* (p. 12).

ECB. (n.d.). *Single Supervisory Mechanism (SSM) Explained*. https://www.bankingsupervision.europa.eu/about/ssmexplained/html/qh.en.html. Accessed April 13, 2024.

Ernst & Young and Copenhagen Economics. (2020). *Study on the Application of the Interchange Fee Regulation* (Commission Final Report), p. 81.

European Court of Justice. (2003). *Commission v Italy*, Judgment of 13 February 2003, Case C-131/01, EU:C:2003:96.

European Court of Justice. (2010). *Schmelz*, Judgment of 26 October 2010, Case C-97/09, EU:C:2010:632.

European Court of Justice. (2015). *CO Sociedad de Gestion y Participación and Others*, Judgment of 25 June 2015, Case C-18/14, EU:C:2015:419.

European Court of Justice. (2019). *Paysera LT*, Judgment of 16 January 2019, C-389/17, EU:C:2019:25.

Expert Group on Regulatory Obstacles to Financial Innovation. (2019). *Thirty Recommendations on Regulation, Innovation and Finance* (Final Report to the European Commission), pp. 67, 68.

Jans, J. A. (2014). *Nieuwe ontwikkelingen in regelgeving betaaldiensten en de barrières voor markttoegang* (Tijdschrift voor Financieel Recht, No. 10), p. 409.

Joosen, E. P. M. (2020). *FinTech, BigTech en de antiwitwaswetgeving* (Tijdschrift voor Financieel Recht, No. 3), pp. 109, 112.

OECD. (2020). *Digital Disruption in Banking and Its Impact on Competition* (p. 24). OECD.

Rank, W. A. K., & Tomé, M. (2020). *PSD2 and the Safeguarding of Clients' Funds: A Comparative Analysis with Respect to Funds of Payment Service Users in the Netherlands and Brazil. Butterworths Journal of International Banking and Financial Law*, p. 621.

The Evaluation Partnership. (2006). *Evaluation of the e-Money Directive (2000/46/EC)* (Final Report), p. 56.

Van Duijvenbode, M. L., & Salemans, C. M. (2019). *De symbiotische relatie tussen de uitgifte van elektronisch geld en het verlenen van betaaldiensten* (Tijdschrift voor Financieel Recht, No. 10), p. 527.

Van Esch, R. E. (2012). *De nieuwe wettelijke regeling voor electronischgeldinstellingen* (Tijdschrift voor Financieel Recht, No. 1/2), p. 29.

Van Zaal, P. J. (2010). *Aanhouden van gelden door beleggingsondernemingen en betaaldienstverleners* (Tijdschrift voor Financieel Recht, No. 9), p. 234.

CHAPTER 5

Security Measures for Banks and Non-Banks

5.1 Background

One of the main requirements for the establishment of an internal market for Payments revolves around the safe processing of Payments. To this end, the European Council suggested in 1997 that the Commission should address fraud and counterfeiting in relation to Payments.[1] The Commission responded by proposing that, as a first step, Member States had to ensure that criminal activities in the Payments market, such as payment fraud, were recognised as a criminal offence under national legislation.[2] In addition, the Commission presented an action plan for PSPs, which would support them in preventing payment fraud to the extent possible.[3] An important action point suggested by the Commission was to provide for a clear allocation of responsibilities between the participants in the Payments ecosystem.[4] In 2001, the Commission took it a

[1] See Commission (1998, p. 1).

[2] See Commission (2004, p. 2).

[3] See Commission (1998).

[4] See Commission (2004, p. 10).

J. A. Jans, *Electronic Payments in the European Market*, EBI Studies in Banking and Capital Markets Law,
https://doi.org/10.1007/978-3-031-64338-5_5

step further and adopted the EU Fraud Prevention Action Plan 2001–2003, which aimed to further enhance the measures on the prevention of fraud in relation to Payments.[5]

Since PSD did not contain specific requirements addressing security risks encountered by PSPs, SecuRe Pay and the EBA published recommendations and guidelines to provide market participants with tools to address these risks in anticipation of PSD2. With the implementation of PSD2, a profound European legislative framework was introduced covering the main security concerns relevant for the Payments market. However, notwithstanding the efforts taken by the European legislature to adopt legal requirements for reducing payment fraud and other types of security risks, these risks continue to be a main concern for a number of reasons. First, the ever-increasing technological complexity of new Payment products continues to create new and unanticipated security risks. Examples include the introduction of account information services and payment initiation services under PSD2, which allow TPPs to request Banks access to the payment accounts of their PSUs (**Paragraph 3.4.3.2**). By introducing a legal obligation for Banks to allow such TPPs access to their IT-infrastructure, the Banks' operational and legal risks relating to the offering of payment services have increased substantially.[6] The same applies to the Banks' fraud risk exposures, which have increased due to the fact that open banking services require the involvement of a TPP in the payment service authorisation process. One might therefore argue that the security standards of the Banks' IT systems have become dependent on the level of sophistication of the security standards applied by TPPs. Second, the increasing appetite for having near real-time processing of Payments has become an important source of security risks for PSPs (**Paragraph 2.2.1**). Near real-time processing makes the execution of Payments more vulnerable to payment fraud as it leaves PSPs with less time to carry out the authorisation process. Moreover, fast payments trigger higher AML/CTF risk exposures for PSPs because near real-time processing does not allow PSPs to conduct proper customer due diligence ('**CDD**') and transaction monitoring (**Paragraph 6.4.4.4**).

[5] Ibid., p. 2.

[6] See Bijlsma, M.J., and Van Veldhuizen, S. (2019, p. 7).

5.2 What Are Security Risks?

Although PSPs are exposed to a variety of security risks when providing payment services, neither PSD nor PSD2 provide for a clear definition of what security risks are. It was not until the EBA published the EBA Guidelines on operational and security risks that a definition of 'security risks' was provided for.[7] According to these guidelines, a security risk entails the risk resulting from inadequate or failed internal processes or external events having an adverse impact on the availability, integrity confidentiality of IT-infrastructures and/or information used for payment services.[8] Prominent examples of security risks to which PSPs are exposed include payment fraud and cyberattacks.

Payment Fraud

Payment fraud involves the execution of a Payment without valid authorisation from the payer.[9] Payment fraud is often committed by imposters using stolen security credentials such as a password, PIN or credit card number. Imposters can for example obtain such security credentials by applying card skimming techniques, which involve the interception of information from a card's magnetic stripe by swiping the card through a device known as the skimmer. An alternative technique that is often used for committing payment fraud is phishing.[10] With phishing, imposters pretend to be a representative of the payer's PSP and trick a PSU into disclosing confidential information.

In 2008, Commissioner McCreevy asked attention to the adverse effects of payment fraud on the internal market for Payments. Commissioner McCreevy stated that '*Payment fraud affects consumer confidence in non-cash means of payment and therefore remains a threat to the success of the single market for payments*'.[11] In 2008, measures against payment fraud were insufficiently effective since Member States applied their own

[7] See EBA (2018). On 30 June 2020, these guidelines have been repealed by EBA (2019c).

[8] See EBA (2019c, p. 3).

[9] See Sullivan, R. (2010, p. 103).

[10] See EPC (2019, p. 18).

[11] See Commission (2008).

definitions of what constituted payment fraud and Member States developed their own legislative framework to address these risks. Not taking an EU-wide approach against payment fraud had an adverse impact on the development of the internal market for Payments. Consequently, the European legislature saw itself encumbered with the task of developing effective legislation addressing the PSPs' exposure to payment fraud and other security-related issues.

The ECB has published numerous reports on payment fraud in Europe, which provide valuable insights into the levels of payment fraud observed in the European market for, in particular, card-based payments. These reports show that Member States which have a more mature cards market appear to be more vulnerable to payment fraud. An explanation for this is that the potential gains to be obtained from payment fraud are much higher in these Member States compared to Member States with a less mature card market.[12] The ECB's seventh report on card fraud shows that so-called CNP transactions provide for the majority of the fraud cases in the European market for card payments.[13] In 2019, 80% of the value was lost because of fraud within the SEPA area related to CNP transactions, compared to 5% at ATMs and 15% at POS terminals.[14]

Cyberattacks

Another main security concern for PSPs revolves around the risk that their IT-infrastructure is temporarily unavailable due to a cyberattack. Examples of cyberattacks are denial of service ('**DoS**') attacks, distributed denial of service ('**DDoS**') attacks and malware attacks. In the event of a DoS attack, a criminal resets or overloads the IT system of a PSP as a result of which it can no longer process Payments.[15] In case of a DDoS attack, the IT systems of a PSP are also overloaded, but the PSP's systems are attacked by multiple computers simultaneously.[16] The attack on multiple systems at the same time makes it more difficult for a PSP to neutralise such cyberattack. DoS and DDoS attacks are often used by criminals

[12] See ECB (2015, p. 3).

[13] See ECB (n.d.).

[14] Ibid.

[15] See EPC (2019, p. 52).

[16] Ibid.

to conceal another attack, such as a malware attack. In the event of a malware attack, criminals steal valuable information (e.g., security credentials) from a PSU using malware such as trojan horses or spyware which is subsequently being used to commit payment fraud.

5.3 Key Initiatives Addressing Security Risks Faced by PSPs

Since one of the objectives of the European legislature is to enhance the markets' confidence in the safe execution of Payments, it is essential to have a financial services regulatory framework in place for safeguarding the security of Payments. To build such confidence throughout the EU, both PSPs and PSUs have to be subject to harmonised legal requirements that ensure the security of the execution of Payments. Initially, the development of security standards for Payments used to be a responsibility of the NCAs on the basis of recommendations issued by SecuRe Pay and the EBA. Since these recommendations do not constitute binding law, a great diversity of security-related standards for PSPs and PSUs were applied. With PSD2, these requirements have first been incorporated into a European legislative framework.

5.3.1 The SecuRe Pay Recommendations

With PSD, the European legislature missed the opportunity to introduce harmonised security requirements for PSPs. Although having efficient security measures was a necessity for PSPs, PSD did not explicitly require PSPs to have such measures in place.[17] The obligation for PSPs to have in place a security policy was first suggested by SecuRe Pay when it published its recommendations on internet payments in 2013 (**'SecuRe Pay Recommendations'**).[18] Since higher levels of fraud were observed

[17] The only reference to the requirement for PIs to have risk management procedures in place could be found in relation to the application for a licence as a PI. As part of the licence application, the applicant was required to submit a description of its risk management procedures.

[18] See ECB (2013, p. 5). The security policy should include *inter alia*: (i) objectives and organisation of information security; (ii) principles for the secure use and management of information and IT resources; and (iii) allocation of responsibilities, security activities and internal processes relating to security.

in relation to Payments that were executed via the internet than with transactions executed using conventional payment methods, the ECB published in 2013 SecuRe Pay Recommendations which provided PSPs with tools to decrease their levels of payment fraud.[19] The SecuRe Pay Recommendations were developed in anticipation of PSD2 and provided PSPs with guidelines on (i) general control and security environment; (ii) specific control and security measures for internet payments; and (iii) customer awareness, education and communication. These Recommendations applied to: (i) card payments executed via the internet (e.g., virtual card payments); (ii) credit transfers executed via the internet; (iii) the issuance of direct debit electronic mandates and (iv) E-money transfers executed via the internet.[20]

The SecuRe Pay Recommendations did not have legal status and therefore needed to be endorsed by the NCA in each of the Member States in order to take effect. Further to the fact that the SecuRe Pay Recommendations only applied to PSPs established in a Member State that endorsed these recommendations, the level playing field was further crossed by its limited scope of applicability as regards the types of Payments covered. The SecuRe Pay Recommendations only applied to PSPs involved in the execution of Payments via the internet.[21] Payments executed at POS (also known as face-to-face transactions) were out of scope and PSPs

[19] Ibid., p. 1.

[20] Ibid., p. 2. Services that are not covered by these guidelines include: (i) other internet services provided by a PSP (e.g. e-brokerage, online contracts); (ii) payments where the instruction is given by post, telephone order, voice mail or using SMS-based technology; (iii) mobile payments other than browser-based payments; (iv) credit transfers where a third party accesses the customer's payment account (a PISP); (v) Payments made via dedicated networks; (vi) payments using anonymous and non-rechargeable physical or virtual pre-paid cards where there is no ongoing relationship between the issuer and the cardholder; and (vii) clearing and settlement of Payments.

[21] The SecuRe Pay Recommendations covered: (i) card payments executed via the internet (e.g. virtual card payments); (ii) credit transfers executed via the internet; (iii) the issuance of direct debit electronic mandates; and (iv) E-money transfers executed via the internet. Services that were not covered by these recommendations included: (i) other internet services provided by a PSP (e.g. e-brokerage, online contracts); (ii) payments where the instruction is given by post, telephone order, voice mail or using SMS-based technology; (iii) mobile payments other than browser-based payments; (iv) credit transfers where a third party accesses the customer's payment account (a PISP); (v) Payments made via dedicated networks; (vi) payments using anonymous and non-rechargeable physical or virtual pre-paid cards where there is no ongoing relationship between the issuer and the cardholder; and (vii) clearing and settlement of Payments.

offering these services were not obliged to comply with the SecuRe Pay Recommendations.

5.3.2 *The EBA Guidelines on Internet Payments*

Notwithstanding the efforts taken by SecuRe Pay to mitigate security risks in the European Payments market in anticipation of PSD2, the EBA considered it expedient to introduce intermediate security requirements and published the EBA Guidelines on internet payments, which included guidelines on security measures for internet payments applicable to PSPs in the EU until PSD2 was implemented into national legislation.[22] With the conversion of the SecuRe Pay Recommendations into the EBA Guidelines on internet payments, was intended to ensure a more consistent application of these principles throughout the EU. However, like the SecuRe Pay Recommendations, the EBA Guidelines on internet payments did not constitute binding law and NCAs had to confirm whether they would endorse these requirements.[23]

Apparently, the EBA was not willing to wait for PSD2 and took the view that immediate action was required to ensure a consistent application of security requirements across the EU and to provide legal certainty for market participants. The EBA concluded that postponing the implementation of certain security requirements until the implementation of PSD2 in 2017 would not have been feasible in view of the growing levels of payment fraud.[24] The EBA Guidelines on internet payments provided minimum requirements that PSPs were obliged to apply to ensure a minimum level of security when offering internet payments.[25] As with the SecuRe Pay Recommendations, the security requirements set out in the EBA Guidelines on internet payments were based on four principles. First, PSPs were required to carry out regular risk assessments to identify the security threats relevant to their business. Second, SCA had to be applied when a PSU initiated a Payment via the internet or requested access to

[22] See ECB (2014).

[23] However, **Article 16(3) EBA Regulation** requires that NCAs and PSPs must make every effort to comply with the guidelines published by the EBA.

[24] See EBA (2014, p. 3).

[25] The EBA Guidelines applied to cards, credit transfers, electronic mandates and E-money.

sensitive payment data. Third, PSPs had to implement effective procedures for authorising and monitoring Payments, identifying abnormal customer payment patterns and preventing fraud. Fourth, PSPs had to make an effort to enhance customer awareness and educate customers regarding security risks in relation to the use of payment instruments.

By introducing new security-related requirements that cover the same elements as the SecuRe Pay Recommendations, the EBA Guidelines on internet payments imposed a disproportionate burden on PSPs by requiring them to amend their business operations for a short transition period only.[26] More importantly, by issuing these guidelines the EBA took a premature step and introduced risk management requirements for PSPs without any legal basis. As rightfully noted by the EPC, the EBA should have awaited its formal legal authority provided under PSD2 since PSD did not provide the EBA with a legal basis to introduce an obligation for PSPs to apply SCA.[27] As a result, these guidelines have had an adverse effect on the level playing field between TPPs and other PSPs. Under the PSD regime, TPPs were not regulated as a result of which TPPs were not obliged to meet the security requirements set out in the EBA Guidelines on internet payments prior to the entering into force of PSD2.

5.3.3 The Revised Payment Services Directive (PSD2)

With the adoption of PSD2, a legal requirement was introduced at a European level for PSPs to take security measures. PSD2 requires PSPs to have, amongst others, a well-documented security policy setting out the security procedures that PSPs must have in place in order to guarantee the safety of Payments. A PSP's security policy must cover all the steps of the execution process in which the PSP is involved.[28] As part of these security procedures, PSD2 explicitly requires PSPs to have a proper risk management framework in place to identify and manage security risks to which their businesses are exposed. **Article 5(1)(j) PSD2** requires the risk management framework to include a detailed description of the security

[26] These amendments were required to cover for the period between august 2015 and January 2018.

[27] The EBA referred to PSD as the legal basis for issuing the EBA Guidelines on internet payments, which did not impose an obligation on PSPs to apply SCA.

[28] The execution process involves all steps from the authentication of the PSU until the moment that sensitive payment data has been transmitted to another PSP.

control and mitigation measures taken by the PSP to safeguard technical security and ensure compliance with data protection requirements.

The PSP's security measures must be proportionate to its business model, which means that it needs to be tailored to *inter alia* the specifics of the payment services provided.[29] Unlike the risk management requirements set out in the SecuRe Pay Recommendations and the EBA Guidelines on internet payments, the PSD2 risk management framework covers a broad range of Payments.[30] **Article 95(1) PSD2 requires** a PSP's risk framework to comprise all types of Payments executed by the relevant PSP and not only Payments executed via the internet.

In order not to hamper innovation, the security requirements laid down in PSD2 are principle based instead of rule based. PSD2 mandates the EBA to prepare guidelines and regulatory technical standards that describe in more detail what these security requirements entail for PSPs. First, the EBA has been mandated to prepare the Regulatory Technical Standards on SCA and secure communication, which the Commission used as a basis for Commission Delegated Regulation (EU) 2018/389 with regard to regulatory technical standards for SCA and common and secure open standards of communication (**'Delegated Regulation on SCA and CSC'**).[31,32] Second, the EBA was mandated to prepare Guidelines on the reporting of major security and operational incidents. Third, the EBA was mandated to prepare the EBA guidelines on operational and security risks. Although the requirements set out in these guidelines and delegated regulations provide more detail than PSD2, these guidelines and delegated regulations are also principle based. This means that PSPs maintain a certain degree of flexibility to determine which security measures are proportionate to cover the risk exposures of their business. Moreover, principle-based requirements enable PSPs to swiftly adapt their

[29] PSD2, Recital 91.

[30] To cover the broader scope under PSD2 compared to the EBA Guidelines on internet payments, the EBA was mandated by PSD2 to prepare separate guidelines on the measures to be taken by PSPs to address operational and security risks under PSD2.

[31] Delegated Regulation (EU) 2018/389 of 27 November 2017 supplementing Directive (EU) 2015/2366 of the European Parliament and of the Council with regard to regulatory technical standards for strong customer authentication and common and secure open standards of communication", OJ L 69, 13.3.2018, pp. 23–43.

[32] The Commission did not adopt all of the EBA's suggestions. Especially with regard to the PSD2 obligation for the AS-PSP to have a dedicated interface available for TPPs, there was a clear difference of opinion as set out in **Paragraph 5.5.2.**

security framework in case of new developments that were not foreseen when these requirements were adopted. Despite these advantages, there are also adverse effects of structuring security requirements as principle-based requirements. An important adverse effect is that principle-based requirements are open to different interpretations. As a consequence, PSPs offering similar payment services and having similar risk profiles may adopt very different risk procedures. This effect can be reinforced if NCAs take different positions as to what adequate security measures must entail. The objective of maximum harmonisation can therefore be counteracted when having principle-based requirements instead of rule-based requirements. The European legislature must therefore always take into account that principle-based requirements may contradict the legislature's maximum harmonisation objective.

5.3.4 The Digital Operational Resilience Act (DORA)

The use of Information and Communications Technology (**'ICT'**) is of critical importance for the daily operations of PSPs.[33] Therefore, security risk exposures such as cyberattacks are a growing concern for PSPs and must be addressed in an adequate manner.[34] In September 2020, the Commission published a proposal for an act on digital operational resilience[35] in response to the joint technical advice of the ESAs on addressing ICT risks in the financial sector.[36] On 16 January 2023, Regulation (EU) 2022/2554 on digital operational resilience for the financial sector (**'DORA'**) entered into force.[37] According to **Article 64 DORA**, the DORA will apply from 17 January 2025 and provides for a regulatory framework on operational resilience and cybersecurity for, amongst others, PSPs.[38] The DORA aims to consolidate and upgrade ICT requirements that have been addressed separately in different European directives

[33] DORA, Recital 2.

[34] See ESAs Joint Committee (2019, p. 3).

[35] See Commission (2020).

[36] See ESAs Joint Committee (2019).

[37] Regulation (EU) 2022/2554 of 14 December 2022 on digital operational resilience for the financial sector (...)", OJ L 333, 27.12.2022, pp. 1–79.

[38] DORA also applies to EMIs and PIs that are exempted from the licence requirement. DORA does not cover system operators of payment systems that are designated under the SFD.

and regulations (e.g., PSD2).[39] An example of a PSD2 ICT requirement involves the obligation under **Article 5(1)(j) PSD2** for an applicant of a PI licence to submit a security document setting out its security control and mitigation measures, including its technical security and ICT systems. In addition, **Article 95 PSD2** requires PSPs to have security measures for operational and security risks related to the provision of payment services. It is generally assumed that these measures also cover ICT risk measures.[40]

The DORA introduces requirements that apply in addition to the ICT and security risk management requirements for PSPs under PSD2. To this end, the DORA contains rules on amongst others, (i) ICT risk management; (ii) major ICT incident reporting; (iii) digital operational resilience testing; (iv) ICT third party risks; and (v) sharing of information on cyber threats.[41]

5.3.5 ICT Risk Management Requirements

To maintain control regarding their ICT risk exposures, PSPs must have an effective ICT risk management and adequate measures for handling and reporting ICT-related incidents.[42] Under **Article 5(1) DORA**, PSPs are obliged to implement a control framework that ensures an effective and prudent management of ICT risk. **Articles 8—14 DORA** provide that this control framework covers amongst others: (i) the identification of sources of ICT risks; (ii) the protection of the PSP's ICT systems and preventing ICT breaches; (iii) the detection of ICT-related incidents; (iv) an ICT business continuity policy; (v) recovery procedures in case ICT systems are down and (vi) a crisis communication plan for the disclosure of major ICT incidents to the market.

[39] DORA, Recital 12.

[40] See ESAs Joint Committee (2019, p. 8).

[41] In line with a general principle of proportionality, **Article 4(1) DORA** allows PSPs to comply with the requirements stipulated under the DORA by taking into account their size and overall risk profile, as well as the nature, scale and complexity of their services, activities and operations.

[42] DORA, Recital 21.

5.3.6 *Major ICT Incident Reporting*

Under **Article 19(1) DORA**, PSPs are obliged to report major ICT incidents to their NCA. Furthermore, **Article 19(2) DORA** provides that PSPs may, on a voluntary basis, notify significant cyber threats to the NCA if they consider this to be of relevance to the financial system.

According to **Article 23 DORA**, the DORA requirements on incidents also cover the operational or security payment-related incidents and major operational or security payment-related incidents as referred to under PSD2. Therefore, PSPs must report all operational or security payment-related incidents that have been previously reported under PSD2 under the DORA regime, irrespective of whether such incidents are ICT-related.[43]

5.3.7 *Digital Operational Resilience Testing*

Article 24(1) DORA requires PSPs to establish a comprehensive digital operational resilience testing programme. By having such programme, PSPs can assess whether they are adequately prepared for handling ICT-related weaknesses and implementing corrective measures.

5.3.8 *ICT Third-Party Risk*

ICT operations are amongst the most commonly outsourced business activities by PSPs.[44] The European legislature noted that financial entities often encounter difficulties in negotiating an outsourcing agreement that fully complies with their regulatory requirements.[45] Moreover, many of the outsourcing agreements do not provide sufficient safeguards to monitor sub-outsourcing.[46] Further to the PSD2 requirements on outsourcing, **Article 28(1) DORA,** therefore, introduces an obligation for PSPs to manage ICT third party risk within their ICT risk management framework in accordance with the following principles: (i) PSPs that have in place contractual arrangements for the use of ICT

[43] DORA, Recital 23.

[44] See EBA (2019a, p. 6).

[45] DORA, Recital 26.

[46] DORA, Recital 28.

services[47] remain at all times fully responsible for compliance with applicable law; and (ii) the PSPs' management of ICT third-party risk must be implemented in accordance with the principle of proportionality. The contractual requirements for outsourcing imposed under the DORA are closely aligned with the EBA Guidelines on outsourcing arrangements.[48]

5.3.9 Information Sharing on Cyber Threats

Article 45(1) DORA allows PSPs to share cyber threat information with other PSPs provided that the sharing of information: (i) aims to enhance the digital operational resilience of PSPs; (ii) takes place within trusted communities of PSPs and (iii) is implemented through information-sharing arrangements that protect the potentially sensitive nature of the information shared, and that are in compliance with the rules on business confidentiality, protection of personal data and competition law.

5.4 Customer Authentication

5.4.1 Introduction

PSPs apply certain safety procedures each time a PSU accesses its payment account or initiates a Payment. A distinction is made between customer authentication and transaction signing or authorisation. Customer authentication is the procedure that enables a PSP to identify the PSU. It provides the PSP with a tool to ensure that the payment account of a PSU is not accessed by an unauthorised person. Transaction signing or authorisation refers to the process of confirming the details of a particular Payment instruction. This involves verifying whether the characteristics of the Payment instruction satisfy the parameters set by the payer, beneficiary and the PSP.[49]

[47] **Article 3(16) DORA** defines 'ICT services' as digital and data services provided through the ICT systems to one or more internal or external users, including provision of data, data entry, data storage, data processing and reporting services, data monitoring as well as data based business and decision support services.

[48] See EBA (2019a).

[49] Example, the PSU should have sufficient balance standing to the credit of its payment account to execute the Payment.

5.4.2 *From Authentication to SCA*

When a PSU initiates a Payment, the payer's PSP is obliged to conduct customer authentication. Under **Article 4(19) PSD**, customer authentication was a procedure that enabled PSPs to verify whether a PSU was allowed to use a particular payment instrument, including its personalised security features. Under **Article 4(29) PSD2**, the concept of customer authentication has been broadened and covers '*a procedure which allows the PSP to verify the identity of a PSU or the validity of a specific payment instrument, including the use of the user's personalised security credentials*'.

To further enhance the safety of the payment execution process, PSD2 provides an improved method for authentication called SCA. SCA was first introduced in the SecuRe Pay Recommendations published by the ECB in 2013. Since the majority of the NCAs in the EU endorsed the SecuRe Pay Recommendations, the concept of SCA was already embraced by a large number of PSPs before it became a legal obligation under PSD2.

SCA is an authentication process that requires a valid combination of at least two authentication elements. According to **Article 4(30) PSD2**, PSPs can choose a combination of two or more elements categorised as knowledge, possession and inherence.

- Knowledge relates to information that only the PSU has, such as a PIN, password or swiping pattern memorised by a PSU and performed on a device.[50]
- Possession is something that only the PSU possesses, such as a smartphone[51], a mobile app (provided that the app includes a device binding process ensuring a unique connection between the app and the device)[52] or a random reader. A one-time password (OTP) sent via SMS to a smartphone can also constitute a possession factor, whereby the possession element would not be the SIM-card associated with the respective mobile number but the SMS containing

[50] See EBA (2019b, p. 8).

[51] It can be questioned whether a smartphone can be considered to constitute a separate authentication element since it is not issued by the PSP. However, the authentication programs/tokens installed on a smartphone can in any case be regarded as a possession element within the meaning of the SCA requirement.

[52] See EBA (2019b, p. 6).

the password.[53] The possession element can have a physical form or may be data as long as this element is non-replicable (i.e., it cannot be duplicated).

- Inherence reflects something that the PSU is, such as fingerprint scanning, voice recognition and key stroke dynamics.[54]

To limit the risk of identity fraud, the elements of knowledge, possession and inherence have to be mutually independent. This means according to **Article 9(1) Delegated Regulation on SCA and CSC** that a security breach of one of these elements should not necessarily lead to a breach of the other element(s). If a PSU uses a multipurpose device for conducting SCA, such as a smartphone, **Article 9(3) Delegated Regulation on SCA and CSC** requires the PSP to use separated secure execution environments via the software installed on such device. In case the smartphone gets stolen, the knowledge or inherence element will not be available to any other person than the PSU. PSPs have to decide for themselves which solution they implement to ensure that the authentication elements are mutually independent.[55]

A valid combination of two authentication elements results in the generation of a unique authentication code, which is, in case of a POS transaction, transmitted from the payment terminal to the payer's PSP. **Article 4(1) Delegated Regulation on SCA and CSC** stipulates that this unique authentication code is accepted only once by the payer's PSP for the execution of a Payment. It is key that the unique authentication code cannot be used to trace back the knowledge element (e.g., the PIN) if it is intercepted by a criminal. Moreover, criminals should not be able to generate a new unique authentication code on the basis of an intercepted authentication code.

In the event SCA is applied for a so-called remote Payment, additional requirements apply regarding the unique authentication code. **Article**

[53] See EBA (n.d.a).

[54] See EBA (2019b, pp. 5–6).

[55] PSPs that apply the inherence element for a particular Payment product are subject to additional security requirements. When applying the inherence element, the Delegated Regulation on SCA and CSC requires that this element must guarantee a sufficiently low likelihood of an unauthorised third party being authenticated as the legitimate PSU. The Delegated Regulation on SCA and CSC does not provide for further guidance on how PSPs should meet this obligation.

4(6) PSD2 qualifies remote Payments are Payments that are initiated via the internet or a device that can be used for distance communication.[56] Since remote Payments are more vulnerable to fraud than Payments initiated at the POS, an additional SCA requirement has been introduced for remote Payments.

In case of a remote Payment, **Article 97(2) PSD2** obliges PSPs to apply so-called dynamic linking. With dynamic linking, the unique authentication code is specific to both the transaction amount and the identity of the beneficiary. The confidentiality of both the transaction amount and the identity of the beneficiary must be ensured so that any change to one of these elements also changes the authentication code. The authentication of transactions on the basis of dynamic codes makes the payer aware of the amount and the beneficiary of the transaction that the payer is authorising.[57] Dynamic linking can however be difficult to apply if the amount of the Payment is not known in advance. In these situations, the unique identification code must be linked to the maximum amount allowed for the Payment rather than the actual transaction amount.

5.4.3 *When Is SCA Required?*

In its recommendations on the security of internet payments, SecuRe Pay suggested that SCA should be applied for the initiation of internet payments and the accessing of sensitive payment data.[58] Although the PSD2 concept of SCA is similar to the SCA requirements set out in the SecuRe Pay Recommendations, PSD2 has a broader scope of applicability. Under **Article 97(1) PSD2**, PSPs are obliged to apply SCA in the event the payer: (i) accesses his payment account online; (ii) initiates a Payment; (iii) creates a list of trusted beneficiaries; or (iv) carries out an action through a remote channel which may imply a risk of payment fraud.

[56] In essence, remote Payments are not initiated at the POS.

[57] PSD2, Recital 95.

[58] See ECB (2013, p. 9).

(i) Online Access to Payment Account

In the event a payer requests access to his online payment account environment, the AS-PSP will have to apply SCA. Where a PSU accesses its payment account without initiating a Payment, the distinction between a payer and beneficiary does not appear to be relevant. One can therefore argue that the SCA requirement applies in case a PSU requests access to its online payment account environment. The requirement to apply SCA is also triggered if payment account access is requested by the PSU using the services of an AISP.

(ii) Initiating a Payment

When a payer initiates a Payment, the AS-PSP must apply SCA before it executes the Payment. The requirement to apply SCA is also triggered if a Payment is initiated by the payer using the services of a PISP. Neither PSD2 nor the Delegated Regulation on SCA and CSC provide guidance as to what constitutes a Payment within the context of this requirement. Since the majority of the Payments are executed using some sort of electronic communication, the scope of what constitutes a Payment requiring SCA is very broad. If a Payment is initiated by the beneficiary, such as with direct debit collections, the AS-PSP does not have to apply SCA.[59]

One can question whether a card payment should be considered a Payment that is initiated by the beneficiary. Card payments are often perceived to be 'beneficiary-initiated' payments since these payments are initiated by merchants. The EBA understands however card payments to be Payments that are initiated by the payer through a beneficiary and therefore within the scope of the SCA requirement.[60]

[59] Under **Article 85(2) PSR Proposal** it is suggested that Payments initiated by the beneficiary shall only not be subject to SCA if those transactions are initiated without any involvement of the payer. This means for example that for direct debits where the mandate is provided through a remote channel with the involvement of a PSP setting up the mandate will be subject to the SCA requirement.

[60] See EBA. (n.d.a).

In the PSR Proposal, it is suggested that SCA must be applied for merchant-initiated transaction (MIT) when setting up the initial mandate, but without any need to reapply SCA for subsequent MITs.[61]

(iii) Creating a List of Trusted Beneficiaries Through its AS-PSP

A PSU can create a list of trusted beneficiaries through its AS-PSP. In the event of a joint payment account[62], each payment account holder can have its own list of trusted beneficiaries. When a PSU creates or amends a list of trusted beneficiaries, **Article 13(1) Delegated Regulation on SCA and CSC** requires the AS-PSP to apply SCA.

If the PSU initiates a Payment to a beneficiary that is included on the list of trusted beneficiaries, **Article 13(2) Delegated Regulation on SCA and CSC** provides that the AS-PSP does not have to apply SCA for the execution of that particular Payment.

(iv) Carrying out any Action, Through a Remote Channel, which May Imply a Risk of Payment Fraud

This category potentially covers a broad range of activities given that it relates to any action via a remote channel that can be considered to imply a risk of payment fraud. An example of an action that falls in this category is the creation of a token or digitised version of a card due to the enrolment of a payment card to an E-wallet.[63] The card issuing PSP is responsible for providing the SCA elements to the PSU and is obliged to apply SCA when adding a card to an E-wallet.[64] This means that the unlocking of a mobile phone using biometrics (e.g., a fingerprint) or with a PIN/password cannot be considered a valid SCA element for the purpose of adding a payment card to an E-wallet, if the screen locking mechanism of the mobile device is not a process under the control of the card issuing PSP.[65] Furthermore, actions that are considered to imply a risk of payment fraud are the activation and deactivation of the payment functionalities of payment instruments.

61 PSR Proposal, Recital 108.

62 Payment account held by two or more PSUs.

63 See BA (n.d.a).

64 Ibid.

65 EBA (n.d.b).

5.4.4 Payments that Are not Covered by the SCA Requirement

When developing their authentication process for the processing of Payments, PSPs have to strike a balance between the following two conflicting objectives: (i) increasing customer convenience; and (ii) enhancing the safety of the authentication process. Imposing higher security standards, such as an additional verification code, increases the reliability of the authentication process but at the same time makes the Payment product more difficult to use and therefore less customer-friendly. From a commercial perspective, PSPs will only be inclined to adopt safer and more secure authentication procedures if they do not require them to make too many concessions in terms of customer experience.

For certain Payment products, applying SCA would have disproportionate adverse effects on the usability of that payment solution. For this reason, there are several situations where PSPs do not have to apply SCA. Situations where no SCA is required include: (i) the payer accessing payment account information without sensitive payment data being disclosed; (ii) the payer accesses payment account information through an AISP; (iii) the payer initiating a contactless POS Payment; (iv) the payer initiating a credit transfer between accounts held by the same (legal) person; (v) low value remote Payments; (vi) secure corporate payments and (vii) Payments that impose a low risk for payment fraud.

(i) Accessing Payment Account Information Without Disclosing Sensitive Payment Data

A PSP does not have to apply SCA if a PSU accesses information regarding its payment account online provided that no sensitive payment data is disclosed. According to **Article 10(1) Delegated Regulation on SCA and CSC**, this exemption only applies in the event the PSU: (i) obtains information regarding its payment account balance; or (ii) obtains information regarding the Payments that were executed in the previous 90 days. **Article 10(2) Delegated Regulation on SCA and CSC** provides that this exemption does not apply in case the PSU: (a) accesses such information for the first time; or (b) accesses the information more than 180 days after the last day on which the PSU accessed the information referred to under (i) and (ii) above and SCA was applied.

(ii) Access to the Payment Account Information Through an AISP

Article 10a Delegated Regulation on SCA and CSC does not require a PSP to apply SCA when a PSU accesses information regarding its payment account online via an AISP provided that no sensitive payment data are disclosed. In these situations, PSPs are not allowed to choose whether or not to apply SCA.[66]

According to **Article 10a(1) Delegated Regulation on SCA and CSC**, the requirement not to apply SCA only applies in the event the PSU: (i) obtains information regarding its payment account balance; or (ii) obtains information regarding the Payments that were executed in the previous 90 days. **Article 10a(2) Delegated Regulation on SCA and CSC** stipulates that SCA must be applied in case the PSU: (a) accesses such information via an AISP for the first time; or (b) accesses the information more than 180 days after the last day on which the PSU accessed the information referred to under (i) and (ii) above via an AISP and SCA was applied.

Article 10a(3) Delegated Regulation on SCA and CSC allows PSPs to apply SCA if a PSU accesses information regarding its payment account online via an AISP and the PSP has objectively justified and duly evidenced reasons relating to unauthorised or fraudulent access to the payment account.

(iii) Contactless Payments at the Point-of-Sale (POS)

A contactless Payment is a transaction that does not involve physical contact between the payment instrument and the POS payment terminal. Contactless payment cards have an NFC antenna for the wireless transfer of payment transaction information to the merchant's payment terminal.[67] No SCA is required according to **Article 11 Delegated Regulation on SCA and CSC** if the payer initiates a contactless POS Payment provided that: (i) the amount of the Payment does not exceed €50; (ii) the cumulative amount of the previous contactless Payments without application of SCA does not exceed €150; and (iii)

[66] Delegated Regulation (EU) 2022/2360, Recital 3.

[67] EMV contactless debit cards and credit cards that have an NFC antenna to communicate with the payment terminal using the ISO/IEC 14443 communication protocol.

since the last application of SCA, no more than five consecutive contactless transactions have been executed. For low value card-based payments, PSPs are also allowed to agree with the PSU in the framework contract that certain other security-related requirements do not apply (**Paragraph 5.5.3**).

(iv) Credit Transfers Between Payment Accounts Held by the Same (Legal) Person

In case the payer and the beneficiary are the same (legal) person, **Article 15 Delegated Regulation on SCA and CSC** provides that the AS-PSP does not have to apply SCA in case that person initiates a transfer of funds between payment accounts held with the same AS-PSP.

(v) Remote Payments Representing a Low Value

No SCA is needed if a payer initiates a remote Payment with a maximum value of €30. **Article 16 Delegated Regulation on SCA and CSC** stipulates that this exemption only applies in case: (i) the cumulative amount of the remote Payments that have been executed without SCA does not exceed €100; and (ii) since the last application of SCA, no more than five consecutive remote Payments have been executed.

(vi) Secure Corporate Payments

According to **Article 17 Delegated Regulation on SCA and CSC** Payments initiated by legal persons are exempted from SCA if they are initiated through the use of dedicated corporate payment processes (machine-to-machine protocols) if the NCA in the relevant Member State takes the view that these processes provide for a similar degree of security as SCA. This exemption requires NCAs to take a view as to whether the dedicated protocols of a PSP provide for a similar degree of security. Absent any further guidance from the Commission, this brings a significant risk that decisions taken by NCAs diverge as a result of which certain machine-to-machine protocols are only approved in certain Member States.[68]

(vii) Low Risk Payments

According to **Article 18 Delegated Regulation on SCA and CSC**, PSPs do not have to apply SCA if a payer initiates a remote

[68] See EBA (2017, p. 6).

Payment that poses a low level of risk. To be eligible for this exemption, PSPs have to implement real-time transaction risk analysis procedures which enable them to verify whether Payments indeed pose a low level of risk.[69] The transaction risk monitoring needs to be completed before the transaction is authorised, which is particularly challenging with regard to fast payments. In case the transaction risk analysis shows that a Payment cannot be qualified as a low risk transaction, the PSP will have to apply SCA for that transaction.

5.4.5 *Using Biometrics as Part of SCA*

The knowledge element is the most commonly used element for authentication purposes. However, this element has the disadvantage that the PSP cannot differentiate between an authorised person and an imposter.[70] In case an imposter presents itself as being one of the PSP's clients by using stolen security credentials, it is difficult for the PSP to identify such a person as not being the authorised PSU. This risk factor can be mitigated by applying a biometric system as part of the SCA requirement.[71]

A biometric system verifies the identity of a person on the basis of biometric data. Biometric data are: '*biological properties, behavioural aspects, physiological characteristics, living traits or repeatable actions where those features and/or actions are both unique to that individual and measurable, even if the patterns used in practice to technically measure them*

[69] **Article 18 Delegated Regulation SCA and CSC** stipulates that a PSP is only eligible for applying this exemption if all of the following requirements are met: (i) the fraud rates for that type of Payments are below the reference fraud rates specified in the Annex to the Delegated Regulation on SCA and CSC. According to **Article 19(1) Delegated Regulation on SCA and CSC**, the fraud rate represents unauthorised and fraudulent remote transactions divided by the total value of all transactions of that particular type of Payment. In case the fraud rates exceed this threshold, the PSP will have to apply SCA and inform the NCA thereof; and (ii) the real-time transaction risk analysis procedures of the PSP should not identify any of the following risks: (a) an abnormal spending or behavioural pattern of the payer; (b) unusual information about the payer's device/software access; (c) malware infection in any session of the authentication procedure; (d) any fraud scenario in the provision of payment services; (e) an abnormal location of the payer; or (f) the location of the beneficiary to be of high risk.

[70] See Jadhav, V. et al. (2015, p. 4957).

[71] See Jans, J. A., and Van den Ende, L. J. J. (2017, p. 205).

involve a certain degree of probability'.[72] A distinction is made between static biometric systems and dynamic biometric systems. Static biometric systems process biometric data of a PSU that remain unchanged, such as a person's fingerprint. A dynamic biometric system captures and processes behavioural biometric data of a natural person such as his typing pattern, the screen pressure he applies on his touchscreen devices or the angle with which a person holds his smartphone when initiating a Payment.

Although PSD2 does not explicitly mention biometric systems as being a suitable element for the SCA requirement, the Delegated Regulation on SCA and CSC refers to the optionality of using biometric systems as part of the SCA requirement.

In 2016, Visa published a research report on consumer readiness for applying biometric systems as part of the SCA requirement.[73] This report shows that consumers are as comfortable with using biometric systems as they are with using a PIN.[74] A possible explanation is that the majority of the smartphones used today are already equipped with sensors that can read biometric information. For example, most smartphones are unlocked using fingerprint recognition. Also, with the increasing popularity of using smartphones as a payment instrument, applying biometric systems for authentication purposes has gained popularity. Biometrics hold the promise of being both fast and safe. Furthermore, PSUs are always in possession of their own biometric data, which makes it easy for them to use. As a result, we observe an increased use of biometric systems as part of the customer authentication process for Payment products.[75]

When using biometrics as part of the authentication process, two different phases can be distinguished, which are called the enrolment phase and the verification phase.

Enrolment Phase:

Before a PSP can use a biometric system for authentication purposes, the PSP must first prepare a biometric template for each of its customers. During the enrolment phase, the PSU presents its biometric data (e.g., fingerprint) to the PSP on the basis of which the PSP will select a number

[72] See Article 29 Data Protection Working Party (2007, p. 8).

[73] See Visa (2016).

[74] Ibid., pp. 3–4.

[75] Payment products that apply a biometric system as part of the SCA procedure include Apple Pay, Samsung Pay and Selfie Pay.

of biometric characteristics that will be stored in the PSU's biometric template. To address data privacy requirements, the biometric characteristics stored in the biometric templates should not enable the PSP to restore the original biometric data that was presented to the PSP during the enrolment phase.[76]

Verification Phase:

If a payer presents his biometric data for the purposes of authenticating a Payment, the PSP compares the biometric data obtained during the verification phase with the biometric parameters stored in the payer's biometric template.[77] In practice, it is not possible to have a 100% match with the biometric template.[78] A situation where a PSP's system often selects different biometric parameters is when using fingerprint recognition. In practice, a payer tends to hold his finger in a slightly different angle each time he uses the fingerprint sensor. As a result, different biometric data is collected during the verification phase and the enrolment phase. To counter this discrepancy, PSPs have to strike a balance between an acceptable false acceptance rate and an acceptable false rejection rate.[79] The false acceptance rate reflects the possibility of an incorrect positive authentication as a result of the biometric system incorrectly identifying an imposter as being one of the PSP's clients.[80] When PSPs use a biometric system as part of the SCA requirement, **Article 8(1) Delegated Regulation on SCA and CSC** requires there to be a very low probability that an imposter can be authenticated as the payer. Ideally, the false acceptance rate should be zero, meaning that no imposter can obtain a positive authentication. However, applying a lower false acceptance rate requires that the PSP's biometric templates contain more parameters. This increases the probability that the biometric system produces a false rejection for a PSU that should obtain a positive authentication.[81] The indicator for this probability is called the false rejection rate.

[76] It is important to emphasize that biometric data obtained during the enrolment phase can constitute sensitive personal data, such as data concerning the customer's health. Additional data privacy requirements apply in such case.

[77] See Jans, J. A., and Van den Ende, L. J. J. (2017, p. 205).

[78] Ibid.

[79] Ibid.

[80] See Article 29 Data Protection Working Party (2012, p. 6).

[81] Ibid.

Because of the trade-off between the false acceptance and rejection rates, PSPs have to strike a balance to ensure that they apply an acceptable composition of these two rates. A potential solution to this trade-off is the use of multiple biometric templates for each individual PSU. PSPs can, for example, use a dynamic biometric system in addition to a static biometric system. Apart from the fact that combining multiple systems improves the PSP's false acceptance and rejection ratio, the reliability of dynamic biometric systems can also be enhanced over time because PSPs can update these templates on a continuous basis by including new information gathered during the authentication phase.[82]

Although the potential of applying biometric systems as part of SCA looks very promising, there are certain security-related concerns that PSPs have to take into account when considering using such systems. As regards the use of static biometrics, the main concern revolves around the reversibility issue in case biometric data is compromised. If for example, an imposter obtains a copy of a PSU's fingerprint, it is no longer safe for that payer to use his fingerprint for authentication purposes going forward.[83] With regard to dynamic biometric systems, the main concern revolves around their verification accuracy.[84] Current technology appears to be not yet sufficiently developed to guarantee a low probability of an unauthorised person being authenticated as the payer.[85] Because having a low false acceptance rate is essential when applying biometrics as part of the SCA requirement, it is not recommended to use dynamic biometric systems for SCA purposes at this moment. Nevertheless, dynamic biometric systems can provide a useful tool to assess the level of risk relating to the authentication of Payments. Profiling clients using dynamic biometric system provides an additional layer of security that can run in the background during the authentication process without interfering with the PSU's experience.[86] This may provide an useful tool in case a PSP wants to rely on the exemption to apply SCA when there is a low risk of payment fraud (**Paragraph 5.4.2.2**). When using a dynamic system, the PSP can for example investigate whether a person conducting SCA shows signs of

[82] See Jans, J. A., and Van den Ende, L. J. J. (2017, p. 206).

[83] Ibid., p. 208.

[84] See Li, Y. et al. (2017, p. 1).

[85] See Jans, J. A., and Van den Ende, L. J. J. (2017, p. 206).

[86] Ibid., p. 207.

abnormal behaviour. In case of abnormal behaviour, the PSP must then immediately request that person to authenticate the transaction on the basis of SCA.

5.4.6 *Apple Pay and SCA*

Apple offers Apple Pay in its capacity as a technical service provider (**Paragraph 4.4.2**). As such, Apple is not licensed as a PSP and does not provide payment services within the meaning of PSD2. The Banks that offer their debit and/or credit cards via the E-wallet of Apple Pay are responsible for the verification of the Payments initiated with their cards and the transfer of the corresponding funds. However, customer authentication takes place within the Apple interface instead of within the interface of the relevant Bank that issued the debit or credit card. In other words, it is Apple who identifies the payer and it is the Bank (acting as card issuer) who verifies the validity of the payment instrument and whether the payer has sufficient balance to initiate the Payment. Therefore, the question arises as to whether the customer authentication procedure conducted by Apple constitutes outsourcing of a part of the SCA requirement by Banks. If this is indeed the case, how Banks must ensure adequate oversight regarding the performance of these outsourced functions? Since there is no contractual relationship between the PSP and the smartphone manufacturer when the smartphone is used for applying SCA and the control of part of the SCA process is with the smartphone manufacturer, this structure gives rise to regulatory concerns as PSPs do not apply any controls or checks on the security measures and their compliance with the requirements of PSD2 and the Delegated Regulation on SCA and CSC.[87] To address these concerns, the PSR Proposal suggests that technical service providers which verify elements of SCA will be subject to: (i) liability for failure to support the application of SCA (**Article 58 PSR Proposal**) and (ii) the requirement to enter into an outsourcing agreement with the PSP regarding its involvement in the SCA process (**Article 87 PSR Proposal**).

[87] See EBA (2022, p. 74).

5.5 Safeguarding Security of Payments

5.5.1 Processing of Sensitive Payment Data

As part of their risk management policy, PSPs have to describe how they store, process and transmit sensitive payment data. **Article 4(32) PSD2** defines sensitive payment data as all data that can be used to carry out fraud. Sensitive payment data includes amongst others information that is used by PSPs to identify and authenticate PSUs. Such information includes *inter alia* the IBAN, log-in name, password, phone number, PIN and e-mail address. The EBA considered it inappropriate to provide detailed guidance as to what type of information constitutes sensitive payment data since it can involve different information for different Payment products.[88] The downside however is that by not providing further guidance, PSPs and NCAs may apply different interpretations as to which information constitutes sensitive payment data.

When a PSU commences the authentication process, **Article 22 Delegated Regulation on SCA and CSC** stipulates that the PSU's PSP must ensure the confidentiality and integrity of the personalised security credentials provided by the PSU during that process to limit the risk of phishing and other fraudulent activities. The PSU must be able to rely on the PSP's procedures for protecting the confidentiality and integrity of its personalised security credentials. For this reason, the PSP's authentication system must ensure that, amongst others, the PSU's password is not visible when it enters its password during the authentication phase.

5.5.2 Tokenisation as a Tool for Protecting Sensitive Payment Data

It is important to emphasise that merchants also have a responsibility when processing sensitive payment data. In the event merchants store sensitive payment data when accepting Payments, the acquirer should contractually require the merchant to have the necessary measures in place to guarantee the confidentiality of such data. The acquirer will have to carry out regular checks to verify whether the merchants have indeed implemented these measures. In case an acquirer notices that a merchant does not have the required security measures in place, the acquirer must

[88] See EBA (2016, pp. 15–16).

either enforce this contractual obligation or terminate its contract with the merchant.

With regard to card payments, tokenisation provides merchants with a practical tool to ensure the security of the communication channel for Payments from the moment the payment is authorised until the moment sensitive payment data is transferred to the acquirer. Tokenisation offers additional security because it replaces sensitive payment data, such as the primary payment account number (IBAN), with a random number called the token.[89] The token is used in the merchant's IT environment instead of the payer's card number. One can use a separate token for each transaction (transaction-based tokens) or a so-called 'card-based' token, which represents a particular card for each transaction initiated with that card. A key characteristic of tokenisation is that imposters cannot obtain the original card number if they intercept the token.[90] The sensitive payment data which is replaced by the token is stored with a third party called the vault. When a Payment is initiated at the POS, the merchant's payment terminal sends the token to the vault, which returns the credit card number. This process is known as detokenisation. The transaction information, including the real card number, is then sent to the acquirer. Detokenisation also takes place if the holder of a credit card initiates a chargeback. In case of a chargeback, the merchant also contacts the vault for the relevant card number since the vault is the only place where the token can be exchanged for the real card number.[91] In general, tokenisation reduces the risk exposures of merchants because merchants are no longer in the possession of sensitive payment data. As a result, tokenisation minimises the compliance burden for merchants.

5.5.3 Secure Communication Between PSPs

Another important security requirement for PSPs is the obligation to use safe and secure means for communicating with other PSPs. When exchanging sensitive payment data via the internet, PSPs must ensure that secure end-to-end encryption is applied to guarantee the confidentiality

[89] See Smart Card Alliance (2016, p. 12).

[90] See First Data (2011, p. 6).

[91] Ibid., p. 9.

and integrity of the data transmitted. With end-to-end encryption, the payment data is encrypted when sent between PSPs.

One of the challenges Banks face when transmitting data to other PSPs revolves around the need to have safe means for communicating with TPPs that offer payment initiation or account information services. By allowing TPPs access to the Banks' IT systems, it has become more difficult for Banks to protect their IT applications with firewalls, leaving them vulnerable to cyberattacks such as DDoS or malware attacks. For this very reason, it is essential that the fraud prevention measures of Banks and TPPs are aligned.[92]

5.5.4 *Screen Scraping*

Under the PSD regime, a main concern for Banks was the use of screen scraping by third-party service providers for accessing the payment accounts of the Banks' customers. Account information and payment initiation services did not qualify as a payment service under PSD and could therefore be provided by non-licensed service providers. At that time, there was no legal provision on the basis of which these service providers could claim payment account access with Banks. In practice, these service providers obtained payment account access by relying on the security credentials of the PSU. This process is known as screen scraping and works as follows. A PSU provides a third party with the security credentials of its payment account. The third party then impersonates that PSU when undergoing the Bank's authentication process. The Bank cannot see that it is a third party accessing its online banking environment on behalf of a PSU.

The banking sector strongly opposed the concept of PSUs sharing security credentials with third parties because it exposes the Banks to a variety of risks.[93] One can even argue that with screen scraping, the safety levels of the Bank's IT-infrastructure are dependent on the safety levels set by the third party gaining access to the Bank's IT-infrastructure. Other main concerns that were raised by the banking sector regarding screen scraping related to: (i) the privacy of client data; and (ii) the allocation of

[92] Although PSD2 allows AS-PSPs to block TPP access in case of fraud, this safeguard only limits the damages caused by payment fraud. It does not enable AS-PSPs to prevent payment fraud.

[93] See EBF (2017).

liability between Banks, third parties and PSUs when screen scraping is applied.

5.5.4.1 Privacy of Client Data

Screen scraping results in third parties having access to the same level of payment account information as the PSU. Screen scraping allows third parties access to, for example, a PSU's salary and online spending behaviour. Such non-payment-related data is often sold to third parties and used to profile financial behaviour.

5.5.4.2 Allocation of Liability

Furthermore, Banks raised concerns regarding the allocation of liability between Banks, third parties and PSUs in case of an unauthorised or erroneous Payment when screen scraping is applied. Under the PSD regime, it was not clear who was to be held responsible in case anything went wrong with a Payment that was initiated using screen scraping. Although PSUs were not allowed to share their security credentials with third parties (suggesting that the PSU is liable in case anything goes wrong when applying screen scraping), it is the Bank that has the primary responsibility of restoring the payment account in case of an unauthorised or erroneous Payment.

One of the objectives of PSD2 was to provide clear rules on the division of responsibilities between TPPs and Banks with regard to the processing of personalised security credentials. According to **Article 22(1) Delegated Regulation on SCA and CSC**, the Bank has a legal obligation to safeguard the confidentiality and integrity of the personalised security credentials of its PSUs. Therefore, allowing its clients to share such information with a TPP would contradict PSD2's objective of enhancing the security for Payments. This was also noticed by the banking sector, who recommended that TPPs should not have direct access to the personalised security credentials of the PSU.[94] **Article 66(3)(e) PSD2** clearly states that a PISP is not allowed to store sensitive payment data of the PSU. Furthermore, **Article 67(2)(e) PSD2** prohibits an AIS-PSP from requesting a PSU to provide sensitive payment data relating to the payment accounts. With these restrictions, PSD2 effectively ended the practice of screen scraping.

[94] See EBA Banking Stakeholder Group (2016, p. 2).

5.5.5 *Unavailability of the Dedicated Interface*

To account for the security risks associated with the introduction of open banking Payment solutions, PSD2 imposed new rules for the sharing of sensitive payment data. According to **Article 30 Delegated Regulation on SCA and CSC**, Banks must have at least one dedicated interface that TPPs can use to access their IT-infrastructure. Banks can use so-called APIs for this purpose. An API is an interface that enables communication between software applications and the exchange of data without human intervention.[95] APIs are a set of requirements defining how software applications can interact with each other.[96] A so-called 'open' API makes the data available to everyone who meets the access requirements set by the Bank. For this reason, the TPP requesting access will have to comply with security standards imposed by the Bank. When applying open API's, Banks remain in control of their IT-infrastructure.

Article 32 Delegated Regulation on SCA and CSC stipulates that if a Bank makes available a dedicated interface for payment account access by a TPP, it is essential that such interface provides the same level of availability and performance as the interface that the Bank offers its own customers. If the dedicated interface for TPPs would not have the same availability or performance, TPPs cannot provide their customers the same processing time limits as Banks, which makes it impossible for them to compete with Banks on an equal footing.[97] The Delegated Regulation on SCA and CSC, therefore, obliges Banks to have a fall-back scenario, which enables TPPs to access payment accounts using the customer-facing interface if the dedicated interface does not meet the required performance levels. According to **Article 33 Delegated Regulation on SCA and CSC**, such customer-facing interface must for example be available in case a TPP is not able to use the dedicated interface for at least 30 seconds.

Notwithstanding the Commission's objective to enable TPPs to obtain a competitive position vis-à-vis Banks, imposing a requirement for Banks to have a customer interface available for TPPs may not be the way

[95] See FSB (2019, p. 6).

[96] See Euro Banking Association (2016, p. 7).

[97] Since one of the main objectives of PSD2 is to foster TPP payment account access, Recital 93 PSD2 states for example that AS-PSPs are not allowed to determine that a TPP should apply a particular business model for obtaining payment account access.

to go. In its opinion on the Commission's proposal, the EBA strongly opposed the obligation for Banks to make available such a fall-back option.[98] According to the EBA, introducing this fall-back option has several adverse effects. First, the EBA was not convinced of the necessity for Banks to develop a separate customer-facing interface for TPPs. Since screen scraping is no longer allowed under PSD2, TPPs have to be able to identify themselves when using a Bank's customer-facing interface. As a result, Banks have to amend their customer-facing interface to enable both PSUs and TPPs to identify themselves using the interface. Having three interfaces available in parallel (one for the PSU and two for the TPP) would create a disproportionate burden for Banks. Second and more importantly, the EBA questioned whether such fall-back scenario improves the reliability of the communication interface for TPPs. The customer-facing interface operating under the fall-back scenario will likely use the same technological infrastructure as the dedicated interface. Consequently, the unavailability of the dedicated interface will in most cases also imply the unavailability of the fall-back option. A better approach would be to oblige Banks to be transparent about the performance levels of their dedicated interfaces. Not meeting predefined performance levels should be made subject to fines, which in itself provides Banks with a strong incentive to meet the predefined performance levels for TPP access. In **Article 35(2) PSR Proposal**, the Commission suggests that Banks must have in place at least one dedicated interface for data exchange with TPPs and will no longer be required to maintain another interface as fall-back.[99] In general, **Article 44(1) PSR Proposal** requires Banks to ensure that their dedicated interface does not create obstacles to the provision of payment initiation or account information services. **Article 36(1) PSR Proposal** stipulates that the dedicated interface for TPPs will have to meet the following security and performance requirements: (i) it must maintain communication sessions between the AS-PSP, TPP and PSU throughout the authentication of the PSU; (ii) it must ensure the integrity and confidentiality of the personalised security credentials and authentication codes transmitted by a PSP; and (iii) the response time of the dedicated interface for TPPs cannot be longer than the response time for the PSU interface. According to **Article**

[98] See EBA (2017, p. 8).

[99] See Commission (2023).

38(1) PSR Proposal, the dedicated interface is considered to be unavailable in case of five consecutive requests for access without any response from the dedicated interface within 30 seconds. During such a period of unavailability, the AS-PSP must allow TPPs access to the PSU interface. To ensure interoperability of these APIs, **Article 35(3) PSR Proposal** requires the dedicated interface to apply standards developed by standardisation organisations such as the ISO. Furthermore, it is proposed in **Article 35(5) PSR Proposal** that Banks must publish on their website quarterly statistics on the availability and performance of their dedicated interface.

5.5.6 Security-Related Rights and Obligations for Card-Based Payments

Further to the security requirements that apply to PSPs and merchants, PSUs also have to abide by certain rules to enhance the safety of the Payment ecosystem. To this end, specific security-related rights and obligations are typically included in the framework contract entered into between the PSP and the PSU.

An important obligation for PSUs is to use their payment instrument in accordance with the terms and conditions of the framework contract.[100] In addition, **Article 69(2) PSD2** requires PSUs to take all reasonable steps to keep the personalised security features of their payment instrument safe. Furthermore, **Article 69(1)(b) PSD2** stipulates that PSUs must notify their PSP without undue delay in case they lose their payment instrument or if there has been misappropriation or unauthorised use of such instrument. To enable PSPs to take immediate action in case a PSU loses its payment instrument or a payment instrument gets stolen, PSPs have to offer PSUs the opportunity to notify their PSP immediately thereof. After such notification has been made to the PSP, the PSP must immediately block the payment instrument in order to minimise financial damages.[101] If provided for in the framework contract, **Article 68(2) PSD2** also allows a PSP to block a payment instrument for other security-related reasons, for example in case of suspicion of unauthorised or fraudulent use of a payment instrument.

[100] Example, a maximum spending limit.

[101] The PSP must unblock or replace the payment instrument in case the reasons for blocking no longer exist.

In case a PSU uses a low value payment instrument[102], **Article 63(1)(a) PSD2** allows the PSP to agree with the PSU that certain PSD2 obligations do not apply if this instrument cannot be blocked. The obligations that the PSP can choose not to apply are: (i) the obligation of the PSU to immediately notify its PSP of loss, theft, misappropriation or unauthorised use of the card; (ii) the obligation of the PSP to enable the PSU to make such notification at all times and to prevent that the card can be used after such notification has been made; (iii) the obligation that the PSU shall not bear any financial consequences resulting from the use of the lost or stolen card after notifying its PSP[103] and (iv) the obligation that the PSU shall not be liable for the financial consequences resulting from using that card if the PSP has not provided means for making a notification of a lost or stolen card.[104]

With regard to cards that can be used anonymously[105] and in situations where a PSP cannot prove that a Payment was authorised, **Article 63(1)(b) PSD2** stipulates that the following obligations do not apply: (i) the obligation for the PSP to prove that a Payment was authenticated, accurately recorded and not affected by a technical breakdown or other deficiency in case the payer denies having authorised an executed Payment or claims that the Payment was not correctly executed; (ii) the obligation for the payer's PSP to refund the amount of an unauthorised Payment; (iii) the liability of the payer up to a maximum of €150, resulting from the use of a lost or stolen payment instrument or, if the payer has failed to keep the personalised security features safe, from the misappropriation of a payment instrument; and (iv) the liability of the payer to bear all losses relating to any unauthorised Payments if he incurred them by acting fraudulently or by failing to fulfil one or more of his obligations with intent or gross negligence.

[102] Low value payment instruments allow for the execution of individual transactions: (i) not exceeding €30; or (ii) which either have a spending limit of €150 or store funds which do not exceed €150 at any time. In **Article 10 PSR Proposal** it is suggested that low value payment instruments allow for the execution of individual transactions: (i) not exceeding €50; or (ii) which either have a spending limit of €200 or store funds which do not exceed €200 at any time.

[103] Except where the payer has acted fraudulently.

[104] Except where the payer has acted fraudulently.

[105] An example of anonymous use of a card is when a payer initiates a contactless Payments using the NFC functionality.

5.5.7 Migration to EMV Technology for Card-Initiated Payments

Before 2010, debit cards and credit cards used to be equipped with a magnetic stripe that transmitted static card security codes for authentication purposes. When using such a card, the cardholder entered his PIN which verified him as the authorised cardholder. Subsequently, the merchant's payment terminal sent the PIN in encrypted form, applying static data authentication, to the payer's PSP.

To enhance the security of card-based Payments in the EU, Europay, Mastercard and Visa jointly developed the EMV chip, which replaced the magnetic stripe in 2010.[106] EMV technology applies a dynamic data element in each card payment.[107] When dynamic data authentication is applied, a unique transaction code is encrypted on the card to create a digital signature.[108] This signature is then decrypted at the merchant's POS terminal to verify the authenticity of the card. Depending on the payment brand, such element is also known as the Card Verification Value or the Card ID. EMV furthermore improves the security of card Payments by means of its advanced microprocessor chip, which stores information in a safe and secure manner and performs cryptographic processing.[109] EMV technology can be used for cards that require physical contact with a POS terminal and for cards that can be used for making contactless Payments. Although contactless Payments do not require the cardholder to enter his PIN for authorising the Payment, cards used for these Payments are more secure than conventional cards with magnetic strips since cards using EMV technology are relatively difficult to counterfeit.[110]

Research reports of the ECB show that the levels of card fraud at both ATMs and POS have decreased considerably in the SEPA countries as a result of the migration to the EMV chip.[111] This technology appears to be especially effective against card skimming,[112] which was a

[106] PSPs in the EU migrated to EMV standards in 2010.

[107] Smart Card Alliance (2014, p. 6).

[108] Ibid., p. 4.

[109] See EMV Connection.

[110] See Sullivan, R. (2010, p. 117).

[111] See ECB (n.d.).

[112] See Smart Card Alliance (2015, p. 4).

common method for conducting payment fraud with payment cards that used magnetic strip technology.

5.6 Monitoring and Reporting of Security Incidents

Article 96 PSD2 obliges PSPs to have effective incident management procedures that enable them to prevent, detect and report major operational and security incidents. The incident management and reporting policy of a PSP must describe in detail how its responsibilities regarding the monitoring and reporting of security incidents are allocated between its business lines. With the EBA report on the revised guidelines on major incident reporting under PSD2 (**'EBA Major Incident Reporting Guidelines'**),[113] the EBA has provided further guidance as to how PSPs must implement this requirement.[114]

Carrying out proper transaction monitoring reduces the possibility of the occurrence of a risk event. One of the main implications that PSPs faced when implementing an internal system for monitoring security incidents under the PSD2 regime was that PSPs had to develop new IT systems to meet these requirements. The EBA recognised this could be too burdensome for, in particular, smaller Non-Banks that already provided payment services prior to the implementation of PSD2. The EBA therefore designed the EBA Major Incident Reporting Guidelines in such a manner that it focusses on the materiality of security incidents rather than the size of the PSP that has to implement the policy. This allows PSPs to tailor their incident policy to the size and complexity of their business. Furthermore, the EBA Major Incident Reporting Guidelines allow PSPs to outsource the reporting obligation regarding incidents to third parties established in the EU. One must bear in mind however that the responsibility to report is not something that can be outsourced.

5.6.1 What Are Major Security Incidents?

The EBA Major Incident Reporting Guidelines define an 'operational or security incident' as a: '*singular event or a series of linked events*

[113] See EBA (2021).

[114] See EBA (2021, p. 26).

unplanned by the PSP which has or will likely have an adverse impact on the integrity, availability, confidentiality and/or authenticity of payment related services'.[115] Operational or security incidents cover situations where *inter alia*: (i) a PSP becomes the victim of a cyberattack; or (ii) the dedicated interface made available for TPP payment account access does not meet the required performance levels. According to **Article 95(1) PSD2**, it is the responsibility of the PSP to determine whether a particular operational or security incident classifies as a 'major' operational or security incident.

The EBA Major Incident Reporting Guidelines provide for quantitative and qualitative criteria that PSPs must apply when determining if a particular incident constitutes a major security incident.[116] By providing such criteria, the EBA aims to create harmonised European standards for the identification of major security incidents.

5.6.2 *The Reporting of a Major Security Incident*

In case a PSP encounters an incident that classifies as a major operational or security incident, the PSP must notify the NCA thereof.[117] Within four hours after the moment the PSP qualifies an incident as a major operational or security incident, the PSP must submit an initial report to the NCA which includes a generic description of the event and its (likely) impact.[118] By obliging PSPs to report incidents on such short notice, the potential damage that may be caused by the incident, such as a substantial

[115] Payment-related services within the meaning of the EBA Major Incident Reporting Guidelines include all payment services regulated under the PSD2 regime and all necessary technical supporting tasks for the correct provision of these services.

[116] The quantitative criteria are: (i) the number of Payments affected; (ii) number of PSUs affected; (iii) whether the incident has compromised the security of network or information systems related to the provision of payment services; (iv) the period of time during which the service was unavailable to PSUs; (v) the monetary impact of the incident. The qualitative criteria include: (i) whether the incident has been or will be reported to the executive management of the PSP; (ii) whether other PSPs or relevant infrastructures were affected; and (iii) the reputational impact of the incident.

[117] An incident does not have to occur in the EU to be eligible for reporting. Incidents that occur outside the EU but affect payment services provided by a PSP in the EU also qualify as incidents that must be reported by such PSP under PSD2.

[118] See EBA (2021, p. 22).

disruption of a payment system, remains limited.[119] Whenever the PSP obtains new relevant information regarding the reported incident, it must submit an intermediate report to the NCA.[120] Ultimately 20 business days after business is deemed to be back to normal, the PSP must file a final report with a detailed description of the incident and the steps that were taken to resolve the situation.[121]

Further to the obligation for PSPs to report major incidents to the NCA, PSPs also have to submit, at least on an annual basis, statistical data on payment fraud to the NCA.[122] In case a major incident affects the financial interests of the PSP's customers, **Article 96(1) PSD2** requires the PSP to also inform its customers about the incident and the measures taken to mitigate its impact.

5.7 Conclusion

Payment solutions provide the most commonly used method for making payments in Europe. In order to ensure that the market continues to use Payment solutions at a large scale, it is essential that all stakeholders in the Payment chain maintain their confidence in the safety and reliability of the processing of Payments. To this end, PSD2 and DORA provide security requirements by which all PSPs have to abide.

PSPs are, amongst others, legally obliged to have a security policy that describes which measures and procedures they have in place to guarantee the safety and reliability of their involvement in the Payment chain. An important security-related measure that PSPs must implement is the obligation to conduct SCA each time a PSU accesses its payment account environment or initiates a Payment.

The market for Payments is a fast-changing market in which technological innovation is a driving factor. In order not to restrict innovation, the European legislature considered that the PSD2 security requirements had to be principle based rather than rule based. Having principle-based requirements gives PSPs flexibility to determine how they can

[119] PSD2, Recital 91.

[120] See EBA (2021, p. 23).

[121] Ibid.

[122] For this reason, the EBA published on 2 August 2017 Draft Guidelines on fraud reporting requirements for PSPs. These guidelines set out the: (i) methodology for reporting; (ii) reporting frequency; and (iii) reporting deadlines.

best comply with the requirements in the context of the continuously changing technological environment. Although principle-based requirements enable PSPs to swiftly adapt their security framework whenever needed, there are also certain adverse effects of principle-based security requirements that should not be neglected. Most importantly, principle-based requirements contradict the European legislature's objective of maximum harmonisation of the PSD2 security requirements in the EU. Since principle-based requirements allow for different interpretations, PSPs offering similar payment services and having similar risk profiles may adopt very different risk procedures. One can argue that such differences could have an adverse impact on the competitive position of PSPs that have more stringent security measures.

The introduction of open banking Payment solutions has increased the complexity for Banks to guarantee the safety of the customer authentication process. For this reason, PSD2 requires that TPPs are able to identify themselves when using a Bank's customer-facing interface. As a consequence, Banks were required to amend their customer-facing interface to enable both PSUs and TPPs to identify themselves using the interface. However, having three interfaces available in parallel (one for the PSU and two for the TPP) creates a disproportionate cost burden for Banks and therefore has a negative impact on the competitive position of Banks *vis-à-vis* Non-Banks. It is therefore suggested in the PSR Proposal that Banks must have in place one dedicated interface and will no longer be required to maintain a fall-back interface.

Moreover, the PSD2 SCA requirement poses challenges to Banks with regard to BigTechs offering Payment-related services as a technical service provider. BigTechs that offer Payment-related services as a technical service provider, such as Apple with the Apple Pay solution, are not licensed as a PSP. In the case of Apple Pay, customer authentication takes place within the IT environment of Apple instead of the Bank that has issued the card that is used via Apple Pay. As a result, the Bank does not have full control over the SCA process regarding the cards that are used via Apple Pay. To address these challenges, the PSR Proposal requires technical service providers that verify elements of SCA to enter into an outsourcing agreement with the PSP regarding their involvement in the SCA process.

Secondary Sources

Article 29 Data Protection Working Party. (2007). *Opinion 4/2007 on the Concept of Personal Data*, 01248/07/EN WP 136, p. 8.

Article 29 Data Protection Working Party. (2012). *Opinion 3/2012 on the Developments in Biometric Technologies*, 00720/12/EN WP 193, p. 6.

Bijlsma, M. J., & Van Veldhuizen, S. (2019). De virtuele bank als onderneming. *Ondernemingsrecht, 10*, p. 7.

Commission. (1998). *Communication from the Commission to the European Parliament, the Council, the European Central Bank and the Economic and Social Committee—A framework for action on combatting fraud and counterfeiting of non-cash means of payment*, COM (1998) 395 final, p. 1.

Commission. (2004). *Communication from the Commission to the Council, the European Parliament, the European and Social Committee, the European Central Bank and Europol—A New EU Action Plan 2004–2007 to Prevent Fraud on Non-cash Means of Payment*, COM (2004) 679 final, pp. 2, 10.

Commission. (2008). *Financial Services: Payment Security Is Key to Improving Consumer Confidence in New Payment Services, Says Commission report*, Press release IP/08/653, 28 April.

Commission. (2020). *Proposal for a Regulation of the European Parliament and of the Council on Digital Operational Resilience for the Financial Sector and Amending Regulations (EC) No 1060/2009, (EU) No 648/2012, (EU) No 600/2014 and (EU) No 909/2014*, COM(2020) 595 final.

Commission. (2023). *Proposal for a Regulation of the European Parliament and of the Council on Payment Services in the Internal Market and Amending (...)*, COM/2023/367 final.

EBA Banking Stakeholder Group. (2016). *Draft BSG Response to EBA/DP/2015/03 on Future Draft Regulatory Technical Standards on Strong Customer Authentication and Secure Communication Under the Revised Payment Services Directive (PSD2)*, p. 2.

EBA. (2014). *Final Guidelines on the Security of Internet Payments*, EBA/GL/2014/12_Rev1, p. 3.

EBA. (2016): *Consultation Paper on the Draft Regulatory Technical Standards Specifying the Requirements on Strong Customer Authentication and Common and Secure Communication Under PSD2*, EBA-CP-2016–11, pp. 15–16.

EBA. (2017). *Opinion of the European Banking Authority on the European Commission's Intention to Partially Endorse and Amend the EBA's Final Draft Regulatory Technical Standards on Strong Customer Authentication and Common and Secure Communication Under PSD2*, EBA/Op/2017/09, pp. 6, 8.

EBA. (2018). *Guidelines on the Security Measures for Operational and Security Risks of Payment Services Under Directive (EU) 2015/2366 (PSD2)*, EBA/GL/2017/17.

EBA. (2019a). *Final Report on the EBA Guidelines on Outsourcing Arrangements*, EBA/GL/2019/02, p. 6.

EBA. (2019b). *Opinion of the European Banking Authority on the Elements of Strong Customer Authentication Under PSD2*, EBA-Op-2019-06, pp. 5, 6, 8.

EBA. (2019c). *Final Report—EBA Guidelines on ICT and Security Risk Management*, EBA/GL/2019/04, p. 3.

EBA. (2021). *Final Report on the Revised Guidelines on Major Incident Reporting Under PSD2*, EBA/GL/2021/03, pp. 22, 23, 26.

EBA. (2022). *EBA Response to the Commission Call for Advice on the Review of the Payment Services Directive*, EBA/REP/2022/14, p. 74.

EBA. (n.d.a). *Single Rule Book Q&A*. https://eba.europa.eu/single-rule-book-qa/-/qna/view/publicId/2018_4039. Accessed April 13, 2024.

EBA. (n.d.b). *EBA Clarifies Application of Strong Customer Authentication Requirements to Digital Wallets*. https://www.eba.europa.eu/eba-clarifies-application-strong-customer-authentication-requirements-digital-wallets. Accessed April 13, 2024.

EBF. (2017). *EBF Asks Commission to Support Ban on Screen Scraping*, EBF_0271732.

ECB. (2013). *Recommendations for the Security of Internet Payments: Final Version After Public Consultation*, pp. 1, 2, 5, 9.

ECB. (2014). *ECB and EBA Step Up Cooperation to Make Retail Payments Safer*, Press release.

ECB. (2015). *Fourth Report on Card Fraud*, p. 3.

ECB. (n.d.). *ECB Card Fraud Report*. https://www.ecb.europa.eu/pub/cardfraud/html/ecb.cardfraudreport202110~cac4c418e8.en.html. Accessed April 13, 2024.

EMV Connection. (2015). *EMV FAQ*. https://www.emv-connection.com/wp-content/uploads/2012/06/EMV-FAQ-update-April-2015.pdf. Accessed April 13, 2024.

EPC. (2019). *2019 Payment Threats and Fraud Trends Report*, EPC302-19, Version 1.0, pp. 18, 52.

ESAs Joint Committee. (2019). *Joint Advice of the European Supervisory Authorities to the European Commission on the Need for Legislative Improvements Relating to ICT Risk Management Requirements in the EU Financial Sector*, JC 2019 26, pp. 3, 8.

Euro Banking Association. (2016). *Understanding the Business Relevance of Open APIs and Open Banking for Banks: Information Paper*, Version 1.0, p. 7.

First Data. (2011). *A Primer on Payment Security Technologies: Encryption and Tokenization* (A First Data White Paper, pp. 6, 9).

FSB. (2019). *FinTech and Market Structure in Financial Services: Market Developments and Potential Financial Stability Implications*, p. 6.

Jadhav, V., et al. (2015). Proposed E-payment System using Biometrics. *International Journal of Computer Science and Information Technologies, 6*(6), p. 4957.

Jans, J. A., & Van den Ende, L. J. J. (2017). *Statische- en dynamische biometrie als onderdeel van sterke cliëntauthenticatie onder PSD2. Tijdschrift voor Financieel Recht*, 5, pp. 205–208.

Li, Y., et al. (2017). *SegAuth: A Segment-based Approach to Behavioral Biometric Authentication*, 2016 IEEE Conference on Communications and Network Security (CNS), p. 1.

Smart Card Alliance. (2014). *Technologies for Payment Fraud Prevention: EMV, Encryption and Tokenization* (White Paper PC-14002, pp. 4, 6).

Smart Card Alliance. (2015). *EMV and NFC: Complementary Technologies Enabling Secure Contactless Payments* (White Paper PC-15002, p. 4).

Smart Card Alliance. (2016). *Contactless EMV Payments: Benefits for Consumers, Merchants and Issuers* (White Paper PC-16001, p. 12).

Sullivan, R. (2010). *The Changing Nature of U.S. Card Payment Fraud: Industry and Public Policy Options*, Federal Reserve Bank of Kansas City Economic Review, Second Quarter, pp. 103, 117.

Visa. (2016). *Visa Biometric Authentication Study*, Research Findings, pp. 3–4.

CHAPTER 6

Anti-Money Laundering and the Allocation of Responsibilities Between Banks and Non-Banks

6.1 Money Laundering and the Financing of Terrorism

In their capacity as gatekeepers of the financial markets, PSPs have a responsibility to take adequate measures to prevent them from being used for laundering money or financing terrorism. Money laundering is a process whereby criminal proceeds are processed to conceal their illegitimate origin.[1] Money laundering involves the transformation of funds with an illegitimate origin into funds that appear to have a legitimate origin.[2] With terrorist financing, the financial system is used to fund a terrorist organisation or a specific terrorist operation.[3] The risks associated with money laundering and terrorist financing differ from other integrity risks to which PSPs are exposed, such as payment fraud (**Paragraph 5.2**), in the sense that a transaction executed for ML/TF purposes appears to be a legitimate transaction. Moreover, ML/TF transactions are, unlike fraudulent payments, in most cases without any direct loss for the PSP(s) or

[1] See Huang, L. (2015, p. 18).

[2] Ibid.

[3] See FATF (2008, p. 7).

J. A. Jans, *Electronic Payments in the European Market*, EBI Studies in Banking and Capital Markets Law,
https://doi.org/10.1007/978-3-031-64338-5_6

PSU(s) involved.[4] In case of payment fraud, the payer's PSP or beneficiary's PSP must redeem the corresponding funds to the payer or beneficiary because such transaction qualifies as an unauthorised transaction within the meaning of PSD2 (**Paragraph 7.2**). Since the costs of redeeming unauthorised transactions can be substantial if a PSP is facing a large number of claims, PSPs have a strong incentive to implement adequate measures to prevent unauthorised transactions from being processed. Such incentive does however not exist, at least directly, in relation to a PSP's exposure to ML/TF risks. ML/TF transactions can be processed by a PSP without the PSP being exposed to the risk that a payer or beneficiary claims a refund. The costs arising from ML/TF activities are borne by society at large rather than by individual PSPs or PSUs. This does however not mean that a PSP's involvement in the processing of ML/TF transactions is without any consequences for the PSP in question. There can be severe adverse effects for PSPs if they fail to take adequate AML/CTF measures. One of these adverse effects is an increased regulatory risk exposure, which involves the risk of a PSP being sanctioned by an NCA for not meeting its AML/CTF requirements. Furthermore, failing to meet AML/CTF requirements is likely to cause reputational damage for the PSP involved. This is true for both Banks and Non-Banks, albeit that the reputation of Banks may be further damaged in case of any wrongdoing by a TPP accessing their IT systems. PSPs can reduce their exposure to regulatory and reputational risks by investing in sophisticated CDD procedures, such as CDD measures based on artificial intelligence. The responsibilities that PSPs have in relation to AML/CTF must not be confused with the AML/CTF responsibilities of NCAs. PSPs are obliged to implement adequate measures to identify ML/TF attempts, prevent such attempts from succeeding and report executed transactions that have an unusual nature to the NCA. Unlike NCAs, PSPs are not responsible for the investigation and prosecution of ML/TF crimes.

Since ML/TF activities often take place in an international context, effective AML/CTF policies require an EU-wide approach. The main legislative frameworks that are currently in force are Directive 2015/849/EC on the prevention of the use of the financial system for the

[4] See Sienkiewicz, S. (2007, p. 7).

purposes of money laundering or terrorist financing (‘**MLD4**’)[5], Directive (EU) 2018/1673 on combatting money laundering by criminal law (‘**MLD6**’)[6], Regulation (EU) 2015/847 on information accompanying transfers of funds (‘**WTR2**’)[7] and the sanction regulations. These directives and regulations impose requirements on PSPs to prevent them from being used for ML/TF purposes. Moreover, these directives and regulations provide NCAs with tools to investigate and prosecute ML/TF activity. To ensure that these directives and regulations do not have an adverse effect on the level playing field between Banks and Non-Banks, it is important that AML/CTF requirements are proportionate to the size and complexity of the business of the relevant PSP. In other words, the investments that a PSP is required to make to meet its AML/CTF obligations have to be aligned with its ML/TF risk exposure. Imposing AML/CTF requirements on Non-Banks, which may be adequate for Banks but are too stringent for Non-Banks, increases the barrier for Non-Banks to enter the Payments market and adversely affects the level playing field between Banks and Non-Banks. Furthermore, imposing disproportionately cumbersome AML/CTF requirements on Non-Banks may trigger a process called ‘de-risking’. With de-risking, a PSP refuses to service prospective high risk clients to minimise the risk that it violates applicable AML/CTF regulations. Unwarranted de-risking by Banks (i.e., the offboarding of PIs and EMIs by Banks without an unacceptable ML/TF risk exposure) is a genuine concern given that it has a detrimental impact on competition between Banks and Non-Banks in the European market.[8] When PIs/EMIs lose access to payment accounts, they are generally no longer able to offer their services, which may ultimately result in business closure. Apart from the fact that de-risking is a genuine concern

[5] Directive (EU) 2015/849 of 20 May 2015 “on the prevention of the use of the financial system for the purposes of money laundering or terrorist financing, (...)”, OJ L 141, 5.6.2015, pp. 73–117.

[6] Directive (EU) 2018/1673 of 23 October 2018 “on combating money laundering by criminal law”, OJ L 284, 12.11.2018, pp. 22–30.

[7] Regulation (EU) 2015/847 of 20 May 2015 “on information accompanying transfers of funds and repealing Regulation (EC) No 1781/2006”, OJ L 141, 5.6.2015, pp. 1–18. On 20 July 2021 the Commission published a proposal for a Regulation of the European Parliament and of the Council on information accompanying transfers of funds and certain crypto assets (recast) COM(2021) 422 final (WTR3).

[8] See EBA (2022b, p. 2).

from a competition perspective, it also makes it more difficult for public authorities to identify criminal behaviour.[9]

With Directive (EU) 2018/843 on the prevention of the use of the financial system for the purposes of money laundering or terrorist financing (‘**MLD5**’),[10] which amends MLD4, the European legislature missed the opportunity to harmonise the national AML/CTF regimes in Europe. Like MLD4, MLD5 is a minimum harmonisation directive, which allows Member States to adopt requirements that are more stringent than the requirements set out in the directive. Not having a coherent AML/CTF framework in all Member States can stimulate regulatory arbitrage, which involves PSPs obtaining their licence in a Member State that imposes less onerous AML/CTF requirements than the Member State in which the PSP is primarily active (**Paragraph 4.2**). Moreover, Non-Banks that are operating on a cross-border basis are confronted with a diversity of AML/CTF requirements and provisions which makes international expansion less attractive. These shortcomings have been acknowledged by the Commission. In its Action Plan for a comprehensive EU policy on preventing money laundering and terrorist financing the Commission proposes to transfer parts[11] of MLD4 to a regulation.[12]

6.2 Money Laundering and Terrorist Financing in the European Payments Market

Although the process of laundering money can take many forms, such process generally consists of three phases referred to as the money laundering cycle. These are the placement phase, the layering phase and the integration phase.[13] During the placement phase, cash with an illegitimate origin is brought into the financial system. Placement occurs for example if a criminal deposits cash on a payment account held with a Bank or

[9] Criminals may operate outside of the financial system using other means for making payments, such as cash.

[10] Directive (EU) 2018/843 of 30 May 2018 “amending Directive (EU) 2015/849 on the prevention of the use of the financial system for the purposes of money laundering or terrorist financing, (…)”, OJ L 156, 19.6.2018, pp. 43–74.

[11] The Commission proposes to transfer amongst others the following requirements to a regulation: (i) CDD requirements; (ii) internal controls and (iii) reporting obligations.

[12] See Commission (2020, p. 5).

[13] See Woda, K. (2006, p. 28).

uses cash to purchase a prepaid card. The main objective of money laundering is to bring illegit funds into the financial system without having the owner of the funds being identified or having to explain the origin of the funds. Nowadays, it is not possible for a person to enter into a contractual relationship with a PSP without being subject to the PSP's CDD procedures. As a result, criminals have to either deceive the PSP during the onboarding process or resort to payment instruments that can be used anonymously. In particular, the payment service 'money transfers' entail relatively high AML risks for PSPs since these services allow PSUs to remain anonymous since the PSU is not required to have a payment account with a PSP.[14] In addition, E-money products are susceptible to high ML/TF risks since these products do not require personal interaction between the holder of the E-money product and the E-money issuer, which makes anonymous use relatively easy.[15] In particular, 'open-loop' E-money instruments have certain characteristics that make them susceptible for being used to launder money or finance terrorism.[16] One of these characteristics is the monetary value that can be loaded on an open-loop E-money instrument. The higher the monetary value that can be loaded on such instrument, the more useful it becomes for criminals to place illegit funds into the financial system. Another characteristic is the method by which open-loop E-money instruments can be funded. Open-loop E-money instruments which allow for anonymous funding (e.g., cash payments) trigger higher ML/TF risks. Cash funding is an ideal way for criminals to bring money into the financial system as it provides no transaction history.[17] Furthermore, the transferability of an open-loop E-money instrument is an important characteristic that triggers higher ML/TF risk exposures. Open-loop E-money instruments that can easily be passed on and used by other persons who are not known to the issuer of the instrument are more susceptible to ML/TF risks. This is of particular concern if such instrument is issued in a country with lower AML/CTF standards and can be used in the EU for making Payments

[14] See Joosen, E. P. M. (2020, p. 110).

[15] See Fan, G. (2010, p. 11).

[16] See ESAs Joint Committee (2017a, p. 46).

[17] See FATF (2013, p. 16).

or ATM withdrawals.[18] Effective measures to reduce the ML/TF risk for open-loop E-money instruments are to limit the monetary value that can be stored on the instrument, limit the geographic scope where such E-money instrument can be used and impose limits on the amounts that can be withdrawn or transferred with such instrument.[19]

The layering phase commences the moment after the illegitimate funds have been successfully placed into the financial system. During the layering phase, the illegit funds are transferred, often multiple times, between payment accounts to further conceal their criminal origin. The payer and the beneficiary of such transactions are often the same person or entity.[20] Payment products provide for a convenient way to transfer funds quickly, which makes them an attractive option for money launderers during the layering phase.[21] An alternative method for layering is to purchase E-money instruments with other E-money instruments that have been purchased during the placing phase.[22] When the layering phase is completed, the funds can be taken out of the financial system and used for making payments without attracting attention from public authorities. This final step, which is referred to as the integration phase, involves for example withdrawing cash from ATMs using E-money instruments.

Because of the short time frame and convenience with which Payments can be processed, Payment products entail a relatively high risk of being used by criminals for ML/TF purposes. This vulnerability creates a necessity to have a legislative framework in place that enables NCAs and PSPs to prevent the Payment ecosystem from being used for these purposes.

[18] Therefore, MLD4 provides that anonymous prepaid cards issued outside the EU can only be used for making payments in the EU in case such instruments can be considered to comply with requirements similar to those set out in the EU.

[19] See FATF (2013, p. 23).

[20] See Woda, K. (2006, p. 29).

[21] See Huang, L. (2015, p. 20).

[22] See Sienkiewicz, S. (2007, pp. 6–7).

6.3 Regulations on Information Accompanying Transfers of Funds

One of the AML/CTF measures taken by the European legislature involves the obligation for PSPs to identify the payer and beneficiary of payment transactions. In this regard, the European legislature adopted two regulations, which oblige PSPs to ensure that Payments are accompanied with relevant information regarding the payer and beneficiary.

6.3.1 The Wire Transfer Regulation (WTR)

The obligation to establish the identity of payers initiating Payments was one of the first AML requirements introduced by the European legislature. The importance of this requirement was first recognised by the Financial Action Task Force (‘**FATF**’)[23] and published by the FATF as Recommendation VII on wire transfers.[24] Since the FATF recommendations do not have legal status and have to be transposed into national legislation in order to take effect, the European legislature adopted FATF Recommendation VII on wire transfers in Regulation (EC) No 1781/2006 on information on the payer accompanying transfers of funds (‘**WTR**’).[25] **Article 5(1) WTR**, which regulation entered into force in 2006, obliged PSPs[26] to pass on certain information regarding the identity of the payer when processing Payments, thereby enabling NCAs to identify the payer of a particular Payment. In case a Payment required the involvement of intermediary PSP(s), **Article 12 WTR** required such intermediary PSP(s) to ensure that the payer's information received from

[23] The FATF was founded by the G7 in 1989 and publishes recommendations regarding AML measures for NCAs and PSPs.

[24] FATF Recommendation VII on ‘wire transfers’ stated that ‘*Countries should take measures to require financial institutions, including money remitters, to include accurate and meaningful originator information (name, address and account number) on funds transfers and related messages that are sent, and the information should remain with the transfer or related message through the payment chain. Countries should take measures to ensure that financial institutions, including money remitters, conduct enhanced scrutiny of and monitor for suspicious activity funds transfers which do not contain complete originator information (name, address and account number)*’.

[25] See Commission (2005, p. 2).

[26] **Article 1 WTR** defines a ‘PSP’ as a natural or legal person whose business includes the provision of transfer of funds services.

the payer's PSP remained attached to the Payment when transferring these funds to another PSP. The WTR covered all Payments carried out in any currency initiated or received by a PSP established in the EEA.[27] Beneficiary initiated Payments, such as direct debit collections, were not in scope of the WTR.

To ensure a consistent application of the FATF Recommendation VII on wire transfers throughout the EU, the European legislature decided to adopt said recommendation in a regulation instead of a directive.[28] Adopting a directive would have prevented a uniform rollout of this recommendation since Member States tend to implement directives differently into their national legislation. Such different implementation would have been particularly detrimental with regard to cross-border Payments involving multiple PSPs. For example, an intermediary PSP that would not receive all relevant details of the payer but was instructed to transfer funds to a beneficiary's PSP in another Member State would not have been authorised to do so. In other words, for FATF Recommendation VII on wire transfers to be effective, it is key that all PSPs in the payment ecosystem are subject to the exact same requirements.

[27] Decision by the EEA Joint Committee No 87/2007 of 6 July 2007 "amending Annex IX (Financial Services) to the EEA Agreement", OJ L 328, 13.12.2007, pp. 32–33. Certain types of fund transfers that represent a low ML/TF risk were explicitly excluded from the scope of the WTR. The WTR did not apply in relation to: (i) transfers initiated using a credit or debit card, provided that the beneficiary had an agreement with the PSP for the provision of goods and services and a unique identifier, allowing the transaction to be traced back to the payer accompanies such fund transfer; (ii) E-money when the relevant Member States applied the derogation of **Article 11(5)(d) of Directive 2005/60/EC** and the amount did not exceed €1,000; (iii) transfers of funds carried out by means of a mobile telephone or any other digital or IT device, when such transfers were prepaid and did not exceed €150; (iv) transfer of funds carried out by means of a mobile telephone or any other digital or IT device, when such transfers were post-paid and met all of the conditions described in **Article 3(5) WTR**; (v) at the discretion of Member States, transfers of funds within that Member State to a beneficiary account permitting payment for the provision of goods or services subject to a number of conditions stipulated in **Article 3(6) WTR**; (vi) cash withdrawals from the payer's account by himself or herself; (vii) direct debit collections when a debit authorisation existed between payer and beneficiary as long as a unique identifier accompanied the transaction allowing the transaction to be traced back to the payer; (viii) transfer of funds resulting from a truncated cheque; (ix) transfers of funds to public authorities for taxes, fines or other levies within a Member State and (x) transaction generated by a PSP to another PSP acting on their own behalf.

[28] See Commission (2005, p. 7).

6.3.1.1 Information on the Payer

Depending on whether the PSPs involved in the processing of a Payment were established in or outside the EEA, different requirements applied regarding the information that had to be attached to the relevant Payment. Three different scenarios could be distinguished.

Scenario I: Payments whereby both the payer's PSP and beneficiary's PSP were established in the EEA

When both the payer's PSP and the beneficiary's PSP were established in the EEA, the information on the payer which had to be attached to the transaction was relatively limited. Pursuant to **Article 6(1) WTR** the transaction only needed to be accompanied with the payer's payment account number or a unique identifier, which consists according to **Article 2(9) WTR** of a combination of letters, numbers or symbols used to effect the Payment.

The payer's PSP was responsible for ensuring the accurateness and completeness of the payer's information attached to the Payment. Before a payer's PSP was allowed to commence the processing of a Payment, **Article 5(2) WTR** obliged the payer's PSP to first verify the payer's information. For this purpose, the payer's PSP had to use information and/or documentation from a reliable and independent source. No verification was required in case: (i) the payer's PSP already verified the information for a particular payer when opening his payment account; or (ii) the respective payer was subject to the CDD requirement under Directive 2005/60/EC on the prevention of the use of the financial system for the purpose of money laundering and terrorist financing ('**MLD3**').[29]

Further to the payer's PSP verification requirement, the beneficiary's PSP was obliged to verify upon receipt of the funds whether any of the required information on the payer was missing or incomplete. In case information was missing or incomplete, **Article 9(1) WTR** required the beneficiary's PSP to either reject the transfer or request the payer's PSP to provide the missing information on the payer. Furthermore, the beneficiary's PSP had to determine, on the basis of a risk-based assessment, whether it needed to report the relevant transaction to the NCA.

[29] Directive 2005/60/EC of 26 October 2005 "on the prevention of the use of the financial system for the purpose of money laundering and terrorist financing", OJ L 309, 25.11.2005, pp. 15–36.

Scenario II: Payments whereby the payer's PSP was established outside the EEA and the beneficiary's PSP in the EEA

Payer's PSPs that were established outside the EEA were not obliged to accompany fund transfers to beneficiary's PSPs in the EEA with information on the payer. Consequently, the beneficiary's PSP did not receive any ML/TF risk related information on non-EEA payers. The European legislature therefore required the beneficiary's PSP to conduct enhanced CDD within the meaning of MLD3 on the beneficiary's PSP on the payer's PSP established outside the EEA.[30]

Scenario III: Payments whereby the payer's PSP was established in the EEA and the beneficiary's PSP outside the EEA

Payer's PSPs established in the EEA were obliged under **Article 7(1) WTR** to accompany fund transfers to beneficiary's PSPs outside the EEA with the name, address[31] and account number of the payer.

6.3.2 The Revised Wire Transfer Regulation (WTR2)

In February 2012, the FATF published its updated recommendations on how PSPs can best mitigate their ML/TF risks. One of the updated recommendations related to the information that PSPs must attach to Payments when processing such transactions. According to FATF Recommendation XVI, the information accompanying fund transfers should also include the identity of the beneficiary. Furthermore, the obligations for intermediary PSPs were expanded by requiring that these PSPs take reasonable measures to identify cross-border fund transfers that are lacking information on the payer or the beneficiary. Moreover, since technological developments enabled new types of service providers to enter the market for Payments, such service providers also had to be covered by FATF Recommendation XVI. FATF Recommendation XVI therefore explicitly refers to businesses that play a role in fund transfers outside the conventional banking system.

[30] WTR, Recital 16.

[31] Pursuant to **Article 4(2) WTR**, the address of the payer could be substituted by: (i) date and place of birth of the payer; (ii) customer identification number of the payer or (iii) national identity number of the payer.

In February 2013, the Commission published a legislative proposal for the WTR2, which was based on the new FATF Recommendation XVI on wire transfers.[32] The WTR2, which entered into force on 26 June 2017, introduced numerous changes to the WTR in order to enhance the traceability of Payments processed in the EEA.[33] First, the WTR2 requirements apply to all PSPs involved in the payment chain, including the payer's PSP, the beneficiary's PSP and intermediary PSPs. The WTR2 applies a broader definition of PSP than the WTR. Under the WTR2, service providers benefitting from a waiver under PSD or EMD2 also qualify as a PSP and are therefore subject to this regulation. Second, fund transfers that are covered by the WTR2 include any Payment that is, at least partially, carried out with a view to making funds[34] available to a beneficiary using a PSP.[35] Unlike the WTR, the WTR2 also covers Payments initiated by the beneficiary. In summary, **Articles 2(1) and 3(9) WTR2** provide that the following Payments are covered by the WTR2: (i) credit transfers; (ii) direct debit collections; (iii) money remittances and (iv) transfers initiated using a payment card, E-money instrument, smartphone or any other digital or IT prepaid or post-paid device that are used to affect a P2P transfer. Fund transfers that are exposed to relatively low ML/TF risks are excluded from the scope of applicability.[36] Moreover, payment services that are out of scope of the

[32] See Commission (2013).

[33] Decision by the EEA Joint Committee No. 250/2018 of 5 December 2018 "amending Annex IX (Financial Services) to the EEA Agreement", OJ L 337, 23.9.2021, pp. 46–47.

[34] Funds within the meaning of WTR2 include banknotes and coins, scriptural money and E-money.

[35] **Article 2(4) WTR2** stipulates that WTR2 does not apply with regard to: (i) cash withdrawals by the payer from its own payment account; (ii) fund transfers to a public authority within a Member State; (iii) fund transfers where both the payer and the beneficiary are PSPs acting on their own behalf or (iv) fund transfers carried out using cheques.

[36] According to **Article 2(3) WTR2** these include transfers carried out using a payment card, e-money instrument, smartphone or any other digital or IT prepaid or post-paid device with similar characteristics, provided that: (i) the card, instrument or device is used exclusively to pay for goods or services; and (ii) the identification number of that payment instrument accompanies all transfers initiated by that payment instrument.

PSD requirements are not covered by the WTR2.[37] Further to the aforementioned exemptions, Member States are allowed to disapply WTR2 in relation to certain fund transfers to a beneficiary's payment account permitting payment exclusively for the provision of goods or services.[38]

6.3.2.1 Information on the Payer and the Beneficiary

Depending on the value of the fund transfer and whether the PSPs involved are established in or outside the EEA, different requirements apply regarding the information that must be attached to said fund transfer.

Scenario I: Payments whereby both the payer's PSP and beneficiary's PSP are established in the EEA

Like the WTR, the WTR2 considers fund transfers between PSPs established in the EEA to be exposed to low ML/TF risks. These fund transfers therefore only have to be accompanied with limited information provided that the transaction amount does not exceed €1,000. If both the payer's PSP and the beneficiary's PSP are established in the EEA, **Article 5(1) WTR2** requires that a transaction between these PSPs is accompanied with the beneficiary's IBAN and the payer's IBAN.[39] For transactions exceeding €1,000, **Articles 4 and 5(2)(a) WTR2** require the payer's PSP to ensure that the following information is attached to each fund transfer: (i) the name of the payer; (ii) the payer's IBAN; (iii) the payer's address, official personal document number, customer identification number or date and place of birth; (iv) the name of the beneficiary and (v) the beneficiary's IBAN. If all PSPs involved in the payment chain are established in the Union, transfers of funds shall be accompanied by at least the payment account number of both the payer and the payee.

[37] According to **Article 2(2) WTR2** transfers of funds corresponding to the payment services referred to in points (a) to (m) and (o) of **Article 3 of PSD** do not fall within the scope of this Regulation.

[38] **Article 2(5) WTR2** stipulates that this option is available provided that: (i) the beneficiary's PSP is subject to MLD4; (ii) the beneficiary's PSP is able to trace the transfer from the person who has an agreement with the beneficiary for the provision of goods or services using a unique transaction identifier and (iii) the maximum amount of the fund transfer does not exceed €1,000.

[39] In the event of a money remittance transaction, the fund transfer must only be accompanied with the unique transaction identifier.

In case a fund transfer involves a money remittance transaction,[40] **Article 4(3) WTR2** requires the payer's PSP to ensure that the fund transfer is accompanied with a unique transaction identifier[41] instead of the IBAN of the beneficiary and the payer.

Scenario II: Payments whereby the payer's PSP is established outside the EEA and the beneficiary's PSP in the EEA

The WTR2 does not apply to PSPs established outside the EEA. Therefore, if the payer's PSP for a particular Payment is situated outside the EEA, the WTR2 cannot oblige the payer's PSP to accompany fund transfers to PSPs in the EEA with information on the payer. In such scenario, **Articles 7(2) and 11(2) WTR2** require the EEA based intermediary and/or beneficiary PSP to only verify whether information on the payer and beneficiary are missing.

Scenario III: Payments whereby the payer's PSP is established in the EEA and the beneficiary's PSP outside the EEA

The WTR2 imposes specific information requirements for Payments to beneficiary's PSPs established outside the EEA. Different information requirements apply depending on the value of the transfer and whether such transfer is executed as a single transaction or included in a batch of multiple payment orders. If executed as a single transaction, **Article 6(2) WTR2** requires fund transfers which do not exceed **€1,000** to be accompanied with at least: (i) the names of the payer and beneficiary; and (ii) the IBAN of the payer and beneficiary.[42] When executed as part of a batch, **Article 6(1) WTR2** states that the individual transactions included in the batch do not have to include the payer's: (i) address; (ii) official personal document number; (iii) customer identification number or (iv) date and

[40] A money remittance transaction is a fund transfer which is not initiated from or to a payment account.

[41] **Article 3 (11) WTR2** defines a 'unique transaction identifier' as a combination of letters, numbers or symbols determined by the PSP, in accordance with the protocols of the payment and settlement systems or messaging systems used for the transfer of funds, which permits the traceability of the transaction back to the payer and the beneficiary.

[42] With regard to money remittance transactions, the IBAN of the payer and the beneficiary can be replaced with a unique transaction identifier.

place of birth. However, these individual transfers must be accompanied with: (i) the name of the payer; and (ii) the payer's IBAN (or a unique transaction identifier in case of a money remittance transaction).

Article 4(4) WTR2 does not allow the payer's PSP to execute a fund transfer in case certain information on the payer or beneficiary is missing or incomplete. Therefore, PSPs must have efficient procedures in place that enable them to identify situations where information is missing or incomplete. To foster a harmonised approach for PSPs in determining whether information is indeed missing or incomplete, the ESA's joint committee published guidelines setting out how PSPs can detect missing or incomplete information and how they should manage fund transfers lacking relevant information.[43] These guidelines are not legally binding for PSPs, unless the NCA of the Member State where the PSP is established has adopted such guidelines.

6.3.2.2 *Obligations of the Beneficiary's PSP and Intermediary PSPs*

According to **Articles 7 and 11 WTR2**, the beneficiary's PSP and, where relevant, intermediary PSPs are also obliged to have effective procedures in place for verifying whether information attached to a particular fund transfer is missing or incomplete. If relevant information is missing, **Article 8(1) WTR2** requires that the PSP which receives the funds rejects the incoming payment or asks the payer's or intermediary PSP for the missing information before or after (depending on a risk-sensitive basis) crediting the beneficiary's payment account. It is for the beneficiary's PSP to decide whether execution, rejection or suspension of the transfer is the appropriate measure for the situation. Furthermore, the PSP must determine whether such transaction is suspicious from an ML/TF perspective and should be reported to the Financial Intelligence Unit ('**FIU**') under **Articles 9 and 13 WTR2**. In case a particular PSP often breaches the information requirement, **Articles 8 and 12 WTR2** require that the other PSP(s) involved in the processing of the fund transfer must issue a warning or impose a deadline before it rejects future fund transfers from that PSP or terminates its business relationship with that PSP.[44]

[43] See ESAs Joint Committee (2017b).

[44] The relevant PSP reports the failure, and the steps taken, to the NCA responsible for monitoring compliance with AML/CTF provisions.

6.4 Customer Due Diligence (CDD)

6.4.1 Introduction

To manage their ML/TF risk exposures, PSPs must have a profound understanding of who their business relationships (e.g., customers) are. To this end, MLD4 requires PSPs to refrain from entering into a business relationship or carrying out Payments without having conducted CDD.[45] In general, the CDD obligation requires PSPs to: (i) identify prospective customers (PSUs) and verify their identity; (ii) carry out a risk assessment when onboarding a prospective customer and (iii) monitor Payments for which their customers act as payer or beneficiary to ensure that these are not processed for ML/TF purposes.

The CDD requirement applies to all PSPs, including Banks, PIs and EMIs[46] that operate on the basis of a licence or an exemption.[47] With E-money products, there is a variety of different service providers involved in the processing of transactions, such as issuers, distributors and agents. The involvement of different service providers raises the question which of these service providers qualifies as an institution within the meaning of MLD4 and should therefore carry out CDD. Although it is obvious that E-money issuers are in any case covered by the CDD obligation, there is no consensus as to whether distributors and agents are subject to AML/CTF requirements.[48] This lack of legal clarity makes it difficult to determine which service providers are responsible for implementing CDD

[45] Moreover, the PSP is not allowed to enter into a business relationship or carry out a transaction if the PSP identifies an unacceptably high risk.

[46] An EMI is not obliged to carry out CDD in case it issues an E-money product that meets all of the following characteristics: (i) the E-money instrument is not reloadable, or has a monthly transactions limit of €150 (which can only be used in the Member State in which the instrument was issued); (ii) the maximum amount that can be stored electronically does not exceed €150; (iii) the E-money instrument can only be used to purchase goods or services (not for making P2P payments; (iv) the E-money instrument cannot be loaded anonymously and (v) the EMI carries out adequate transaction monitoring. Moreover, E-money issuers that solely issue closed-loop cards remain out of scope of the CDD requirements.

[47] The scope of applicability of the CDD requirement is not limited to licensed PSPs. Non-licensed PSPs, such as PIs operating on the basis of a waiver, also qualify as an 'institution within the meaning of MLD4 and are therefore subject to AML requirements. **Article 9(8) EMD2** stipulates that non-licensed EMIs proving payment services on the basis of a waiver are subject to the AML requirements.

[48] See ESAs Joint Committee (2012b, pp. 11–12).

measures in relation to E-money products.[49] In 2013, the FATF provided some guidance as to which service provider should conduct CDD in relation to E-money products. According to the FATF, the entity that enters into the contractual arrangement with the user of the E-money instrument is responsible for carrying out CDD (e.g., the programme manager or the issuer).[50]

6.4.2 PSU Risk Categorisation

A PSP's ML/TF risk exposure is to a large extent determined by factors such as the type of payment services provided, the countries in which the PSP is active and the composition of the PSP's customer base. In general, Banks are exposed to larger ML/TF risks than Non-Banks given the size and complexity of their business operations. Imposing the same AML/CTF requirements on Banks and Non-Banks would therefore be disproportionate for (especially smaller) Non-Banks.

To ensure that the AML/CTF requirements for PSPs are proportionate to their ML/TF risk exposures, the CDD requirement is structured as a risk-based responsibility. This means that PSPs have to identify and assess the ML/TF risks to which they are exposed and implement the measures and procedures they deem appropriate to mitigate these risks in an adequate manner.[51] Amongst others, a customer's risk profile and the nature of the business relationship determine to a large extent the scope of a PSP's CDD requirement. More stringent CDD measures better safeguard the integrity of the financial sector but at the same time increase the PSP's regulatory burden. PSPs therefore must strike a balance between being exposed to acceptable levels of ML/TF risks and providing payment services to PSUs in a cost-efficient and customer friendly manner. Although a risk-based approach for the CDD requirement provides PSPs with flexibility to adequately address ML/TF risks, there is a risk of having too much diversity in the application of the AML/CTF requirements by PSPs. Providing a certain level of consistency regarding the interpretation of these requirements is therefore essential.[52]

[49] See FATF (2013, p. 11).

[50] Ibid, p. 34.

[51] See FATF (2014, p. 6).

[52] See ESAs Joint Committee (2017c, p. 6).

When PSPs establish their AML/CTF measures and procedures, **Article 8 MLD4** requires they first identify the ML/TF risks that are associated with the Payment products they intend to offer, the (geographical) markets in which they want to be active and the customers they intend to service. In order to identify their ML/TF risk exposures, PSPs carry out a systemic integrity risk assessment ('**SIRA**'), which involves an integrity risk assessment as well as the development of mitigation measures to manage the risks identified.[53] Subsequently, PSPs define their risk appetite, which is in essence the maximum ML/TF risk exposure that PSPs are willing to accept when providing payment services.

After a PSP has carried out its SIRA, it divides its customers into risk categories on the basis of their perceived risk levels. PSPs specify the relevant risk categories in their risk policy, which is based on the PSP's SIRA. In general, PSPs categorise their customers as low, medium or high risk customers. The obligation to create a risk profile for each prospective customer is not a one-of obligation but it is a requirement that must be met on an ongoing basis.[54] It is for the PSP to decide which parameters it uses to determine a prospective customer's risk profile. An approach often taken by PSPs is to define customer peer groups on the basis of certain customer characteristics, such as the countries where the customer is active or the legal form of the customer. To promote consistency, it is recommended that PSPs use the risk factors identified by the ESA's Joint Committee, such as: (i) is the customer a high risk customer given his reputation; (ii) does the relationship involve countries which are high risk and (iii) whether there are politically exposed persons (PEPs) involved.[55]

Moreover, a customer's risk profile is determined on the basis of a customer's transactional behaviour. Since it is difficult to foresee transactional behaviour of prospective customers, PSPs predict such behaviour

[53] The PSP must update its SIRA on a regular basis because the risks to which it is exposed are not static. In case new or different risks are identified, the PSP should incorporate the results thereof in the benchmarks that it applies for monitoring transactions.

[54] During the business relationship, the PSP must periodically verify whether the risk profile and transaction pattern of the client is still in line with the PSP's expectations. In case expectations have changed, the PSP must update the client's profile. In other words, the PSP must monitor the business relationship with each client on a continuous basis and include in its internal procedures how and with which frequency it ensures that the client's profile is kept up to date.

[55] See ESAs Joint Committee (2017a).

on the basis of information received from a prospective customer on his expected incoming, outgoing payments and transaction volumes. After the ML/TF risk exposure of a prospective customer has been identified, the PSP must weigh each of these factors and determine whether the customer qualifies as a low, medium or high risk customer.[56] Depending on the risk classification of a particular prospective customer, PSPs may consider to apply simplified or enhanced CDD.

6.4.3 Client Identification and Verification

If PSPs have proper client identification screening measures in place, they can, to a certain extent, prevent criminals from gaining access to the financial sector. Therefore, when onboarding a prospective customer, CDD requires the PSP to first identify its customer and to verify his identity.[57] If the prospective customer is a legal entity, the PSP must also identify and verify the identity of the members of the management board and the ultimate beneficial owner. Carrying out CDD on the ultimate beneficial owner is a statutory requirement since it is not uncommon for criminals to use structures involving (foreign) legal persons to conceal the criminal source of their funds.[58] By identifying the ultimate beneficial owner, PSPs can assist public authorities with tracing criminals that would have otherwise been able to hide their identity behind a corporate structure.[59]

Nowadays, most PSPs no longer have physical offices where they can onboard prospective PSUs in person. It has become the standard for

[56] The PSP must assess the importance of each factor for the particular business relationship and score it accordingly.

[57] This also involves, where relevant, identifying the ultimate beneficial owner(s) and verifying their identity.

[58] Business relationships with politically exposed persons (PEPs) require additional measures since these persons generally present a higher risk from an ML/TF perspective. A politically exposed person is a natural person who is or who has been entrusted with prominent public functions, such as (non-exhaustive list): (i) heads of State, heads of government, ministers and deputy or assistant ministers; (ii) members of parliament or of similar legislative bodies; (iii) members of the governing bodies of political parties; (iv) members of supreme courts, of constitutional courts or of other high-level judicial bodies, the decisions of which are not subject to further appeal, except in exceptional circumstances; (v) members of courts of auditors or of the boards of central banks; (vi) ambassadors and high-ranking officers in the armed forces and (vi) members of the administrative, management or supervisory bodies of State-owned enterprises.

[59] MLD4, Recital 14.

PSPs to establish new customer relationships online. With the transition of the PSPs' interaction with PSUs to the online environment, it has become more challenging for PSPs to carry out diligent CDD.[60] The FATF recognised that the absence of face-to-face contact with prospective customers has an increasing effect on a PSP's exposure to ML/TF risks.[61] For this reason, customers which are onboarded non-face-to-face are considered potentially high risk situations under MLD4 and PSPs have to determine on a case by case basis whether such customer qualifies as a high risk customer. To address their increased risk exposure in case of non-face-to-face onboarding, PSPs often require prospective customers to provide a qualified electronic seal or qualified electronic signature[62] within the meaning of Regulation (EU) No 910/2014 on electronic identification and trust services for electronic transactions in the internal market (**'eIDAS Regulation'**).[63,64] With MLD4, the use of electronic certificates under the eIDAS Regulation has been first recognised as a valid means for customer identification purposes.[65] To address different applications of remote customer onboarding procedures between Member States, the EBA issued in 2023 guidelines for PSPs on the use of technological solutions in the non-face-to-face onboarding of PSUs.[66]

After a PSP obtained all relevant information for identifying a prospective customer, it must verify his identity.[67] The identity of the customer must be verified on the basis of 'reliable and independent' sources. MLD4 does not provide any guidance as to what reliable and independent

[60] It is easier for criminals to commit identity fraud by pretending to be someone else in case of non-face-to-face onboarding.

[61] See FATF (2013, p. 14).

[62] For natural persons an electronic signature is required and for a legal person an electronic seal. An electronic seal is the same as an electronic signature, however an electronic seal only applies to legal persons and corporate entities. It enables organisations to sign documents.

[63] Regulation (EU) No 910/2014 of 23 July 2014 "on electronic identification and trust services for electronic transactions in the internal market and repealing Directive 1999/93/EC", OJ L 257, 28.8.2014, pp. 73–114.

[64] See ESAs Joint Committee (2018, p. 16).

[65] eIDAS Regulation, Recital 22.

[66] See EBA (2022a, p. 3).

[67] Where relevant, the identity of such beneficial owner should also be verified.

sources are. In principle, a PSP can use documents which it considers to adequately address its ML/TF risk exposures, such as a passport or identity card. During the verification phase the PSP also assesses the purpose and nature of the business relationship.[68]

6.4.3.1 *Simplified CDD*

If the ML/TF risks associated with a prospective customer are relatively low, the risk-based approach justifies the use of simplified CDD measures. PSPs must assess on a customer-by-customer basis whether it is appropriate to carry out simplified CDD. Considering a prospective customer to be a low risk customer only because it falls within a certain customer category or obtains a particular payment service does in itself not justify the application of simplified CDD.

MLD4 does not specify what simplified CDD for a particular customer should look like. In general, simplified CDD allows PSPs to, amongst others, adjust the timing of the CDD screening or the level of detail of information required from the prospective customer to complete the CDD process.[69] Different timing involves the optionality for the PSP to verify a customer's identity during the establishment of the business relationship instead of prior to the establishment of the business relationship. Another example of simplified CDD involves the verification of a customer's identity using a single source of information. Simplified CDD can also mean that a PSP carries out transaction monitoring with a lower frequency or limited scope. It is important to emphasise that simplified CDD does not allow PSPs to skip one or more of the CDD requirements.

6.4.3.2 *Enhanced Customer Due Diligence (CDD)*

In case a PSP qualifies a prospective customer as a high risk customer, the PSP must apply a more stringent form of CDD before it is allowed to onboard such customer. Prospective customers can, for example, be labelled high risk because of the nature of their business. Especially if a customer's business is cash intensive, the risk that the PSP will be used for ML/TF purposes is relatively high. Moreover, prospective customers from countries that have been identified by the Commission as high risk

[68] The purpose of the relationship is often evident because of the products or services requested by the customer. However, in case there are ambiguities, it is important that the PSP asks further questions to obtain a clear understanding of the customer's intentions.

[69] See ESAs Joint Committee (2017a, pp. 23–24).

countries are labelled high risk by the PSP.[70] It is important to emphasise that a high risk classification does not necessarily mean that such client is indeed involved in ML/TF activities. A high risk classification is merely an indication of an increased risk that such client could be involved in ML/TF activities.

Enhanced CDD provides for a proportionate tool to cater for this increased risk exposure. As with simplified CDD, MLD4 does not specify how a PSP must carry out enhanced CDD. On the basis of the PSP's anticipated ML/TF risk exposures, the PSP determines what is needed to meet the enhanced CDD obligation for a particular customer. Depending on the prospective customer in question, enhanced CDD can take many forms and often involves an obligation to obtain additional information on a prospective customer and/or the nature of the business relationship.[71] Unlike simplified CDD, enhanced CDD does not allow the PSP any flexibility regarding the timing of the CDD process. The PSP cannot enter into a business relationship before the enhanced CDD process has been completed. Whether a PSP can onboard a high risk customer after completion of the enhanced CDD process is ultimately a decision for the PSP. However, the PSP should in any case refrain from onboarding a prospective customer who fails to provide the required information/documentation or exposes the PSP to unacceptable ML/TF risks.

6.4.4 Transaction Monitoring

The risk that a criminal uses the services of a PSP for ML/TF purposes is reduced significantly if PSPs apply proper customer identification and verification measures. There are however no guarantees that customers who have passed the identification and verification clearance process do not have criminal intentions. It is therefore of profound importance for PSPs to also have procedures in place to monitor customer behaviour on an ongoing basis and to identify and report transactions that are unusual.[72]

[70] MLD4, Recital 29.

[71] See FATF (2019, p. 65).

[72] Indications of unusual transactions include *inter alia*: (i) a PSU makes frequent or large transactions; or (ii) transactions with counterparties in high risk countries. Further to the obligation to carry out transaction monitoring for AML/CTF purposes, PSPs can also be subject to an obligation to monitor transactions from a security perspective (**Paragraph 5.3**).

This goes for both outgoing and incoming Payments. Instructions for outgoing payments can constitute an attempt to launder money or finance terrorism whereas incoming payments can represent funds that have been laundered or are in the process of being laundered.

Transaction monitoring is a risk mitigating tool that addresses the integrity risks identified by a PSP in its SIRA and which provides the PSP with an effective instrument to identify transactions that are initiated or executed for ML/TF purposes. It involves the gathering of information on Payments on the basis of which the PSP can determine whether it should process a particular transaction. Moreover, transaction monitoring enables PSPs to intervene in the execution of suspicious Payments. PSPs can carry out transaction monitoring before it processes Payments (ex-ante transaction monitoring) or after these Payments are processed (ex-post transaction monitoring). Ex-post transaction monitoring has the disadvantage that the PSP cannot intervene if a particular transaction turns out to be unusual. In other words, the possibility for PSPs to recover funds that are labelled suspicious is reduced substantially when conducting ex-post transaction monitoring instead of ex-ante transaction monitoring.

6.4.4.1 Implementing an Adequate Transaction Monitoring Framework

The challenge with transaction monitoring is to distinguish illegal Payments from Payments that are legitimate. MLD4 does not provide any guidance as to what an adequate transaction monitoring process should look like. In line with the risk-based approach, PSPs are responsible for determining what transaction monitoring procedures are adequate and proportionate for their business.[73] This means that transaction monitoring procedures can be tailored to *inter alia*: (i) the type of clients serviced by the PSP[74]; (ii) the type of Payments executed on behalf of clients; and (iii) the risk profile of the PSP's clients. There is no legal obligation for PSPs to implement an automated system for monitoring transactions. However, conducting manual transaction monitoring is no

[73] It is important to note that PSPs are not entirely free to determine how they structure their transaction monitoring process. The Home CA verifies the adequateness of a PSP's transaction monitoring procedure as part of its licence application and gives instructions to licensed PSPs in case it considers such procedures to be inadequate.

[74] For example, a PSP is exposed to higher ML/TF risks in case a PSU qualifies as a PEP.

longer a realistic option given the large number of transactions that the average PSP processes daily and the speed with which these transactions are cleared and settled.

For smaller Non-Banks it is often too onerous to develop and maintain their own transaction monitoring process. It is therefore not uncommon for smaller PSPs to outsource part of their transaction monitoring process to, for example, FinTechs, which have advanced technologies that enable them to monitor transactions more effectively and efficiently.[75] It is important to emphasise that PSPs cannot outsource their legal transaction monitoring responsibility. This means that PSPs which outsource part of their monitoring process have to ensure that the insourcing party continues to meet all legal requirements. Moreover, the outsourcing PSP must at all times be able to intervene in case the agreed service levels are not met by the insourcing party.

6.4.4.2 *Transaction Monitoring—Threshold Setting*

Conventional transaction monitoring techniques use pre-set rules with regard to thresholds and patterns.[76] These techniques use information that a PSP receives during the customer onboarding phase in order to create risk profile segments by which customers are categorised. Based on its SIRA, the PSP applies certain triggers that are used during the transaction monitoring process to identify transactions that are unusual.[77] Such triggers can be of a qualitative nature, a quantitative nature or a combination of both. An example of a quantitative threshold is the minimum transaction amount of €15,000. Transactions that represent a value of at least €15,000 qualify in any case as unusual and have to be reported to the national FIU. A minimum transaction amount of €15,000 is however not necessarily a trustworthy indication of ML/TF activity. Criminals can, for example, make multiple Payments of less than €15,000 to circumvent a red flag in a PSP's transaction monitoring system that applies only such quantitative threshold.[78] More reliable are qualitative thresholds, which include *inter alia*: (i) black lists of compromised or stolen card data; and

[75] See Institute of International Finance (2016, p. 3).

[76] See ESAs Joint Committee (2018, p. 5).

[77] Such triggers can include: (i) frequent use of the same credit card with a single merchant; (ii) the time periods between payment and refunds or charge backs; (iii) payments from Internet Protocol (IP) addresses in high risk countries.

[78] This ML technique is also known as micro laundering or smurfing.

(ii) abnormal behaviour patterns of a customer's access device (such as a change of Internet Protocol (IP) address).[79] If a transaction initiated by a customer deviates from his risk profile, the transaction monitoring system generates an alert and the PSP must determine whether the payment order constitutes an unusual transaction which needs to be reported to the national FIU.[80]

Conventional monitoring procedures, which are based on quantitative and qualitative thresholds, have several shortcomings. An important shortcoming is that these procedures are backward looking since they use historical data to identify unusual transactions. Another shortcoming of these monitoring techniques is that they are generally not very accurate in distinguishing legitimate transaction patterns from ML/TF patterns and, as a result, create a relatively high number of false positives. False positives are transactions that are labelled unusual but are legitimate and should have passed the transaction monitoring screening. It is important that a PSP keeps the number of false positives to a minimum since false positives often result in payment accounts being wrongfully blocked or legitimate transactions not being executed.

More sophisticated transaction monitoring systems use artificial intelligence to determine their ML/TF triggers. When analysing transaction data, artificial intelligence applies algorithms that collect and interpret data from a variety of different sources to identify abnormal patterns.[81] Subsequently, the transaction monitoring system produces a risk score of the perceived level of unusualness and provides a measure of confidence regarding this risk score. The level of confidence increases based on previous experiences, which means that the accuracy of the categorisation of transactions by the monitoring process enhances overtime. Unlike conventional monitoring tools, which do not have this learning capacity and can only identify what they are programmed to identify, artificial intelligence can draw conclusions and improve future outcomes

[79] To provide the market with guidance and stimulate a more homogenous approach throughout the EU, the Wolfsberg group, which is an initiative of Banks against ML/TF, and the FATF regularly publish guidance papers on the indicators that PSPs should use for monitoring transactions.

[80] An alternative conclusion could be that the customer's risk profile is no longer up to date.

[81] Information can be obtained from internal sources (e.g., account information and transaction history) and/or external sources (e.g., public registers).

based on past experience. This increases the accurateness of the unusual transactions identified by the system and reduces the number of false positives. Another key advantage of using artificial intelligence for transaction monitoring purposes is that artificial intelligence can identify complex fraud patterns real-time, which makes it an essential technology for PSPs offering fast payments.

6.4.4.3 Transaction Monitoring in Case of Open Banking

With regard to open banking, the main objective of the European legislature appears to be to achieve the highest possible level of customer convenience. PSD2 mainly focusses on ensuring smooth payment account access by TPPs and little attention is paid to the potential implications of open banking on, for example, transaction monitoring and the allocation of CDD responsibilities between Banks and Non-Banks. By involving a PISP in the execution process of a Payment, open banking de facto increases the ML/TF risk exposures of Banks. These exposures are further increased by the fact that AML/CTF requirements are often relatively new to TPPs. In 2019 the ESAs published a research report in which they identified several ML/TF risk-increasing factors associated with FinTechs involved in the provision of payment services. According to the ESAs, key risk-increasing factors are that FinTechs tend to have very different compliance cultures and a lack of understanding of the overall legislative framework in the field of Payments.[82]

MLD4 requires Banks, PISPs and AISPs to carry out transaction monitoring when offering an open banking Payment solution. Transaction monitoring is in my opinion a relevant requirement for PISPs given their role in the processing of payment initiation services. PISPs can monitor payment orders before these are processed and intervene in case such order has an unusual nature. In practice this means that a PISP screens a payment order prior to releasing it into the Bank's IT system. Subsequently, the same payment order is screened by the Bank before it is being executed. One can question whether it is necessary to have both the PISP and Bank carrying out transaction monitoring regarding the same transactions. Absent any legal provision allowing the transaction monitoring of one PSP to replace the transaction monitoring obligation of another PSP, the better view seems to be that all PSPs involved in the payment

[82] See ESAs Joint Committee (2019, p. 12).

chain have to perform transaction monitoring.[83] A benefit of having multiple PSPs screening the same transactions is that it increases the likelihood that unusual transactions are identified as such. Unlike Banks, PISPs also have oversight over the transactions initiated by a payer with other Banks, which provides them with a comprehensive overview of a payer's transaction history. A disadvantage of having multiple PSPs screening the same transaction is that it increases the likelihood of generating false positives. Transactions have a higher probability of being incorrectly labelled as unusual if screened by multiple monitoring systems. Collaboration between PSPs with regard to transaction monitoring would in my opinion allow the market to benefit from the advantage of having all PSPs conducting transaction monitoring without creating too many false positives.

Transaction monitoring does not seem to be particularly relevant in relation to account information services since no funds are being transferred as part of this payment service. Because AISPs do not process payment orders, AISPs only have access to transaction information relating to payments that have already been cleared and settled. The mutations on the payment accounts in the dashboard of an AISP have successfully passed the transaction monitoring of the PSPs involved in the processing of these mutations. Perhaps even more important, AISPs are not authorised to intervene in case it considers a transaction to be unusual. For example, an AISP is not authorised to freeze a particular payment. Since transaction intervention is one of the main objectives of the transaction monitoring obligation, it defeats the purpose to make AISPs subject to the transaction monitoring obligation. However, AISPs do not benefit from exemptions under the MLD4 but are allowed to adjust their AML//CFT procedures on a risk-sensitive basis.[84] As EBA considers the ML/TF risks associated with AISPs, EBA recommended the Commission to further assess whether these entities should qualify as 'obliged entities' under the MLD framework.[85]

[83] See Joosen, E. P. M. (2020, p. 108).

[84] See EBA (n.d.).

[85] See EBA (2021, p. 212).

6.4.4.4 Transaction Monitoring and Fast Payments

Fast payments cater for the (perceived) need of consumers and businesses to have near real-time settlement of Payments. A main concern with fast payments revolves around the difficulty to carry out proper transaction monitoring before these payments are released. Unlike conventional credit transfers, which are generally settled in batches (**Paragraph 8.2.2**) within one business day (in the retail market), fast payments are processed individually (gross settlement) within a matter of seconds (**Paragraph 2.2.1**). This means that payment orders for executing fast payments are not queued by the payer's PSP, which makes it nearly impossible for the payer's PSP to assess whether such transaction is suspicious before it is released for processing.[86] Since conventional transaction monitoring procedures are by definition inadequate for monitoring fast payments, PSPs offering fast payment products require real-time monitoring procedures in order to detect and report any ML/TF activity. To date, the technology for carrying out real-time transaction screening is not yet available. This means that fast payments are currently subject to ex-post transaction monitoring, which makes it impossible for PSPs to intervene in case a particular transaction turns out to be unusual. It is interesting to see how little attention is paid to this issue by the European legislature. A possible solution to this problem could be to offer fast payments on the basis of a payment guarantee. With a payment guarantee, the payer's PSP guarantees the beneficiary's PSP that the beneficiary's payment account will be credited with the transaction amount after the transaction monitoring process has been completed. Although this increases the processing time from a couple of seconds to a few hours, it will provide for better safeguards that PSPs will not be used by criminals for ML/TF purposes.

Further to the increased ML/TF risk exposures, having inadequate transaction monitoring procedures for fast payments also triggers practical issues that reduce the commercial attractiveness of these products. When offering fast payments, PSPs have to clear payment orders within a matter of seconds in order to offer the PSU the agreed service level. Conducting transaction monitoring under such time pressure tends to increase the risk of generating large numbers of false negatives. False negatives are payment orders that are cleared but should have been flagged as unusual transactions. The number of false negatives could be reduced by enhancing the

[86] See Balani, H. (2017, p. 245).

clearing thresholds for fast payments. The downside however is that it increases the number of false positives. From a commercial perspective, having a large number of false positives is unacceptable since it makes fast payments unreliable and, as a result thereof, less attractive to use.[87]

6.4.4.5 Allocation of AML/CTF Responsibilities between Non-Banks, Branches and Agents

Licensed Non-Banks can provide payment services in other Member States: (i) on a cross-border basis; (ii) via a branch; or (iii) via a payment agent (**Paragraph 4.3**). If a PSP provides payment services in another Member State on a cross-border basis (i.e., the host Member State), the PSP does not have a physical presence in the host Member State. Such PSP is therefore subject to home Member State AML/CTF regulations when providing payment services on a cross-border basis in another Member State.

In the event a non-Bank provides payment services in another Member State via a branch, said branch qualifies as an 'institution' for AML/CTF purposes. This means that the branch must comply with the AML/CTF rules and regulations applicable in the host Member State. **Article 20 PSD2** stipulates that the PSP is responsible for the branch's compliance with the host Member State AML/CTF rules and regulations.

It is less clear whether home Member State or host Member State AML/CTF regulations apply in case a non-Bank provides payment services in another Member State via an agent. An agent does not qualify as an institution for AML/CTF purposes, which suggests that it is not subject to host Member State AML/CTF regulations.[88] The Commission takes the view however that an agent must comply with host Member State AML/CTF provisions.[89] The legal basis for this being the contractual arrangement that usually exists between PSPs and their agents.[90] Such contractual arrangement is required pursuant to **Article 20 PSD2** since Non-Banks must assume responsibility and liability for their agents' compliance with host Member State AML/CTF regulations. Moreover,

[87] Ibid, p. 252.

[88] National AML legislation in certain Member States (e.g., the Netherlands) qualify payment agents as an 'institution'.

[89] See Commission (2011, p. 2).

[90] See ESAs Joint Committee (2012a, p. 7).

the Commission considers Non-Banks operating in other Member States via an agent to have a form of establishment in the host Member State, which would also justify the necessity to comply with host Member State ML/TF regulations.[91]

6.4.4.6 Customer Due Diligence (CDD) in Case of a Correspondent Banking Relationship

If a non-Bank uses the services of another PSP for the offering of payment services, the latter PSP is considered to be providing a payment service to the non-Bank instead of to the non-Bank's customers. According to **Article 3(8)(b) MLD4** such business relationship between PSPs is called a correspondent banking relationship or correspondent relationship and is often used for processing cross-border Payments (**Paragraph 8.1**). In a correspondent banking relationship, one PSP (the correspondent PSP) holds deposits owned by another PSP (the respondent PSP) and provides payment services to the respondent PSP. In most cases, the correspondent PSP does not have a contractual relationship with the respondent PSP's customers, which are the end users on whose behalf fund transfers are executed.[92] Often, the correspondent PSP does not even know the identity of the respondent PSP's customers, let alone having carried out CDD regarding these customers. Not having a contractual relationship with a respondent PSP's customer makes it difficult for a correspondent PSP to verify the identity of the customer on whose behalf a Payment is executed.[93] This is of particular concern in case such respondent PSP is established in a country that has less stringent AML/CTF requirements than the country where the correspondent PSP is established.[94] The correspondent PSP only has information on a respondent PSP's customer insofar as this is included in the payment order that the correspondent PSP receives from the respondent PSP.[95] A correspondent PSP cannot verify the legitimacy of the source of the funds it is requested

[91] See Commission (2011, p. 5).

[92] For this reason, correspondent banking arrangements are often used during the layering phase of the money laundering process.

[93] See Hoppe, T. (2013, p. 53).

[94] Criminals generally prefer to be onboarded by a Bank established in a country that has relatively low CDD standards.

[95] See ESAs Joint Committee (2017a, p. 33).

to transfer, which leaves the correspondent PSP exposed to the accurateness of the CDD process carried out by the respondent PSP. This makes correspondent banking a 'high risk' activity from an AML/CTF perspective.

To avoid being used for ML/TF purposes, the correspondent PSP should have a profound understanding of the respondent PSP with which it enters into a correspondent banking relationship.[96] From an AML/CTF perspective, the correspondent PSP's customer is the respondent PSP and not the respondent PSP's customer.[97] This means that the correspondent PSP carries out (enhanced) CDD on the respondent PSP rather than the respondent PSP's customers. The fact that the respondent PSP holds a licence, and is therefore subject to AML/CTF supervision, is generally perceived to be a risk mitigant for the correspondent PSP's CDD procedure.[98] However, **Article 19 MLD4** requires that if a respondent PSP is established outside the EEA, the correspondent PSP must carry out enhanced CDD due to the risk that the respondent PSP itself has less effective AML/CTF policies and procedures.[99] Enhanced CDD is also required in case the respondent PSP is established in the EEA but is classified as a high risk customer based on the correspondent PSP's internal risk classification.[100]

[96] **Article 24 MLD4** prohibits PSPs to enter into a correspondent relationship with a shell Bank. PSPs must therefore also take appropriate measures to ensure that they do not engage in correspondent relationships with a PSP that is known to allow its accounts to be used by a shell Bank.

[97] See BIS (2017, p. 23).

[98] See FATF (2016, p. 44).

[99] Carrying out enhanced CDD means that the correspondent PSP must: (i) obtain sufficient information about the respondent PSP to fully understand the nature of the respondent's business and to determine from publicly available information the reputation of the PSP and the quality of supervision; (ii) assess the respondent PSP's AML/CTF controls; (iii) obtain approval from senior management before establishing new correspondent relationships; (iv) document the respective responsibilities of each institution and (v) with respect to payable-through accounts, be satisfied that the respondent PSP has verified the identity of, and performed ongoing CDD on, the clients having direct access to accounts of the correspondent PSP, and that it is able to provide relevant CDD data to the correspondent PSP, upon request.

[100] For Banks it is particularly important to stay alert for the potential use of a correspondent Bank's payable-through account, which is a payment account used directly by the respondent to transact business on its own behalf. This requires a Bank's attention because it involves in essence the provision of payment services at a distance.

6.5 Sanctions Regulations

Further to the AML/CTF requirements, PSPs are also obliged to carry out sanctions screening to ensure compliance with European sanctions regulations. Sanctions screening is the process of verifying whether a relation (e.g., (prospective) customer) is included on a European or national sanctions list issued by *inter alia* the Council of the European Union and NCAs.[101] Sanctions screening involves both relation screening and transaction screening. When monitoring transactions as part of the sanctions screening process, the PSP aims to identify transactions between targeted customers.

When a PSP onboards a prospective customer, the PSP first verifies whether the customer is a targeted individual or company. To this end, the PSP screens the prospective customer against the relevant sanctions lists.[102] A match with a sanctions list means that the PSP is not allowed to onboard the customer and has to notify the NCA thereof without undue delay. Furthermore, the PSP must intervene by either freezing the financial assets of the relevant person or refrain from providing payment services to that person.

Sanctions screening is an obligation for both the payer's PSP and the beneficiary's PSP. Since the selection of relevant sanctions lists is a national responsibility, it is not uncommon for a beneficiary's PSP to be legally obliged to screen cross-border Payments against different lists than a payer's PSP. In case a beneficiary's PSP has a match with a sanctions list for a particular transaction which has been cleared by the payer's PSP, the beneficiary's PSP will have to investigate the relevant transaction. This process delays the execution of the Payment, which is particularly a concern in case of a fast payment. The execution timeline of a fast payment does not allow the beneficiary's PSPs to investigate transactions prior to the crediting of the beneficiary's payment account. Since such investigation may take hours to complete, this issue was flagged by the

[101] Examples include the sanction measures imposed on Iran, Russia and North Korea. It is however prudent for PSPs to also establish their own sanction list based on past experience.

[102] Whenever there is a relevant change regarding the customer or a sanction list has been updated, new sanctions screening may be required.

ECB's Advisory Group on Market Infrastructures for Payments (AMI-Pay).[103] Adopting an EU-wide list instead of working with national lists could provide for a better solution since this would take away the need for the beneficiary's PSP to screen the same transactions.

6.6 Conclusion

Since 1990, the European legislature has adopted numerous directives and regulations to address the ML/TF risk exposures in the market for Payments. The main legislative frameworks that are currently in force include MLD4, MLD6, WTR2 and the sanction regulations.

In their capacity as gatekeepers of the financial markets, all PSPs have to implement adequate policies and procedures to limit the risk of being used for ML/TF purposes. A main AML/CTF requirement for PSPs is the obligation to conduct CDD prior to entering into a business relationship with a prospective PSU or processing a Payment. The CDD requirement applies to Banks and Non-Banks since both categories of PSPs qualify as an 'institution' within the meaning of MLD4. By subjecting both Banks and Non-Banks to the CDD requirement, the European legislature tried to limit the risk that ML/TF activity remains unnoticed. By subjecting all PSPs to the AML/CTF framework, it becomes significantly more difficult to bring funds with an illegit origin into the financial system without being detected, especially if transactions are screened by multiple PSPs.

The CDD obligation requires PSPs to: (i) identify prospective PSUs and verify their identity; (ii) carry out a risk assessment when onboarding a prospective PSU and (iii) monitor Payments for which their customers act as payer or beneficiary. The obligation to conduct CDD is a risk-based requirement, which means that the PSP in question must identify and assess the ML/TF risks to which it is exposed and take the measures it deems appropriate to mitigate these risks in an effective manner. This means for example that PSPs are allowed to conduct simplified or enhanced CDD based on the risk qualification of a particular PSU. MLD4 does not prescribe what the CDD process of a PSP should look like, as a result of which different approaches between PSPs are not uncommon.

As part of the CDD requirement, Banks and Non-Banks are obliged to conduct transaction monitoring. A benefit of having multiple PSPs

[103] See ECB (2018, p. 5).

screening the same transactions is that it increases the likelihood that unusual transactions are identified. For example, in case of a payment initiation service, the PISP screens a payment order prior to releasing it into the Bank's IT system. Subsequently, the payment order is screened by the Bank before it is executed. An advantage of having both PSPs screening the same transaction is that PISPs often have additional data regarding transactions initiated by the relevant payer with other Banks. As a result, the PISP may have a more comprehensive overview of the payer's transaction history and can therefore screen transactions from a different perspective. Moreover, due to the risk-based approach different PSPs have different CDD procedures in place and apply different thresholds and indicators for determining whether a particular transaction is unusual. However, a distinction should be made between PSPs that process Payments and PSPs that only process data. Transaction monitoring is not particularly relevant for AISPs since these PSPs do not have any involvement in the transfer of funds. Subjecting AISPs to the obligation to conduct transaction monitoring does not decrease the ML/TF risk exposures in the Payments market because: (i) AISPs only have access to transaction information relating to payments that have already been cleared and settled; and (ii) AISPs are not authorised to intervene in case it considers a transaction to be unusual.

Secondary Sources

Balani, H. (2017). What Faster Payments Means for Anti-Money Laundering Compliance. *Journal of Financial Compliance, 1*(3), pp. 245, 252.

BIS. (2017). *Guidelines Sound Management of Risks Related to Money Laundering and Financing of Terrorism*, p. 23.

Commission. (2005). *Proposal for a Regulation of the European Parliament and of the Council on Information on the Payer Accompanying Transfer of Funds*, COM (2005) 343 final, pp. 2, 7.

Commission. (2011). *Commission Staff Working Paper on Anti-money Laundering Supervision of and Reporting by Payment Institutions in Various Cross-border Situations*, SEC(2011) 1178 final, pp. 2, 5.

Commission. (2013). *Proposal for a Regulation of the European Parliament and of the Council on Information Accompanying Transfers of Funds*, COM (2013) 44 final.

Commission. (2020). *Communication from the Commission on an Action Plan for a Comprehensive Union Policy on Preventing Money Laundering and Terrorist Financing*, C(2020) 2800 final, p. 5.

EBA (n.d.). Single Rule Book Q&A: Question ID 2019_4712. https://www.eba.europa.eu/single-rule-book-qa/qna/view/publicId/2019_4712. Accessed April 13, 2024.

EBA. (2022a). *Final Report Guidelines on the Use of Remote Customer Onboarding Solutions under Article 13(1) MLD4*, (EBA/GL/2022/15), p. 3.

EBA. (2022b). *Opinion of the European Banking Authority on 'de-risking'*, EBA/Op/2022/01, pp. 2, 22, 23.

EBA (2021). *Guidelines on customer due diligence and the factors credit and financial institutions should consider when assessing the money laundering and terrorist financing risk associated with individual business relationships and occasional transactions ('The ML/TF Risk Factors Guidelines') under Articles 17 and 18(4) of Directive (EU) 2015/849*, EBA/GL/2021/02, p. 212.

ECB. (2018). *12 March 2018 AMI-Pay Workshop on Issues Related to Instant Payments—Outcome*, p. 5.

ESAs Joint Committee. (2012a). *Supervisory Cooperation Protocol between Home Supervisor and Host Supervisor(s) of Agents and Branches of Payment Institutions in Host Member State*, p. 7.

ESAs Joint Committee. (2012b). *Report on the Application of AML/CTF Obligations to, and the AML/CTF Supervision of E-money Issuers, Agents and the Distributors in Europe*, JC 2012 086, pp. 11–12.

ESAs Joint Committee. (2017a). *Joint Guidelines under Articles 17 and 18(4) of Directive (EU) 2015/849 on simplified and enhanced customer due diligence and the factors credit and financial institutions should consider when assessing the money laundering and terrorist financing risk associated with individual business relationships and occasional transactions (The Risk Factors Guidelines)*, Final Guidelines, JC 2017 37, pp. 23–24, 33, 46.

ESAs Joint Committee (2017b). *Joint Guidelines under Article 25 of Regulation (EU) 2015/847 on the measures payment service providers should take to detect missing or incomplete information on the payer or the payee, and the procedures they should put in place to manage a transfer of funds lacking the required information*, Final Guidelines, JC/GL/2017/16.

ESAs Joint Committee (2017c). *Joint Opinion on the Risks of Money Laundering and Terrorist Financing Affecting the Union's Financial Sector*, JC/2017/07, p. 6.

ESAs Joint Committee. (2018). *Opinion on the Use of Innovative Solutions by Credit and Financial Institutions in the Customer due Diligence Process*, JC 2017 81, pp. 5, 16.

ESAs Joint Committee. (2019). *Joint Opinion of the European Supervisory Authorities on the Risks of Money Laundering and Terrorist Financing Affecting the European Union's Financial Sector*, JC2019 59, p. 12.

Fan, G. (2010). *Risks of Electronic Money Misuse for Money Laundering and Terrorism Financing*, Eurasian Group on Combating Money Laundering and Terrorism Financing (EAG), p. 11.

FATF. (2008). *Financial Action Task Force—Terrorist Financing*, p. 7.

FATF. (2013). *Guidance for a Risk-based Approach: Prepaid Cards, Mobile Payments and Internet-based Payment Services*, pp. 11, 14, 16, 23, 34.

FATF. (2014). *Guidance for a Risk-based Approach: The Banking Sector*, p. 6.

FATF. (2016). *Guidance for a Risk-based Approach: Money or Value Transfer Services*, p. 44.

FATF. (2019). *International Standards on Combating Money Laundering and the Financing of Terrorism & Proliferation*, the FATF recommendation, p. 65.

Hoppe, T. (2013). Correspondent Banking en KYC. *Tijdschrift Voor Compliance, No., 1*, 53.

Huang, L. (2015). Countermeasures against Internet-based Money Laundering: A Conceptual Study. *Journal of Information Technology Management, XXVI*(4), pp. 18, 20.

Institute of International Finance. (2016). *Regtech in Financial Services: Technology Solutions for Compliance and Reporting*, p. 3.

Joosen, E. P. M. (2020). *FinTech, BigTech en de antiwitwaswetgeving*, Tijdschrift voor Financieel Recht, No. 3, pp. 108, 110.

Sienkiewicz, S. (2007). *Prepaid Cards: Vulnerable to Money Laundering*, Discussion Paper Payment Cards Center, pp. 6–7.

Woda, K. (2006). Money Laundering Techniques with Electronic Payment Systems. *Information & Security: An International Journal, 18*, pp. 28–29.

CHAPTER 7

Allocation of Liability in Case of Unauthorised or Erroneous Payments

7.1 Background

In case the payer and beneficiary of a particular Payment do not hold their payment account with the same PSP, the execution of the Payment requires the involvement of at least two PSPs. Further to the payer's AS-PSP and beneficiary's AS-PSP, other PSP's, such as PISPs or AISPs, may also be involved in the execution process of a Payment. A key responsibility by which all PSPs in the Payment chain have to abide is the obligation to ensure correct and timely execution of Payments that have been authorised. It is important to note that PSUs also have a responsibility when it comes to warranting the sound functioning of the Payments market in general. The responsibilities of PSUs in this regard revolve mainly around the safe use of payment instruments.

A well-functioning Payments market requires PSPs and PSUs to have complete confidence in the correct and timely execution of authorised Payments. Since each of the PSPs involved in the processing of Payments fulfils a pivotal role, PSPs should be held accountable if they fail to act in accordance with their responsibilities. It is therefore of paramount importance to have clear rules on the allocation of responsibilities and liabilities between the PSPs involved in the execution of Payments. Not having clear rules creates unacceptable ambiguities and impedes a proper functioning

J. A. Jans, *Electronic Payments in the European Market*, EBI Studies in Banking and Capital Markets Law,
https://doi.org/10.1007/978-3-031-64338-5_7

of the Payments market. In particular, it is essential to have comprehensive rules on the allocation of liability between the participants in the Payments ecosystem for unauthorised and incorrectly executed Payments. Running the risk of having too many disputes over unauthorised or incorrectly executed Payments could have adverse effects on the reliability of that particular Payment solution and, as a result, commercial attractiveness of Payment products in general.

The first legislative initiatives on the allocation of liability between PSPs and PSUs in case of non- or incorrectly executed Payments were taken by the European legislature during the nineties of the last century. With the adoption of Directive 97/5/EC, a first step was taken to provide clear rules on the allocation of liability between PSPs for cross-border credit transfers (**Paragraph 3.2.1**).[1] **Article 8(1) Directive 97/5/EC** obliged the payer's PSP was obliged to refund a payer in case a cross-border credit transfer was not successfully completed. With PSD, the scope of the refund obligation of Directive 97/5/EC was broadened and also covered direct debit collections and national credit transfers. Moreover, the cap on the maximum amount that could be refunded under Directive 97/5/EC was abandoned with **Articles 60, 62 and 63 PSD**. Although one-leg Payments were not covered by PSD, PSD did provide Member States the option to also apply the liability requirements to one-leg Payments executed by PSPs located in their jurisdiction.

Under the PSD2 regime, the liability provisions for unauthorised and incorrectly executed Payments cover all Payments regardless of the currency in which they are carried out. Moreover, one-leg Payments are covered by the PSD2 liability provisions for the part of the transaction that is being carried out in the EEA (**Paragraph 3.4.3.1**). In addition, PSD2 describes how liability must be allocated between Banks and TPPs if something goes wrong with the execution of an open banking Payment solution.

When analysing the allocation of legal liabilities for unauthorised and incorrectly executed Payments between Banks and Non-Banks, a distinction is made between: (i) executed Payments that lack the payer's consent and should not have been executed (unauthorised Payments); and (ii) Payments that have been authorised by the payer but were executed incorrectly or not executed at all (erroneous Payments).

[1] Directive 97/5/EC did not provide for a right of refund for national credit transfers or (national) direct debit collections.

7.2 Unauthorised Payments

7.2.1 *What Are Unauthorised Payments?*

A PSP is only allowed to process a Payment if the payer agreed to the execution of that particular Payment. This means that authorisation of a Payment requires the consent of the payer, which must be provided by the payer to his PSP in the agreed form according to **Article 64 PSD2**.

The procedure for giving consent is set out in the framework contract entered into between the PSP and the PSU. In principle, the payer must provide his consent to his PSP prior to the execution of the transaction. However, if agreed between the payer and the PSP, Payments can also be authorised after they have been executed. With so-called 'push transactions', which are credit transfers initiated by the payer via his online banking environment, the payer provides his consent by: (i) stating the name of the beneficiary and the amount to be transferred; and (ii) entering his identification code. With so-called 'pull transactions', which are credit transfers initiated by the payer at a POS terminal using a debit or credit card, the payer typically provides his consent by entering his PIN after the merchant has inserted the transaction amount into the POS terminal. For direct debit collections, which are initiated by the beneficiary, the payer's consent is provided by means of the direct debit mandate.

An executed Payment that lacks the payer's consent qualifies as an unauthorised Payment. There are numerous reasons why a disputed transaction can lack payer's consent. Obviously, a transaction lacks consent if the person initiating the payment order for the execution of the transaction is unauthorised to do so. This typically involves situations where transactions are initiated by imposters using a lost or stolen payment instrument.[2] Alternatively, an executed transaction can be unauthorised because the characteristics of the transaction do not match the characteristics of the payment order. This can for example be the case if an executed direct debit collection does not correspond with the amount specified in

[2] To this end, **Article 2 Delegated Regulation on SCA and CSC** stipulates that PSPs are required to carry out transaction monitoring to detect attempts to use security credentials that were lost or stolen. Such process takes at least the following risk-based factors into account: (i) list of comprised or stolen authentication elements; (ii) the amount of each Payment; (iii) known fraud scenarios in the provision of payment services; (iv) signs of malware infection in any sessions of the authentication procedure.

the relevant mandate. Furthermore, an executed transaction can be unauthorised because the payer has revoked his consent prior to execution and the execution process was not cancelled by the PSP in accordance with the terms laid down in the framework contract.[3] If a payer does not want to proceed with the execution of a transaction after submitting the order for that transaction, the payer is, under certain conditions, allowed to revoke his consent.[4] For one-off credit transfers, the payer can revoke his consent until the moment the payer's PSP receives the payment order.[5] However, **Article 80(5) PSD2** allows the PSU and PSP to agree to a moment of irrevocability that is later than the moment on which the PSP receives the order. In case of a direct debit collection, the payer may revoke his consent at the latest by the end of the business day preceding the day on which the transaction amount is debited from his payment account. Two weeks before the collection is debited from the payer's payment account, the payer receives a pre-notification of the scheduled collection. This pre-notification enables the payer to revoke his consent within the mandatory time limit should he disagree with the forthcoming collection.

The above-mentioned situations provide for clear indications as to when a disputed transaction is unauthorised. There are however situations where it is more difficult to assess whether an executed transaction qualifies as an unauthorised transaction. Especially transactions whereby the payer was misled to make a payment to an imposter instead of the intended beneficiary and which have been authorised in accordance with the PSPs rules and procedures appear to be difficult to categorise. This practice is also known as spoofing. In case of spoofing, the payer initiates the transaction in accordance with the PSP's authentication procedures, as a result of which the PSP has a legal obligation to execute the payment order. With spoofing, the question arises as to whether the disputed

[3] Payment products where transactions are often executed without consent because consent has been revoked are so-called continuous payment authorities. These are recurring payments (credit transfers) which are authorised by the payer who gives his debit card or credit card details to a merchant to which the payer intends to make payments.

[4] This moment is known as the moment of irrevocability. In case the execution of the payment order starts on a specific day (a warehoused payment order), the PSU can revoke the order until the end of the business day preceding the day on which the order would be executed.

[5] **Article 80(2) PSD2** stipulates that if a Payment is initiated by a PISP, the payer is not allowed to revoke the payment order after it has provided the PISP with its consent to initiate the Payment.

transactions are unauthorised transactions for which the payer can seek recourse against his PSP. Clearly, the payer does not intent to transfer funds to an imposter and the argument could therefore be made that the payer has not provided his consent for such payment. However, the common view is that such payment does not qualify as an unauthorised payment within the meaning of PSD2, even though the consent provided by the payer does not match his intentions.[6] It is not for the PSP to question each payment order it receives from its PSUs to verify whether it corresponds with their intentions. A similar view is taken in relation to payments made to the wrong person, which can be the result of the payer providing his PSP with an incorrect unique identifier. If a payer realises that he provided an incorrect unique identifier, the payer's PSP is obliged to cooperate on a best efforts basis and help recover the funds but it cannot be held liable in case it does not succeed in reclaiming the full transaction amount. If the payer's PSP cannot reclaim the funds, it must provide the payer with all relevant information regarding the beneficiary of that transaction so that the payer can reclaim the transaction amount in a civil proceeding. To limit the number of payments that are made to wrong persons via mobile banking solutions, several Dutch Banks introduced a useful tool named the IBAN name check. The IBAN name check triggers a pop-up in the online environment in case the name of the beneficiary and the provided IBAN number do not correspond. The obligation to offer an IBAN name check for instant euro payments has been included in **Article 50(8) PSR Proposal**. The obligation to offer an IBAN name check for all other credit transfers is laid down in the PSR Proposal. Where the payer wants to make use of this service, **Article 57(1) PSR Proposal** provides that the payer's PSP will be liable for any unauthorised Payment if it fails to inform the payer of any discrepancy between the name of the beneficiary and the IBAN. If the payer authorises the Payment after being informed about any discrepancy between the name of the beneficiary and the IBAN and the Payment is executed in accordance with the unique identifier given by the payer, the Payment is considered to be correctly executed according to **Article 50(3) PSR Proposal**.

[6] However, there could still be grounds for liability for the PSP on the basis of its duty of care under national law (**Paragraph 7.2.2**).

7.2.2 *Liability in Case of an Unauthorised Credit Transfer*

Regardless of what causes a particular credit transfer to be unauthorised, the basic rule is that such transaction should not have been executed. This is only different in case the PSU is not a consumer and the PSP has agreed with the PSU that a transaction lacking consent may nevertheless be executed.[7]

If a payer realises that a credit transfer has been executed without his consent, the payer must notify his PSP immediately thereof. It is essential that such notification is made as soon as possible in order to mitigate the financial damages resulting from the unauthorised transaction.[8] **Article 71(1) PSD2** stipulates that the notification should in any case be made within 13 months after the date on which the payer's payment account was debited.[9] **Article 61(1) PSD2** allows PSPs to agree with their corporate clients to apply a shorter notification time limit than 13 months. The question that arises is if the payer has an active duty to investigate whether a specific transaction has been executed without its consent in order to comply with the obligation to notify the PSP immediately of an unauthorised transaction. In this context, a distinction can be made between objective awareness, whereby the payer is considered to be aware of an unauthorised transaction when it has been informed of the executed transaction by his PSP, and subjective awareness, whereby the payer is considered to be aware of the unauthorised transaction when it has taken notice thereof (i.e., regardless of the moment the payer was informed by his PSP of the relevant transaction).[10] In 2021, the Netherlands Supreme Court ruled that under the PSD regime, the moment at which the notification requirement for the payer is triggered is determined by the subjective awareness of the payer with the transaction in

[7] Pursuant to **Article 61(1) PSD2**, the PSP and the non-consumer PSU may agree that the Payment shall also be authorised in the absence of consent (corporate opt-out).

[8] PSD2, Recital 70.

[9] The notification time limit of 13 months does not apply when the PSP fails to make available the relevant transaction information.

[10] See Rank, W. A. K., and Wijnstekers, B. W. (2021, pp. 421–422).

question.[11] Given that the PSD2 equivalent of this notification requirement is similar to the PSD requirement, it is fair to assume that the same interpretation applies in the Netherlands under the PSD2 regime.[12]

If a payer's PSP receives a notification regarding an unauthorised transaction, the PSP is in principle obliged under **Article 73(1) PSD2** to restore the payer's payment account to the state it would have been in case the disputed transaction was not executed. This means that the payer's PSP must refund the payer and apply a credit value date which is the same date on which the payer's payment account was debited as a result of the unauthorised transaction.[13] The payer's payment account must be restored by the end of the following business day after the payer notified his PSP.[14] Having such immediate refund right for PSUs is essential to ensure that PSUs maintain their confidence in the reliability of Payment solutions in general.

A more difficult question to answer is whether a payer's payment account must be restored in case of spoofing. Unlike unauthorised pull transactions, push transactions involving fraud are authorised in accordance with the PSP's procedures. For this reason, the payer can in principle not claim a refund from its PSP in case of spoofing. However, under certain circumstances, the payer may be able to claim damages from his PSP based on a breach of the PSP's duty of care. The payer's PSP could for example breach its duty of care *vis-à-vis* the PSU if it had (or should have had) reasonable grounds to suspect fraud but nevertheless executed the transaction without any further investigation.[15] The payer can in any case not seek compensation from the imposter's PSP to which the funds have been transferred since there is no contractual arrangement between the payer and said PSP. If, for example, the imposter's PSP

[11] See Hoge Raad [Supreme Court of the Netherlands] (2021).

[12] See Rank, W. A. K., and Wijnstekers, B. W. (2021, p. 424).

[13] The payer and his PSP can agree that additional financial compensation is paid if allowed under applicable law.

[14] The payer's PSP is however not to be held liable in cases of abnormal and unforeseeable circumstances beyond the control of the PSP of which the consequences are unavoidable. Furthermore, no liability exists in case the PSP is bound by other legal obligations.

[15] Under certain circumstances, the payer's PSP may be obliged to investigate a particular instruction and to refrain from executing the order on a no-questions asked basis.

was not allowed to provide the imposter with a payment account under the AML/CTF regulations, said PSP may incur a fine from the NCA but it cannot be held responsible *vis-à-vis* the payer for executing the transaction. In **Article 59 PSR Proposal** it is suggested that good-faith consumers who are victim of spoofing whereby the fraudster pretends to be an employee of the consumer's PSP, should be entitled to a refund of the full amount unless the consumer has acted fraudulently or with gross negligence.

7.2.2.1 Limitation of the PSP's Liability

There are situations where the payer's PSP is exonerated from the obligation to refund the payer in case of an unauthorised transaction. The PSP does not have to refund the payer in case it can prove that: (i) contrary to the claim made by the payer, the transaction was authorised; (ii) the payer acted fraudulently or with gross negligence; or (iii) the payer failed to inform his PSP within 13 months after the moment on which the transaction amount was debited from his payment account.[16]

(i) *PSP claims the transaction was authorised*

From a consumer protection point of view, it is essential that a PSP cannot unfairly reject a payer's refund claim in case a payer considers an executed transaction to be unauthorised. According to **Article 72(1) PSD2** it is therefore the payer's PSP that has to prove that the payer did provide his consent for a transaction in case the payer's PSP challenges that the relevant transaction was unauthorised. In principle, the PSP is not allowed to contractually limit its burden of proof or to shift its burden of proof to the payer.[17] Transactions that are not subject to this rule are: (i) transactions initiated with an anonymous payment instrument; and (ii) transactions for which the PSP cannot prove that a credit transfer was authorised, provided that the PSP has agreed with the cardholder that it will not be obliged to prove that a credit transfer was authorised in case this is questioned by the cardholder. In case a PSU is not a consumer, **Articles 61(1) and 72(1) PSD2** allow

[16] The notification time limit of 13 months does not apply if the payer's PSP fails to make available the relevant transaction information.

[17] According to Recital 72 PSD2 such provision should be null and void.

the payer's PSP to contractually limit its burden of proof or to shift the burden of proof to the payer.

A logical interpretation of PSD2 would be that the payer's PSP has until the end of the following business day after the moment on which the payer notified his PSP to prove that, contrary to the claim made by the payer, the transaction was authorised. In case the payer's PSP does not succeed in providing such evidence within that deadline, the payer's PSP must refund the payer and reclaim these funds from the payer at a later date should the payer's PSP succeed in providing the necessary evidence.[18]

Handing over evidence of the mere use of a payment instrument does not suffice to prove that a transaction was authorised. To avoid liability, the PSP will have to provide convincing evidence that it was indeed the payer who used the security credentials for initiating the transaction. Since it is difficult for the payer's PSP to prove that a transaction was actually authorised, it is important for PSPs to build transaction evidence in anticipation of a potential dispute with a PSU. To counter claims from payers, the payer's PSP often applies so-called 'non-repudiation', which is an IT-tool for connecting a person to a particular action of that person. When a payer submits a payment order to his PSP, non-repudiation ensures that the payer cannot deny having submitted that payment order. In case of a dispute, non-repudiation enables the payer's PSP to hold a payer to his commitments. In addition, it is relevant to mention that with certain authentication methods it is easier for the payer's PSP to prove that the person giving the payment order is the authorised payer. For example, if PSPs use biometric authentication methods for authorising payments instead of conventional methods such as a PIN, it is more difficult for imposters to use the PSU's authentication tool. This makes a successful claim by a payer that an imposter authenticated a transaction less likely.

(ii) *Payer acted fraudulently or with gross negligence*

In case a transaction is unauthorised because the payer committed fraud or acted with gross negligence, it is the payer who is to be held accountable for the financial consequences thereof. Provided that a payer's PSP has reasonable grounds for suspecting

[18] The refund by the payer's PSP would then constitute an undue payment.

fraud, e.g., because the PSP suspects that a payer has deliberately made a false claim that a particular payment was unauthorised, **Article 73 PSD2** allows the PSP to investigate the transaction before restoring the payer's payment account to determine whether the unauthorised transaction was indeed caused by fraudulent behaviour. Such investigation must be carried out within a reasonable time frame to protect the payer against any adverse effects caused by such investigation.[19] The PSP has to make sure that if there is a refund once the investigation is completed, the credit value date of that refund is the same date on which the respective amount was debited.[20]

Further to situations where a payer has acted fraudulently, PSPs can avoid liability if they can prove that a payer has acted with gross negligence. Like PSPs, PSUs also have a responsibility to ensure the safety of Payments. Not meeting such responsibilities can have consequences for the allocation of liability between the PSP and PSU in case something goes wrong with the execution of a Payment. First, **Article 69 PSD2** obliges PSUs to use their payment instrument in accordance with the terms of the framework contract and keep their personalised security features safe.[21] Second, PSUs are obliged under **Article 69(1)(b) PSD2** to notify their PSP in case their payment instrument is compromised (lost or stolen). The PSU does in principle not bear any financial consequences from the use of its lost or stolen payment instrument after it has notified its PSP thereof.[22] However, it

[19] Recital 77 of the PSR Proposal suggests that the PSP should be able to conduct such investigation before refunding the payer in case there is a high suspicion that the unauthorised Payment is caused by fraudulent behaviour of the payer and the NCA has been informed thereof. **Article 56(2) PSR Proposal** requires the payer's PSP to refund the payer or provide the payer with supportive evidence for refusing the refund within 10 business days after becoming aware of the unauthorised transaction.

[20] PSD2, Recital 71.

[21] **Article 70(1)(a) PSD2** requires the PSP issuing the payment instrument to ensure that the personalised security features of these payment instruments cannot be accessed by others than the PSU to which the payment instrument is issued. This means that when, for example, the PSP sends the security credentials for a particular payment instrument to a PSU by mail, the PSP will be held responsible if another person obtains access to these credentials.

[22] The payment instrument issuing PSP has to have means available at all times that enable the PSU to make such notification. In addition, the PSP must have measures in

is important that a PSU does its utmost best to limit potential damages during the period prior to making such notification. For this reason, the European legislature aimed to strike a balance between: (i) protecting PSUs against potentially severe losses due to a compromised payment instrument; and (ii) providing PSUs with a financial incentive to notify their PSP as soon as possible after they become aware that their instrument is compromised. In general, PSUs tend to be more cautious if acting negligently triggers a liability on their side. The European legislature considered it appropriate that PSUs should incur losses of the use of a lost or stolen payment instrument up to a maximum of €50[23] until the moment on which they have notified their PSP thereof.[24] For obvious reasons, the liability cap of €50 does not apply in case a payer acted fraudulently or with gross negligence. The concept of gross negligence has not been defined by the European legislature and is therefore interpreted in each Member State on the basis of national law. Consequently, the concept of gross negligence may be applied very differently by PSPs, which could prevent PSUs in certain Member States from exercising their right of reduced liability. PSD2 provides some guidance by stating that acting with gross negligence involves conduct exhibiting a considerable degree

place to immediately block a payment instrument in case a PSU notifies its PSP regarding a lost or stolen payment instrument. In case a PSP does not offer PSUs appropriate means for making such notification, the PSP will be held liable for the financial consequences resulting from the unauthorised use of the payment instrument. For obvious reasons, the PSP and PSU can agree with regard to low value payment instruments, which cannot be blocked, that there is no obligation for the PSU to notify its PSP without undue delay when becoming aware of the loss, theft, misappropriation or unauthorised use of its payment instrument. The payment instrument issuing PSP must unblock or replace the payment instrument once the reasons for blocking no longer exist.

[23] With PSD2, this maximum amount has been reduced from €150 to €50. One might argue whether this reduction of the payer's liability provides for sufficient consumer protection. In the Netherlands, the liability of the payer has been reduced to €0.

[24] **Article 74(1) PSD2** states that there is no such liability for the payer in case: (i) it was not possible for the payer to detect the loss or theft of the payment instrument; or (ii) the loss of the payment instrument was caused by conduct of an employee, agent or branch of the PSP or of an entity to which the PSP has outsourced relevant activities. Furthermore, **Article 74(2) PSD2** states that the payer can always claim full reimbursement from their PSP (does not have a maximum liability of €50) in case: (i) of an unauthorised payment due to a lost or stolen payment instrument; where (ii) the payer's PSP did not require SCA; and (iii) the payer has not acted fraudulently.

of carelessness.[25] An example of behaviour that constitutes gross negligence is if a PSU fails to report the loss or theft of its payment instrument. Another example of behaviour that constitutes gross negligence is if a PSU keeps the security credentials for its payment instrument next to its payment instrument.[26] If the payer's PSP believes that a PSU has acted with gross negligence, it is for the payer's PSP to prove that the PSU has indeed acted with gross negligence.

(iii) *Payer did not notify the PSP of the unauthorised transaction within 13 months*

In case an executed transaction is unauthorised and the payer did not act fraudulently or with gross negligence, **Article 71(1) PSD2** requires the payer's PSP to refund the payer unless the payer fails to report the unauthorised transaction to the payer's PSP within 13 months. It is important to emphasise that the 13 month time limit does not apply in case the payer's PSP has not provided the payer with the relevant information after the execution of the transaction. Since PSD2 does not provide for a time limit, the national law of the relevant Member State determines the time period in which a refund can be claimed.

7.2.3 Unauthorised Credit Transfer Initiated via a PISP

In case of a payment initiation service, the credit transfer is initiated via a PISP instead of by the payer to the AS-PSP directly (**Paragraph 3.4.3.2**). This means that the initiation of a payment initiation service requires the involvement of both the AS-PSP and the PISP, whereby the PISP acts as the payer's first point of contact.

In case a payer challenges the authorisation of a Payment initiated via a PISP, **Article 71(2) PSD2** requires the payer to submit the refund claim to his AS-PSP, even though the disputed transaction was initiated via the PISP. Regardless of whether the AS-PSP or PISP is responsible for the unauthorised transaction, **Article 73(2) PSD2** requires the AS-PSP to restore the payer's payment account by the end of the following business

[25] PSD2, Recital 72.

[26] Ibid.

day.[27] This makes sense from a consumer protection point of view since PSUs are generally not aware of the level of involvement that each PSP has in the execution of a Payment, let alone the responsibility that each PSP has in this regard. Given these circumstances, the European legislature apparently considered it to be too onerous for the payer to claim a refund from the PISP. By allowing the payer to claim a refund from his AS-PSP, the payer is also protected against situations where neither the PISP nor the AS-PSP consider themselves to be liable for the unauthorised transaction. From a level playing field perspective, one can question whether it is proportionate for the AS-PSP to be the first point of contact for unauthorised transactions initiated via a PISP. There can be situations where an AS-PSP refunds a payer and the PISP is responsible for the unauthorised transaction. Such situation leaves the AS-PSP with a credit exposure *vis-à-vis* the PISP, even though the AS-PSP might not have been able to prevent the unauthorised transaction from being executed.

What happens after an AS-PSP has refunded its PSU for an unauthorised transaction? The basic rule is that each PSP takes responsibility for its role in the execution process of a Payment.[28] In case the PISP turns out to be responsible for the unauthorised transaction, the PISP will have to compensate the AS-PSP for refunding the payer. According to **Article 90(2) PSD2**, such compensation must cover the transaction amount as well as any other expenses[29] incurred by the AS-PSP in relation thereto. PISPs are obliged to hold a professional indemnity insurance or some other comparable guarantee against liability to ensure that they can cover their financial liabilities *vis-à-vis* AS-PSPs for situations like these (**Paragraph 4.2.3.3**). PSD2 does not provide any guidance regarding the recourse available for the AS-PSP in case a PISP successfully denies any wrong doing. If a PISP successfully claims not to be responsible, the AS-PSP sees itself exposed to liability unless it can successfully claim that another PSP (e.g., the beneficiary's PSP) is to blame for the unauthorised transaction.

An important determent regarding the scope of responsibility for a PISP is who issued the security credentials that were used for initiating

[27] Restoring the payment account involves bringing the payment account to the state in which it would have been if the unauthorised Payment would not have been executed.

[28] PSD2, Recital 74.

[29] For example, if it involves a credit card transaction, the payer may have incurred interest expenses.

the unauthorised transaction. In other words, whether the AS-PSP or the PISP was responsible for the authentication of the transaction. PISPs have a right to use the authentication process of the AS-PSP and are therefore not legally obliged to develop their own authentication process when offering payment initiation services.[30] However, if a PISP decides to use its own authentication procedure, this increases the PISP's scope of responsibility and therefore its potential liability *vis-à-vis* the AS-PSP.

(i) *Transaction authorised on the basis of the AS-PSP's authentication procedure*

In case a PISP relies on the authentication procedure of the AS-PSP, authentication takes place within the sphere of influence of the AS-PSP. In such case, the PISP instructs the AS-PSP to commence the authentication process. An advantage for the PISP to use the AS-PSP's authentication procedure is that it is not required to develop and maintain its own authentication process.

Since it is the AS-PSP that confirms the authentication of the transaction, the AS-PSP must prove that a disputed transaction has been authenticated. As a consequence, the AS-PSP is in principle liable *vis-à-vis* the payer in case of an unauthorised transaction.[31] An example of a situation where the PISP could be held responsible even though it relies on the authentication process of the AS-PSP is if the PISP would, at its own discretion, change a feature of the transaction, such as the transaction amount or the beneficiary.[32] In

[30] In other words, an AS-PSP cannot force a PISP to develop its own authentication process.

[31] Prior to PSD2, there was no legal provision allowing PISPs to demand access to the payment accounts of an AS-PSP's clients. At that time, PISPs commonly obtained access to these accounts using the security credentials of the PSU (also known as screen scraping). An interesting question is what happens with the allocation of liability in case the PISP applies screen scraping. A payment instrument may only be used by the person(s) on who's name said instrument has been issued. To this end, the terms and conditions of AS-PSPs typically include provisions that the PSU is not allowed to share its personal security credentials with third parties. As a result, screen scraping introduces in particular liability issues for the PSU since it is not allowed to share its security credentials with a PISP.

[32] It is important to note that the AS-PSP cannot delay refunding the payer in case it considers the PISP to be responsible and has not yet received compensation from the PISP.

accordance with **Article 66(3)(h) PSD2**, such transaction would be unauthorised because its lacking the payer's consent.

(ii) *Transaction authorised on the basis of the PISP's authentication procedure*

If a PISP decides to issue its own security credentials, authentication takes place within the sphere of influence of the PISP. This triggers an obligation for the PISP **under Article 66(3)(b) PSD2** to ensure that the personalised security credentials of its PSUs are not accessible to other persons than the relevant PSUs and that these are transmitted by the PISP via safe and efficient channels.

In case a PISP issues its own security credentials, the AS-PSP is no longer in control of the authentication process. If authentication takes place within the IT environment of the PISP, the AS-PSP receives limited information from the PISP regarding the payer (i.e., only the name and IBAN of the payer).[33] Consequently, the AS-PSP cannot verify whether it is indeed the authorised payer that initiates a particular transaction. This means that the AS-PSP has no choice but to rely on the PISP's authentication process. Since the AS-PSP has a risk exposure which it cannot mitigate itself, PSD2 offers the AS-PSP in such situations the possibility to block a PISP's access to its payment accounts in case there are clear indications of unauthorised or fraudulent payment account access by that PISP.[34] Even if a PISP issues its own security credentials, the AS-PSP remains liable for the processing of the transactions and continues to act as the first point of contact for the payer if anything goes wrong with a particular payment.[35] But what happens after the payer's AS-PSP restores the payer's payment account because of an unauthorised payment? It is impossible for the AS-PSP to prove that the transaction was authorised in accordance with the PISP's authentication procedure. According to **Article 72 PSD2** it is therefore the PISP that will have to provide evidence that it was the authorised payer that used his

[33] See Wolters, P. T. J., and Jacobs, B. P. F. (2018, p. 7).

[34] In case access is blocked by the AS-PSP, the AS-PSP informs the relevant PSU thereof.

[35] This imbalance triggers the need to have contractual arrangements in place between the AS-PSP and the PISP.

security credentials in case the payer challenges that the transaction was unauthorised.[36]

Given the increased scope of liability for PISPs when using their own security credentials for the authorisation of credit transfers, it is not very likely that a large number of PISPs will issue their own security credentials. Also, contractual arrangements with AS-PSPs are required in case a PISP decides to issue its own security credentials, which PISPs may not be able to enter into on favourable terms.

7.2.4 *Unauthorised Direct Debit Collections*

Like credit transfers, direct debit collections qualify as unauthorised if executed without the payer's consent. Since direct debit collections are executed on the basis of instructions received from the beneficiary, without these instructions being verified against the characteristics of the mandate[37], it is of paramount importance to have legal safeguards in place to protect the payer against collections that are unauthorised. These legal safeguards are provided for in the form of: (i) a generic refund right for authorised collections on a no-questions asked basis within the meaning of **Article 77(1) PSD2**; and (ii) a separate refund right for unauthorised collections (as with unauthorised credit transfers). Not having such refund rights would have weakened the payer's trust in direct debit collections as a Payment solution, thereby making it a commercially unattractive Payment product for PSPs to offer.

In case a payer denies having consented to the execution of a particular direct debit collection, the payer can ask his PSP to reverse the transaction. **Article 71 PSD2** allows a payer to request a refund of an unauthorised direct debit collection within 13 months after the date on which the funds were debited from his payment account, but in the event such a request is made after eight weeks the payer must substantiate his claim. It is important to emphasise that the refund right is not available for corporate clients that use the direct debit product in accordance with the EPC DD B2B Scheme. The EPC DD B2B Scheme therefore requires

[36] Showing records of the use of a particular payment instrument for initiating the transaction is not sufficient to claim authentication.

[37] Unless the collection is executed under EPC DD B2B Scheme.

that the payer's PSP verifies each individual collection against the mandate before executing the collection.

If a payer's PSP receives a refund request, the beneficiary of that direct debit collection will be asked to share the mandate on the basis of which the disputed collection was executed so that the payer's PSP can verify whether the mandate provides for the payer's consent.[38] In case no consent was given by the payer or the consent given does not correspond with the collection, **Article 77(2) PSD2** requires the payer's PSP to restore the payer's payment account within ten business days or provide justification for refusing such refund.[39] The EPC DD Core Scheme provides a contractual entitlement for the payer's PSP to recover the amount of the refund from the beneficiary's PSP. The beneficiary's PSP can recover the amount of the refund from the beneficiary in accordance with its contractual arrangement with the beneficiary. It is important to emphasise that the refund does not discharge the payer of its responsibility to resolve any issues in respect of the disputed collection with the beneficiary.

7.3 Erroneous Execution of Payments

If a payer provides his consent for the execution of a particular transaction and the payer's PSP authorises said transaction, both the payer and beneficiary should be able to rely on its correct execution. For this reason, the payer's PSP and the beneficiary's PSP are obliged to provide for timely and correct execution once a transaction has been authorised. Not executing or wrongly executing an authorised transaction triggers a liability for the PSP responsible for the erroneous payment.

In general, a transaction is considered to be erroneous in case one of the PSPs fails to process the transaction in accordance with the payer's payment order. Such failure can, for example, be caused by a technical issue, such as IT-infrastructure failure causing late execution. Alternatively, a transaction can be erroneous because the full transaction amount has not been transferred or the execution of the transaction did not take place within the prescribed execution time limit.

[38] It can be agreed with non-consumer clients (corporate opt-out) that there is no right to request a refund regarding an executed direct debit collection.

[39] Such clarification should also be provided within ten business days after receipt of the request.

7.3.1 *Liability in Case of an Erroneous Credit Transfer*

With regard to credit transfers, **Article 89(1) PSD2** provides that it is the payer's PSP that is in principle responsible *vis-à-vis* the payer for the timely and correct execution of the transaction. This means that if a payer challenges the correct execution of a particular credit transfer, the payer must notify his PSP thereof without undue delay and at the latest within 13 months after the debit date of the disputed transaction.[40] Upon receipt of such notification, the payer's PSP must either correct the Payment or restore the payer's payment account.[41]

If the payer's PSP claims that the execution of a disputed credit transfer was not erroneous, **Article 72(1) PSD2** obliges the payer's PSP to prove that the payment was executed correctly. To avoid liability, the payer's PSP must provide the payer with evidence that the credit transfer was indeed authenticated, correctly executed and not influenced by any shortcomings on the side of the payer's PSP. In addition, the payer's PSP must prove that the beneficiary's PSP received the corresponding funds. PSD2 does not allow PSPs to contractually limit their burden of proof or to shift their burden of proof to the payer.[42]

Alternatively, a situation could occur where the payer's PSP agrees with the payer that a disputed credit transfer was incorrectly executed but the payer's PSP denies responsibility. For example because the payer's PSP considers the error to be caused by the beneficiary's PSP or a PISP (in case of a payment initiation service). Since each PSP assumes responsibility for its own role in the processing of a credit transfer, liability for an erroneous transaction may in such case shift from the payer's PSP to the beneficiary's PSP or PISP.

The beneficiary's PSP is to blame for the erroneous payment

In case the payer's PSP succeeds in proving that the beneficiary's PSP received the transaction amount in good order, the payer's PSP is

[40] The PSP can agree with non-consumers (corporate opt-out) on a different timeline. The notification time limit of 13 months does not apply when the PSP fails to make available the relevant transaction information.

[41] **Article 91 PSD2** stipulates that further financial compensation for an erroneous Payment may be determined in accordance with the law applicable to the contract concluded between the payer and its PSP.

[42] According to Recital 72 PSD2 such provision is null and void.

no longer liable *vis-à-vis* the payer for the incorrect execution of the credit transfer. If the beneficiary's PSP is to blame for the incorrect execution, for example, because it has credited the payment account of another person than the beneficiary, the beneficiary's PSP is liable *vis-à-vis* the beneficiary and must immediately credit his payment account.[43] According to **Article 89(1) PSD2** this does not trigger a liability on the side of the beneficiary's PSP *vis-à-vis* the payer.

It is relevant to mention that in case of late execution, whereby the funds are at the disposal of the beneficiary but the beneficiary's payment account is not credited within the mandatory time limit, the payer cannot request a refund.[44] This makes sense since there is already a liability on the side of the beneficiary's PSP *vis-à-vis* the beneficiary, which would make it not proportional to also have a liability *vis-à-vis* the payer for the same transaction. Having a right of refund for the payer would in this situation amount to an unjustified sanction for the payer's PSP.[45]

The PISP is to blame for the erroneous payment

In case of an incorrectly executed payment initiation service, the payer cannot request a refund from his PISP directly. This means that, similar to the situation of an unauthorised transaction initiated via a PISP (**Paragraph 7.2.3**), the payer will have to seek recourse against the AS-PSP and the AS-PSP will have to refund the payer in accordance with **Article 90(1) PSD2**, even though the PISP may be responsible for the erroneous payment.

In case the PISP turns out to be liable for the erroneous transaction, the AS-PSP can only seek recourse against the PISP after it has refunded the payer. In other words, it is not allowed for the AS-PSP to delay payment to the payer until it receives the corresponding funds from the PISP. According to **Article 90(1) PSD2**, the PISP must prove to the

[43] When funds are transferred between a payer and a beneficiary holding their payment account with the same PSP, the execution of the transaction only requires the involvement of a single PSP, acting both as payer's PSP and beneficiary's PSP. Therefore, the PSP is not liable *vis-à-vis* the payer but is liable *vis-à-vis* the beneficiary in its capacity as beneficiary's PSP.

[44] However, in case the payer incurred damages as a result of late payment, the payer may request compensation for such damages from his PSP.

[45] See Commission (2016), question 76.

AS-PSP that the transaction was accurately recorded, not affected by a technical breakdown or other deficiency and has been accurately received by the AS-PSP. In case the PISP does not succeed in proving this or in case it is evident that the PISP caused the transaction to be erroneous, **Article 90(2) PSD2** requires that the PISP compensates the AS-PSP for the costs incurred in relation thereto.[46]

7.3.2 Incorrectly Executed Direct Debit Collections

The allocation of liability is somewhat different in case an erroneous transaction involves a collection under a direct debit scheme. If something goes wrong with the execution of a direct debit collection, e.g., the payment order was not transmitted by the beneficiary's PSP to the payer's PSP within the agreed time limit or the beneficiary's PSP fails to have the transaction amount at the beneficiary's disposal immediately after it is credited to the beneficiary's PSP, **Article 89(2) PSD2** provides that it is the beneficiary's PSP that is in principle liable *vis-à-vis* the beneficiary. In case the beneficiary's PSP caused the collection to be incorrectly executed, it shall immediately re-transmit the payment order to the payer's PSP. Furthermore, the beneficiary's PSP must ensure that the value date of the funds credited to the beneficiary's account is no later than it would have been in case the transaction was correctly executed.

In situations where the beneficiary's PSP is not liable for the erroneous payment, **Article 89(2) PSD2** stipulates that the payer's PSP shall in principle be liable to the payer for that transaction. This means that the payer's PSP must restore the payer's payment account to its situation prior to the execution of the erroneous payment. No such refund obligation exists however for the payer's PSP in case it can prove that the beneficiary's PSP received the corresponding funds, even though, for example, these funds have not been transferred within the mandatory time limit. In such case, the payer's PSP will no longer be liable *vis-à-vis* the payer but the beneficiary's PSP will have to restore the beneficiary's payment account and claim compensation for this effort from the payer's PSP.

[46] Such compensation would include the transaction amount and damages incurred by the AS-PSP.

7.4 Account Information Services

The business model of an AISP is very different from that of a PISP or an AS-PSP. The business model of AISPs is based on the processing of (personal) data instead of the transferring of funds between payers and beneficiaries. Since no funds are transferred when account information services are provided, the legal provisions on the allocation of liability regarding unauthorised and erroneous transactions are not relevant for AISPs. However, PSUs that use the services of an AISP can nevertheless incur damages in case their AISP does not provide its services in accordance with the legal standards. One of such legal standards is the requirement for AISPs to obtain explicit consent from a PSU prior to accessing, using and processing its payment account information. A PSU may incur damages if an AISP obtains access to its payment account without the PSU having provided its explicit consent.

The AS-PSP that manages the payment account of the PSU on whose behalf an AISP demands access cannot verify whether such explicit consent has been provided by the PSU. This is an undesirable side effect of PSD2, which does not allow AS-PSPs to demand a contractual agreement with AISPs for such payment account access. From a competition perspective, it makes sense to prohibit AS-PSPs to demand such contractual agreement since this would enable AS-PSPs to impose barriers for AISPs to enter the market. The downside however is that an AS-PSP cannot verify whether a request from an AISP to access a certain payment account is authorised by the PSU. In practice, this means that when an AS-PSP receives a request from an AISP to grant access to certain payment accounts, the AS-PSP will have to trust the AISP that the necessary consent has been given. However, if an AS-PSP provides an AISP unauthorised access, the AS-PSP breaches its duty *vis-à-vis* the PSU to safeguard the security of its payment account. This in itself could provide for a legal basis for the PSU to claim damages from the AS-PSP.

A situation where an AISP may be exposed to damages is if it cannot ensure the safety of the PSU's security credentials. The AISP has a right to use the authentication process of the AS-PSP. However, **Article 67(2)(b) PSD2** requires the AISP to ensure that these credentials are not, with the exception of the PSU and the AS-PSP, accessible to other persons and that when they are transmitted by the AISP, this is done via safe and efficient channels. Not meeting these standards may trigger liability issues on the side of the AISP. Furthermore, **Article 67(2)(e) PSD2** stipulates that the AISP can be held liable in case an AISP requests sensitive payment data linked to a PSU's payment account, which an AISP is not allowed to have in its possession. It is important to emphasise that such request may also trigger a liability for the AS-PSP in case it provides the AISP with such information.[47] Moreover, liability could arise under **Article 67(2)(f) PSD2** in case the AISP uses or stores personal data for other purposes then performing the account information service requested by the PSU.

7.5 Liability in Case of Non-availability

What happens in case the online banking environment of a PSP is temporarily unavailable for its PSUs due to a cyberattack (e.g., DDos) or an IT failure? Since PSUs will not be able to access their online banking environment and initiate Payments from their payment account, the question arises as to whether non-availability triggers a liability of the PSP *vis-à-vis* its PSUs.

Although the wording of the PSD2 liability provisions suggests that not being able to initiate a transaction is not covered by the liability provisions for non-execution, some argue that these rules also apply in case of unavailability of a PSP's online banking environment.[48] No legal evidence can be found however to support this statement. Since the non-execution provisions of PSD2 only cover situations where a payment order has been initiated, these provisions do in my opinion not provide for a legal basis to hold a PSP liable in case of unavailability of its online environment.

Under **Articles 6:74 and 6:75 of the Dutch Civil Code**, PSUs can hold their PSPs liable for the unavailability of their online banking environment in case it constitutes a breach of contract and said breach is caused by an external event that is attributable to the PSP. Whether or not the PSP can be held liable requires a factual assessment of the case at hand that takes into consideration, amongst others, the precautionary measures that the PSP could have reasonably taken to prevent the unavailability of its online environment. Most Banks address the potential risk of liability for unavailability of their online environment by including in their terms

[47] The AS-PSP loses control over highly sensitive information which makes it difficult to ensure the confidentiality of said information.

[48] See Tjong Tjin Tai, E. (2013, p. 4).

and conditions that such availability is not guaranteed and that unavailability will not result in liability. One can question however whether such contractual provision will hold in court if the PSP has not implemented adequate measure to safeguard its online environment against unavailability. Such condition could be unreasonably onerous within the meaning of **Article 6:236 (a) Dutch Civil Code**.

In addition, a PSP could be held liable by a PSU in case of unavailability of its online banking environment if such unavailability constitutes a breach of its duty of care. Given the pivotal role that Payments fulfil in the European economy, not offering a minimum level of availability could constitute a breach of a PSP's duty of care. This is particularly relevant for Banks since Banks have a special duty of care *vis-à-vis* PSUs because of their function in society.[49]

7.6 Conclusion

Because the execution of Payments often requires the involvement of multiple PSPs, it is essential to have clear rules on the allocation of liability between PSPs in case of an unauthorised or erroneous Payments. A transaction is unauthorised if its lacking the payer's consent. Erroneous Payments are Payments that have not been executed in a timely and correct manner.

The European legislature's objective for the current rules on the allocation of legal liabilities between Banks and Non-Banks for unauthorised and erroneous Payments appears to be to provide for maximum PSU protection. It is the payer's PSP that is in principle responsible *vis-à-vis* the payer in case a Payment is unauthorised or erroneous. This means that the payer's PSP is obliged to restore the payer's payment account unless it can demonstrate that the transaction was authorised or correctly executed. The same applies in case the disputed Payment has been initiated by a PISP. Regardless of which PSP is responsible for the execution of an unauthorised or erroneous transaction, the payer's Bank will have to restore the payer's payment account. The payer's Bank is in first instance liable *vis-à-vis* the payer since the European legislature considered safeguarding the interests of PSUs to be the highest priority in case of an unauthorised or erroneous Payment. By allowing the payer to approach

[49] See Van Zandvoort, M. A. H. (2018, p. 251).

his Bank in case of a disputed transaction, the payer is protected against situations where neither the PISP nor the Bank considers themselves to be liable for the relevant transaction. The current allocation of liabilities between Banks and Non-Banks with regard to payment initiation services can however be considered disproportionate in the context of the competitive position between Banks and Non-Banks. There can be situations where a Bank refunds a payer and the PISP turns out to be responsible for the execution of the disputed transaction. Banks are under all circumstances the payer's first point of contact in case of an unauthorised or erroneous Payment, even in situations where there is no doubt the PISP is to be held liable. Allowing the payer to submit his refund claim to his Bank, even in situations where the PISP is responsible for the disputed transaction, is not proportionate in the context of the competitive position between Banks and Non-Banks. Such situation leaves the Bank in question with a credit exposure *vis-à-vis* the PISP, even though the Bank might not have been able to prevent the disputed transaction from being executed.

Secondary Sources

Commission. (2016). Questions and Answers on the Payment Services Directive—Last Updated 22 February 2011, question 76.

Hoge Raad [Supreme Court of the Netherlands]. (2021). HR 21 May 2021, ECLI:NL:HR:2021:749 (ING Bank/Van den Hurk).

Rank, W. A. K., & Wijnstekers, B. W. (2021). Aansprakelijkheid voor niet-toegestane betalingstransacties: wie betaalt de rekening? *Maandblad Voor Vermogensrecht, 2021*(12), pp. 421–422, 424.

Tjong Tjin Tai, E. (2013). Zorgplichten van banken tegen DDoS-aanvallen. *NJB*, 2013/1969, p. 4.

Van Zandvoort, M. A. H. (2018). Fintechs getemd? Zorgplichten en aansprakelijkheden van betaaldienstverleners na invoering van PSD II. *Tijdschrift voor Financieel Recht*, 5, p. 251.

Wolters, P. T. J., & Jacobs, B. P. F. (2018). De toegang tot betaalrekeningen onder PSD2. *Ondernemingsrecht*, 38, p. 7.

CHAPTER 8

Payment Systems and Non-Banks Access to Payment Systems

8.1 Background

The processing of Payments requires a technical infrastructure that enables PSPs to transfer funds between each other. Banks play a key role in the processing of Payments since Banks were the first PSPs to offer payment accounts and Payment products to PSUs in the EU. It was therefore a logical step for the banking sector to develop and maintain the first infrastructures for clearing and settlement of national and cross-border Payments in the EU.

Initially, Banks used to settle Payments using bilateral arrangements called correspondent banking arrangements (**Paragraph 6.4.6**).[1] Banks applied such arrangements when instructed to transfer funds to a beneficiary holding a payment account with a different Bank.[2] The rules and regulations on the settlement of Payments via correspondent banking arrangements were primarily based on self-regulation. Absent a European legal framework on the basis of which Non-Banks could claim a role in these correspondent banking arrangements, Non-Banks did not have any involvement in these arrangements. The fact that both the settlement

[1] See ECB (2010, p. 39).

[2] In the eighties and nineties of the last century, correspondent banking networks such as Eurogiro enabled Banks to process cross-border Payments.

J. A. Jans, *Electronic Payments in the European Market*, EBI Studies in Banking and Capital Markets Law,
https://doi.org/10.1007/978-3-031-64338-5_8

infrastructures and the rules governing these infrastructures were developed by the banking sector made it difficult for Non-Banks to enter the market for Payments.

Although correspondent banking arrangements continue to be used by Banks today, its importance for settling Payments has decreased over the years.[3] Higher costs as well as increased regulatory restrictions on correspondent banking arrangements have resulted in Banks seeking alternatives.[4] Since the nineties of the last century, there has been a substantial increase in the use of payment systems as an alternative to correspondent banking arrangements. Nowadays, payment systems clear and settle the vast majority of the Payments executed between PSPs. Subsequently, a shift has taken place from the self-regulation framework for correspondent banking arrangements implemented by the banking sector towards a European legislative framework governing clearing and settlement by payment systems.

One of the main reasons for carrying out supervision on payment systems is to ensure the stability and operational reliability of these systems. These objectives are part of the Eurosystem's's[5] responsibility for carrying out indirect supervision on payment systems called 'oversight'. However, with the increasing involvement of Non-Banks in the European market for Payments, the scope of payment system supervision has been broadened to also cover aspects of sound competition between Banks and Non-Banks. Allowing Non-Banks access to payment systems is considered to be essential by the European legislature for levelling the playing field between Banks and Non-Banks. However, one should also consider the fact that non-Bank payment system access increases the security risk exposure for payment systems and their participants. Given the interconnectedness of PSPs and payment systems, there can be circumstances in which facilitating non-Bank payment system access exposes the market to systemic risks, which in turn can have adverse effects on the stability of the financial markets in general. Systemic risk involves the risk of a PSP's failure leading to considerable adverse effects on one or several

[3] See BIS (2016a, p. 9).

[4] Ibid., p. 12.

[5] According to **Article 282(1) TFEU**, the Eurosystem consists of the ECB together with the national central banks of the Member States whose currency is the euro.

other PSPs.[6] Because this risk is of particular importance for the banking sector, the European legislature adopted amongst others Directive 2014/59/EU establishing a framework for the recovery and resolution of Banks and investment firms (**'BRRD'**)[7], which allows for the intervention in a failing Bank to ensure the continuity of the Bank's critical functions[8] and to minimise the impact of a Bank's failure on the economy and financial system.[9] The Payments business is a function that qualifies as a Bank's critical function within the meaning of BRRD.[10]

Although the business of a non-Bank is generally smaller compared to Banks, failure of a non-Bank may also have a contagion effect on other PSPs and an adverse impact on financial stability. Such risk exists because of the interconnectedness between PSPs in the Payments market and the dominant market position that certain Non-Banks have in the market for Payments. In this regard, the case of the Dutch FinTech Adyen is worth mentioning. Adyen is a PSP founded in 2006 that was initially licensed as a PI. Since 25 April 2017, Adyen operates as a PSP on the basis of a banking licence. It is generally assumed that the Dutch Central Bank (*De Nederlandsche Bank*), which is the NCA in the Netherlands, fulfilled a steering role by demanding that Adyen would upgrade its PI licence to a banking licence. Although we do not know the specific facts, the general perception is that the Dutch Central Bank instructed Adyen to obtain a banking licence so that the Dutch Central Bank would be better able to conduct adequate supervision on the business operations of Adyen. The premise is that this was necessary because of the impressive growth of Adyen's Payments business and the large volume of Payments that were being processed.

[6] See ECB (2000b, pp. 10–11).

[7] Directive 2014/59/EU of 15 May 2014 "establishing a framework for the recovery and resolution of credit institutions and investment firms (...)", OJ L 173, 12.6.2014, pp. 190–348.

[8] **Article 2(1)(35) BRRD** defines 'critical functions' as activities, services or operations the discontinuance of which is likely in one or more Member States, to lead to the disruption of services that are essential to the real economy or to disrupt financial stability due to the size, market share, external and internal interconnectedness, complexity or cross-border activities of an institution or group, with particular regard to the substitutability of those activities, services or operations.

[9] BRRD, Recital 5.

[10] See FSB (2013, p. 7).

Despite the fact that sound competition between Banks and Non-Banks is a key priority, this should never result in the European legislature making unacceptable concessions regarding the safety of the Payment infrastructure. In practice, the European legislature must therefore strike a balance between: (i) safeguarding the reliability of the clearing and settlement process; and (ii) fostering competition between Banks and Non-Banks by allowing Non-Banks access to payment systems.

8.2 Payment Systems as a Means for Clearing and Settlement of Payments

8.2.1 *What Is a Payment System?*

Payment systems provide clearing and/or settlement services to PSPs. However, different definitions are used to describe the business activities of a payment system. For example, the ECB takes a holistic view and considers a payment system to be the '*complete set of payment instruments, intermediaries, rules, procedures, processes and interbank funds transfer systems that facilitate the circulation of money*'.[11] This broad definition encompasses all layers of the life cycle of a Payment (**Paragraph 2.1**). A narrower definition can be found in **Article 2(6) SEPA Regulation** and **Article 4(7) PSD2**, which define a payment system as '*a funds transfer system with formal and standardised arrangements and common rules for the processing, clearing or settlement of payment transactions*'. An argument for using a more restricted definition of a payment system is that it better captures the addressees of oversight supervision, which focusses on service providers responsible for the clearing and settlement of Payments.

Figure 8.1 illustrates the involvement of a payment system in the processing of a Payment.

If a payer wants to make a payment to a beneficiary (**1**), the payer submits a payment order to the payer's Bank (**2**). Upon receipt of the payment order, the payer's Bank debits the payer's payment account and submits a payment order into the payment system, which validates the order before it is accepted for processing (**3**).[12] After the order has been

[11] See ECB (2010, p. 25).

[12] The payment system validates amongst others the key data elements of the Payment message and the security measures for ensuring the identification of the payer's Bank and the integrity and non-repudiation of the payment order.

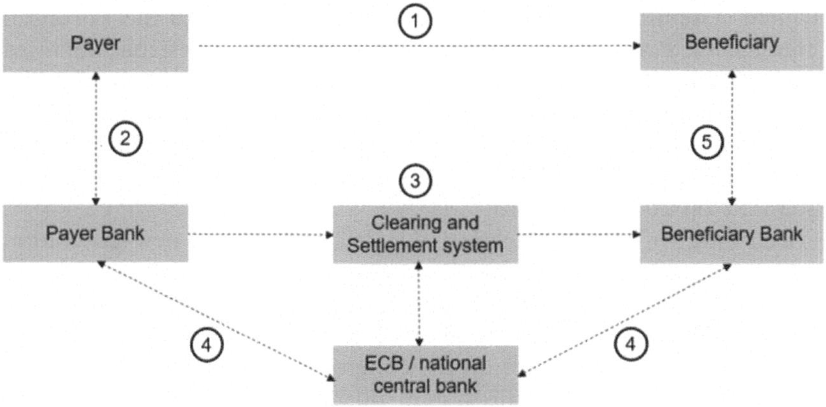

Fig. 8.1 Flowchart payment system

validated, the payment system calculates the impact of the order on the mutual positions of each of its participants.[13] Subsequently, the Payment is settled by the debiting of the payer's Bank payment account with the ECB/national central bank and the crediting of the beneficiary's Bank payment account with the ECB/national central bank (**4**). Subsequently, the beneficiary's Bank credits the payment account of the beneficiary (**5**).

Notwithstanding the lack of agreement as to how a payment system should be defined, there appears to be consensus as regards the different types into which payment systems can be categorised. A payment system can be categorised as a large-value payment system (**'LVPS'**) or a retail payment system.[14] According to **Article 2(18) SEPA Regulation**, LVPSs clear and settle Payments of high priority and urgency, which often represent a large transaction amount. The first LVPS in the EU was TARGET[15], which was founded by the Eurosystem in 1999. TARGET settled Payments using a decentralised technical infrastructure that connected 16 national Real-Time Gross Settlement (**'RTGS'**)

[13] See ECB (2010, p. 41).

[14] Ibid., p. 48.

[15] Trans-European Automated Real-time Gross settlement Express Transfer system.

payment systems[16] with the ECB's payment system called the European Central Bank Payment Mechanism (EPM).[17] With the establishment of TARGET2 in 2007, a centralised platform was introduced, known as the Single Shared Platform, which replaced the function of the national RTGS payment systems used in TARGET.[18] In order to improve the technical aspects of TARGET2, TARGET2 has been replaced by the new RTGS system T2 on 20 March 2023.[19]

According to ECB Guideline (EU) 2022/912 on a new-generation Trans-European Automated Real-time Gross Settlement Express Transfer system (TARGET) (**'ECB Guideline T2'**).[20] According to **Article 3(1) ECB Guideline T2**, T2 is structured as a combination of different payment systems which make up the component systems of T2, whereby each central bank of the Eurosystem operates its own T2 component system. According to **Article 1 ECB Guideline T2**, T2 provides the settlement of central bank operations through Main Cash Accounts (**'MCAs'**) maintained by participants.[21] Furthermore, **Article 1 ECB Guideline T2** requires participants to maintain an RTGS Dedicated Cash Account (**'RTGS DCA'**) for large value real-time gross settlement of Payments. For the settlement of instant payments, **Article 1 ECB Guideline T2** requires participants to maintain a TARGET Instant Payment Settlement (TIPS) Dedicated Cash Account (**'TIPS DCA'**). According to **Article 1(2) Part II of Annex I ECB Guideline T2**, Participants must maintain at least one MCA with the national central bank and may

[16] The following national RTGS systems are a part of TARGET: (i) ELLIPS (Belgium); (ii) CHAPS Euro (UK); (iii) RTGS^{plus} (Germany); (iv) TOP (Netherlands); (v) SPGT (Portugal); (vi) ARTIS (Austria); (vii) TBF (France); (viii) SORBNET- EURO (Poland); (ix) LIPS- Gross (Luxembourg); (x) BoF-RTGS (Finland); (xi) New BIREL (Italy); (xii) IRIS (Ireland); (xiii) HERMES (Greece); (xiv) SLBE (Spain); (xv) ERIX (Sweden) and (xvi) Kronos (Denmark).

[17] See CPSS (2012, p. 94).

[18] The Single Shared Platform was developed by the national central banks of Germany, France and Italy.

[19] See ECB (n.d.).

[20] ECB Guideline (EU) 2022/912 of 24 February 2022 "on a new-generation Trans-European Automated Real-time Gross Settlement Express Transfer system (TARGET) and repealing (...)", OJ L 163, 17.6.2022, pp. 84–185.

[21] Under the TARGET2 account structure the accounts for RTGS and liquidity management were the same.

also hold one or more RTGS DCAs and/or TIPS DCAs.[22] As part of the replacement of TARGET2, the balances of participants held on the account in the payments module of TARGET2 (PM accounts) and the HAM account have been transferred to the relevant MCAs.

An alternative LVPS for processing euro Payments in the EEA is EURO1. EURO1 is a privately held system operated and owned by EBA Clearing.[23] EURO1 is a clearing system for interbank and commercial euro Payments and uses the services of T2 to settle the outstanding positions between the participants in EURO1 at the end of each day. To this end, EURO1 sends the netted amounts of the intraday transactions to T2 for settlement. Depending on the preferences of the participants, such as the urgency of a particular transaction, participants can send their large-value payment orders to T2 directly or indirectly via EURO1.

LVPSs such as T2 settle Payments in central bank money. Central bank money is issued by a central bank and represents a claim on the central bank in the form of bank notes/coins or deposit liabilities.[24] The ECB is the only central bank in Europe that is allowed to issue central bank money in euro. Using central bank money as settlement asset has important advantages. For example, using central bank money reduces liquidity risk exposures for the participants in the payment system.[25] Liquidity risk is the risk that a participant in the payment system does not have sufficient financial means to cover its financial obligations *vis-à-vis* other participants.[26] Using central bank money as settlement asset reduces a participant's liquidity risk exposure as participants can dispose of central bank money easily and without loss of value. Central bank money can be exchanged for commercial bank money at par, which means that there is a one-to-one conversion rate between central bank money and commercial bank money.

According to **Article 2(22) SEPA Regulation** Retail payment systems are systems that clear and settle primarily low value and low priority

[22] It must be noted that T2 also offers a Dedicated Cash Account for the settlement of securities.

[23] EBA Clearing is a bank owned provider of pan-European payment infrastructure solutions and was founded by the Euro Banking Association in June 1998.

[24] Deposit liabilities are credit balances held by a Bank with the central bank.

[25] See BIS (2003, p. 11).

[26] See ECB (2010, p. 122).

Payments. Retail payment systems also play a prominent role in the stability of the European financial system since the majority of the Payments in the EU are carried out between individuals and companies.[27] The European market for retail payment systems is relatively fragmented compared to the market for LVPSs.[28] Whereas only a few LVPSs clear and settle large-value payments in the EU, EU retail payment systems operate predominantly at a national scale. The only retail payment systems that currently operate across Europe are STEP1[29] and STEP2.[30]

Retail payment systems typically settle transactions in commercial bank money, which is money issued by Banks that represents a claim on these Banks in the form of deposit liabilities.[31,32] The market generally trusts the use of commercial bank money as settlement asset because Banks can easily convert these liabilities into either: (i) other commercial bank money (the balance standing to the credit of payment accounts held with other Banks); or (ii) central bank money.[33] Since commercial bank money can be exchanged for central bank money at par, PSUs do not notice any differences in case their Payments are executed using commercial bank money or central bank money as settlement asset.[34]

8.2.2 Gross Settlement Versus Net Settlement

Payment systems that settle Payments can apply gross settlement or net settlement. With gross settlement, each individual Payment is cleared and settled separately.[35] An important advantage of gross settlement is that it

[27] See ECB (2016b, p. 7).

[28] See CPSS (2012, p. 78).

[29] STEP1 is operational since November 2000 and complements EURO1 by offering the processing of retail and commercial payments.

[30] STEP2 is operational since April 2003 and was developed as the first pan- European ACH (PE-ACH) for bulk payments in euro.

[31] Credit balances on payment accounts held with Banks.

[32] Retail payment systems can however also use central bank money as settlement asset.

[33] A situation where commercial bank money is converted into central bank money is when a person withdraws money from an ATM.

[34] See BIS (2003, p. 8).

[35] See Bank of England (1996, p. 21).

enables Payments to be processed in near real-time.[36] This reduces the credit risk exposures for the participants in the payment system substantially.[37] Gross settlement is therefore the standard for LVPSs such as T2, since it better caters the urgent and high value nature of the Payments settled by LVPSs.

In case of net settlement, the payment system, such as an automated clearing house ('**ACH**'), collects payment orders that have been submitted during a particular day in batches. Subsequently, the payment system calculates the individual claims of each participant by netting the payment orders received intraday instead of having these cleared individually.[38] Only the net positions of each participant in the payment system are settled (e.g., by an LVPS such as T2). Net settlement is primarily used for settling retail Payments as these payments are less urgent and represent a relatively low value. An advantage of net settlement is that it reduces the number and size of the Payments that have to be settled and hence the settlement cost per transaction.[39] Furthermore, net settlement limits the liquidity exposures for the participants in the payment system.[40] Although net settlement has important advantages when it comes to processing non-urgent payments, one should take into consideration that net settlement increases the legal risks to which the payment system and its participants are exposed. Legal risks entail the uncertainty regarding the applicability of national laws and the risk that a contract cannot be legally enforced. In case of net settlement, it is essential that settlement arrangements between participants and the payment system are legally enforceable in all relevant countries.[41] This is particularly important in case of cross-border Payments where the netting arrangement is subject to multiple legal regimes. A main concern of payment systems and their participants is that the insolvency laws of a Member State may require a particular Payment, which already entered the payment system,

[36] According to Principle 8 of the CPSS-IOSCO Principles it is desirable to provide for real-time settlement whenever possible.

[37] Nevertheless, Principle 4 of the CPSS-IOSCO Principles requires that payment systems maintain sufficient financial resources to address credit exposures to participants.

[38] See Bank of England (1996, p. 22).

[39] See BIS (1990, p. 2).

[40] Ibid.

[41] Ibid., p. 11.

to be reversed in case of the insolvency of a participant located in their jurisdiction (**Paragraph 8.2.4**).

Because retail payment systems generally apply net settlement, the introduction of fast payment products triggered the need to adopt a new system for processing retail payments. Unlike standard credit transfers, fast payments have to be processed within a matter of seconds, which requires each individual transaction to be executed separately.[42] In other words, unlike conventional Payments, fast payments cannot be processed in batches. To facilitate the processing of Payments within such extremely short time limit, the Eurosystem developed a new retail payment system called the Target Instant Payments Settlement System (**'TIPS'**), which settles euro retail payments on an individual basis 24/7/365. TIPS is in essence an RTGS system for retail payments.

Since TIPS cannot settle retail Payments within the required time limit of ten seconds, the beneficiary's payment account must be credited before the beneficiary's PSP receives the transaction amount from the payer's PSP. This process is called prefunded settlement and requires the beneficiary's PSP to advance payment. Consequently, participating in a fast payment system such as TIPS increases the credit risk exposure of the beneficiary's PSP *vis-à-vis* the payer's PSP substantially. The proposed solution for limiting the beneficiary's PSP's credit exposure is to include in the regulations of the fast payment scheme that each participant must maintain a prefunded balance standing to the credit of the TIPS DCA from which instant payments can be settled.[43] Such balance represents an estimate of the anticipated volume of instant payments to be initiated by PSUs of the relevant participant and provides the beneficiary's PSP with a guarantee that it will receive its advance payment from the payer's PSP. According to **Article 1(2) Part V of Annex I ECB Guideline T2** it is not allowed for the participant to maintain a debit balance on a TIPS DCA. Therefore, the participant's TIPS DCA is connected to its MCA to receive liquidity for the settlement of instant payments. It is only possible for participants to add funds to their TIPS DCA accounts during T2 opening hours.[44]

[42] See BIS (2016b, p. 15).

[43] See ECB (2020a, p. 14).

[44] To this end, **Article 13(1) ECB Guideline T2** requires participants to monitor and manage the liquidity on their TIPS DCA in line with the T2 operating schedule as set

8.2.3 Interoperability as a Requisite for Efficient Payments

Payment messages are an important element of the payment infrastructure since the processing of Payments requires data to be exchanged between the participants in the payment chain.[45] Information contained in Payment messages includes amongst others, the transaction amount, details of the payer and the beneficiary and the BIC of the receiving PSP.[46] Currently, different standards are used for Payment messages, of which the most commonly used are the ISO 15022 standard (SWIFT MT) and the ISO 20022 standard.[47]

Since timely processing is key, it is unhelpful if PSPs apply different technical standards when communicating with each other or with payment systems.[48] This is of particular importance in case the execution of a single transaction requires the involvement of multiple payment systems. Unlike LVPSs, retail payment systems operate primarily at a national level. As a result, the processing of a cross-border retail Payment often requires the involvement of multiple retail payment systems established in different Member States. Interoperability between payment systems allows PSPs to process Payments involving multiple payment systems without the need to be a participant in all of these systems.[49] Ensuring that PSPs and payment systems communicate on the basis of common standards is therefore even more relevant for retail Payments.

The obligation to apply the same technical standards is known as the interoperability requirement and was first introduced for retail payment systems by the SEPA Regulation in 2012 (**Paragraph 3.5.2**).[50] Under **Article 4(2) SEPA Regulation**, retail payment systems established in the EU have to be technically interoperable with other EU based retail

out in Appendix V of the ECB Guideline T2 and perform reconciliation at least once a day.

[45] See J. A. Jans (2023, p. 13).

[46] Ibid.

[47] Ibid., p. 14.

[48] Principle 22 of the CPSS-IOSCO Principles requires payment systems to use internationally accepted standards for communication to accommodate effective interaction between payment systems and their (in)direct participants.

[49] See C. Boar et al. (2021, p. 1).

[50] Interoperability represents the ability of participants in the payment chain to be accessible for other participants in the payment ecosystem.

payment systems. The European legislature considered it disproportionate to also capture LVPSs by the interoperability requirement since large-value Payments are incomparable to retail credit transfers and direct debit collections.[51] Since Payments processed by LVPSs are characterised by their high priority, urgency and high value, the European legislature did not see a need to also cover these Payments by the interoperability requirement.[52]

The interoperability requirement applies to payment schemes and retail payment system operators. However, retail payment systems that are systemically important and therefore designated under the SFD (**Paragraph 8.2.4.2**) are only required to be interoperable with other retail payment systems that have been designated under the SFD. In practice, this means that designated retail payment systems do not have to apply the same standards as non-systemically important retail payment systems, which makes communication between these different types of payment systems less efficient. To ensure interoperability, payment schemes and retail payment systems have to oblige their participants to use identical technical standards to ensure that data can be exchanged between participants in an efficient manner.[53] These standards are typically laid down in the payment scheme of the relevant Payment product, such as the SEPA schemes developed by the EPC.[54] The SEPA Regulation allows additional standards to be introduced at a European level provided that these are applied consistently. Such standards cannot differentiate between national and cross-border Payments according to **Article 4(1)(a) SEPA Regulation**. For example the European Automated Clearing House Association (EACHA), which is a forum of European ACHs, developed a technical framework for interoperability of payment systems which applies to Payments between PSPs involving more than one clearing and settlement mechanism. Further to the obvious benefits that the use of common standards has on processing efficiency,

[51] SEPA Regulation, Recital 6.

[52] **Article 1(2)(b) SEPA Regulation** stipulates that the requirement of interoperability does apply in case a direct debit collection is processed via an LVPS where the payer has not requested this transaction to be routed via an LVPS.

[53] One of the main standards introduced by the SEPA Regulation (Article 5(1)(b)) is the ISO 20022 XML standard for transmitting orders for direct debit collections and credit transfers to other PSPs or via a retail payment system.

[54] E.g., the EPC CT Scheme.

it can also have adverse effects on innovation and can restrict the market in developing better standards. One should for example be cautious that the interoperability requirement does not result in PSPs being forced to apply obsolete standards.

Initially, the SWIFT MT messaging standard was primarily used to support interoperability between payment systems regarding cross-border Payments. However, frictions in the translations between these standards and national messaging standards often resulted in delayed processing of cross-border Payments and increased costs.[55] In 2020, the FSB published a roadmap for enhancing cross-border Payments of which one its building blocks is to enhance interoperability between payment systems by making ISO 20022 the new standard for Payment messages.[56] This proposal also fits within the ambition of the FSB to have 75% of the cross-border Payments worldwide settled within one hour after initiation (or on the agreed settlement date).[57] T2 applies the ISO 20022 messaging standard, as was already the case for T2S and TIPS, thereby increasing efficiency for cross-border Payments and reducing the costs for the clearing and settlement of these Payments.

8.2.4 Finality of Payments

8.2.4.1 The Risk of Insolvency Proceedings Against a Participant in a Payment System

When settling Payments via a payment system, the participating PSPs must have certainty that the transactions which entered the system will not be reversed. This is of paramount importance since insolvency laws of numerous Member States stipulate that the insolvency of a PSP on a particular day is assumed to have occurred at 0:00 hours on that day.[58] This rule, which is known as the zero-hour rule, implies that a payment order submitted by a PSP to a payment system on the day the PSP is declared insolvent is automatically ineffective by operation of law

[55] See BIS (2023, p. 2).

[56] See FSB (2020, p. 27).

[57] See FSB (2022, pp. 14, 19).

[58] This is particularly important in case of Payments whereby the beneficiary's PSP prefunds the transaction amount by crediting the beneficiary's payment account before its own account is credited with the transaction amount, such as with fast payments (**Paragraph 8.2.2**).

and can therefore not be settled. Consequently, a beneficiary's PSP that has received funds from a payer's PSP which is declared insolvent on that day is required to refund these funds. Depending on the transaction amounts involved, such reversals could disrupt the continuity of the payment system processing these transactions, which in itself can have a domino effect to other payment systems or participants. In other words, a disruption in the continuity of a single payment system can have severe adverse effects on other participants in the payment chain and, as a result thereof, the stability of the financial system as a whole. This risk, which is known as systemic risk[59], is reduced considerably by ensuring that participants in payment systems have certainty as to the validity of payment orders submitted by a payer's PSP that is declared bankrupt.

8.2.4.2 The Settlement Finality Directive (SFD)

For the very reasons set out in **Paragraph 8.2.4.1**, it is essential that a beneficiary's PSP is not exposed to the risk that payment orders, which have entered the payment system, can be revoked in case of an insolvent payer's PSP. To this end, the European legislature adopted the SFD in 1998, which limits the disruption effects for a payment system that can be caused by an insolvency proceeding against a participant in that system.[60] **Article 7 SFD** prohibits EEA Member States[61] to apply the zero-hour rule for designated payment systems since insolvency proceedings should not have retroactive effects on the rights and obligations of the participants in these systems. The SFD sets out the moment on which a Payment can no longer be reclaimed by the payer or the payer's PSP in case of the insolvency of the payer's PSP. This moment is known as the moment of finality. As a principle rule, **Article 3(1) SFD** provides that payment orders that have entered a designated payment system prior to

[59] **Article 2(3) SIPS Regulation** defines a 'systemic risk' as the risk of a participant or the SIPS operator not meeting their respective obligations in an SIPS will cause other participants and/or the SIPS operator to be unable to meet their obligations when they become due.

[60] SFD, Recital 4.

[61] Decision of the EEA Joint Committee No 53/1999 of 30 April 1999 "amending Annex IX (financial services) to the EEA Agreement", OJ L 284, 9.11.2000, pp. 12–12 and Decision of the EEA Joint Committee No 50/2010 of 30 April 2010 "amending Annex IX (Financial services) and Annex XII (Free movement of capital) to the EEA Agreement", OJ L 181, 15.7.2010, pp. 18–18.

the opening of insolvency proceedings against one of its direct participants[62] in the system or the system operator is binding on third parties and can therefore not be revoked. It is important to emphasise that the moment of finality is not affected by whether or not the beneficiary has received the corresponding funds.[63]

The SFD does not prescribe the moment at which a payment order is assumed to have entered a payment system. According to **Article 3(3) SFD** it is for payment systems themselves to determine their moment of finality. Payment systems commonly consider a payment order to have entered their system when such order has become irrevocable and unconditional according to the payment system's scheme rules. A payment order is irrevocable after it has been validated by the payment system.[64] In case the payer's PSP is no longer allowed to revoke its order under the scheme rules, the payment system verifies *inter alia* whether the payer's PSP has sufficient funds to execute the transaction. If the payer's PSP has sufficient funds and meets all other requirements set out in the scheme rules, the payment order becomes unconditional and the moment of finality enters into effect. For obvious reasons, the time between the submission of a payment order to the payment system and the moment of finality of the transaction must be as short as possible. In an RTGS system, payments are settled with immediate finality. Therefore, an RTGS system eliminates the credit risk exposures of its participants and, as a result thereof, the systemic risk for the market in general. In case of a net settlement system there is a time lag between the moment of acceptance of a payment order by the payment system and the moment of finality. In principle, payment orders are only protected against an insolvency proceeding of a participant in a net settlement system if they have entered the system prior to the opening of the insolvency proceedings. Under certain conditions, the SFD does allow however payment orders, which have entered the payment system after the opening of insolvency proceedings, to be binding on third parties. According to **Article 3(1) SFD**, this is only allowed provided that the Payment is: (i) carried out the same day during which the opening of the insolvency proceedings of

[62] Depending on the national regimes, payments initiated by indirect participants in TARGET2 may also covered by the SFD.

[63] See BIS (2003, p. 11).

[64] See BIS (2005, p. 13).

the payer's PSP occurs; and (ii) the payment system can prove that it was not aware and should not have been aware of these proceedings at the moment the payment order became irrevocable.

Because of the increasing involvement of Non-Banks in the processing of Payments, one can question whether it would be appropriate to extend the scope of applicability of the SFD to Non-Banks. Unlike Banks, Non-Banks cannot qualify as participants within the meaning of the SFD and therefore cannot benefit from the same safeguards. At the time the SFD entered into force, limiting the scope of protection to Banks seemed adequate as Non-Banks were ineligible to participate directly in payment systems. However, with PSD a legal obligation was introduced for payment systems to allow, under certain circumstances, Non-Banks (in)direct access to their systems (**Paragraph 8.4**). Non-Banks that have (in)direct access to payment systems do not benefit from the protection granted under the SFD as they cannot be a direct participant in payment systems designated under the SFD. At first glance, it does not appear to be an omission not to grant the same level of protection to Non-Banks. However, the view on whether Non-Banks should be allowed direct access to designated payment systems is subject to change. Although no longer relevant from a European point of view, the Bank of England announced in 2017 that licensed PIs and EMIs should also be eligible for holding a settlement account[65] in the RTGS system of the Bank of England.[66] The Bank of England considered that competition and innovation would be enhanced when enabling Non-Banks direct access to an LVPS that settles in central bank money. If this line of reasoning will be embraced by Member States, it becomes relevant to investigate whether there is a need to extend the scope of applicability of the SFD safeguards to Non-Banks.

[65] A settlement account is an account maintained with a central bank for the purpose of settling payments in central bank money.

[66] Provided that such non-Bank complies with the risk management framework of the Bank of England.

8.3 Oversight of Payment Systems Established in the EU

8.3.1 Why Is Supervision on Payment Systems Relevant?

With the decreasing use of correspondent banking arrangements for the clearing and settling of Payments in the EU, payment systems have become responsible for the clearing and settling of the vast majority of Payments in the EU. Since there are only a limited number of payment systems established in the EU, the European market for payment systems is characterised by a relatively high degree of market concentration. An explanation for this market situation could be that payment systems require a relatively high transaction volume to operate on a cost-efficient basis. In other words, Payments can only be cleared and settled in a cost-efficient manner if the market is serviced by only a few payment systems that process large volumes of Payments. This economic characteristic makes it difficult for new payment systems to enter the market and be commercially successful immediately upon commencing their activities. Since market entrants typically generate lower transaction volumes, newly established systems are required to charge higher costs per transaction to operate break-even and are therefore unable to be competitive at that stage if they need to cover their costs from the start. It is therefore fair to assume that the market for payment systems in the EU will remain relatively concentrated in the foreseeable future.

The fact that the market for payment systems is concentrated and payment systems play a prominent role in the processing of Payments, leaves the financial market exposed to relatively high systemic risk in case a payment system were to fail. Payment system failure can occur because of many different reasons. For example, inadequate internal operational processes and procedures can result in failure of a payment system's IT system. Moreover, a payment system's exposure to adverse external events can impact the reliability of a payment system's internal processes.[67] An example of such external event is the level of competition between payment systems, which can be a driver for generating operational risks for payment systems. Although this is less of a risk in a concentrated market, there remains a risk that payment systems pay insufficient attention to

[67] Principle 17 of the CPSS-IOSCO Principles requires that payment systems have procedures in place that identify, monitor and address operational risks.

their safety measures in order to reduce their costs and thereby attract more business. Such behaviour can result in a 'race to the bottom' as it comes to rule setting in case the initiative is followed by competing payment systems.[68]

Given the importance of mitigating systemic risk in the financial markets to the largest extent possible, carrying out adequate supervision on the operational reliability of payment systems is a top priority. Such supervision on payment systems is referred to as oversight.

8.3.2 *What Is Oversight and Who Is Responsible for Carrying Out Oversight?*

Despite that there appears to be consensus regarding the importance of having adequate supervision on payment systems, there is no harmonised EU legislative framework that imposes standards by which payment systems have to abide. There is however a European legal basis designating NCAs that are responsible for carrying out supervision on payment systems. According to the TFEU, the Eurosystem is charged with the responsibility to promote the smooth operation of payment systems in the EU.[69] In other words, the Eurosystem is responsible for supervising the safety and operational reliability of EU payment systems.[70] This responsibility is embedded in the Eurosystem's task of carrying out indirect supervision on payment systems, which is called oversight.[71] Oversight is defined by the Eurosystem as '*a central bank function whereby the objectives of safety and efficiency are promoted by monitoring existing and*

[68] See London Economics (2014, p. 48).

[69] According to **Article 127(2) TFEU** and **Articles 3 and 22 of the Statute of the European System of Central Banks and of the ECB**, the Eurosystem is charged with promoting the smooth operation of payment systems.

[70] ECB (2016b, p. 7).

[71] The scope of oversight supervision in the payments market by the Eurosystem is not limited to payment systems. Further to payment systems, oversight also covers payment instruments. In 2009, the ECB published the Eurosystem's oversight framework for credit transfer schemes. In 2010, the ECB published the Eurosystem's oversight framework for direct debit schemes. Both framework documents established five standards that credit transfer and direct debit schemes should apply. These schemes are required to: (i) have a sound legal basis in each relevant country; (ii) ensure that all relevant information is available to the participants in the scheme; (iii) maintain an adequate degree of security, operational reliability and business continuity; (iv) have effective governance arrangements and (v) manage and contain financial risks regarding the clearing and settlement process.

planned systems. Assessing them against these objectives and, where necessary, inducing change'.[72]

The legal authority to carry out oversight of a particular payment system is based on the agreement entered into between the payment system and the NCA, which is: (i) the central bank of the Member State where the payment system is established; or (ii) the ECB.[73] When determining which authority is primarily responsible for carrying out oversight of a particular payment system, a distinction is made between systemically important payment systems (**'SIPS'**) and systems that do not share that level of importance (**'Non-SIPS'**).[74] As a rule of thumb, payment systems qualify as an SIPS in case failure of that system could result in the transmission of shocks throughout the financial system (i.e., the failure of a system could impose systemic risk). When assessing if a particular payment system qualifies as an SIPS, the following factors are taken into consideration: (i) the size of the payment system; (ii) the importance of the payment system for the (national) payment market; (iii) the cross-border dimension of the payment system and (iv) the level of interdependencies with other payment systems.[75] An SIPS can be an LVPS or a retail

[72] ECB (2016b, p. 2).

[73] Oversight supervision does not provide NCAs with enforcement instruments against payment systems that are not compliant with the applicable oversight requirements.

[74] ECB (2016b, p. 7).

[75] **Article 1(3) SIPS Regulation** defines an 'SIPS' as a payment system that: (i) is eligible to be designated under the SFD by a Member State whose currency is the euro or its operator is established in the euro area, including establishment by means of a branch, through which the system is operated; and (ii) at least two of the following occur over a calendar year: (a) the total daily average value of euro- denominated payments processed exceeds €10 bln; (b) the total euro/denominated Payments processed represents at least one of the following: 15% of total volume of euro-denominated Payments, 5% of total volume of euro-denominated cross- border Payments or 75% of total volume of euro-denominated Payments at the level of a Member State whose currency is the euro; (c) its cross-border activity (participants established in a country other than that of the SIPS operator and/or cross-border links with other payment systems) involves five or more countries and generates a minimum of 33% of the total volume of euro-denominated payments processed by that SIPS; (d) it is used for the settlement of other FMIs. **Article 1(3-a) SIPS Regulation** stipulates that the ECB, exercising sound and reasoned judgement, may also decide that a payment system shall be identified as an SIPS in either of the following cases: (a) if such qualification would be appropriate taking into account the nature, size and complexity of the payment system; the nature and importance of its participants; the substitutability of the payment system and the availability of alternatives to it; and the relationship, interdependencies and other interactions the system has with

payment system. Because LVPSs process large-value transactions, which are often executed cross-border, these systems can impose systemic risks by default and are therefore considered to be an SIPS. SIPS that are established in the EU are subject to oversight by the ECB. This means that the ECB is responsible for oversight regarding the LVPSs T2 and EURO1.

Non-SIPS are supervised by the central bank of the Member State where the payment system is established. The majority of the retail payment systems are Non-SIPS and therefore subject to oversight by a national central bank. However, in case a retail payment system has a high market penetration and can have severe cross-border implications, such system will likely qualify as an SIPS. In such case, the responsibility for carrying out oversight is transferred from the national central bank to the ECB.[76] Retail payment systems such as STEP1 and STEP2 qualify as SIPS and therefore fall within the remit of the ECB.

8.3.3 The Standards Used for Oversight of Payment Systems

The Eurosystem conducts oversight of payment systems on the basis of recommendations and standards developed by the Committee on Payment and Settlement Systems (‘**CPSS**’)[77] and the International Organization of Securities Commission (‘**IOSCO**’).[78] In January 2001, the CPSS published its Core Principles for Systemically Important Payment Systems[79], which provided for minimum standards on governance and business operations applicable to SIPS established in the EU.[80] In 2012,

the wider financial system; or (b) where a payment system does not meet the criteria set out under (i) and (ii) above solely because these criteria occur over a period of less than a calendar year and it is plausible that the payment system will continue to meet the criteria when assessed in the next verification review.

[76] See ECB (2000a, p. 3).

[77] On 1 September 2014, the CPSS was renamed the CPMI.

[78] See CPSS (2012, p. 77).

[79] See BIS (2001).

[80] These principles included amongst others: (i) principle 1: the payment system should have a sound legal basis; (ii) principle 2: the rules of the payment system should enable participants to assess the impact of the payment system on the participant's financial risks; (iii) principle 3: the payment system should have procedures for addressing credit and liquidity risks; (iv) principle 4: the payment system has to provide prompt final settlement on the day of value; (v) principle 5: payment systems applying multilateral netting have to be capable of ensuring timely settlement in case the participant with the largest settlement

these principles were replaced by a larger set of standards published by the CPSS and IOSCO.[81] Nowadays, the Principles for financial market infrastructures published by the BIS and International Organization of Securities Commissions ('**CPSS-IOSCO Principles**')[82] are the most widely accepted oversight standards for payment systems that are systemically important.[83] Although the CPSS-IOSCO Principles are addressed to SIPS, the Eurosystem also applies a number of these principles for carrying out oversight of retail payment systems that qualify as Non-SIPS.[84] To determine which of the CPSS-IOSCO Principles apply to a particular Non-SIPS retail payment system, such system is categorised as a: (i) prominently important retail payment system[85]; or (ii) other retail payment system.[86,87] Prominently important retail payment system are required to comply with the majority of the CPSS-IOSCO Principles.[88]

obligation is not able to settle; (vi) principle 6: if possible, the settlement asset should be central bank money; (vii) principle 7: the payment system should guarantee a high level of security and operational reliability; (viii) principle 8: the payment system should enable making payments that are practical for its users; (ix) principle 9: payment systems have to have objective criteria for payment system access and (x) principle 10: the governance arrangements of the payment system have to be effective and transparent.

[81] I.e., the CPSS-IOSCO Principles.

[82] See BIS and International Organization of Securities Commissions (2012).

[83] The CPSS-IOSCO Principles are not only addressed to payment systems established in the EU.

[84] See ECB (2016a).

[85] These are retail payment systems that do not qualify as an SIPS within the meaning of the SIPS Regulation but have a minimum market share of 25% of the euro denominated payments processed in a Euro area Member State.

[86] These are retail payment systems that have a market share of less than 2% of the euro denominated payments processed in a Euro area Member State.

[87] See ECB (2016a, p. 3).

[88] These principles include: (i) principle 1: legal basis; (ii) principle 2: Governance; (iii) principle 3: framework for the comprehensive management of risks; (iv) principle 8: settlement finality; (v) principle 9: money settlement; (vi) principle 13: participant default rules and procedures; (vii) principle 15: general business risk; (viii) principle 17: operational risk; (ix) principle 18: access and participation requirements; (x) principle 21: efficiency and effectiveness; (xi) principle 22: communication procedures and standards and (xii) principle 23: disclosure of rules, key procedures and market data.

Other retail payment systems have to comply with only a few of the CPSS-IOSCO Principles.[89] Certain retail payment systems are also required to meet other standards than those set out in the CPSS-IOSCO Principles. For example, retail payment systems processing card payments, such as Visa, Mastercard and Maestro, also have to adhere to the principles set out in the ECB Oversight framework for card payment schemes.[90] In order to have proportionate requirements for smaller card schemes, the Eurosystem provides for a waiver which allows smaller card schemes to be excluded from the applicability of the oversight standards.[91] In 2020, the ECB published a draft oversight framework for Payment instruments, schemes and arrangements for public consultation.[92] The draft framework complements the oversight of payment systems for the aspects that are relevant from a payment scheme perspective.[93] The framework covers payment instruments used for payments to beneficiaries within the euro area and/or Non-euro Member States which are denominated in euro.[94] To avoid overlap with oversight on the basis of the CPSS-IOSCO Principles, payment system operators that are subject to oversight on the basis of these principles will not be assessed on the basis of the draft oversight framework for Payment instruments, schemes and arrangements.

To ensure that the main standards of the CPSS-IOSCO Principles are applied by all SIPS in the same manner, the ECB adopted Regulation

[89] These principles include: (i) principle 1: legal basis; (ii) principle 2: Governance; (iii) principle 3: framework for the comprehensive management of risks; (iv) principle 8: settlement finality; (v) principle 13: participant default rules and procedures; (vi) principle 17: operational risk; (vii) principle 18: access and participation requirements; (viii) principle 21: efficiency and effectiveness and (ix) principle 23: disclosure of rules, key procedures and market data.

[90] See ECB (2008).

[91] Ibid., p. 6. A card scheme is eligible for a waiver in case: (i) the number of cards issued per year over the past three years was on average less than 1 mln; or (ii) the annual average value of transactions of the card scheme over the past three years was less than 1 billion. However national central banks are allowed to apply stricter rules to the schemes that are eligible for a waiver on the basis of risk considerations and the relevant importance of the scheme in that Member State.

[92] See ECB (2020b).

[93] Ibid., p. 7.

[94] Ibid., p. 3. Excluded from the framework are: (i) cash payments; (ii) paper cheques or other comparable instruments and (iii) paper-based vouchers or cards issued with a view to place funds at the disposal of the beneficiary.

(EU) No 795/2014 on oversight requirements for systemically important payment systems ('**SIPS Regulation**')[95] in 2013.[96] In line with the CPSS-IOSCO Principles, the SIPS Regulation imposes legal requirements on the operators of an SIPS to have *inter alia* adequate governance arrangements and a sound risk management framework. Since the SIPS Regulation does not cover Non-SIPS, there is no European legal requirement obliging Non-SIPS in the EU to comply with any of the standards set out in the CPSS-IOSCO Principles. The necessity for these payment systems to apply (some of) the CPSS-IOSCO Principles follows from the individual contractual arrangements entered into by each Non-SIPS and its NCA.

Moreover, there are certain service providers that offer essential services to payment systems and can therefore expose these systems to significant risks. A well-known service provider for payment systems is SWIFT[97], which acts as an intermediary by transmitting Payment messages electronically between the participants in a payment system. These 'critical service providers' do not qualify as a payment system themselves and are therefore not required to comply with the standards set out in the CPSS-IOSCO Principles. However, allowing such service providers to operate without any form of supervision is undesirable since interaction between critical service providers and payment systems could constitute a source of operational risk for the payment system in question. To address these risks in an adequate manner, the CPSS-IOSCO Principles provide for five 'oversight expectations' by which critical service providers such as SWIFT have to abide.[98]

[95] ECB Regulation (EU) No 795/2014 of 3 July 2014 "on oversight requirements for systemically important payment systems", OJ L 217, 23.7.2014, pp. 16–30.

[96] ECB. (2013). Decisions taken by the Governing Council of the ECB (in addition to decisions setting interest rates). Available at: https://www.ecb.europa.eu/press/govcdec/otherdec/2013/html/gc130621.en.html (Accessed: April 13, 2024). **Article 132 TFEU** provides for a legal basis for the ECB to issue regulations for ensuring efficient and sound payment systems in the EU.

[97] Society for Worldwide Interbank Financial Telecommunication.

[98] These expectations are set out in Annex F to the CPSS-IOSCO Principles and include: (i) service providers have to have an adequate risk management process; (ii) service providers have to ensure the confidentiality and integrity of the information that it processes; (iii) the critical services provided have to remain available, reliable and resilient; (iv) the service provider must have effective technology and (v) the service provider must communicate with others in a clear and transparent manner.

8.4 Access to Payment Systems by Non-Banks

8.4.1 The Importance of Payment System Access

Since payment systems fulfil a pivotal role in the processing of Payments, having access to such systems is of paramount importance for Non-Banks that want to compete with Banks on an equal footing.[99] For Non-Banks providing end-to-end Payment products, it is preferable to have direct payment system access instead of indirect access.[100] End-to-end providers, such as three-party card schemes and E-money issuers, have a direct relationship with both the payers and beneficiaries of their Payment products.[101] Direct payment system access allows an end-to-end non-Bank to provide payment services to its PSUs without the involvement of a Bank. There is less of an upside for front-end Non-Banks to have direct payment system access since these Non-Banks need to maintain a payment account with a Bank for the offering of their services. Front-end providers focus on the interaction between the Bank and the PSU and typically offer Payment products to PSUs holding a payment account with a Bank. Having direct payment system access does not enable these Non-Banks to operate on a stand-alone basis without any Bank involvement.

Being unable to obtain direct payment system access could have significant adverse competition effects for Non-Banks since it potentially constrains their offering of payment services. Moreover, not having direct access to payment systems implies that Non-Banks do not have any involvement in the payment network decision making process. As a result, the scheme rules of payment systems can develop in directions that are not beneficial to Non-Banks and Non-Banks are not able to exercise any form of influence over the rulemaking process.[102]

The European legislature considered access to payment systems by Non-Banks to be an important step to enhance the competitive position of Non-Banks *vis-à-vis* Banks. The European legislature took the view that any PSP should be able to access the technical infrastructure of payment systems provided that it meets the minimum access

[99] See Commission (2003, p. 13).

[100] See ACM (2017, p. 21).

[101] Ibid., p. 20.

[102] See Commission (2007, p. 153).

requirements.[103] In 2009, **Article 28 PSD** introduced a legal obligation for payment system operators to allow Non-Banks non-discriminatory (in)direct access to their system, which obligation continues to apply under **Article 35 PSD2**.[104] Although payment system access by Non-Banks is important for levelling the playing field between Banks and Non-Banks, such access should not endanger the integrity and operational reliability of the payment system involved. In other words, the obligation to provide Non-Banks access should never result in system operators applying inadequate access requirements that expose the payment system to unacceptable risks, even if applying adequate access requirements means that (particular) Non-Banks will not be able to obtain payment system access. In this regard, it is suggested in the PSR Proposal that payment system operators conduct a risk assessment regarding the PSP that applies for direct payment system access.[105] According to **Article 31(1) PSR Proposal**, such risk assessment should cover all relevant risks, including settlement risk, operational risk, credit risk, liquidity risk and business risk. Under **Article 31(3) PSR Proposal**, Payment system operators can only reject an application for direct access in case the PSP cannot adhere to the rules of the payment system or poses an unacceptable high risk. For payment systems that are subject to oversight supervision, these payment system access rules are supervised by the central bank responsible for conducting oversight.[106] For payment systems that are not subject to oversight, **Article 31(7) PSR Proposal** requires the Member State to appoint an NCA that will be responsible for supervising compliance by payment system operators with these rules.

8.4.2 Direct Payment System Access by Non-Banks

In case of direct payment system access, a PSP can submit its payment orders directly into the payment system. Direct access therefore requires the PSP to have an IT connection with the payment system's IT-infrastructure. Since such connection can expose the payment system and

[103] PSD, Recital.

[104] For SIPS, **Article 16 SIPS Regulation** also imposes an obligation on the operator of the system to have non-discriminatory access and participation criteria for direct and indirect participation.

[105] PSR Proposal, Recital 31.

[106] PSR Proposal, Recital 32.

its participants to operational, legal and security risks, system operators only allow PSPs direct access to their system if they comply with the system's access criteria. These access criteria, also known as the scheme-level criteria, ensure that the risks associated with PSPs accessing the payment system remain at an acceptable level.[107]

The payment system access criteria are of a legal, financial and operational nature. Legal requirements typically involve the need for a participant to have a certain regulatory status (e.g., hold a banking licence). Financial requirements aim to reduce the liquidity risk exposure for the participants in the system. These requirements are particularly important for PSPs participating in a gross-settled payment system or in a payment system for which pre-funding is required.[108] Operational requirements involve *inter alia* the obligation to have a reliable and secure IT-infrastructure that communicates with the payment system's IT-infrastructure.[109] Payment system operators have a certain degree of freedom to determine which access criteria they consider appropriate and proportionate to safeguard the operational reliability of their payment system. However, PSD2 provides for certain parameters within which payment systems have to determine their access criteria.[110] PSD2 stipulates that the access criteria for payment systems must be objective, non-discriminatory and proportionate.[111] Having non-discriminatory access criteria means that system operators have to apply the same criteria for PSPs that share similar characteristics.[112] System operators are allowed to impose different access requirements on Banks and Non-Banks due

[107] Principle 18 of the CPSS-IOSCO Principles imposes a principle based obligation on payment systems to have objective and risk-based access criteria for (in)direct participants. PSD2 does not provide for a comprehensive list of the relevant risks, but according to **Article 35 PSD2** one should in any case think of settlement risk, operational risk and business risk.

[108] This is for example an obligation for participants in instant payments schemes.

[109] The PSP's IT-infrastructure should for example be able to adequately deal with security threats.

[110] Since payment system access is primarily a competition test, payment system access is supervised by the national competition authorities.

[111] The PSD2 provision on payment system access does not apply to systems that are operated by a single PSP (e.g., three-party card schemes).

[112] Recital 50 PSD2 states that differences in pricing are for example only allowed when the payment system incurs different costs when allowing different types of PSP access to their system.

to the differences in *inter alia* their financial capacity and the degree of sophistication of their IT systems. This rule setting flexibility is desirable since it allows system operators to determine which conditions are elementary to ensure the reliability of their system.[113] Furthermore, access criteria have to be proportionate, which means that these criteria should not go beyond what is needed to protect the financial and operational stability of the payment system and to safeguard the system against risks such as settlement risk, operational risk and business risk.[114] Without the proportionality requirement, system operators could impose onerous access requirements on all Non-Banks without breaching the payment system access obligation. This would unlevel the playing field between Banks and Non-Banks.[115] One can question however whether the European legislature's attention for direct access by Non-Banks is expedient since Non-Banks will always have to meet high security standards that are difficult for them to comply with.

8.4.2.1 Direct Access Criteria of Large-Value Payment Systems (LVPSs) and Retail Payment Systems

According to the access criteria of LVPSs such as T2 and EURO1, Non-Banks are by default ineligible to become a direct participant. The access criteria for these systems contain numerous requirements that Non-Banks cannot fulfil. First, LVPSs use central bank money for settling Payments[116], which means that direct participants are required to maintain a payment account with a national central bank. For example, T2 requires direct participants to maintain an MCA with their national central bank. Non-Banks, other than ACHs, are ineligible for having such accounts with T2. A similar access requirement applies for the LVPS EURO1. Transactions processed by EURO1 are settled in central

[113] See J. A. Jans (2010, p. 155).

[114] According to **Article 35(1) PSD2**, payment systems are in any case not allowed to impose: (i) any restrictive rule on effective participation in other payment systems; (ii) any rule which discriminates between authorised PSPs or between registered PSPs in relation to the rights, obligations and entitlements of participants or (iii) any restriction on the basis of institutional status.

[115] See Commission (2007, p. 151).

[116] According to Principle 9 of the CPSS-IOSCO Principles, payment systems should settle in central bank money when practical and available.

bank money in T2. Therefore, EURO1 also requires its direct participants to hold an MCA with their national central bank. Second, LVPSs settle Payments (near) real-time, which implies that direct participants in such system are exposed to relatively high intraday liquidity risks.[117] To counter these liquidity exposures, direct participants in an LVPS must comply with stringent liquidity requirements to ensure their financial soundness. Since Non-Banks are subject to less stringent capital requirements than Banks, Non-Banks are in most cases unable to comply with an LVPS's liquidity requirements.

Similar requirements apply for direct access regarding European retail payment systems. For example, the access criteria of the retail payment systems STEP1, STEP2 and RT1[118] do not allow Non-Banks direct access to their IT-infrastructure. Furthermore, direct participation in the retail payment system TIPS is not available for Non-Banks.

8.4.3 Indirect Payment System Access by Non-Banks

In case of indirect access, a PSP obtains access to a payment system via another PSP, which is called the sponsor. The sponsor is a direct participant in the payment system. The indirect participant does not have a direct connection into the payment system's IT-infrastructure but sends its payment orders via the sponsor to the system. For example, with T2, indirect participants can only send and receive Payments via a direct participant.[119] For this purpose, a direct participant is allowed to maintain a separate RTGS DCA for settlement of Payments on behalf of indirect participants.[120] Payment orders submitted or funds received by the indirect participant are according to **Article 7(2) Part I of Annex I ECB Guideline T2** deemed to have been submitted or received by the sponsor. Indirect participants of T2 therefore have to maintain a payment account with a sponsor.[121]

[117] See ECB (2010, p. 52).

[118] RT1 is a retail payment system founded by SWIFT and EBA Clearing for processing instant payments.

[119] See ECB (2020a, p. 26).

[120] Ibid., p. 17.

[121] The arrangements between the sponsor and the indirect participant setting out the conditions for indirect access are laid down in a participation agreement which both parties enter into.

Non-Banks that obtain indirect access must comply with two sets of rules. First, Non-Banks must adhere to the indirect access criteria of the payment system. Since indirect access exposes payment systems to lower risks than direct access, the criteria for indirect access are less stringent. However, indirect participation can trigger substantial risk exposures for a payment system, especially if the system has many indirect participants compared to direct participants. CPSS-IOSCO therefore urges payment systems to pay particular attention to the risks associated with indirect participation.[122] As with direct participation, most payment systems therefore require indirect participants to hold a banking licence. As a result, **Article 4 Part I of Annex I ECB Guideline T2** does for example not allow Non-Banks to obtain access to T2 as an indirect participant. Second, a non-Bank that seeks indirect payment system access must adhere to the sponsor's rules and regulations, also known as the sponsor-level criteria. A non-Bank requesting indirect access will have to enter into a contractual arrangement with a sponsor on the basis of which it can submit payment orders into the system.[123] A main concern with indirect access is that these contractual arrangements allow sponsors to gather strategic information regarding competing Non-Banks, such as payment volumes and growth rates.[124] Furthermore, with correspondent relationships there is a risk that sponsors charge prices or impose other terms on Non-Banks which limit the profitability of Non-Banks and hence their competitive position.

To ensure sound competition between Banks and Non-Banks, it is essential that sponsors apply objective access criteria for Non-Banks. For this reason, **Article 35(2) PSD2** requires that the sponsor-level criteria for indirect payment system access are also objective, proportionate and non-discriminatory. Moreover, it is elementary that sponsors process payment orders received from Non-Banks swiftly. With indirect access, payment orders submitted by a PSU to a non-Bank may take longer to process than a payment order which is submitted directly to the Bank. The transaction amount must first be transferred from the payer's payment account to the non-Bank's account maintained with the sponsor before

[122] Principle 19 of the CPSS-IOSCO Principles.

[123] These contracts typically contain legal, technical and financial requirements.

[124] See D. Awrey (2021, p. 34).

these are subsequently transferred via the payment system to the beneficiary's PSP. Sound competition between Banks and Non-Banks also requires that the sponsor does not charge Non-Banks excessive fees in comparison to the costs it incurs for offering Non-Banks indirect payment system access.[125]

8.4.4 Payment System Access and Competition Between Banks and Non-Banks

The PSD evaluation report revealed that none of the Non-Banks interviewed obtained access to a payment system since PSD was implemented into national legislation.[126] Although it is unclear whether these numbers have changed with PSD2, one can question whether the initiatives from the European legislature to date on non-Bank payment system access have been effective in levelling the playing field.

Two main limitations preventing non-Bank payment system access appear to stand out. First, the PSD2 payment system access obligation only covers systems that are not designated under the SFD.[127] Since the majority of the payment systems are designated under the SFD, the payment system access obligation is in practice a hollow phrase. The Expert Group on Regulatory Obstacles to Financial Innovation suggested that the Commission should investigate whether the SFD must be revised to allow for the participation in payment systems by any type of PSP on the basis of risk-based criteria such as operational resilience and risk management.[128] The Commission picked up the gauntlet and suggests in **Article 46(1) PSD3 Proposal** that the SFD will be amended by including licensed PIs as eligible institutions for direct participation in payment systems designated under the SFD. Second, the majority of the payment systems in the EU are either owned by national central banks

[125] See International Telecommunication Union (2016, p. vi).

[126] See London Economics and iff in association with PaySys (2013, p. 215).

[127] Although the obligation to allow access also doesn't apply regarding payment systems: (i) composed exclusively of PSPs belonging to a group composed of entities linked by capital where one of the linked entities enjoys effective control over the other linked entities; and (ii) operated by a single PSP (e.g., in-house banking systems), the effect of these restrictions are less relevant from a competition perspective. Unlike PSD, PSD2 does not exempt three-party card schemes from the access requirement.

[128] See Expert Group on Regulatory Obstacles to Financial Innovation (2019, p. 79).

or Banks.[129] For example, the main retail payment systems in the EU, STEP1 and STEP2, are both owned and operated by EBA Clearing, which was founded by Banks and only has Banks as members. In their capacity as indirect sole shareholders of payment systems, Banks can exercise influence over the development of access criteria applicable to their direct competitors (e.g., Non-Banks) that intend to access their payment system. By requiring for example that (in)direct participants need to have a banking licence, the PSD2 provision that Non-Banks must be allowed non-discriminatory access remains without effect. It therefore appears that the current ownership structures of the main payment systems have an adverse effect on level playing field between Banks and Non-Banks.

In my opinion, the European legislature should take a more holistic approach for regulating payment system access. Instead of limiting its focus on market access criteria, the European legislature should also take account of the ownership structure of payment systems. To level the playing field between Banks and Non-Banks, payment systems should have a more independent position *vis-à-vis* their participants.[130]

8.5 Conclusion

Nowadays, payment systems are responsible for the clearing and settlement of the vast majority of the Payments executed in Europe, which makes these systems a crucial component of the Payment infrastructure. Since payment systems fulfil such a pivotal role in the processing of Payments, the European legislature considers it essential that Non-Banks are able to access the technical infrastructures of payment systems to ensure sound competition between Banks and Non-Banks. To this end, PSD introduced a legal obligation for payment system operators to allow Non-Banks (in)direct access to their systems.

The payment system access requirement, which obligation continues to apply under PSD2, stipulates that the rules on payment system access have to be objective, non-discriminatory and proportionate. In practice, direct payment system access requires the participant to comply with the eligibility criteria of the relevant Payment scheme as well as the eligibility

[129] E.g., EURO1.

[130] Such separation of ownership from Banks has already taken place with Mastercard and Visa.

criteria for obtaining a payment account at the central bank. Indirect access requires the participant to adhere to both the payment system's indirect access criteria as well as the sponsor-level criteria.

The rationale for imposing payment system access requirements on PSPs is to safeguard the stability of the Payment infrastructure without excluding certain categories of PSPs. To ensure sound competition between PSPs, it is essential that PSPs with similar business propositions and risk profiles encounter the same payment system access requirements. As long as the payment system access requirements do not discriminate between PSPs sharing similar characteristics, such access criteria can be stringent if required to safeguard the integrity and operational reliability of the payment system in question. Although unfavourable for the competitive position of Non-Banks *vis-à-vis* Banks, having stringent access criteria does not harm the level playing field between Banks and Non-Banks provided that these are objective, non-discriminatory and proportionate. Allowing PSPs that do not fulfil certain legal criteria access to payment systems would make such systems vulnerable to security breaches, credit risk exposures and, as a result thereof, discontinuity of the system. Although payment system access strengthens the competitive position of Non-Banks, allowing Non-Banks payment system access should never endanger the integrity and operational reliability of the payment system in question. In other words, the legal obligation for payment system operators and sponsors to provide Non-Banks access should never result in payment systems being exposed to unacceptable risks.

To safeguard the operational reliability of payment systems that are elementary for the Payments sector, the PSD2 requirement on direct payment system access does not apply to payment systems that are designated under the SFD. Since most payment systems in Europe are designated under the SFD, the PSD2 payment system access requirement remains without effect. With regard to these payment systems, Non-Banks are only eligible for indirect payment system access, which means that Non-Banks are dependent on competitors for this elementary element of the Payment process and are required to submit payment instructions to the Banks with which they compete in the Payments market. Being dependent on competing Banks for payment system access may raise anti-competitive concerns, even though PSD2 also requires that sponsor-level criteria are objective, non-discriminatory and proportionate. This concern appears to have materialised since most sponsor-level criteria require applicants for indirect access to hold a banking licence. Although imposing such requirement does not constitute a breach of the PSD2 obligation to have objective, proportionate and non-discriminatory criteria, it withholds Non-Banks from obtaining indirect payment system access. Because access to payment systems is of paramount importance for Non-Banks that want to compete with Banks on an equal footing, allowing Non-Banks to become a direct participant in an SFD-designated payment system could contribute to the creation of a level playing field between Banks and Non-Banks. The Commission has therefore suggested in the PSD3 Proposal to amend the SFD by recognising licensed PIs as eligible institutions for direct access to payment systems designated under the SFD.

The majority of the payment systems in the EU are either owned by national central banks or Banks. For example, STEP1 and STEP2 are both owned and operated by EBA Clearing, which was founded by Banks and only has Banks as members. In their capacity as indirect sole shareholders of payment systems, Banks are able to exercise influence over the development of access criteria applicable to direct competitors (e.g., Non-Banks) that intend to access these payment systems. Payment systems develop access criteria to ensure that PSPs obtaining access to their system are subject to appropriate requirements to ensure the integrity and stability of the payment system. However, with regard to payment systems whereby Banks are involved both as participant and shareholder, there is a risk that these Banks may exercise improper influence on the rule setting by these systems, which could harm the competitive position between Banks and Non-Banks. The main objective of payment system operators is to safeguard the operational reliability of their system, whereas Banks may also have an incentive to limit payment system access by Non-Banks. Imposing access criteria with which a non-Bank cannot comply effectively rules out that competing Non-Banks can obtain payment system access. It is therefore worth investigating whether it would be feasible to prohibit PSPs that are a direct participant in a payment system to be able to also have any form of control over such payment system in another capacity. In practice, this could mean for example that PSPs should not be allowed to be a (in)direct shareholder of the payment system in question. By introducing such prohibition, a potential conflict of interest can easily be avoided, thereby reducing potential obstacles for sound competition between Banks and Non-Banks. A downside of implementing such prohibition is that less Bank involvement could hamper innovation within payment system infrastructures since Banks have been a driving force behind innovation regarding the IT-infrastructure of payment systems in recent decades.

In order to eliminate private sector involvement in payment systems altogether, one may even consider nationalising payment systems. Although the Payments market is a private sector business, the IT-infrastructure of the Payments market can be regarded as a public utility function since it serves the public interest of enabling citizens and companies to make Payments. By nationalising payment systems, these systems are no longer exposed to anti-competitive incentives regarding the rule setting for payment system access. In other words, nationalising payment systems better guarantees that rule setting regarding payment system access is non-discriminatory, as required by **Article 35 PSD2**. A potential downside of nationalising payment systems however is that it may hamper innovation in the Payments market. Because of a lack of competitive incentives, governments are less inclined to be innovative and further enhance the Payments infrastructure. Moreover, governments do not have the same in-depth knowledge as Banks regarding the Payments market and its technical specifications.

Secondary Sources

ACM. (2017). *Report Fintechs in the Payment System: The Risk of Foreclosure*, pp. 20–21.

Awrey, D. (2021). *Unbundling Banking, Money, and Payments*, ECGI, Law Working Paper No. 565/2021, p. 34.

Bank of England. (1996). *Payment Systems*. Handbooks in Central Banking No. 8, pp. 21-22.

BIS and International Organization of Securities Commissions. (2012). *Principles for Financial Market Infrastructures*.

BIS. (1990). *Report of the Committee on Interbank Netting Schemes of the Central Banks of the Group of Ten countries*, pp. 2, 11.

BIS. (2001). *Core Principles for Systemically Important Payment Systems*.

BIS. (2003). *The Role of Central Bank Money in Payment Systems*, pp. 8, 11.

BIS. (2005). *New Developments in Large-Value Payment Systems*, p. 13.

BIS. (2016a). *Correspondent Banking*, pp. 9, 12.

BIS. (2016b). *Fast Payments—Enhancing the Speed and Availability of Retail Payments*, p. 15.

BIS. (2023). *ISO 20022 Harmonisation Requirements for Enhancing Cross-Border Payments*. Consultative Report, p. 2.

Boar, C., et al. (2021). *Interoperability Between Payment Systems Across Borders*. BIS Bulletin, No. 49, p. 1.

Commission. (2003). *Communication from the Commission to the Council and the European Parliament Concerning a New Legal Framework for Payments in the internal market (Consultative Document)*. COM (2003) 718 final, p. 13.

Commission. (2007). *Report on the Retail Banking Sector Inquiry, Commission Staff Working Document Accompanying the Communication from the Commission—Sector Inquiry Under Art 17 of Regulation 1/2003 on Retail Banking (Final Report)*. SEC (2007) 106, pp. 151, 153.

CPSS. (2012). *Payment, Clearing and Settlement Systems in the Euro Area* (pp. 77, 78, 94). Red Book.

ECB. (2000a). *Role of the Eurosystem in the Field of Payment System Oversight*, p. 3.

ECB. (2000b). *Systemic Risk: A Survey*. Working Paper No. 35, pp. 10–11.

ECB. (2008). *Oversight framework for Card Payment Schemes—Standards*, p. 6.

ECB. (2010). *The Payment System*, pp. 25, 39, 41, 48, 52, 122.

ECB. (2016a). *Revised Oversight Framework for Retail Payment Systems*, p. 3.

ECB. (2016b). *Eurosystem Oversight Policy Framework*. Revised Version, pp. 2, 7.

ECB. (2020a). *T2-T2S Consolidation*, Business Description Document, Version 2.1, pp. 14, 17, 26.

ECB. (2020b). *Eurosystem Oversight Framework for Electronic Payment Instruments, Schemes and Arrangements*. Draft for Public Consultation, pp. 3, 7.

ECB. (n.d.). *TARGET Consolidation*. https://www.ecb.europa.eu/paym/target/consolidation/html/index.en.html. Accessed April 13, 2024.

Expert Group on Regulatory Obstacles to Financial Innovation. (2019). *Thirty Recommendations on Regulation, Innovation and Finance*. Final Report to the European Commission, p. 79.

FSB. (2013). *Recovery and Resolution Planning for Systemically Important Financial Institutions: Guidance on Identification of Critical Functions and Critical Shared Services*, p. 7.

FSB. (2020). *Enhancing Cross-Border Payments: Stage 3 Roadmap*, p. 27.

FSB. (2022). *Developing the Implementation Approach for the Cross-Border Payments Targets*. Final Report, pp. 14, 19.

International Telecommunication Union. (2016). *Access to Payment Infrastructures*. Focus Group Technical Report, ITU, p. vi.

Jans, J. A. (2010). *Harmonisering Van Regels Voor Markttoegang Betaalinstellingen*. Tijdschrift voor Financieel Recht, No. 6, p. 155.

Jans, J. A. (2023). *ISO 20022 als standaard voor interoperabiliteit tussen betalingssystemen*. Tijdschrift voor Financieel Recht, No. 1/2, pp. 13–14.

London Economics and iff in association with PaySys. (2013): *Study on the Impact of Directive 2007/64/EC on Payment Services in the Internal Market and on the Application of Regulation (EC) No 924/2009 on Cross-Border Payments in the Community*. Final Report, p. 215.

London Economics. (2014). *Competition and Collaboration in UK Payment Systems*. Final Report, p. 48.

CHAPTER 9

EU Competition Enforcement in the Payments Sector

9.1 Competition Law in the European Payments Sector

Prior to the adoption of PSD, EU competition law was the only area of law regulating competition in the Payments market. Main objectives of EU competition law include: (i) the protection of competition; and (ii) the enhancement of the internal market. To this end, EU competition law provides for rules on *inter alia* antitrust and merger control. Under **Article 101 TFEU**, PSPs are prohibited to enter into agreements with other undertakings[1] which can adversely affect trade between Member States and restrict competition. Moreover, **Article 102 TFEU** prohibits PSPs that hold a dominant position in a particular market to abuse their position. **Article 4 EC Merger Regulation** requires prospective mergers in the Payments sector, which have an EU dimension, to be cleared by the Commission.[2] When assessing the level playing field between Banks and

[1] An undertaking within the meaning of EU competition law is an entity engaged in economic activity, regardless of the legal status of the entity and the way in which it is financed (See European Court of Justice (1991), paragraph 21).

[2] Regulation (EC) No 139/2004 of 20 January 2004 "on the control of concentrations between undertakings (the EC Merger Regulation)", *OJ L 24*, 29.1.2004, pp. 1–22.

J. A. Jans, *Electronic Payments in the European Market*, EBI Studies in Banking and Capital Markets Law,
https://doi.org/10.1007/978-3-031-64338-5_9

Non-Banks in the market for Payments, the legal requirements on anti-competitive agreements and abuse of dominant market positions appear to be of higher relevance than the legal requirements on merger control. This chapter therefore focusses on EU antitrust rules in the market for Payments.

Contrary to the financial services regulatory framework, EU antitrust rules are sector agnostic, which means that antitrust rules do not take into account any of the characteristics that are specific to the European Payments market, let alone the different types of PSPs. Nonetheless, the Commission has identified the financial services sector as one of its key sectors of interest. In 2005, the Commission conducted a sector inquiry on competition in the financial services sector, which covered amongst others the European cards business.[3] This sector inquiry revealed the existence of significant competition issues in the European cards market.[4] One of the main issues identified was the existence of a significant discrepancy with regard to merchant fees, cardholder fees and interchange fees charged by card schemes in different Member States. The Commission considered this to be an indication of the existence of competition barriers. According to the Commission, antitrust enforcement provides for an effective tool to address these competition issues.[5]

Nowadays, the financial services regulatory framework and the competition framework share the same objective of enhancing competition in the market for Payments. However, these legal frameworks do not provide for any form of coordination. This raises the question whether a form of interaction between these areas of law would be beneficial to address competition issues in the Payments sector.[6] For example, when adopting legal provisions impacting competition between Banks and Non-Banks from a financial services perspective, the legislature could benefit from the knowledge and experience that competition authorities have developed in this area over the past decades.

[3] See Commission (2007a).

[4] Ibid., p. 4.

[5] Ibid., p. 9.

[6] See European Parliament (2018, p. 105).

9.2 Defining the Relevant Market

At a European level, the Commission is responsible for overseeing anti-competitive behaviour and enforcing EU competition law. When assessing potential anti-competitive behaviour by PSPs, the Commission first defines the relevant market in which the PSP in question is offering its products or services. The main purpose of defining the relevant market is to identify the competitive constraints that PSPs face in a particular market.[7] Defining the relevant market is particularly important when verifying whether a PSP holds a dominant market position in a particular market (**Paragraph 9.4**).[8]

The Commission defines the relevant market as a combination of: (i) the product market; and (ii) the geographical market. The product market covers all Payment products and services which PSUs consider to be a substitute on the basis of their product characteristics, price and intended use.[9] When assessing the level of substitutability of a particular Payment product or service, the Commission verifies whether PSUs can easily switch to a similar product in case of a small price increase (demand-side substitutability) and whether competing PSPs can easily commence offering similar Payment products on the same relevant market (supply-side substitutability). The geographical market covers the geographical area in which the conditions of competition for a specific Payment product or service are homogenous.[10]

9.3 Anti-competitive Agreements

Collaboration between competing PSPs can benefit the market in general if it leads to new and improved Payment products. However, if such collaboration is of an anti-competitive nature, collaboration tends to weaken competition and, as a result thereof, the level playing field between Banks and Non-Banks. **Article 101(1) TFEU** prohibits agreements between PSPs, decisions by associations of PSPs and concerted parties which may affect trade between Member States and have as their 'object' or 'effect' the restriction of competition. Any agreement between

[7] See Commission (1997b), paragraph 2.

[8] See Commission (2013c).

[9] See Commission (1997b), paragraph 7.

[10] Ibid., Paragraph 8.

PSPs that is in violation of this prohibition is automatically void according to **Article 101(2) TFEU**.

The prohibition to enter into anti-competitive agreements applies with regard to horizontal agreements and vertical agreements. Horizontal agreements are according to **Paragraph 1 Guidelines on Horizontal Agreements** agreements between potential or actual competitors.[11] Examples of horizontal agreements in the Payments market are the EPC rulebooks and the scheme rules of four-party card schemes. According to **Article 1(1)(a) of the Treaty on the functioning of the European Union to categories of vertical agreements**, vertical agreements are agreements between two or more undertakings each of which operates at a different level of the production or distribution chain.[12] In the Payments market, vertical relations exist *inter alia* between Banks and TPPs in relation to open banking solutions, whereby TPPs require the services of Banks in order to provide payment initiation or account information services. In general, the Commission considers vertical agreements which are restrictive of competition to be less harmful than horizontal agreements that are anti-competitive.[13]

Agreements that restrict competition by 'object' have by their nature the potential to restrict competition.[14] For these agreements, the Commission does not have to demonstrate the anti-competitive effects to establish a violation of the prohibition to enter into anti-competitive agreements. Agreements that restrict competition by object include price fixing, market sharing and output restrictions. For agreements restrictive by 'effect', an extensive analysis on a case by case basis is required to determine whether such agreement is in violation of the prohibition

[11] Under the Guidelines on Horizontal Agreements, actual competitors are PSPs that are active in the same relevant market. A PSP is a potential competitor of another PSP if a small but permanent increase in price will likely result in the PSP entering the market.

[12] Regulation (EU) No 330/2010 of 20 April 2010 "on the application of Article 101(3) of the Treaty on the Functioning of the European Union to categories of vertical agreements and concerted practices", *OJ L 102*, 23.4.2010, pp. 1–7.

[13] See Commission (2010a), paragraph 6.Vertical agreements are exempted from the prohibition to enter into anti-competitive agreements provided that: (i) these are not entered into between competing undertakings; (ii) the market share of the supplier does not exceed 30% of the relevant market and (iii) the market share of the buyer does not exceed 30% of the relevant market.

[14] See Commission (2014d, p. 3).

on anti-competitive agreements. For these agreements, the Commission considers the anti-competitive effect not to be present in case the market shares of the PSPs involved are relatively small. In other words, the prohibition to enter into anti-competitive agreements does not apply where the impact of the agreement on competition is not appreciable.[15] To this end, the Commission adopted a Notice on agreements of minor importance which do not appreciably restrict competition (**'De Minimis Notice'**)[16], which contains guidelines on how the Commission determines whether a particular agreement has an appreciable effect on competition.[17] The De Minimis Notice provides for a safe harbour for agreements between PSPs that remain below certain market share thresholds.[18] The Commission emphasised that horizontal agreements between actual or potential competitors are not subject to the prohibition on anti-competitive agreements if the combined market share does not exceed 10% of the relevant market affected by the agreement.[19] For vertical agreements between actual or potential competitors, the Commission applies a market share threshold of 15% of the relevant market.[20] It should be emphasised that the safe harbour is not available for agreements that restrict competition by object.[21]

Some agreements that have an anti-competitive nature can generate objective economic benefits that outweigh the adverse effects of the restriction on competition.[22] For this reason, **Article 101(3) TFEU** states that agreements that are in violation of the prohibition on anti-competitive agreements may be allowed in case the PSP(s) involved

[15] See Commission (2014e, p. 1).

[16] See Commission (2014a).

[17] See Commission (2014a), paragraph 3. The De Minimis Notice is not legally binding for national competition authorities.

[18] According to Commission (2014a), paragraph 6, these principles also apply to decisions by associations of undertakings and to concerted parties.

[19] See Commission (2014a), paragraph 8(a).

[20] See Commission (2014a), paragraph 8(b).

[21] See European Court of Justice (2012a).

[22] See Commission (n.d.a).

provide evidence that four cumulative criteria are met.[23] First, the agreement in question must contribute to the improvement of the production or distribution of Payment products and services or promote technological or economic progress. To this end, the PSP must provide evidence of efficiency gains, such as cost efficiencies or qualitative efficiencies, that can be realised by entering into this agreement.[24] Second, PSUs should get a fair share of the benefits realised as a result of the relevant agreement. Third, the agreement must be necessary to achieve these benefits and must not go beyond what is needed to realise these benefits. Fourth, the agreement should not eliminate competition in a substantial part of the relevant market in question.

With regard to the European Payments market, the Commission's focus has primarily been on the competition effects of horizontal agreements. The Commission has challenged in particular the horizontal price setting agreements by card schemes such as Visa and Mastercard. In addition, standard setting practices by PSPs is a main area of concern for the Commission.

9.3.1 Interchange Fees for Card Payments

Card schemes compete with each other by onboarding as many as possible card issuing PSPs under their scheme rules. Card schemes attract issuers by offering them a high interchange fee, which results in an increased cost base for the execution of card payments.[25] In order to incentivise PSUs to use these relatively expensive cards, card schemes tend to offer cardholders certain benefits, such as air miles and bonuses. The costs of these benefits are included in the interchange fee and are often invisible to the cardholder.[26] Because the interchange fee is part of the merchant service charge, which is the fee that merchants pay for accepting card payments, merchants tend to pass these costs on to their customers. This means that interchange fees have a price increasing effect on the goods

[23] Moreover, it should be noted that Commission Regulation (EU) No 1217/2010 provides a block exemption from the prohibition of **Article 101(1) TFEU** for certain types of research and development agreements.

[24] See Commission (2004a), para. 50.

[25] Commission. (n.d.b).

[26] See Commission (2012a, p. 12).

and services offered by merchants.[27] Since consumers are unaware of the actual costs of the benefits offered to them by card schemes, consumers are generally not inclined to use cheaper cards that do not offer such benefits.

An argument often used by issuers to justify the use of higher interchange fees is that an issuer's loss of revenue with lower interchange fees would be compensated by charging cardholders higher banking fees.[28] Issuers often argue that higher banking fees incentivise PSUs to use payment products that are less cost efficient, such as cash. Moreover, it is argued that merchants do not reduce their prices in case of lower interchange fees. In other words, issuers claim there are no guarantees that lowering interchange fees has a price decreasing effect on products and services offered by merchants.[29]

However, instead of being an effective tool for balancing fees between merchants and cardholders, interchange fees appear to provide for a direct source of income for issuers since there is no obligation for issuers to pass on (part of) the interchange fee to the cardholders.[30] Furthermore, interchange fees can impose obstacles for new card schemes to enter the European market for card-based payments. To compete successfully with existing card schemes, new schemes entering the market have to offer issuers similar interchange fees and cardholders similar benefits as incumbent card schemes. Consequently, the price reducing effect that we normally see with increased competition does not appear to exist in the European market for card payments. Moreover, interchange fees distort price competition between acquirers since it leads to the transfer of revenues from acquirers to issuers.[31] For these reasons, European card schemes have been scrutinised by competition authorities since the 1990s.

9.3.1.1 Visa

Visa operates the largest four-party card scheme in the EEA. Under the Visa scheme rules, Visa used to apply a MIF for cross-border payments with Visa debit cards and credit cards which was set as a percentage of

[27] See Commission (2014c, p. 1).

[28] See Hayashi, F. (2013, p. 90).

[29] Ibid., p. 91.

[30] See J. D. Mathis (2015, p. 102).

[31] See Commission (2007b, p. 115).

net sales. In 1997, the Commission received a formal complaint by Euro-Commerce[32] about Visa's price setting rules, which marked the beginning of numerous competition cases against Visa.[33]

In 2000, the Commission sent Visa a formal statement of objections in which the Commission ruled that the multilateral setting of interchange fees between competing Banks affiliated to the Visa network constituted an anti-competitive collective price agreement.[34] To address the Commission's concerns, Visa proposed to amend its scheme rules by: (i) reducing the intra-regional MIFs; (ii) using three categories of issuers costs as a benchmark against which the intra-regional MIFs could be assessed and (iii) increasing transparency on MIFs *vis-à-vis* merchants.[35] In 2002, the Commission concluded that the proposed amendments to the Visa scheme rules justified the granting of an exemption of the prohibition to enter into an anti-competitive agreement (**Paragraph 9.3**).[36] The exemption applied from the moment Visa amended its Visa scheme rules until 31 December 2007 and only covered cross-border transactions initiated with Visa consumer cards.[37]

In 2008, after the exemption expired, the Commission opened antitrust investigations against Visa in relation to its MIFs for cross-border POS transactions.[38] In 2009, the Commission sent a statement of objections to Visa containing the Commission's preliminary view that Visa's MIFs weakened competition between acquirers.[39] Following the Commission's statement of objections, Visa offered to reduce its MIFs for debit card payments to 0.2% of the transaction value, which represented an average reduction of 60% for national MIFs and 30% for cross-border

[32] EuroCommerce is a European organisation representing the retail and wholesale sector across the EU.

[33] See Commission (2002b, p. 2).

[34] See Commission (2000).

[35] See Commission (2001).

[36] See Commission (2002a).

[37] I.e., credit cards, deferred debit cards and debit cards. The exemption did not apply with regard to corporate Visa cards that were used by employees to pay for business expenditures.

[38] See Commission (2008a).

[39] See Commission (2009b).

MIFs.[40] These commitments were made legally binding by the Commission for a period of four years.[41] The Commission's proceedings against Visa's MIFs for credit card payments continued, which resulted in the Commission issuing a supplementary statement of objections in 2012.[42] Besides the MIFs for credit card payments, the Commission was also concerned about Visa's rules on cross-border acquiring, which is the offering of acquiring services to merchants located in another Member State. Visa's rules on cross-border acquiring prevented merchants from benefitting from lower merchant service charges of acquirers located in other Member States, which restricted cross-border competition in a significant manner. Visa addressed the Commission's concerns by complementing its previous commitment by: (i) capping its credit card MIFs at 0.3%; and (ii) allowing acquirers to apply the national rates or a reduced cross-border interchange fee of 0.2% for debit card transactions and 0.3% for credit card transactions when competing for merchants cross-border.[43] These commitments were subsequently made legally binding by the Commission and were in force for a period of four years.[44]

On 3 August 2017, the Commission sent another supplementary statement of objections to Visa relating the Visa's inter-regional interchange fees, which are fees charged to payments made in the EU using Visa cards that are issued outside the EU.[45] These cards are not covered by the IFR and therefore not subject to the IFR caps on interchange fees (**Paragraph 3.7.3**). Visa committed itself to *inter alia*: (i) cap its inter-regional debit MIF for CP transactions at 0.2% and for CNP transactions at 1.15%; and (ii) cap its inter-regional credit MIF for CP transactions at 0.3% and for CNP transactions at 1.50%.[46] These commitments were made legally binding by the Commission in 2019 for a period of five years and six months.[47]

[40] See Commission. (2010b).

[41] See Commission (2010c).

[42] See Commission (2012b).

[43] See Commission (2014b).

[44] See Commission (2014f).

[45] Commission (n.d.c).

[46] See Commission (2019b).

[47] See Commission (2019c).

9.3.1.2 Mastercard

Mastercard operates the second largest four-party card scheme in the EEA. Like Visa, Mastercard has been subject to numerous competition investigations. The Commission commenced its investigations into Mastercard's pricing structure in 1992 due to a complaint received from British Retail Consortium and EuroCommerce.[48]

In 2007 the Commission examined the effects of Mastercard's interchange fees on cross-border acquiring in the EEA. The Commission ruled that the interchange fees set by the Banks affiliated to the Mastercard network for cross-border card payments with Mastercard and Maestro debit and credit cards restricted competition and therefore infringed the prohibition to enter into an anti-competitive agreement.[49] The Commission's decision addressed only one specific type of interchange fee called the 'intra-EEA fallback interchange fee', which was charged for almost all cross-border card payments executed in the EEA with Mastercard and Maestro.[50] Subsequently, Mastercard temporarily repealed its interchange fees for cross-border card payments and searched for evidence to demonstrate to the Commission the benefits of charging this interchange fee in order to be eligible for the exemption under **Article 101(3) TFEU**.[51] In addition, changes were made by Mastercard to its pricing method.[52] As a result, the Commission decided not to pursue investigations into Mastercard for infringing the antitrust rules at that moment.[53]

Mastercard appealed the Commission's decision of 2007 that Mastercard's interchange fees for cross-border card payments infringed the prohibition to enter into anti-competitive agreements, but the decision was upheld by the General Court in 2012.[54] Like the Commission,

[48] See A. De Matteis & S. Giordano (2015, p. 85).

[49] See Commission (2009c).

[50] See Commission (2007c).

[51] See Commission (2008b).

[52] An important change included using a different methodology for calculating cross-border MIFs which ensures that these MIFs reflect transactional benefits to merchants when accepting card payments instead of cash payments.

[53] See Commission (2009a).

[54] See European Court of Justice. (2012b).

the General Court rejected the claim by Mastercard that these interchange fees were objectively necessary for operating a card scheme.[55] In 2014, the CJEU confirmed the General Court's decision that the Mastercard's interchange fees for cross-border transactions in the EEA restrict competition.[56]

In 2013, the Commission opened investigations into: (i) the Mastercard rules on cross-border acquiring; and (ii) Mastercard's inter-regional interchange fees, which are fees charged for payments with Mastercard cards that were issued outside the EU.[57] Under the Mastercard rules for cross-border acquiring, acquirers were obliged to pay the issuer the interchange fee applicable in the Member State where the merchant was established.[58] Consequently, merchants could not benefit from lower merchant fees charged by acquirers in other Member States.[59] On 9 July 2015, the Commission adopted a statement of objections against Mastercard stating *inter alia* that the high levels of inter-regional interchange fees were not justified and the Mastercard rules on cross-border acquiring limited acquirers to compete cross-border on price.[60] Like Visa, Mastercard committed itself to: (i) cap its inter-regional debit MIF for CP transactions at 0.2% and for CNP transactions at 1.15%; and (ii) cap its inter-regional credit MIF for CP transactions at 0.3% and for CNP transactions at 1.50%.[61] In 2019, the Commission imposed a fine of €570 mln. on Mastercard for the adverse competitive effects of its rules on cross-border acquiring.[62]

9.3.2 *Standardisation and Its Effect on Competition*

Because the market for Payments is a network-based market, PSPs must cooperate with each other to ensure efficient processing of Payments.[63]

[55] See Commission (2012c).

[56] See European Court of Justice (2014).

[57] See Commission (2013a).

[58] See Commission (2012a, p. 9).

[59] See (Commission (2015a, p. 3).

[60] See Commission (2015b).

[61] See Mastercard (2018).

[62] Commission (2019a).

[63] See OECD (2013, p. 23).

To maximise the reach between PSPs, interoperability between PSPs and Payment schemes is an absolute necessity.[64] Interoperability can only be achieved if Payment schemes and PSPs apply the same standards for transmitting Payment messages and processing Payments.[65] With regard to open banking solutions, interoperability also requires the use of standardised APIs by Banks to ensure frictionless payment account access by TPPs.

In the market for Payments, the main initiatives on standardisation have been taken by market participants. Examples of such market initiatives are the SEPA schemes that have been developed by the EPC. These SEPA standards have played a substantial role in the development of an efficient European market for direct debit collections and credit transfers (**Paragraph 3.5**). Another example of a market initiative on standardisation is the recommended functionalities published by the Application Programming Interface Evaluation Group (**'API EG'**).[66] The main objectives of the API EG are to ensure that: (i) the API specifications developed by the main API initiatives[67] are compliant with PSD2 and the RTS SCA; and (ii) these specifications function well for TPPs that need to rely on them. Examples of standardisation can also be found in the European financial services regulatory framework. For example, the European legislature adopted the SEPA Regulation to ensure that, amongst others, the use of the ISO 20022 standard became mandatory for in-scope Payments.[68]

Standardisation enhances the efficiency of the Payments market and holds the promise of increasing competition.[69] Nevertheless, it should be emphasised that collaboration between (potential) competitors for standardisation purposes can raise competition concerns. Standards are not neutral since they reflect the technology and preferences of the PSPs that

[64] See Commission (2013d, p. 2).

[65] See Commission (2004b, p. 6).

[66] See EPC (2018). The API EG was established by the Commission in 2018 and consists of representatives from AS-PSPs, TPPs, PSUs and NCAs.

[67] I.e., the Berlin Group, Open Banking UK, Polish API initiative, Slovak Banking API initiative and STET.

[68] SEPA Regulation, Recital 14.

[69] See Commission (2004b, p. 5).

developed these standards.[70] Technological standards that are developed by non-participating PSPs are often not taken into consideration. Another risk with standardisation is that it can lead to an oligopolistic market structure if PSPs agree to apply certain standards to divide the market between them.[71] Another competition concern is that the standardisation process can lead to competing PSPs sharing more information than strictly required for ensuring interoperability.[72] Moreover, imposing standards on all PSPs holds the risk of increasing barriers to market entry for Non-Banks.

To address these concerns, **Paragraph 319 Guidelines on Horizontal Agreements** requires standardisation agreements between PSPs to include adequate safeguards for mitigating competition risks. According to **Paragraph 280 Guidelines on Horizontal Agreements**, standard setting practices between PSPs are not in violation of the prohibition to enter into anti-competitive agreements provided that: (i) participation by PSPs in standard setting is unrestricted; (ii) the procedure for adopting the standard is transparent; (iii) there is no obligation for PSPs to comply with the standard and (iv) access to the standard is on fair, reasonable and non-discriminatory terms.

9.3.2.1 The European Payments Council (EPC)

An example of an antitrust case regarding standardisation in the Payments market is the Commission's antitrust investigations into the standardisation process of the EPC. The EPC is one of the main standard setting organisations in the European Payments market. One of the standardisation initiatives launched by the EPC was the development of a Payment framework containing standards and rules for interoperability between Payment schemes in various Member States. The Payment framework rules did not allow Non-Banks to become a participant in this framework.

In 2011, the Commission opened antitrust investigations into the standardisation activities of the EPC based on a complaint received from the FinTech Sofort, which stated that the Payment framework imposed barriers on market entry for Non-Banks.[73] Commissioner

[70] See ISO standards (2012, p. 9).

[71] See European Parliament (2018, p. 13).

[72] See OECD (2013, p. 23).

[73] See Commission (2011).

Joaquín Almunia explained: '*The use of the internet is increasing rapidly making the need for secure and efficient online payment solutions in the whole Single Euro Payments Area all the more pressing. I therefore welcome the work of the European Payments Council to develop standards in this area. In principle, standards promote interoperability and competition, but we need to ensure that the standardisation process does not unnecessarily restrict opportunities for non-participants*'.

According to the Commission, standardisation must be fair and should recognise the needs of all stakeholders in the payment chain, which also involves non-participants such as Non-Banks. After the EPC announced that it would stop its work on the Payments framework, Sofort withdrew its complaint. The Commission closed its investigations into the EPC in 2013 as a result of which the opportunity was lost to gain inside into the Commission's view on standardisation practices by PSPs.[74]

9.3.2.2 APIs as a Means for Ensuring Interoperability Between Banks and TPPs

Interoperability is a main requirement for TPPs that need to align their IT-infrastructure with the IT-infrastructure of Banks. If each AS-PSP designs its own API, it becomes very challenging for TPPs to develop services that are capable of communicating with each of these different APIs.[75] It is therefore essential that harmonised standards are developed which are used by all market participants.

PSD2 is however technology neutral and does not prescribe how data must be exchanged between AS-PSPs and TPPs. The Banking industry is therefore required to develop their own sets of APIs. As a result, TPPs often face different API standards with which they must comply in order to obtain access to the payment accounts of its PSUs. This is considered to be one of the reasons why the potential of PSD2 for stimulating the development of open banking solutions remains to a large extent unused.[76]

To foster the level playing field between Banks and TPPs, it is elementary that larger Banks adopt common standards for open APIs. A standardised API can increase competition by making it easier for TPPs to

[74] See Commission (2013b).

[75] See G. Colangelo and O. Borgogno (2018, p. 24).

[76] See Commission (2020b, p. 15).

access APIs of different Banks. However, the use of standardised APIs can also have adverse effects on innovation and the level playing field between Banks and TPPs. Using standardised APIs could hinder innovation if it prevents PSPs from developing new APIs that are better than these standardised API.[77] The use of standardised APIs may harm the level playing field between Banks and TPPs since, from a Bank's perspective, investing in standardised APIs increases the Banks' costs and brings the competition in a better position. As a result, it has an adverse impact on the profitability of the Bank's Payment business.

9.4 Abuse of a Dominant Market Position

9.4.1 Background

PSPs that hold a dominant position in a particular segment in the market for Payments have a special responsibility to ensure that their conduct does not impair competition.[78] A dominant position is defined as '*a position of economic strength enjoyed by an undertaking which enables it to prevent effective competition being maintained on the relevant market by giving it the power to behave to an appreciable extent independent of its competitors, customers and ultimately of consumers*'.[79] A dominant position is determined on the basis of a PSP's market share in the relevant market and the existence of entry barriers in that market. The higher the market share of a PSP, and the longer the period of time over which it is held, the more likely that such PSP holds a dominant position. A PSP is in any case assumed to hold a dominant position when it has a market share of at least 50%.[80]

Holding a dominant position is by itself not in violation of EU antitrust rules. **Article 102 TFEU** prohibits PSPs holding a dominant position to abuse such position.[81] Examples of behaviour that constitute abuse if conducted by a PSP holding a dominant position include *inter alia*: (i) charging excessive prices, which are prices that do not reasonably relate to the economic value of the product or service; (ii) charging extremely low

[77] See G. Colangelo and O. Borgogno (2018, p. 24).

[78] See European Court of Justice (1983), paragraph 57.

[79] See European Court of Justice (1978), paragraph 65.

[80] See A. Van der Beek (2017, p. 171).

[81] This article corresponds to **Article 54 of the EEA Agreement**.

prices as a result of which (potential) competitors can no longer compete or (iii) tying[82] and bundling[83] practices.

The European market for Payments used to be dominated by Banks. Being a first mover in the Payments market enabled Banks to obtain a prominent market position. Competition authorities have therefore been particularly concerned about the potential abuse of market power by Banks. However, with BigTechs entering the market for Payments, Banks are no longer the only PSPs holding a dominant position. BigTechs trigger anti-competitive foreclosure risks if they use their networks as leverage to obtain a dominant position and use that position to squeeze out the competition. An example of behaviour that may constitute abuse of a dominant market position by a BigTech is the case of Apple Pay. Apple does not allow PSPs access to the NFC antenna installed on iOS devices. As a result, PSPs are not able to offer E-wallets like Apple Pay which can be used for making contactless payments with an iOS device. One of the objectives of the Commission is to enable PSPs to obtain access to technical infrastructures relevant for the development of innovative Payment solutions. In 2020, the Commission announced that it opened antitrust investigations into Apple Pay to assess whether Apple abuses its dominant market position with the Apple Pay app.[84] In 2022, the Commission informed Apple of its preliminary view that it indeed abuses its dominant position in markets for E-wallets on iOS devices by limiting access to the NFC antenna installed on these devices.[85] To address the Commission's concerns, Apple has offered certain commitments, which include: (i) allowing PSPs free of charge access with the NFC functionality on iOS devices through APIs; and (ii) applying fair, objective, transparent and non-discriminatory eligibility criteria for NFC access by such PSPs.[86]

In case of abuse of a dominant market position, the competition authorities can only intervene ex-post, which means that intervention is in

[82] In case of tying, PSUs can only purchase a particular payment product if they also purchase another (payment) product from the same PSP.

[83] In case of bundling, PSPs sell different (payment) products only jointly.

[84] See Commission (2020a).

[85] See Commission (2022).

[86] See Commission (2024).

most cases only possible after any damage has materialised.[87] To address this risk the ACM suggested in 2019 to include an ex-ante competition tool in Regulation 1/2003[88] aimed to prevent competition problems with dominant companies.[89] Such tool would consist of measures that the NCA can take to prevent undesired situations and should be available without the need of identifying an infringement of **Article 102 TFEU**.

9.4.2 La Poste / SWIFT + GUF

A relevant example of an antitrust case on the prohibition to abuse a dominant market position is the Commission's antitrust case against the global financial messaging services provider SWIFT. SWIFT is the main international system for transmitting payment instructions between PSPs. SWIFT develops standards such as SWIFT MT102[90], which PSPs use for straight-through processing of credit transfers. Initially, only Banks were allowed access to SWIFT services. The French post office La Poste operated a retail banking system in France but was not allowed to grant loans and therefore not regulated as a Bank. For this reason, La Poste was denied SWIFT membership. In 1996, La Poste filed a complaint with the Commission for being denied access to the SWIFT network. In 1997, the Commission initiated a formal procedure against SWIFT. According to the Commission, SWIFT qualified as an 'essential facility' because it was the only international network available for the transmission of Payment messages between PSPs. SWIFT was therefore considered to have a dominant market position and abused its position by imposing unlawful admission criteria. Pending the Commission's investigations, SWIFT issued a formal undertaking to grant full access to all entities fulfilling European Monetary Institute criteria for admission to

[87] See ACM (2020, p. 5).

[88] Council Regulation (EC) No 1/2003 of 16 December 2002 "on the implementation of the rules on competition laid down in Articles 81 and 82 of the Treaty", *OJ L 1*, 4.1.2003, pp. 1–25.

[89] See ACM (2019).

[90] SWIFT MT102 is a messaging format for bundling multiple payment instructions sent between PSPs for executing credit transfers.

national payment systems.[91] Subsequently, the Commission suspended its investigations into the anti-competitive behaviour of SWIFT.[92]

9.4.3 Interpay

Another relevant example of an antitrust case on the prohibition to abuse a dominant market position is the antitrust case of the Dutch competition authorities against the Dutch payment system Interpay. Interpay[93] was a Dutch joint venture founded by eight Banks in 1994.[94] Interpay was responsible for the clearing and settlement of Payments in the Netherlands. To this end, Interpay: (i) licensed Banks to issue debit cards; (ii) processed the transactions initiated with these debit cards and (iii) entered into contractual arrangements with merchants for debit card acceptance.

In 2002, the Dutch competition authority[95] opened an investigation into potential infringements by Interpay and its shareholding Banks of *inter alia* the prohibition to abuse a dominant market position.[96] The Dutch competition authority ruled that Interpay had a dominant position in the market for network services for PIN transactions in the Netherlands since the Interpay network was the sole supplier of support services for Payments in the Netherlands.[97] The Dutch competition authority ruled that Interpay charged excessive fees since the return made by Interpay over the period 1998–2001 was five to seven times higher than the calculated benchmark return. This excessive pricing constituted abuse by

[91] See Commission (1997c).

[92] See Commission (1997a).

[93] In 2006 Interpay merged with the German Transaktioninstitut für Zahlungsdiensleistungen and was renamed Equens. In 2016 equensWorldline was created following the merger between Equens and Worldline.

[94] (i) ING Bank N.V.; (ii) ABN AMRO Bank N.V.; (iii) Coöperatieve Raiffeisen—Boerenleenbank B.A.; (iv) Fortis Bank (Nederland) N.V.; (v) SNS Bank N.V.; (vi) F. van Lanschot Bankiers N.V.; (vii) Friesland Bank N.V. and (viii) N.V. Bank Nederlandse Gemeenten.

[95] De Nederlandse Mededingingsautoriteit (NMa), which was renamed De Autoriteit Consument & Markt (ACM) after a merger with the Onafhankelijke Post en Telecommunicatie Autoriteit (OPTA) on 1 April 2013.

[96] Within the meaning of **Article 24 of the Dutch Competition Act (*Mededingingswet*)**.

[97] See ACM. (n.d.a).

Interpay of its dominant market position.[98] Although Interpay was fined for abusing its dominant position, the Dutch competition authority later repealed this fine because it considered that further research was required to demonstrate the charging of excessive fees by Interpay.[99]

To enhance competition in the Dutch Payments market, Interpay divided its business into two separate legal entities. To this end, Currence[100] was established which became the certification institution and the product owner of Payment products such as PIN, Chipknip and iDEAL. However, the measures taken by Interpay were inadequate to address the competition concerns since the shareholding Banks of Interpay were also the sole shareholders of Currence. Furthermore, 70% of the supervisory board members of Currence were representatives from the shareholding Banks. As a result, Interpay's shareholding Banks were able to exercise substantial influence over Currence's decision making process on allowing competing PSPs access to the Dutch market for debit card payments.[101] In 2006, the Dutch competition authority (NMa) opened investigations into the ownership structure of Currence and the level of influence that the shareholding Banks had on the decision making process of Currence.[102] After Currence had the representatives for the shareholders resign from the supervisory board, the Dutch competition authority concluded that there were no longer sufficient indications for a violation of Dutch competition rules.[103]

[98] See NMa (2004).

[99] See NMa (2005b). It must be emphasised that Interpay was also fined for breaching the prohibition to enter into agreements restrictive of competition. The Dutch competition authority ruled that the shareholding Banks of Interpay infringed this prohibition because the sale of network services for PIN transactions via Interpay, instead of in competition with each other, eliminated competition in the relevant market. The agreement to offer these services via Interpay resulted in Dutch merchants having to obtain acquiring services from a single supplier.

[100] Currence was established under the name Brands & Licences Betalingsverkeer Nederland. In 2005 Brands & Licences Betalingsverkeer Nederland was renamed Currence.

[101] See NMa (2005a).

[102] See ACM. (n.d.b).

[103] Ibid., ACM.

9.5 The Digital Markets Act (DMA)

9.5.1 Introduction

BigTechs that operate a platform and are active in the Payments market, either as PSP or technical service provider, can obtain a dominant position. As part of its Digital Single Market Strategy, the Commission published on 15 December 2020 a draft regulation on the digital markets.[104] Regulation (EU) 2022/1925 (**'DMA'**)[105] applies as of 2 May 2023 and aims to eliminate unfair practices by companies that act as gatekeepers in the online platform economy.[106]

9.5.2 Gatekeepers and the Payments Market

The DMA introduces rules for BigTech platforms that qualify as 'gatekeepers' in the digital market to prevent these undertakings from imposing unfair conditions on businesses and consumers. According to **Article 3(1) DMA**, gatekeepers are platforms that provide so-called core platform services[107] and: (i) have a significant impact on the internal

[104] See Commission (2020c).

[105] Regulation (EU) 2022/1925 of 14 September 2022 "on contestable and fair markets in the digital sector (…)", OJ L 265, 12.10.2022, pp. 1–66.

[106] See Commission (n.d.d).

[107] According to **Article 2(2) DMA**, core platform services are: (i) online intermediation services as defined in point 2 of Article 2 of Regulation (EU) 2019/1150; (ii) online search engines as defined in point 5 of Article 2 of Regulation (EU) 2019/1150; (iii) online social networking services; (iv) video-sharing platform services as defined in point (aa) of Article 1(1) of Directive (EU) 2010/13; (v) number-independent interpersonal communication services as defined in point 7 of Article 2 of Directive (EU) 2018/1972; (vi) operating systems (system software that controls the basic functions of the hardware or software and enables software applications to run on it); (vii) web browsers (software application that enables end users to access and interact with web content hosted on servers that are connected to networks); (viii) virtual assistants (a software that can process demands, tasks or questions); (ix) cloud computing systems as defined in point 19 of Article 4 of Directive (EU) 2016/1148 and (x) online advertising services, including any advertising networks, advertising exchanges and any other advertising intermediation services, provided by a provider of any of the core services listed in points (i) to (ix).

market[108]; (ii) operate a core platform service which serves as an important gateway for business users to reach end users[109] and (iii) enjoys a durable position in its operations or it is foreseeable that it will enjoy such position in the near future.[110,111] Examples of BigTechs that qualify as gatekeepers under the DMA and which are active in the market for Payments include Apple, Amazon and Google.

The DMA introduces, amongst others, restrictions that gatekeepers need to implement in their daily operations. Although the objective of the DMA is not to regulate the Payments market, the DMA introduces an interoperability requirement for BigTechs that may be of particular importance for the competitive position of PSPs *vis-à-vis* BigTechs.

9.5.3 Interoperability Requirement for BigTechs Acting as Gatekeeper

In addition to their core platform services, gatekeepers often provide ancillary services such as payment services or technical services that support payment services.[112] Although competition law requires companies that operate a platform with a dominant market position to allow other companies access to their platform under objective, reasonable and non-discriminatory terms, PSPs cannot claim access to the ecosystems of gatekeepers. Therefore, if a platform offers a new payment solution, it

[108] According to **Article 3(2)(a) DMA**, a platform is considered to have a significant impact on the internal market if it provides a core platform service in at least three Member States and: (i) it achieves an annual EU turnover of EUR 7.5 billion or more in each of the last three financial years; or (ii) where the average market capitalisation or the equivalent fair market value of the undertaking amounted to at least EUR 75 billion in the last financial year.

[109] According to **Article 3(2)(b) DMA**, a platform is considered to operate a core platform service which serves as an important gateway for business users to reach end users if the core platform service has more than 45 million monthly active end users in the EU and more than 10,000 yearly active business users in the EU in the last financial year.

[110] According to **Article 3(2)(c) DMA**, a platform is considered to enjoy an entrenched and durable position if the thresholds of **Articles 3(2)(a) and 3(2)(b) DMA** were met in each of the last three financial years.

[111] If a platform meets all these requirements but does not meet all the relevant thresholds, **Article 3(6) DMA** allows the Commission to qualify such platform as a gatekeeper on the basis of a qualitative assessment.

[112] See Commission (2020c, p. 18).

works with software or hardware that is only available to its own payment solution. This unlevels the playing field since gatekeepers, if licensed or registered as a TPP, can claim access to the payment accounts of Banks.

To address this issue, the DMA provides for an interoperability obligation for gatekeepers. If a gatekeeper provides an ancillary service such as a payment service, **Article 6(7) DMA** requires the gatekeeper to provide PSPs access to and operability with the same operating system that is used by the gatekeeper for the same service. Having such interoperability requirement for BigTechs could be helpful for situations like Apple Pay, whereby PSPs are denied access to the NFC antenna installed on iOS devices.

9.6 Conclusion

In a network-based sector like the Payments sector, collaboration between competing PSPs with regard to standard setting is essential to enhance interoperability between PSPs and Payment schemes (which involves PSPs applying the same standards for exchanging Payment messages and processing Payments) and, as a result thereof, ensure efficient processing of Payments (i.e., processing Payments swiftly and with low costs). Without any form of collaboration between competitors regarding the standards that are to be used by PSPs, PSPs cannot process Payments in an efficient manner.

In general, standardisation enhances the efficiency by which Payments are executed. However, one must take into account that standardisation agreements between PSPs can also have an anti-competitive nature and, as a result thereof, restrict the level playing field between Banks and Non-Banks.

Under the EU antitrust rules, PSPs are prohibited to enter into agreements which have as their 'object' or 'effect' the restriction of competition. The prohibition to enter into anti-competitive agreements applies with regard to horizontal agreements and vertical agreements, albeit that the Commission's focus in the European Payments market has been primarily on the competition effects of horizontal agreements. The Commission scrutinises in particular: (i) the horizontal price setting agreements by four party card schemes; and (ii) standard setting practices by PSPs.

According to the Commission's Guidelines on the applicability of **Article 101 TFEU** to horizontal cooperation agreements (**'Guidelines**

on Horizontal Agreements')[113], standard setting practices between PSPs are not in violation of the prohibition to enter into anti-competitive agreements provided that: (i) participation by PSPs in standard setting is unrestricted; (ii) the procedure for adopting the standard is transparent; (iii) there is no obligation for PSPs to comply with the standard and (iv) access to the standard is on fair, reasonable and non-discriminatory terms.

In the market for Payments, the main initiatives on standardisation have been taken by market participants, such as the SEPA project, which was initially launched by the European banking sector. As part of the SEPA project, the EPC published numerous rulebooks containing standards by which PSPs have to abide when transmitting Payment messages and processing Payments. Although these rulebooks have contributed substantially to the efficiency of the European Payments market, the SEPA project only allows for limited non-Bank involvement. For example, Non-Banks cannot participate in the development process of new standards and are therefore confronted with the EPC requirements as a matter of fact. Moreover, the practical implication of the EPC's adherence policy is that PIs cannot join the EPC schemes as a direct participant. This means that PIs can only obtain indirect access via a banking competitor, as a result of which it is more difficult for PIs to compete with Banks on costs. Standardisation initiatives can also be found in the European financial services regulatory framework. An example is the obligation imposed by the SEPA Regulation on PSPs to use the ISO 20022 standard.

To ensure that standard setting initiatives do not adversely impact competition between Banks and Non-Banks, Non-Banks also need to be involved in the standard setting process. As mentioned in **Paragraph 9.3.2**, standards are not neutral since they reflect the technology and preferences of the PSPs that developed these standards. To date, Non-Banks are underrepresented in standardisation bodies that issue standards that are mandatory in the Payments market. As a consequence, the interests of these stakeholders are not (or to a lesser extent) taken into consideration when new market standards are developed.

In order to foster sound competition between Banks and Non-Banks, it is therefore essential to also have non-Bank involvement in standard setting processes. Involving Non-Banks in standardisation serves two

[113] Communication from the Commission "Guidelines on the applicability of Article 101 of the Treaty on the Functioning of the European Union to horizontal co-operation agreements", *OJ C 11*, 14.1.2011, pp. 1–72.

purposes. First, it enhances innovation since non-Bank participation may result in different ideas being developed that can be beneficial for the market as a whole. Second, it enables Non-Banks to promote their interests and introduce topics that are of particular relevance to them. By ensuring that the interests of Non-Banks are also taken into account, there is a lower risk that the competitive position of Non-Banks *vis-à-vis* Banks deteriorates as a result of standard setting practices by Banks. As a consequence, the status quo is better safeguarded which is beneficial for achieving a level playing field between Banks and Non-Banks. A downside of non-Bank participation in standard setting processes is that it makes the decision making process less efficient if there are too many different stakeholders involved. By allowing a larger group of different stakeholders to participate in the decision making process, it becomes more difficult to find common ground and to agree on standards that are useful to the market as a whole. There is an increased risk of conflicting interests as a result of which standardisation bodies have to reach a compromise. By reaching a compromise that is acceptable to all stakeholders, standards may be introduced which are not the most efficient for the Payments market as a whole.

Moreover, EU antitrust rules prohibit PSPs which hold a dominant position in a particular market to abuse their position. PSPs holding a dominant position in a particular segment of the Payments market have a special responsibility to ensure that their conduct does not impair competition. The European market for Payments used to be dominated by Banks. However, nowadays BigTechs such as Apple often have dominant positions in the market for Payments. In case of abuse of a dominant market position, the competition authorities can only intervene ex-post, which means that intervention is only possible after potential damages have materialised. With the interoperability requirement of the DMA, the Commission may have a valuable instrument to intervene in case of anticipated market abuse by a BigTech that qualifies as a gatekeeper.

Secondary Sources

ACM. (2019). *Ex-ante Tool for the Assessment of Sustainability Initiatives*. https://www.acm.nl/sites/default/files/documents/2019-08/ex-ante-tool.pdf. Accessed April 13, 2024.

ACM. (2020). *Rapportage BigTechs in Het Betalingsverkeer*, p. 5.

ACM. (n.d.a). NMa Obtains Information and Starts Consultation in Investigation into Debit Card Transactions. https://www.acm.nl/en/publications/publication/5936/NMa-Obtains-Information-and-Starts-Consultation-in-Investigation-into-Debit-Card-Transactions. Accessed April 13, 2024.

ACM. (n.d.b). *NMa rondt onderzoek naar Currence af*. https://www.acm.nl/nl/publicaties/publicatie/4761/NMa-rondt-onderzoek-naar-Currence-af. Accessed April 13, 2024.

Colangelo, G., & Borgogno, O. (2018). *Data, Innovation and Transatlantic Competition in Finance: The Case of the Access to Account Rule*. Stanford-Vienna European Union Law Working Paper No. 35, p. 24.

Commission. (1997a). *Following an Undertaking by S.W.I.F.T. to Change Its Membership Rules, the European Commission Suspends Its Action for Breach of Competition Rules*. Press release IP/97/870.

Commission. (1997b). *Commission Notice on the Definition of Relevant Market for the Purposes of Community Competition Law* (1997 97/C 372/03) (OJ C 372, 9.12.1997), Paragraphs 2, 7, 8.

Commission. (1997c). Case IV/36.120, *La Poste / SWIFT + GUF*. Commission decision of 6 November, Official Journal, 1997 C 335/3.

Commission. (2000). *Commission Plans to Clear Certain Visa Provisions, Challenge Others*. Press Release IP/00/1164.

Commission. (2001). *Notice Pursuant to Article 19(3) of Council Regulation No 17—Case COMP/29.373 – Visa International*. Official Journal, C 226, 11.8.2001.

Commission. (2002a). *Case COMP/29.373—Visa International MIF, Commission Decision*, 22 November.

Commission. (2002b). *Commission Exempts Multilateral Interchange Fees for Cross-Border Visa Card Payments*. Press Release IP/02/1138, p. 2.

Commission. (2004a). *Communication from the Commission—Guidelines on the Application of Article 81(3) of the Treaty* (2004/C 101/08). Official Journal of the European Union, C 101, 27.4.2004, para. 50.

Commission. (2004b). *Communication from the Commission to the European Parliament and the Council on the role of European Standardisation in the Framework of European Policies and Legislation*. COM (2004) 674 final, pp. 5, 6.

Commission. (2007a). *Communication from the Commission: Sector Inquiry under Article 17 of Regulation (EC) No 1/2003 on Retail Banking (Final Report)*. COM (2007) 33 final, pp. 4, 9.

Commission. (2007b). *Report on the Retail Banking Sector Inquiry*. Commission Staff Working Document Accompanying the Communication from the Commission—Sector Inquiry Under Art 17 of Regulation 1/2003 on Retail Banking (Final Report), SEC (2007) 106, p. 115.

Commission. (2007c). *Antitrust: Commission Prohibits Mastercard's Intra-EEA Multilateral Interchange Fees*. Press release IP/07/1959.

Commission. (2008a). *Antitrust: Commission Initiates Formal Proceedings Against Visa Europe Limited*. MEMO/08/170.

Commission. (2008b). *Antitrust: Commission Notes Mastercard's Decision to Temporarily Repeal Its Cross-Border Multilateral Interchange Fees Within the EEA*. MEMO/08/397.

Commission. (2009a). Antitrust: *Commissioner Kroes Takes Note of Mastercard's Decision to Cut Cross-Border Multilateral Interchange Fees (MIFs) and to Repeal Recent Scheme Fee Increases*. Press release IP/09/515.

Commission. (2009b). *Antitrust: Commission Sends Statement of Objections to Visa*. MEMO/09/151.

Commission. (2009c). Mastercard, Case COMP/34.579, Summary of Commission Decision 2009/C 264/04, *Official Journal*. [2009] OJ C 264/8, paragraph 30.

Commission. (2010a). Guidelines on Vertical Restraints, 19 May 2010 (2010/C 130/01) (Official Journal, C 130, 19.5.2010), paragraph 6.

Commission. (2010b). *Antitrust: Commission Makes Visa Europe's Commitments to Cut interbank Fees for Debit Cards Legally Binding*. Press release IP/10/1684.

Commission. (2010c). Case COMP/39.398—Visa MIF, Commission Decision, 8 December.

Commission. (2011). *Antitrust: Commission Opens Investigation in e-Payment Market*. Press release IP/11/1076.

Commission. (2012a). *Green Paper: Towards an Integrated European Market for Card, Internet and Mobile Payments*. COM (2011) 941 final, pp. 9, 12.

Commission. (2012b). *Antitrust: Commission Sends Supplementary Statement of Objections to Visa*. Press release IP/12/871.

Commission. (2012c). *Antitrust: Commission Welcomes General Court Judgement in Mastercard Case*. MEMO/12/377.

Commission. (2013a). *Antitrust: Commission Opens Investigation into Mastercard Inter-bank Fees*. Press release IP/13/314.

Commission. (2013b). *Antitrust: Commission Closes Investigation of EPC but Continues Monitoring Online Payments Market*. MEMO/13/553.

Commission. (2013c). *Competition: Antitrust Procedures in Abuse of Dominance*. Factsheet.

Commission. (2013d). *Summary of the Impact Assessment Accompanying the Document Proposal for a Directive of the European Parliament and of the Council on Payment Services in the Internal Market and Amending Directives 2002/65/EC, 2013/36/UE and 2009/110/EC and Repealing Directive 2007/64/EC and Proposal for a Regulation of the European Parliament and*

of the Council on Interchange Fees for Card-Based Payment Transactions. SWD(2013) 289, p. 2.
Commission. (2013e). *Antitrust: Commission Opens Investigation into Mastercard Inter-bank Fees*. Press release IP/13/314.
Commission. (2014a). *Communication from the Commission—Notice on Agreements of Minor Importance Which Do Not Appreciably Restrict Competition Under Article 101(1) of the Treaty on the Functioning of the European Union (De Minimis Notice), Official Journal*. C 291, 30.8.2014, paragraphs 3, 6, 8.
Commission. (2014b). *Antitrust: Commission Makes Visa Europe's Commitments to Cut Inter-Bank Fees and to Facilitate Cross-Border Competition Legally Binding*. Press release IP/14/197.
Commission. (2014c). *Antitrust: Commission Makes Visa Europe's Commitments Binding—Frequently Asked Questions*. MEMO/14/138, p. 1.
Commission. (2014d). *Guidance on Restrictions of Competition "by Object" for the Purpose of Defining Which Agreements May Benefit from the De Minimis Notice*. Commission Staff Working Document, SWD(2014) 198 final, p. 3.
Commission. (2014e). *Antitrust: Commission Adopts Revised Safe Harbours for Minor Agreements ('De Minimis Notice') and Provides guidance on "by Object" Restrictions of Competition—Frequently Asked Questions*. MEMO/14/440, p. 1.
Commission. (2014f). Case COMP/39.398—Visa MIF. Commission Decision.
Commission. (2015a). *Competition Policy Brief*. Issue 2015–3, p. 3.
Commission. (2015b). *Antitrust: Commission Sends Statement of Objections to Mastercard on Cross-Border Rules and Inter-regional Interchange Fees*. Press Release IP/15/5323.
Commission. (2019a). Case AT.40049 Mastercard II. Commission Decision of 22 January.
Commission. (2019b). *Antitrust: Commission Accepts Commitments by Mastercard and Visa to Cut Inter-Regional Interchange Fees*, Press Release IP/19/2311.
Commission. (2019c). Case COMP/39.398 - Visa MIF. Commission Decision, 29 April.
Commission. (2020a). *Antitrust: Commission Opens Investigation into Apple Practices Regarding Apple Pay*, Press release IP/20/1075.
Commission. (2020b). *Communication from the Commission to the European Parliament, the Council, the European Economic and Social Committee and the Committee of the Regions on a Retail Payments Strategy for the EU*. COM(2020) 592 final, p. 15.
Commission. (2020c). *Proposal for a Regulation of the European Parliament and of the Council on Contestable and Fair Markets in the Digital Sector (Digital Markets Act)*. COM(2020) 842 final, p. 18.

Commission. (2022). *Antitrust: Commission Sends Statement of Objections to Apple Over Practices Regarding Apple Pay*. Press Release IP/22/2764.

Commission. (2024). *Antitrust: Commission Seeks Feedback on Commitments Offered by Apple Over Practices Related to Apple Pay*. Press Release IP/24/282.

Commission. (n.d.a). *Article 101(3) of the Treaty on the Functioning of the European Union*. Available at: https://ec.europa.eu/competition/antitrust/legislation/art101_3_en.html. Accessed: April 13, 2024.

Commission. (n.d.b). *Antitrust: Regulation on Interchange Fees*. https://ec.europa.eu/commission/presscorner/detail/en/MEMO_16_2162. Accessed April 13, 2024.

Commission. (n.d.c). *Daily News 03/08/2017*. https://ec.europa.eu/commission/presscorner/detail/en/MEX_17_2341. Accessed April 13, 2024.

Commission. (n.d.d). *Press Release IP/22/6423*. https://ec.europa.eu/commission/presscorner/detail/en/ip_22_6423. Accessed April 13, 2024.

De Matteis, A., & Giordano, S. (2015). Payment Cards and Permitted Multilateral Interchange Fees (MIFs): Will the European Commission Harm Consumers and the European Payment Industry? *Journal of European Competition Law & Practice*, *6*(2), 85.

EPC. (2018). *Recommended Functionalities*. https://www.europeanpaymentscouncil.eu/sites/default/files/kb/file/2018-12/API%20EG%20045-18%20Recommended%20Functionalities%2010%20December%202018.pdf. Accessed April 13, 2024.

European Court of Justice. (1978). Judgment of 14 February 1978, *United Brands v Commission*. Case C-27/76, EU:C:1978:22, paragraph 65.

European Court of Justice. (1983). Judgment of 9 November 1983, *Michelin*. Case C-322/81, EU:C:1983:313, paragraph 57.

European Court of Justice. (1991). *Höfner and Elser v Macrotron*, Judgment of 23 April 1991, Case C-41/90, EU:C:1991:161, paragraph 21.

European Court of Justice. (2012a). *Expedia*. Judgment of 13 December 2012, Case C-226/11, EU:C:2012:795.

European Court of Justice. (2012b). Mastercard v European Commission, Case T-111/08, [2012] OJ C 200/11.

European Court of Justice. (2014). *Mastercard and Others v Commission (2014)*. Judgment of 11 September 2014, Case C-382/12 P, EU:C:2014:2201.

European Parliament. (2018): *Competition Issues in the Area of Financial Technology (FinTech)*. IP/A/ECON/2017–20, pp. 13, 105.

Hayashi, F. (2013): *The New Debit Card Regulations: Effects on Merchants, Consumers, and Payments System Efficiency*. Federal Reserve Bank of Kansas City Economic Review, First Quarter, pp. 90–91.

ISO Standards. (2012). *What's the Bottom Line?*, p. 9.

Mastercard. (2018). Case AT.40049 Mastercard II, Commitments Offered to the European Commission Pursuant to Article 9 of Council Regulation No 1/2003, 26 November.

Mathis, J. D. (2015). Het Europees 'Betaalpakket' – Gevolgen voor de interne markt en het betalingsverkeer in Nederland. *Nederlands Tijdschrift Voor Europees Recht, No., 4*, p. 102.

NMa. (2004). Case 2910–700, *Interpay*, 28 April 2004.

NMa. (2005a). Case 4174/32.O105, *Interpay*, NMa Informal Opinion, 19 April 2005.

NMa. (2005b). Case 2910–864, *Interpay*, 21 December 2005.

OECD. (2013). *Competition and Payment Systems*. DAF/COMP(2012)24, p. 23.

Van der Beek, A. (2017). *FinTech en Mededingingsrecht: FinTech als 'Driver of Competition'*, Tijdschrift voor Financieel Recht, No. 5, p. 171.

CHAPTER 10

Concluding Remarks

10.1 Introduction

Because of the role that Banks traditionally played in the circulation of money, Banks have been able to build a dominant position in the European Payments market during the last few decades. Since the nineties of the last century, the market for Payments has become more diverse, as a result of which we have seen Non-Banks entering the market and starting competing with Banks.

With Non-Banks entering the Payments market, the European legislature considered it important to develop a financial services regulatory framework that contributes to the establishment of a level playing field between Banks and Non-Banks. This book covers the normative background of the European financial services regulatory framework that has been adopted for the Payments market between January 1990 and March 2024.

A holistic interpretation of the concept level playing field is applied that takes into account the six intermediate objectives described in **Paragraph 1.3.1**. A level playing field is defined as the extent to which the rules and regulations covering these intermediate objectives are proportionate in the context of competition between Banks and Non-Banks.

The premise of this book is that the rules and regulations covering the six intermediate objectives described in **Paragraph 1.3.1** are of relevance

J. A. Jans, *Electronic Payments in the European Market*, EBI Studies in Banking and Capital Markets Law,
https://doi.org/10.1007/978-3-031-64338-5_10

when assessing the extent to which there is a level playing field between Banks and Non-Banks in the market for Payments. More specifically, the legal implications of these rules and regulations need to be in proportion to these objectives in order to contribute to the level playing field between Banks and Non-Banks.

Overall, the rules and regulations covering the intermediate objectives described in **Paragraph 1.3.1** appear to be in proportion to these objectives and therefore supportive of the level playing field between Banks and Non-Banks, albeit that some of these rules turn out to be more supportive than others.

10.2 Non-Bank Market Access

Chapter 4 of this book describes the access requirements that apply to Non-Banks that wish to enter the European market for Payments. A main condition for achieving a level playing field between Banks and Non-Banks is that Non-Banks are able to enter the market on the basis of objective and proportionate requirements. With the introduction of the PSD licensing regime for PIs, which is tailored to the business model of service providers that only offer payment services, the European legislature first provided for such proportionate market entry requirements for Non-Banks.

With PSD2, the scope of activities that qualify as a payment service has been extended to also cover the open banking solutions account information services and payment initiation services. By extending the scope of the services that qualify as payment services, PSD2 has enabled new service providers, such as FinTechs, to enter the Payments market and start offering their services under a PI licence.

However, the level playing field between Banks and Non-Banks has not (yet) reached its full potential under PSD2. One of the shortcomings in the financial services regulatory framework that appears to have prevented the level playing field from reaching its full potential is the widespread use of the technical services provider exemption by BigTechs offering PSU interfaces as a front-end service provider. Since these BigTechs do not operate on the basis of a PI or EMI licence, they are not subject to the financial services regulatory framework applicable to PSPs. Although these BigTechs are not receiving any PSU funds, their business proposition often involves more than supporting PSPs in their business activities. Therefore, the scope of the technical service provider exemption under

PSD2 provides for an undesirable legal vacuum that contradicts the objective of creating a level playing field between PSPs operating in the Payments market. Unfortunately, this issue has not been addressed by the Commission in the PSD3 Proposal.

10.3 Security Measures for Banks and Non-Banks

Chapter 5 covers the allocation of the PSD2 security requirements between Banks and Non-Banks. A prerequisite for a well-functioning Payments market is that the safety and reliability of the processing of Payments is guaranteed. To this end, PSD2 contains security requirements for PSPs, such as the obligation to conduct SCA each time a PSU initiates a Payment or accesses its payment account. The allocation of the PSD2 security requirements between Banks and Non-Banks is generally in proportion to the objective of safeguarding the security of the Payments market and therefore proportionate in the context of the competitive position between Banks and Non-Banks. However, it is important to note that the customer authentication process has become more complex for Banks with the introduction of open banking solutions. PSD2 requires TPPs to identify themselves when accessing the customer-facing interface of a Bank. Consequently, Banks had to amend their customer-facing interface to ensure that both PSUs and TPPs can identify themselves using the interface. As a result, Banks are required to have three interfaces available in parallel (one for PSUs and two for TPPs), which creates a disproportionate cost burden for Banks. To address this issue, the Commission suggests in the PSR Proposal that Banks must have in place one dedicated interface and will no longer be required to maintain a fall-back interface.

With regard to certain products, such as the E-wallet Apple Pay, the application of the SCA requirement appears to create challenges for Banks as certain steps in the SCA process are executed by a third party service provider that does not hold a PSP licence nor agrees to enter into an outsourcing arrangement with the Banks. With Apple Pay, customer authentication takes place within the Apple interface instead of within the interface of the relevant Bank that issued the debit or credit card. Since the card issuing Bank is responsible for the SCA process, it is essential that the Bank in question is able to conduct adequate oversight to ensure that Apple complies with all relevant requirements under the financial services regulatory framework. Since this appears not to be possible in practice, vulnerabilities are created in the Payment ecosystem which, amongst others, adversely impacts the competitive position of Banks. This concern has however not been left unnoticed by the Commission. To address these challenges, the PSR Proposal requires technical service providers that verify elements of SCA to enter into an outsourcing agreement with the PSP regarding their involvement in the SCA process.

10.4 Anti-money Laundering and the Allocation of Responsibilities Between Banks and Non-Banks

Chapter 6 covers the AML/CTF requirements that apply to Banks and Non-Banks. In their capacity as gatekeepers of the financial markets, PSPs have to implement adequate CDD procedures to limit the risk of being used for ML/TF purposes. By subjecting both Banks and Non-Banks to the CDD requirement, it is significantly more difficult for criminals to bring funds with an illegit origin into the financial system. This is especially the case if a single transaction is screened by multiple PSPs. For example, contrary to Banks, PISPs often have data regarding transactions initiated by a particular payer with a number of different Banks. Therefore, PISPs often have a more comprehensive overview of a payer's transaction history and are therefore able to screen transactions from a different perspective. As a result, an additional security layer is added to the AML/CTF process. Moreover, because of the risk-based approach of the AML/CTF framework, each PSP has different CDD procedures in place and applies different thresholds and indicators for determining whether a particular transaction is unusual. Involving multiple PSPs in the screening of a particular transaction therefore reduces the risk that unusual transactions remain unnoticed. A disadvantage of having multiple PSPs screening the same transaction is that it generates more false positives.

By requiring that all PSPs conduct CDD on their business relationships, the AML/CTF framework does not appear to have created a disproportionate burden for Non-Banks other than AISPs. For example, the obligation to conduct transaction monitoring may not be very relevant for AISPs since these PSPs only have access to transaction information relating to payments that have already been cleared and settled. Furthermore, AISPs are not authorised to intervene in case it considers a transaction to be unusual.

10.5 Allocation of Liability in Case of Unauthorised or Erroneous Payments

Chapter 7 describes the allocation of legal liabilities for unauthorised and incorrectly executed Payments between Banks and Non-Banks under PSD2. Since the processing of Payments often requires the involvement of multiple PSPs (i.e., in case the payer and payee hold their payment account with a different PSP), PSD2 contains rules on the allocation of liabilities for unauthorised and incorrectly executed Payments between PSPs. With regard to these rules, the emphasis of the European legislature appears to have been primarily on safeguarding the interests of PSUs. For example, with open banking solutions Banks remain in all circumstances the PSU's first point of contact in case of an unauthorised or erroneous Payment, which is not helpful for achieving a level playing field between Banks and Non-Banks. Allowing the payer to submit all refund claims to his Bank, even in situations where it is clear that for example a PISP is responsible for the disputed transaction, can be regarded disproportionate in the context of the competitive position between Banks and Non-Banks. Such situation leaves the Bank in question with a credit exposure *vis-à-vis* the PISP, even though the Bank in question might not have been able to prevent the transaction from being executed. In general however, the rules and regulations on the allocation of liability for unauthorised and erroneous Payments are in proportion to the objective of enhancing PSU protection in case of an unauthorised or erroneous Payment.

10.6 Payment Systems and Non-Bank Access to Payment Systems

Chapter 8 of this book covers the PSD2 requirements for (in)direct payment system access by Non-Banks. Being able to compete with competitors on an equal footing is one of the key requisites for a level playing field. In order for Non-Banks to compete with Banks on an equal footing, the European legislature considers it elementary that Non-Banks have access to the technical infrastructures of payment systems. For this very reason, PSD introduced a legal obligation for payment system operators to allow Non-Banks access to their systems. The payment system access requirement stipulates that the rules on payment system access have to be objective, non-discriminatory and proportionate. This means that rules on payment system access can be stringent as long as they are not subjective, discriminatory or disproportionate. Having stringent requirements for payment system access is not detrimental to the level playing field since allowing PSPs which do not fulfil certain minimum criteria access to payment systems would make such systems vulnerable to security breaches and credit risk exposures.

To date, not a single non-Bank has obtained direct access to an EU payment system, which means that Non-Banks are dependent on Banks for this element of the Payment process. Since the PSD2 provisions on payment system access do not apply to payment systems that are designated under the SFD and most European payment systems are designated under the SFD, the PSD2 payment system access requirement remains in practice without effect. Furthermore, Non-Banks appear not to be able to meet the access requirements imposed by most payment system operators since they often require the applicant to hold a banking licence.

As a result of not being able to obtain direct payment system access, Non-Banks can only apply for indirect payment system memberships using a Bank as sponsor. In case of indirect payment system access, the non-Bank must adhere to both the payment system's indirect access criteria and the sponsor-level criteria imposed by the Bank that allows the non-Bank indirect access. Being dependent on competing Banks for payment system access may raise anti-competitive concerns, even though PSD2 also requires that sponsor-level criteria are objective, non-discriminatory and proportionate. This appears to be a justified concern since most sponsor-level criteria require applicants for indirect access to hold a banking licence. Although such requirement is in accordance with the PSD2 obligation to have objective, proportionate and non-discriminatory criteria, it prevents Non-Banks from obtaining indirect payment system access.

To address these issues, the Commission suggests in the PSD3 Proposal to amend the SFD by recognising licensed PIs as eligible institutions for direct access to payment systems designated under the SFD. Although this will ensure the eligibility of licensed PIs to obtain payment system access, it does not prevent payment system operators from requiring applicants to hold a banking licence.

Since a number of payment systems in the EU are owned by Banks (e.g., STEP1 and STEP2 are both owned and operated by EBA Clearing, which was founded by Banks and only has Banks as members), Banks find themselves in a position in which they can exercise influence over the development of access criteria applicable to direct competitors (e.g., Non-Banks) that intend to access these payment systems. In such situation, there is a risk that these Banks may exercise improper influence on the rule setting by these systems, which could harm the competitive position between Banks and Non-Banks. Although no evidence has been found of this happening in practice, the possibility of having such conflict of interest constitutes a vulnerability in the Payment infrastructure that needs to be addressed.

Like other network industries, such as the railway or gas industry, competitors in the Payments market rely on the same technical infrastructure for the processing of Payments. Nowadays, the majority of Payments are processed via payment systems, which makes these systems a crucial component of the Payment infrastructure. In recent decades, Banks have been able to build an almost monopolistic position in the development and establishment of payment systems and infrastructures. With Non-Banks entering the Payments market, market dynamics have changed and Banks started to face competition from Non-Banks. With this development, it has become important to evaluate the role of Banks in the Payments infrastructure. One may even consider nationalising payment systems. Although the Payments market is a private sector business, the IT-infrastructure of the Payments market can be regarded as a public utility function since it serves the public interest of enabling citizens and companies to make Payments. By nationalising payment systems, these systems would be no longer exposed to anti-competitive incentives regarding the rule setting for payment system access. A potential downside of nationalising payment systems however is that it may hamper innovation in the Payments market due to a lack of competitive incentives.

As described in **Paragraph 8.4.4**, the majority of the payment systems in the EU are either owned by national central banks or Banks. In their capacity as indirect sole shareholders of payment systems, Banks are able to exercise influence over the development of access criteria applicable to direct competitors (e.g., Non-Banks) that intend to access these payment systems, which could harm the competitive position between Banks and Non-Banks. Although there appears to be no supporting evidence of this happening in practice, it may be worth investigating whether it would be feasible to prohibit PSPs that are a direct participant in a payment system to be able to also have any form of control over such payment system in another capacity.

10.7 EU Competition Enforcement in the Payments Sector

Chapter 9 describes the conditions under which collaboration between competing PSPs can be advantageous for the Payments market. In a network-based sector like the Payments sector, collaboration between competing PSPs is a key requirement to ensure efficient processing of Payments. An example of such collaboration is the standard setting practices for ensuring interoperability between PSPs and Payment schemes. One of the main standardisation initiatives developed by PSPs is the SEPA project, which was initially launched by the European banking sector. As part of the SEPA project, the EPC develops rulebooks containing standards for the transmission of Payment messages and the processing of Payments, which apply to PSPs that have adhered to these rulebooks. Although the SEPA project contributed significantly to the efficiency of the European Payments market, there are only limited possibilities for non-Bank involvement. For example, Non-Banks are not allowed to participate in the development process of new standards. Furthermore, the EPC's adherence policy does not allow PIs to join the EPC schemes as a direct participant.

According to the Guidelines on Horizontal Agreements, standard setting practices between PSPs are not in violation of the prohibition to enter into anti-competitive agreements provided that: (i) participation by PSPs in standard setting is unrestricted; (ii) the procedure for adopting the standard is transparent; (iii) there is no obligation for PSPs to comply with the standard and (iv) access to the standard is on fair, reasonable and non-discriminatory terms. Although EU antitrust rules require that participation by Non-Banks in standard setting must be unrestricted, the financial services regulatory framework does not contain any requirement of a similar nature. To date, Non-Banks are underrepresented in standardisation bodies that issue standards for the Payments market. As a consequence, the interests of Non-Banks are not (or to a lesser extent) taken into consideration when new market standards are developed. To ensure that standard setting initiatives do not adversely impact the competitive position of Non-Banks, Non-Banks should also have some level of involvement in the standard setting process, for example by being able to propose agenda items for meetings relating to the determination of standards and to cast votes with regard to decisions taken during these meeting. By allowing Non-Banks to participate in standard setting processes, Non-Banks will be able to promote their interests and introduce topics that are of particular relevance to them. By ensuring that the interests of Non-Banks are also taken into account, there is a lower risk that the competitive position of Non-Banks *vis-à-vis* Banks deteriorates as a result of standard setting practices in the Payments market.

10.8 The PSD3/PSR Proposal

The launch of an evaluation of PSD2 was first announced in the digital finance strategy and the retail payments strategy.[1] As part of its evaluation, the Commission assesses the application and impact of PSD2 to determine whether amendments are required to ensure that the legislative framework remains at par with the current developments in the Payments market. To conduct its review, the Commission has requested input from different stakeholders, including: (i) PSPs, PSUs and other participants in the Payments market such as operators of payment systems, card schemes and technical services providers; and (ii) the ECB and the EBA.[2]

On 20 October 2021, the Commission sent a call for advice to the EBA with the objective to gather evidence on the application and impact of the PSD2.[3] As part of its evaluation, the Commission asked the EBA to identify PSD2 provisions for which amendments are appropriate.[4] The EBA has identified a substantive number of shortcomings that must be addressed in order for PSD2 to reach its objectives of enhancing competition between PSPs, facilitating innovation, increasing security of Payments

[1] **Article 108 PSD2** obliged the Commission to already report on the application of PSD2 by 13 January 2021. According to the Commission, this deadline could not be met due to the late transposition of PSD2 by certain Member States.

[2] As part of the PSD2 review, the Commission aimed to gather feedback and evidence by amongst others: (i) an external study; (ii) a public consultation and (iii) a call for advice to the EBA.

[3] See EBA. (n.d.).

[4] See EBA (2022, p. 2). The Commission invited the EBA to provide advice on the application of the following elements of PSD2: (i) scope and definitions; (ii) licensing of PIs and supervision of PSPs under PSD2; (iii) transparency of conditions and information requirements; (iv) rights and obligations; (v) strong customer authentication; (vi) access to and use of payment accounts data in relation to payment initiation services and account information services; (vii) access to payment systems and access to accounts maintained with a Bank; (viii) core-sectoral topics and (ix) enforcement of PSD2.

and enhancing customer protection.[5] An overview of the main proposals suggested by the EBA is included in **Annex II**.

In addition, the Commission launched a consultation on 10 May 2022 on the application of PSD2 to identify possible amendments that will serve as input for an impact assessment accompanying a legislative proposal for revising PSD2.[6] Elements of particular interest that have been identified by the Commission include:[7]

i. Whether the scope and definitions of PSD2 are still appropriate to ensure a level playing field because of new market players, such as Fintechs and BigTechs, that were not active in the Payments market when PSD2 was adopted;
ii. Whether the SCA requirements are adequate to address new forms of payment fraud that have emerged since the adoption of PSD2 (e.g., social engineering);
iii. Whether the PSD2 transparency requirements and rules related to rights and obligations (e.g., the right of refunds) are adequate in the context of current market developments;
iv. The challenges related to payment account access;
v. The challenges related to payment system access; and
vi. The main differences in cross-border Payments rules between the EU and other countries.

On 2 February 2023, the Commission published a study on the application and impact of PSD2.[8] This study contains a comprehensive assessment of the implementation and application of PSD2 and contains recommendations on possible revisions.[9] An overview of the main proposals suggested by the Commission is included in **Annex II**.

An important observation of both the EBA and the Commission is that PSD2 should better reflect recent market developments whereby in particular BigTechs claim a prominent role in the provision of payment services. In addition, with regard to payment account access by TPPs, the

[5] See EBA (2022, p. 3).

[6] See Commission (n.d.).

[7] See Commission (2022).

[8] See Commission (2023a).

[9] Ibid., p. 10.

legal framework must provide for a fair distribution of costs and the possibility of new revenue streams for all PSPs involved. Under the current framework, payment account access by TPPs results in a disproportionate investment burden for AS-PSPs. Another main recommendation involves the merging of PSD2 and EMD2. Since PSD2 provides for many requirements that also apply to EMIs offering payment services, both the EBA and the Commission suggest to merge both directives to enhance clarity on the applicable legal requirements for PIs and EMIs.

On 28 June 2023 the Commission published the Financial data access and payments package, which includes amongst others the PSD3 Proposal and PSR Proposal.[10] With these proposals, the Commission aims to address the PSD2 and EMD2 shortcomings that have been identified in the evaluation and impact assessments of these directives.

The Commission considered it appropriate to include the rules applicable to PSPs in a regulation to ensure a coherent implementation of these rules and to cover the market access requirements and rules on supervision of Non-Banks in a directive.[11] With these legislative proposals, the Commission aims to achieve the following four objectives:[12]

1. Strengthen the protection of PSUs and enhance the confidence in the use of Payment products by introducing, amongst others, improvements to the application of SCA and an extension of the obligation for the payer's PSP to apply the IBAN verification tool to all credit transfers;
2. Improve the competitiveness of open banking services by, amongst others, requiring Banks to ensure that: (i) their dedicated data access interface for TPPs meet certain performance criteria; and (ii) they provide PSUs with a 'permissions dashboard' that enables PSUs to manage their open banking access permissions;
3. Improve implementation and enforcement of the legislative framework on Payments in Member States by: (i) replacing a large part of PSD2 with a regulation; (ii) further clarifying the PSD2 definitions

[10] Further to the PSD3 Proposal and the PSR Proposal, the Financial data access and payments package includes a proposal for a regulation on a framework for financial data access.

[11] PSD3 Proposal, p. 3.

[12] Ibid., pp. 5–6.

that are ambiguous and (iii) integrating the licence requirement for PIs and EMIs; and

4. Improve non-Bank access to payment systems and bank accounts by strengthening the rights of PIs to obtain a payment account with a Bank and providing for the possibility of direct payment system access by PIs.

Secondary Sources

Commission. (2022). *Call for Evidence for an Evaluation and Impact Assessment Run in Parallel*, Ares(2022)3556263.

Commission. (2023a). *A Study on the Application and Impact of Directive (EU) 2015/2366 on Payment Services (PSD2)*, FISMA/2021/OP/0002, p. 10.

Commission. (2023b). *Proposal for a Directive of the European Parliament and of the Council on Payment Services and Electronic Money Services in the Internal Market Amending Directive 98/26/EC and Repealing Directives 2015/2366 and 2009/110/EC*, COM(2023) 366 final, pp. 3, 5, 6.

Commission. (n.d.). *Payment Services: Review of EU Rules*. https://ec.europa.eu/info/law/better-regulation/have-your-say/initiatives/13331-Payment-services-review-of-EU-rules_en. Accessed April 13, 2024.

EBA. (2022). Opinion of the European Banking Authority on Its Technical Advice on the Review of Directive (EU) 2015/2366 on Payment Services in the Internal Market (PSD2), EBA/Op/2022/06, 23 June, pp. 2–3.

EBA. (n.d.). *EBA Replies to the European Commission's Call for Advice on the Review of the Payment Services Directive*. https://www.eba.europa.eu/eba-replies-european-commission%E2%80%99s-call-advice-%C2%A0-review-payment-servicesdirective#:~:text=As%20part%20of%20the%20review,challenges%20that%20may%20have%20arisen. Accessed April 13, 2024.

Annex I

PSD2 Transparency and Information Requirements

Transparency and information requirements for payment services covered by a framework contract

In due time before a PSU enters into such framework contract, the PSP has to inform the PSU on paper or on another durable medium regarding:[1]

1. the contact details of the PSP;[2]
2. the use of the payment service;[3]

[1] *See* **Article 52 PSD2**.

[2] Information includes: (i) the name of the PSP; (ii) geographical address of the PSP's head office and, where applicable, the geographical address of its agent or branch established in the Member State where the payment service is provided and any other address, including electronic mail address, relevant for communication with the PSP; (iii) the particulars of the relevant NCA and of the relevant public register of authorisation of the PSP and (iv) the registration number, or equivalent means of identification in that register.

[3] Information includes: (i) a description of the main characteristics of the payment service; (ii) specification of the information or unique identifier that has to be provided

J. A. Jans, *Electronic Payments in the European Market*, EBI Studies in Banking and Capital Markets Law,
https://doi.org/10.1007/978-3-031-64338-5

3. applicable charges, interest rates and exchange rates;[4]
4. the manner of communication between the PSP and the PSU;[5]
5. safeguards and corrective measures;[6]
6. changes in and termination of the framework contract;[7] and

by the PSU in order for a payment order to be properly initiated or executed; (iii) the form of and procedure for giving consent to initiate a payment order or execute a Payment and withdrawal of such consent; (iv) a reference to the time of receipt of a payment order and the cut-off time, if any, established by the PSP; (v) the maximum execution time for the payment services to be provided; (vi) whether there is a possibility to agree on spending limits for the use of the payment instrument and (vii) in case of co-badged cards, the PSU's rights under **Article 8 IFR**.

[4] Information includes: (i) all charges payable by the PSU to the PSP and, where applicable, the breakdown of the amounts of any charges; (ii) where applicable, the interest and exchange rates to be applied or, if reference interest and exchange rates are to be used, the method of calculating the actual interest, and the relevant date and index or base for determining such reference interest or exchange rate and (iii) if agreed, the immediate application of changes in reference interest or exchange rate and information requirements relating to the changes.

[5] Information includes: (i) where applicable, the means of communication, including the technical requirements for the PSU's equipment and software, agreed between the parties for the transmission of information or notifications under PSD2; (ii) the manner in and frequency with which information under PSD2 is to be provided or made available; (iii) the language in which the framework contract is concluded and the communication undertaken during the contractual arrangement and (iv) the PSU's right to receive the contractual terms of the framework contract and information and conditions.

[6] Information includes: (i) where applicable, a description of steps that the PSU is to take to keep safe a payment instrument and how to notify the PSP in case of loss, theft, misappropriation or unauthorised use of the payment instrument; (ii) the procedure for notification of the PSU by the PSP in the event of suspected or actual fraud or security threats; (iii) if agreed, the conditions under which the PSP reserves the right to block a payment instrument for security related reasons; (iv) the liability of the payer regarding unauthorised Payments, including information on the relevant amount; (v) how and within what period of time the PSU is to notify the PSP of any unauthorised or incorrectly initiated or executed Payment as well as the PSP's liability for unauthorised Payments; (vi) the liability of the PSP for the initiation or execution of Payments and (vii) the conditions for refund.

[7] Information includes: (i) if agreed, information that the PSU is deemed to have accepted changes in the conditions, unless he notifies the PSP that he does not accept them before the date of their proposed date of entry into force; (ii) the duration of the framework contract and (iii) the right of the PSU to terminate the framework contract and any agreements relating to termination.

7. the redress procedures available to the PSU.[8]

A PSU can at any time request its PSP to provide any of the information and conditions specified under 1–7 above on paper or on another durable medium.[9]

Information to be provided before and after the execution of a Payment

There are three moments at which a payer's PSP or beneficiary's PSP is obliged to provide its PSU with certain Payment-related information. This is when: (i) the payer initiates a Payment; (ii) the amount of the Payment is debited from the payer's payment account and (iii) the Payment is executed.

When a Payment is initiated by the payer under a framework contract, the payer can request its PSP to provide information on the maximum execution time, the fees payable and a breakdown of these fees.[10] After the transaction amount of a Payment is debited from the payer's payment account, the payer's PSP has to inform the payer without undue delay on the specifications of the transaction.[11] After the execution of the Payment, the beneficiary's PSP informs the beneficiary without undue delay on the specifications of the transaction.[12]

[8] Information includes: (i) any contractual clause on the law applicable to the framework contract and/or the competent courts; and (ii) the alternative dispute resolution procedures available to the PSU.

[9] *See* **Article 53 PSD2**.

[10] *See* **Article 56 PSD2**.

[11] According to **Article 57(1) PSD2**, the PSP must provide the following information: (i) a reference enabling the payer to identify each Payment and, where appropriate, information relating to the beneficiary; (ii) the amount of the Payment in the currency in which the payer's payment account is debited or in the currency used for the payment order; (iii) the amount of any charges for the Payment and, where applicable, a breakdown thereof, or the interest payable by the payer; (iv) where applicable, the exchange rate used in the Payment by the payer's PSP, and the amount of the Payment after that currency conversion and (v) the debit value date or the date of receipt of the payment order.

[12] According to **Article 58(1) PSD2**, this information includes: (i) a reference enabling the beneficiary to identify the Payment and, where appropriate, the payer, and any information transferred with the Payment; (ii) the amount of the Payment in the currency in which the beneficiary's payment account is credited; (iii) the amount of any charges for the Payment and, where applicable, a breakdown thereof, or the interest payable by the

Changes to the framework contract

During the term of the framework contract it is allowed for the PSP to introduce amendments to the framework contract.[13] In case the framework contract contains a negative consent clause, the PSP can inform the PSU that he is deemed to have accepted the changes proposed if he does not inform the PSP within a certain period that he does not accept these changes. The PSP has to specify that the PSU has the right to terminate the framework contract immediately and without charge before these changes enter into force.

Termination of a framework contract

Both the PSP and the PSU are allowed to terminate the framework contract. Different notice periods apply depending on who terminates the contract.

In case a PSU wants to terminate the contract, it can do so according to **Article 55(1) PSD2** at any time provided that the PSP and PSU have not agreed a specific notice period. PSPs and PSUs are not allowed to agree on a notice period exceeding one month. **Article 55(6) PSD2** allows Member States to apply more favourable provisions for PSUs that want to terminate their framework contract.

Article 55(3) PSD2 allows the PSP to terminate a framework contract concluded with a PSU for an indefinite period if the following conditions are met: (i) the framework contract contains a provision that the PSP can terminate the contract; and (ii) the PSP notifies the PSU at least two months prior to terminating the contract.

beneficiary; (iv) where applicable, the exchange rate used in the Payment by the beneficiary's PSP, and the amount of the Payment before that currency conversion and (v) the credit value date.

[13] **Article 54(1) PSD2** requires that the PSP informs the PSU regarding any changes no later than two months before these become effective: (i) on paper or on another durable medium; (ii) in understandable words and in a clear and comprehensible form and (iii), in an official language of the Member State where the payment service is provided or in any other language agreed upon. **Article 54(2) PSD2** provides that changes to the framework contract relating to the interest or exchange rates can be applied immediately and without notice provided that: (i) this has been agreed in the framework contract; and (ii) the changes are based on the reference interest or exchange rates that the PSP and PSU agreed on. In case the new interest or exchange rate is more favourable for the PSU, such changes can be applied by the PSP without notice to the PSU.

Information requirements for low value payment instruments

To keep low value payment instruments a cheap and easy-to-use means for initiating Payments, PSD2 provides that certain information requirements do not apply when these payment instruments are used.[14]

With regard to multifunctional cards (e.g., a debit card or credit card that also has a contactless function (NFC) which can be used for small payments under the thresholds for low value payment instruments), different information regimes apply depending on the function used to initiate a particular Payment. In other words, in case the holder of the multifunctional card initiates a Payment using the NFC function, the information regime for low value payment instruments applies. If a Payment is initiated with a multifunctional card using PIN authorisation, the standard regime for information requirements applies since the potential spending limit of such payment exceeds the thresholds for low value payment instruments.

Transparency and information requirements for payment services not covered by a framework contract

Different information requirements apply with regard to Payments that are not executed under a framework contract. These transactions are also referred to as single transactions. With single transactions, the payer is usually present when giving the payment order.[15]

Before a PSU is bound by a single payment service contract, the PSP provides the PSU with relevant information regarding the payment

[14] **Article 42 PSD2** provides that: (i) the PSP only has to provide the payer with information on the main characteristics of the payment service (e.g., the way in which the payment instrument can be used, liability, charges levied and other material information); (ii) the PSP can agree with the PSU that it will not be required to propose changes in the conditions of the framework contract in the same way as required in relation to pre-contractual information; (iii) the PSP can agree with the PSU that after the execution of a Payment: (a) the PSP provides only a reference that enables the PSU to identify the Payment, the amount of the Payment, any charges and/or, in case of several Payments of the same kind made to the same beneficiary, information on the total amount and charges for those Payments; (b) the PSP is not required to provide or make available information referred to in point (i) if the payment instrument is used anonymously or if the PSP is not otherwise technically in a position to provide it. However, the PSP must provide the payer with a possibility to verify the amount of funds stored.

[15] *See* Recital 58 PSD2.

service offered.[16] The payer's PSP can provide this information orally or via a board or sign in the physical store where the PSU initiates the Payment.[17] **Article 44(1) PSD2** stipulates that, upon request, the PSP must provide the PSU with the relevant information on paper or another durable medium.

After receipt of the payment order, the payer's PSP informs the payer regarding the main characteristics of the Payment.[18] In case of a payment initiation service, the PISP informs the payer and, where applicable, the beneficiary immediately after initiation regarding the main characteristics of the payment initiation service.[19] In addition, **Article 47 PSD2** requires the PISP to provide the payer's AS-PSP with a reference of the Payment.

[16] **Articles 44(1) and 45 PSD2** require that the PSP informs the PSU regarding: (i) the information or unique identifier that the PSU has to provide for a payment order to be properly initiated or executed; (ii) the maximum execution time for the Payment; (iii) the charges payable by the PSU and, where applicable, a breakdown of the charges and (iv) where applicable, the actual or reference exchange rate to be applied to the Payment. In case of a payment initiation service, the PISP shall provide the payer prior to initiation with the following information: (i) the name of the PISP; (ii) address of its head office; (iii) any other contact details relevant for communication with the PISP.

[17] As long as the information provided is understandable, clear, comprehensible and in an official language of the Member State where the payment service is provided.

[18] According to **Article 48 PSD2**, said information includes: (i) a reference enabling the payer to identify the Payment and, where appropriate, information relating to the beneficiary; (ii) the amount of the Payment in the currency used in the payment order; (iii) the amount of any charges for the Payment payable by the payer and, where applicable, a breakdown of the amounts of such charges; (iv) where applicable, the exchange rate used in the Payment by the payer's PSP or a reference thereto, when different from the rate provided, and the amount of the Payment after that currency conversion and (v) the date of receipt of the payment order.

[19] According to **Article 46 PSD2**, said information includes: (i) confirmation of the successful initiation of the payment order with the AS-PSP; (ii) a reference enabling the payer and beneficiary to identify the payment transaction and, where appropriate, the beneficiary to identify the payer, and any information transferred with the Payment; (iii) the transaction amount and (iv) where applicable, the amount of the charges payable to the PISP for the transaction, and where applicable a breakdown of these charges.

Immediately after the execution of the Payment, the beneficiary's PSP informs the beneficiary regarding the main characteristics of the Payment.[20]

[20] According to **Article 49 PSD2**, said information includes: (i) the reference enabling the beneficiary to identify the Payment and, where appropriate, the payer and any information transferred with the Payment; (ii) the amount of the Payment in the currency in which the funds are at the beneficiary's disposal; (iii) the amount of any charges for the Payment payable by the beneficiary and, where applicable, a breakdown of the amount of such charges; (iv) where applicable, the exchange rate used in the Payment by the beneficiary's PSP, and the amount of the Payment before that currency conversion and (v) the credit value date.

Annex II

Evaluation of PSD2

Table A.1 contains an overview of the main recommendations for improvement suggested by the EBA:

Table A.2 contains an overview of the main recommendations for improvement suggested by the Commission:

J. A. Jans, *Electronic Payments in the European Market*,
EBI Studies in Banking and Capital Markets Law,
https://doi.org/10.1007/978-3-031-64338-5

Table A.1 EBA recommendations on PSD2

No	*Subject*	*Recommendation*	*Feedback provided by*
1	Scope of applicability	Clarify the place of provision of payment services (in particular when provided online).	EBA[21]
2	Scope of applicability	Clarify the application of the following exclusions from the scope of PSD2: • limited network exemption; • commercial agent exemption; and • independent ATM providers exclusion.	EBA[22]
3	Scope of applicability	Clarify the application of PSD2 provisions to one-leg transactions, in particular: • the application of SCA to one-leg transactions; and • the circumvention by EU merchants of SCA requirement by contracting non-EEA acquirers.	EBA[23]
4	Scope of applicability	Merge PSD2 and EMD2 to harmonise the legal framework for PIs and EMIs and: • clarify the distinction between payment accounts and E-money accounts; • distinguish between scriptural money and E-money; • clarify the difference in some of the applicable legal requirements (e.g., authorisation, own funds and safeguarding; and • clarify the legal status of distributors of E-money.	EBA[24]

[21] EBA, 'EBA response to the Commission call for advice on the review of the Payment Services Directive', EBA/REP/2022/14, 23 June 2022, p. 7.

[22] Ibid., pp. 18–21.

[23] Ibid., pp. 21–23.

[24] Ibid., pp. 27–31.

No	*Subject*	*Recommendation*	*Feedback provided by*
5	Definitions	Clarify the definitions of the following payment services: • credit transfers and money remittance; • placing and withdrawing cash from a payment account and related services of operating a payment account; • execution of payment transaction where ancillary credit is provided those where it is not; and • issuing of payment instruments and acquiring of payment instruments.	EBA[25]
6	Definitions	Clarify the following PSD2 terms: • payment account; • payment instrument; • payment channel; • electronic payment transactions; • initiation of a payment transaction; • remote payment transactions; and • sensitive payment data.	EBA[26]
7	Licensing of PIs	Align the initial capital requirement for money remittance services with the requirements for payment services (1) to (5) of Annex I to PSD2.	EBA[27]
8	Licensing of PIs	Introduce for the calculation of the own funds requirement: • a single default calculation method; and • a uniform calculation method to determine own funds requirement for credit risk based on the standard method under CRR for PIs and EMIs that grant credit.	EBA[28]

(continued)

[25] Ibid., pp. 8–11.
[26] Ibid., pp. 12–18.
[27] Ibid., pp. 33–35.
[28] Ibid., pp. 35–37.

Table A.1 (continued)

No	*Subject*	*Recommendation*	*Feedback provided by*
9	Licensing of PIs	Introduce a simplified framework for recovery and wind-down for significant PIs and EMIs.	EBA[29]
10	Licensing of PIs	Assess the advantages and challenges of introducing consolidated group supervision in PSD2.	EBA[30]
11	Transparency requirements	Introduce a requirement for PSPs to inform payers that their PSP and the PSP of the beneficiary are not required to check whether the IBAN of the beneficiary and the name of the beneficiary match.	EBA[31]
12	Rights and obligations	Clarify regarding the distribution of liability between PSPs: • how liability is allocated between a PISP and an AS-PSP in case of an incorrectly executed transaction; and • the distribution of liability between PSPs when an SCA exemption has been applied.	EBA[32]
13	Rights and obligations	Clarify the following terms used in relation to evidence of authentication and execution of Payments: • reasonable grounds to suspecting fraud; • fraudulent act; and • gross negligence.	EBA[33]
14	Rights and obligations	Adjust the legal framework to fit the nature of fast payments, such as execution time, instant finality and the specific risks faced.	EBA[34]

29 Ibid., pp. 41–42.

30 Ibid., pp. 53–54.

31 Ibid., p. 63.

32 Ibid., pp. 66–67.

33 Ibid., pp. 67–69.

34 Ibid., pp. 69–70.

No	*Subject*	*Recommendation*	*Feedback provided by*
15	SCA	Clarify whether the use of third party technology (e.g., smartphone) for applying SCA would require an outsourcing agreement.	EBA[35]
16	SCA	Clarify that delegation of SCA to technical service providers (including E-wallet providers) is allowed but that it requires an outsourcing agreement between the PSP and the technical service provider.	EBA[36]
17	SCA	Clarify whether refunds should be considered as a stand-alone Payment for which SCA must be applied.	EBA[37]
18	SCA	Clarify the application of the liability requirements in case an SCA exemption has been applied by either the payer's PSP or the beneficiary's PSP.	EBA[38]
19	Access to payment account data	Explore the possibility of having a common API standard across the EU.	EBA[39]
20	Access to payment account data	Clarify the following aspects regarding access to payment accounts: • revocation of consent by the PSU via the AS-PSP; • scope of the information to be shared with TPPs; • exchange of information from TPPs to the AS-PSP; • what 'online access' means; and • the use of agents by AISPs.	EBA[40]

[35] Ibid., p. 74.

[36] Ibid, p. 74.

[37] Ibid., p. 79.

[38] Ibid., p. 80.

[39] Ibid., p. 86.

[40] Ibid., pp. 91–94.

Table A.2 Commission recommendations on PSD2

No	*Subject*	*Recommendation*	*Feedback provided by*
1	Scope of applicability	Improve consistent application of PSD2 and align licensing requirements. In this regard, it is suggested to establish a: • standing committee for coordination with a schedule of meetings between the EBA and the NCAs; and • standing committee with a schedule of meetings amongst the central banks of the ESCB.	Commission[41]
2	Scope of applicability	Address competition issues. The following recommendations are proposed: • schedule continued antitrust scrutiny; • NCAs to provide the European Parliament with regular updates on the results of investigations on BigTechs; • create a public register with regard to antitrust investigations; • schedule regular meetings between the ECB, NCAs and competition authorities; • address the operation of payment systems as a regulated business; and • Setting up and information structure on Member State choices on surcharging.	Commission[42]
3	Scope of applicability	Address legal uncertainty regarding the scope of PSD2. The following recommendations are proposed to address legal uncertainty: • include a residual normative clause in the PSD2 annex on payment services; • the residual normative clause must have a broad scope and not exclude any future payment initiation or account initiation like services; and • guidelines to be provided by the EBA on the approach to the normative clause.	Commission[43]

[41] Commission, 'A study on the application and impact of Directive (EU) 2015/2366 on Payment Services (PSD2)', FISMA/2021/OP/0002, 2023, pp. 181–182.

[42] Ibid., p. 182.

No	*Subject*	*Recommendation*	*Feedback provided by*
4	Scope of applicability	Address legal uncertainty within PSD2. The following recommendations are proposed: • establish a legislative consolidation process between the Regulation on markets in crypto assets (MiCA) and PSD2; • ensure that the definition of 'funds' in PSD2 also covers e-money tokens; • include a chapter in PSD2 on authorisation and supervision of issuers of: (i) asset referenced tokens; and (ii) e-money tokens; • extent of the application of the information requirements to payment transactions by means of e-money tokens and asset referenced tokens; and • exclude the application of Title IV PSD2 to payment transactions by e-money tokens and asset referenced tokens.	Commission[44]
5	Scope of applicability	Merge PSD2 and EMD2 by: • including a chapter in PSD2 on authorisation and supervision of EMIs; • extending the application of Titles III and IV PSD2 to e-money payment transactions; • removing recital 6 EMD2; and • introducing a single set of core definitions that apply to both e-money and payment services.	Commission[45]
6	Scope of applicability	Adopt more consistent definitions for: (i) access to accounts; (ii) access to payment systems and (iii) agents/outsourcing by means of EBA guidelines.	Commission[46]

(continued)

[44] Ibid.

[45] Ibid., pp. 183–184.

[46] Ibid., p. 184.

Table A.2 (continued)

No	*Subject*	*Recommendation*	*Feedback provided by*
7	Scope of applicability	Strengthen cooperation between NCAs regarding payment platforms. To this end, the following recommendations are proposed: • provide for a legal framework for digital platforms providing payment services as foreseen in the DMA; and • establish a cross-border supervision committee of platforms coordinated by the EBA.	Commission[47]
8	Open banking	Address standardisation and interoperability issues. To this end, the following recommendations are proposed: • vesting the EPC with a coordinating task; and • establish a SEPA-like incentive mechanism to ensure that market participants apply the regulatory and technical standards.	Commission[48]
9	Open banking	Ensure that new PSPs are covered by the regulatory framework governing retail payments. To this end, the following recommendations are proposed: • define a three-tier payment service concept based on: (i) the transfer and custody of monetary assets; (ii) transfer and custody of data associated with Payments and (iii) managing of Payment platforms; and • provide for closer cooperation between NCAs via the EBA.	Commission[49]
10	Open banking	Address FinTech concern that PSD2 raises a range of obstacles by amending Article 97 PSD2 to ensure that a PSUs authorisation for an AISP to access its payment account is valid on an ongoing basis until the PSU revokes the permission.	Commission[50]

47 Ibid.

48 Ibid.

49 Ibid., p. 185.

50 Ibid.

No	*Subject*	*Recommendation*	*Feedback provided by*
11	Data and consumer protection	Provide for a more efficient data authorisation and customer identity control system by improving coordination between the EBA and data protection authorities.	Commission[51]
12	Data and consumer protection	Improve protection of PSUs. To this end, the following recommendations are proposed: • introduce different levels of protection and liability based on the degree of vulnerability of the PSU; • enhance the effectiveness of cross-border alternative dispute resolution mechanisms; • extent data protection safeguards in PSD2; • ensure that PSPs providing licence as a service are liable for the custody/transfer of funds/data *vis-à-vis* the supervisory authorities; and • streamline information requirements by introducing a single Title in PSD2 on information obligations for: (i) PIs; (ii) EMIs and (iii) issuers of asset referenced tokens and e-money tokens.	Commission[52]

51 Ibid.

52 Ibid., pp. 185–186.

Annex III

Information/Documentation to be Submitted for Authorisation as PI for the Provision of Services 1–8 of Annex I PSD2

J. A. Jans, *Electronic Payments in the European Market*,
EBI Studies in Banking and Capital Markets Law,
https://doi.org/10.1007/978-3-031-64338-5

No	*Requirement*	*Comments*
1	Generic information regarding the PI	Information on the applicant should include *inter alia*: • corporate name; • status of incorporation of the PI; • national identification number (if applicable); • the PI's legal status and (draft) articles of association and/or constitutional documents; • addresses of its head office and registered office; • the website; • contact person (contact details of the person(s) in charge of dealing with the application file); • current regulatory status (under the supervision of an NCA in the financial services sector); • intentions to join a trade association(s) in relation to the provision of payment services; • register certificate of incorporation; and • payment of any fees or of the deposit of funds to file an application for authorisation as a PI (when required).
2	Payment services to be provided	Relevant information to be provided includes *inter alia*: • description of the payment services that will be provided; • copy of the framework agreement; • description of ancillary services to the payment services, if applicable; • declaration of whether the PI intends to grant credit; and • declaration of whether the PI plans to provide payment services in other Member States.

(continued)

(continued)

No	*Requirement*	*Comments*
3	A business plan	The business plan contains *inter alia*: • a marketing plan; • a forecast budget calculation for the first three financial years; • description of ancillary services to be provided by the PI; • the PI's strategy; • a chart of anticipated cash flows for each payment service;[53] and • calculation of the PI's own funds.
4	PI's structural organisation	Relevant information to be provided includes *inter alia*: • an organisational chart; • a description of outsourcing arrangements; and • a description of the branches and agents used by the PI for offering payment services.
5	Initial capital	Evidence can be provided by submitting: • an audited account statement; or • a bank statement certifying that the funds are deposited in the PI's bank account.
6	Safeguarding of PSU funds[54]	Description of the measures to safeguard the funds of PSUs covers: • depositing funds in a separate account with a Bank or through an investment in secure, liquid, low risk assets; or • insurance policy or guarantee from an insurance company or Bank.

(continued)

[53] This requirement does not apply to PIs that only provide account information or payment initiation services.

[54] This requirement does not apply regarding the provision of account information or payment initiation services.

(continued)

No	*Requirement*	*Comments*
7	Governance arrangements and internal control mechanisms	Description must cover *inter alia*: • the risks to which the PI is exposed; • monitoring of outsourcing arrangements; • composition of management board and internal governance; and • accounting procedures for recording and reporting of financial information.
8	The procedures for monitoring and handling security incidents	Such procedures provide for: • measures and tools used by the PI to prevent fraud; and • means for reporting incidents to the NCA.
9	The procedures for the processing of sensitive payment data	Procedures must describe how the PI monitors and restricts access to sensitive payment data.
10	Business continuity arrangements	Such arrangements consist of *inter alia*: • recovery procedures in case of an interruption; • backup systems; • access to IT systems; and • regular testing of IT systems on sensitivity for disruptions.
11	Procedures for the collection of statistical data regarding performance, transactions and fraud	Description must cover *inter alia*: • type of data collected; and • means and frequency of data collection.
12	The internal control mechanisms in relation to AML/CTF obligations	Information to be provided includes: • assessment of the PI's ML/TF risks; • risk mitigating measures that are in place; • controls in place to ensure that the PI's branches and agents also meet the AML/CTF standards; • periodic review of the internal AML/CTF procedures; and • AML/CTF manual for the PI's staff.
13	Identity and suitability of the holders of a qualifying holding in the PI	Information must be provided on the change in control filing with the NCA.

(continued)

(continued)

No	*Requirement*	*Comments*
14	Identity and suitability of the members of the management board/executive directors of the PI	Information must be provided on the applications with the NCA for the integrity and suitability screening of the day-to-day policymakers.
15	Statutory auditors and audit firms	Contact details of the statutory auditors and audit firms must be provided.
16	The professional indemnity insurance or guarantee	PIs offering account information or payment initiation services have to provide evidence of the professional indemnity insurance or guarantee.
17	The security policy	The security policy must contain a description of: • the PI's IT systems; • risk assessment of the payment services to be provided; • physical security measures to safeguard the institution's data centre; • safeguards to ensure the security of the processing of Payments, which covers, amongst others, SCA procedures; and • mitigation measures to adequately protect PSUs against identified risks, including fraud and illegal use of sensitive and personal data.

Annex IV

Information/Documentation to be Submitted for Authorisation as PI for the Provision of Service 8 of Annex I PSD2

J. A. Jans, *Electronic Payments in the European Market*,
EBI Studies in Banking and Capital Markets Law,
https://doi.org/10.1007/978-3-031-64338-5

No	*Requirement*	*Comments*
1	Generic information regarding the PI	Information on the applicant should include *inter alia*: • corporate name; • status of incorporation of the PI; • national identification number (if applicable); • the PI's legal status and (draft) articles of association and/or constitutional documents; • addresses of its head office and registered office; • the website; • contact person (contact details of the person(s) in charge of dealing with the application file); • current regulatory status (under the supervision of an NCA in the financial services sector); • intentions to join a trade association(s) in relation to the provision of payment services; • register certificate of incorporation; and • payment of any fees or of the deposit of funds to file an application for authorisation as a PI (when required).
2	Programme of operations	Relevant information to be provided includes *inter alia*: • description of the account information services that will be provided; • terms and conditions of the account information services; • description of ancillary services to the account information services, if applicable; and • declaration of whether the PI plans to provide account information services in other Member States.
3	A business plan	The business plan contains *inter alia*: • a marketing plan; • certified annual accounts for the previous three years or a summary of the financial situation; and • a forecast budget calculation for the first three financial years.

(continued)

(continued)

No	*Requirement*	*Comments*
4	PI's structural organisation	Relevant information to be provided includes *inter alia*: • a forecast of staff numbers for the next three years; • a description of outsourcing arrangements; • an organisational chart; and • a description of the branches and agents used by the PI for offering payment services.
5	Governance arrangements and internal control mechanisms	Description must cover *inter alia*: • the risks to which the PI is exposed; • monitoring of outsourcing arrangements; • composition of management board and internal governance; and • accounting procedures for recording and reporting of financial information.
6	The procedures for monitoring and handling security incidents	Such procedures provide for: • measures and tools used by the PI to prevent fraud; and • means for reporting incidents to the NCA.
7	The procedures for the processing of sensitive payment data	Procedures must describe how the PI monitors and restricts access to sensitive payment data.
8	Business continuity arrangements	Such arrangements consist of *inter alia*: • recovery procedures in case of an interruption; • backup systems; • access to IT systems; and • regular testing of IT systems on sensitivity for disruptions.

(continued)

(continued)

No	*Requirement*	*Comments*
9	The security policy	The security policy must contain a description of: • the PI's IT systems; • risk assessment of the account information services to be provided; • physical security measures to safeguard the institution's data centre; • safeguards to ensure the security of the processing of Payments, which covers, amongst others, SCA procedures; and • mitigation measures to adequately protect PSUs against identified risks, including fraud and illegal use of sensitive and personal data.
10	Identity and suitability of the members of the management board/executive directors of the PI	Information must be provided on the applications with the NCA for the integrity and suitability screening of the day-to-day policymakers.
11	The professional indemnity insurance or guarantee	PIs offering account information services have to provide evidence of the professional indemnity insurance or guarantee.

Annex V

Information/Documentation to be Submitted for EMI Licence Application

J. A. Jans, *Electronic Payments in the European Market*, EBI Studies in Banking and Capital Markets Law,
https://doi.org/10.1007/978-3-031-64338-5

No	*Requirement*	*Comments*
1	Generic information regarding the EMI	Information on the applicant should include *inter alia*: • corporate name; • status of incorporation of the EMI; • national identification number (if applicable); • the EMI's legal status and (draft) articles of association and/or constitutional documents; • addresses of its head office and registered office; • the website; • contact person (contact details of the person(s) in charge of dealing with the application file); • current regulatory status (under the supervision of an NCA in the financial services sector); • intentions to join a trade association(s) in relation to the provision of payment services; • register certificate of incorporation; and • payment of any fees or of the deposit of funds to file an application for authorisation as an EMI (when required).
2	Programme of operations	Relevant information to be provided includes *inter alia*: • indication of the E-money services that the EMI intends to provider (issuance, redemption and/or distribution); • description of the E-money services and payment services that will be provided; • description of ancillary services to the E-money services/payment services, if applicable; and • declaration of whether the EMI plans to provide payment services in other Member States.

(continued)

(continued)

No	*Requirement*	*Comments*
3	A business plan	The business plan contains *inter alia*: • a marketing plan; • certified annual accounts for the previous three years or a summary of the financial situation; • a forecast budget calculation for the first three financial years and • calculation of the EMI's own funds
4	EMI's structural organisation	Relevant information to be provided includes *inter alia*: • an organisational chart; • a description of outsourcing arrangements; and • a description of the branches and agents used by the EMI for offering payment services.
5	Initial capital	Evidence can be provided by submitting: • an audited account statement; or • a bank statement certifying that the funds are deposited in the EMI's bank account.
6	Safeguarding of PSU funds	Description of the measures to safeguard the funds of PSUs covers: • depositing funds in a separate account with a Bank or through an investment in secure, liquid, low-risk assets; or • insurance policy or guarantee from an insurance company or Bank.
7	Governance arrangements and internal control mechanisms	Description must cover *inter alia*: • the risks to which the EMI is exposed; • monitoring of outsourcing arrangements; • composition of management board and internal governance; and • accounting procedures for recording and reporting of financial information.
8	The procedures for monitoring and handling security incidents	Such procedures provide for: • measures and tools used by the EMI to prevent fraud; and • means for reporting incidents to the NCA.

(continued)

(continued)

No	*Requirement*	*Comments*
9	The procedures for the processing of sensitive payment data	Procedures must describe how the EMI monitors and restricts access to sensitive payment data.
10	Business continuity arrangements	Such arrangements consist of *inter alia*: • recovery procedures in case of an interruption; • backup systems; • access to IT systems; and • regular testing of IT systems on sensitivity for disruptions.
11	Procedures for the collection of statistical data regarding performance, transactions and fraud	Description must cover *inter alia*: • type of data collected; and • means and frequency of data collection.
12	The security policy	The security policy must contain a description of: • the EMI's IT systems; • risk assessment of the payment services to be provided; • physical security measures to safeguard the institution's data centre; • safeguards to ensure the security of the processing of Payments, which covers, amongst others, SCA procedures; and • mitigation measures to adequately protect PSUs against identified risks, including fraud and illegal use of sensitive and personal data.
13	The internal control mechanisms in relation to AML/CTF obligations	Information to be provided includes: • assessment of the EMI's ML/TF risks; • risk mitigating measures that are in place; • controls in place to ensure that the EMI's branches and agents also meet the AML/CTF standards; • periodic review of the internal AML/CTF procedures; and • AML/CTF manual for the EMI's staff.
14	Identity and suitability of the holders of a qualifying holding in the EMI	Information must be provided on the change in control filing with the NCA

(continued)

(continued)

No	*Requirement*	*Comments*
15	Identity and suitability of the members of the management board/executive directors of the EMI	Information must be provided on the applications with the NCA for the integrity and suitability screening of the day-to-day policymakers.
16	Statutory auditors and audit firms	Contact details of the statutory auditors and audit firms must be provided.
17	The professional indemnity insurance or guarantee	EMIs offering account information or payment initiation services have to provide evidence of the professional indemnity insurance or guarantee.

Index

J. A. Jans, *Electronic Payments in the European Market*, EBI Studies in Banking and Capital Markets Law, https://doi.org/10.1007/978-3-031-64338-5

D

E

Q

R

S

SPRINGER NATURE

GPSR Compliance

The European Union's (EU) General Product Safety Regulation (GPSR) is a set of rules that requires consumer products to be safe and our obligations to ensure this.

If you have any concerns about our products, you can contact us on ProductSafety@springernature.com

In case Publisher is established outside the EU, the EU authorized representative is:

Springer Nature Customer Service Center GmbH
Europaplatz 3
69115 Heidelberg, Germany

The manufacturer's authorised representative in the EU is Springer Nature Customer Service Centre GmbH, Europaplatz 3, 69115 Heidelberg, Germany. If you have any concerns regarding our products, please contact ProductSafety@springernature.com

Printed and bound by CPI Group (UK) Ltd, Croydon, CR0 4YY
01/10/2026
02225903-0016